# OFFICIAL REPORT

OF THE

# United States' Expedition

TO EXPLORE THE

# DEAD SEA AND THE RIVER JORDAN,

BY

LIEUT. W. F. LYNCH, U. S. N.

*Published at the National Observatory*, Lieut. M. F. Maury, U. S. N., *Superintendent*,

BY AUTHORITY OF THE HON. WM. A. GRAHAM, SECRETARY OF THE NAVY.

BALTIMORE:

PRINTED BY JOHN MURPHY & CO.

No. 178 MARKET STREET.

1852.

Baltimore, *Sept.* 1, 1851.

Sir:

I transmit herewith my final Report of the Expedition to the Dead Sea and the River Jordan, and request you to submit it to the Hon. Secretary of the Navy, and obtain his consent to have it published by the Observatory under your superintendence.

The Report embraces a maritime survey, and therefore comes peculiarly within the province of the National Observatory.

Very respectfully, your ob't serv't,

W. F. LYNCH, *U. S. Navy.*

To Lieut. M. F. Maury, U. S. N.,

*Superintendent of the National Observatory, Washington, D. C.*

---

National Observatory, Washington, *8th Sept.*, 1851.

Sir:

I have the honor to transmit herewith, the final Report of Commander Wm. F. Lynch, concerning the Expedition to the Dead Sea.

This Report has been referred to this office. It contains much useful and interesting information, and I therefore recommend its publication.

Respectfully, &c.

M. F. MAURY.

Hon. Wm. A. Graham, *Secretary of the Navy.*

The following Report was printed, in part, by order of the United States Senate, in 1849, but the Geological portion was not finished until September, 1851. With the consent of the Honorable Secretary of the Navy the whole has been submitted to, and published under the auspices of the National Observatory.

The Ornithological Report is unaccompanied with plates, as from the intense heat, and other causes, but few birds were preserved and brought to the United States.

The Botanical Report is also without plates, as the plants, although sufficiently well preserved for classification, were many of them too much mutilated to be *truly* represented by drawings.

# TABLE OF CONTENTS.

# REPORT OF THE SECRETARY OF THE NAVY,

WITH A

# REPORT MADE BY LIEUTENANT W. F. LYNCH,

# OF AN EXAMINATION OF THE DEAD SEA.

February 26, 1849. *Read February 27, referred to the Committee on Commerce, and ordered to be printed.*

Navy Department, *February* 24, 1849.

Sir: In compliance with a resolution of the Senate, of the 8th instant, I have the honor to transmit herewith a copy of the report made to this department by Lieutenant William F. Lynch, of the United States Navy, of the examination by himself, and other officers of the Navy, of the Dead Sea.

I have the honor to be, very respectfully, your obedient servant,

J. Y. MASON.

Hon. Geo. M. Dallas,
*Vice-President of the United States, and President of the Senate.*

Washington, *February* 3, 1849.

Sir: In obedience to your order, I herewith submit my official report of the late expedition to the Dead Sea. It does not include the geological portion which will not be complete for several months. The maps and appendix will be sent as soon as copies can be taken.

The report is but a synopsis of my copious notes, but comprehends all that is material of a scientific nature. *They* embrace much matter, incidentally elicited by visiting such interesting places, which is wholly unfit for an official paper.

I therefore respectfully ask permission to publish a narrative *after* the official report has been called for.

I have the honor to be, your obedient servant,

W. F. LYNCH,
*Lieutenant United States Navy.*

Hon. J. Y. Mason,
*Secretary of the Navy.*

UNITED STATES STORE SHIP SUPPLY,
*At Sea, November*, 1848.

SIR: I have the honor to report that, in obedience to your order of September 30, 1847, I assumed the command of this ship on the 2d day of October following. By your special order, I had previously contracted for two metallic boats, and while the ship was being equipped, procured mathematical instruments and various articles deemed necessary for the successful result of the contemplated attempt to descend the Jordan and explore the Dead Sea, should the Ottoman government grant the required firman. By your further order, Lieutenant J. B. Dale and Passed Midshipman Richmond Aulick, reported to me for the same special service, and, with your permission, I shipped ten seamen as crews to the boats. I was very particular in selecting young, native born Americans, of sober habits, from each of whom, I exacted a pledge to abstain from all intoxicating drinks.

On the 26th November, 1847, having received your final orders, with a case of books from the State Department for our minister at Constantinople, we sailed from New York for Smyrna.

On the 29th November, the deep color of the water, its higher temperature, and the light mist which shrouded its surface, showed that we were crossing the gulf stream. During this time our chronometer, being invariably ahead of the reckoning, proved that we were accelerated about half a mile an hour.

December 2d. We experienced a northwest gale with a heavy sea; it was indicated by a barometrical depression of 1.14th of an inch. On the approach of an easterly gale, a few days prior to our departure from New York, the barometer fell 7.14ths of an inch.

In latitude 38° 40′ north, longitude 43° 16′ west, we tested the thermometrical barometer, No. 2; temperature of the air, 68°, of the surface of the water of the sea, 70°, of do. at the depth of 100 fathoms, 63°. Water boiled at 212° 95′. Barometer 30.6.

December 8. The barometer had reached its minimum 29.72; compelled to heave to, in consequence of the fierce wind and excessively heavy sea.

December 9. The weather moderated, and on the 11th, we made the islands of Corvo and Flores, the northwesternmost of the Azores; on the 12th, we passed the island of Graciosa, one of the same group, and on the 17th December, made Cape St. Vincent, on the coast of Portugal.

December 19. Made Cape Trafalgar, and at 4, P. M., anchored in the bay of Gibraltar. We touched at that place for some instruments that had been ordered from London, and it was my purpose to have proceeded thence direct to Smyrna, but through the United States Consul, I received a message from Commodore Read, informing me that the squadron was short of provisions. As I knew that you would regard the wants of the squadron as of paramount importance, I proceeded to Port Mahon, without a moment's unnecessary delay.

We arrived at Mahon on the 4th January, where, in consequence of two cases of small-pox having occurred on board, this ship was subjected to a quarantine of fourteen days. Immediately on receiving pratique, we commenced delivering stores, Commodore Read evincing every disposition to facilitate our departure.

On February 4, 1848, at midnight, we sailed from Mahon; stopping at Malta for a few hours on the 9th, we sailed the same day for the Archipelago, and arrived at Smyrna on the 16th. Not finding any safe conveyance for the case under my charge, I proceeded in a steamer to Constantinople on the 19th, and immediately after my arrival waited upon the Hon. Dabney Carr, our resident minister.

In Constantinople, I associated in the expedition Henry Bedlow, Esq., a young fellow-countryman of high honor and great intelligence; and received some valuable geological suggestions from Dr. Smith, an American gentleman, employed as geologist by the Ottoman government. The application for the firman in behalf of a national expedition being considered unusual, was referred by the Divan for the decision of the Sultan. Through the deserved high standing of our minister, that being favorable, the firman was made out on the 8th of March, and I left the same afternoon for Smyrna.

On the 10th, I rejoined the ship, and sailed for the coast of Syria on the 11th. Twice compelled to put back by stress of weather, we reached Beïrût, on the coast of Syria, on the 25th. There engaging a dragoman or interpreter, and receiving two chronometers forwarded from London, we sailed on the 27th, and arrived the next day in the bay of Acre, and anchored under Mount Carmel, near the walled village of Haifa. In Beïrût, I engaged the services of Henry James Anderson, M. D., a citizen of the United States, and formerly professor in Columbia College, New York, as physician to the expedition, with the agreement that he should take charge of the geological department, and remain with us until the Dead Sea had been explored. He was to join us on the route, and I left a letter for him at Acre, a copy of which is annexed, marked A.

For two days we were detained by tempestuous weather, but on the afternoon of March 31st, we succeeded in landing the boats and all our effects. The next day, with great difficulty, we transported them to the banks of the river Belus, near Acre, where we pitched our tents.

While encamped near Acre, we heard the most alarming accounts of the hostile spirit of the Arab tribes on each bank of the Jordan. These reports were in a measure confirmed by a party of American travellers, who had been attacked two nights previous under Mount Tabor. The governor of Acre, Sa'id Bey, endeavored to take advantage of this state of things. Advancing the opinion that we could not proceed in safety with less than 100 soldiers to guard us, he offered to secure us from molestation, and procure means for the transportation of the boats, if I would pay him 20,000 piastres, (about $800). This I declined, stating that I scorned to buy protection; that if draught horses could be procured, or oxen furnished, I would pay fairly for them, and for a few soldiers to act as scouts—but, that we were well armed and able to protect ourselves. Finding that I would not embrace his terms, although he mitigated them, he urged me to abandon the enterprise; to which I replied that we were ordered to explore the Dead Sea and were determined to obey. He then advised me to go by the way of Jerusalem: As he was too ignorant to understand the geographical difficulties of that route, I merely answered that we had set our faces towards the Sea of Galilee, and were not disposed to look back. Finally, he evinced such a spirit of extortion, that I declined further communication with him and refused a small escort he offered.

I can give a very inadequate idea of my feelings. To turn back was out of the question, and my soul revolted at the thought of bribing Sa'id Bey, even if I had been authorized to spend money for such a purpose. I felt sure that he had exaggerated in his statement, and yet the attack on our countrymen, so far this side of the Jordan, staggered me.

From all the information I could gain of the Arab character, I had arrived at the conclusion that it would tend more to gain their good-will if we threw ourselves among them without an escort, than if accompanied by a strong armed force. But the attack on our countrymen indicated danger of collision at the very outset, and I determined to be prepared for it.

On leaving the "Supply" I had placed a sum of money in charge of Lieutenant-Commanding Pennock, with the request that he would, in person, deliver it to H. B. M. Consul at Jerusalem. Partly for that purpose, and in part to make some simultaneous barometrical observations, he had sailed for Jaffa, which is about thirty miles distant from the Holy City. To him, therefore, I despatched a messenger, asking him to call upon the Pasha of Jerusalem, and request a small body of soldiers to be sent to meet us at Tiberias or on the Jordan. This precaution taken, my mind was at ease, and indeed, I was half ashamed of the previous misgivings.

At our Consul's I was introduced to a fine old man, an Arab nobleman, called Sherîf Hazzâ of Mecca, the thirty-third lineal descendant of the Prophet. He was about 50 years of age, of a dark Egyptian complexion, small stature, and intelligent features. His father and elder brother had been Sherîfs or Governors of Mecca, until the latter was deposed by Mehemet Ali. He was dressed in a spencer and capacious trowsers of olive-green cloth—a color only worn by the descendants of Mohammed. His appearance was very prepossessing, and he evinced much enlightened curiosity with regard to our country and its institutions. We were told that from his descent he was held in great veneration by the Arabs; and I observed that every Muslim who came in, first approached him and kissed his hand with an air of profound respect. He was as communicative about his own affairs as he was inquisitive with respect to us and our country. Finding that he was now doing nothing, but inactively awaiting the decision of a law-suit, I proposed that he should accompany us. At first he smiled as if the proposition were an absurd one; but when I explained to him that, instead of a party of private individuals, we were sent by a far distant but powerful country, to solve a scientific question, he became interested. I further added that, with us, I knew he believed in the writings of Moses; and that with solutions of scientific questions, we hoped to convince the incredulous that Moses was a true prophet. He listened eagerly, and after some further conversation, rose abruptly, and saying that he would very soon give me an answer, took his departure.

Sooner even than in my impatience, I had anticipated, he returned and accepted the invitation, leaving the remuneration of his services entirely to my own appraisement.

I also engaged the services of a magnificent savage, who was the handsomest, and I soon thought also, the most graceful being I had ever seen. His complexion was of a rich, indescribable olive tint, his hair was glossy black, his teeth were regular and of the whitest ivory, and the glance of his eye was keen at times, but generally soft and lustrous. He was a distinguished Sheikh of the Bedawin; and had been the year before at the head of several tribes in rebellion against the Turkish Government, which, unable to subdue him, had bought him in with a pelisse of honor and a commission corresponding to that of Colonel of the Irregular Arabs.

There seemed to be no alternative but to take the boats apart and transport them in sections to the Sea of Galilee, unless camels could be made to draw in harness, and I determined to try the experiment. It was tried and *proved successful;* and our hearts throbbed with gratitude, as the huge animals, three to each, marched off with the trucks, the boats upon them, with perfect ease. The first attempt to substitute camels for draught horses, was a novel sight, witnessed by an eager crowd of people. The successful result taught them the existence of an unknown accomplishment in that patient and powerful animal, which they had before thought fit only to plod along with its heavy load upon its back.

On the 4th of April we broke up our camp on the banks of the Belus, and started with the boats for the Sea of Galilee. Our course was first east, then gradually round to south, over an extensive plain enamelled with flowers, and struck into a rolling country of gentle undulations. Besides the profusion of flowers, a stunted tree was here and there presented. The village of Abelin was soon visible on the summit of a high hill, rising abruptly from the southern slope of the plain. To the east and southeast, in the far distance, were two other villages; all else was nearly a level plain, with broken ground in front. Crossing the shoulder of a hill, we opened upon the head of a ravine,—wide at first, but narrowing to a gorge as it descended and swept around the bases of the hills. The village of Abelin, perched upon the highest one, commands an extensive view from the "Album Promontorium" to the Convent of Mount Carmel. But the place is indescribably poor and filthy. The houses are built of uncemented stones, are mostly but one story high, and have flat, mud roofs;—and without, encircling the whole, is a row of small, dome-roofed hovels, made entirely of mud, and used for baking bread;—all enveloped in a most offensive atmosphere, tainted by the odor of the fuel—the sun-dried excrement of camels. There appeared to be as many as one of these little hovels to each dwelling.

Leaving Abelin on the right, we came in half an hour to the Blowing Valley, or Valley of the Winds, with forests of white oak on the flanks of the hills, where we pitched our tents.

Here our allies joined us. They had assumed the garb of the desert, and each, with a flowing dark aba (cloak) and the yellow Koofeeyeh upon his head, bound round with a cord of camels' hair, dyed black, and bearing a spear eighteen feet in length, some of them tufted with ostrich feathers, looked the wild and savage warrior.

We this day passed through the narrow tract on the coast of Syria, which was never subdued by the Israelites, and through the narrowest part of the land of the tribe of Asser into that of Zebulon.

Wednesday, April 5. We were early on the move. The carriages with the boats upon them were drawn by three camels each, two abreast and one as leader, with twelve spare ones to relieve every half hour. Our party numbered sixteen in all, including dragoman and cook, with eleven camels, laden with provisions, tents, instruments, &c., and fifteen Bedawin, all well mounted, the followers and servants of the Sherif of Mecca and Sheikh 'Akil Aga el Hasseé. Our course was at first down a narrow gorge. Through this we found it impossible to drag the boats, and therefore deploying to the left we drew them to the summit of a hill, and then taking out the camels, lowered them down by hand.

Passing along this ravine in a southeasterly direction, we came at 9.30, A. M., upon the great plain of Buttauf. Winding around a green hill tufted with oak, we reached Khan el Diellil, now in ruins, with an excellent well beside it. A few hundred yards beyond, we came to a shallow pond of water, the collection of winter rains, where we stopped to water the caravan. Here we took chronometer observations, having to remove some distance in consequence of the vibration caused by the movement of the animals. From this ruined

Khan, across the plain, bearing south, cresting a lofty hill, was the castle of Sefûrieh, (Sephoris,) the Dio Cesarea of the Romans. Thence southeast over a hill was Nazareth, but three hours distant from us. To the left, almost due east, one hour distant, was Cana of Galilee.

Starting again, our route was east-northeast along the plain. Coming to a broken, rocky country, we encountered much difficulty with the boats. At length, making a detour to the right, breaking off a projecting crag here, and filling up a hollow there, we got them over the first ridge. It was shortly, however, succeeded by another and another, and the trains were obliged to abandon the road, or rather mule track, altogether. Winding along the flanks of several hills, we came upon an elevated plain of cultivated fields. Turning then more to the north and skirting a ridge of rocky limestone, we gradually ascended a slope covered with olive orchards and reached the walled village of Turân, near which, on the brow of a hill, we encamped. In the plain, immediately beneath, was fought the battle between the Syrians and the French, when Napoleon rescued Kleber. Mount Tabor bore south-southwest. We were in the land assigned to the tribe of Zebulon.

We had thus far ascended upwards of fifteen hundred feet, which, better than any description, will give an idea of the steepness but not of the ruggedness of the road.

Thursday, April 6. Wind light and weather pleasant. Our course was first east, down a long descent, and thence over a rolling plain, to a large artificial reservoir, with an area of about three acres, partly filled with rain water. Thence we passed immediately north of the village of Lubieh, differing only in its less conspicuous position from Turân and Abelin.

Since leaving the olive groves of Turân, we had not seen a tree nor a bush, except on the hill sides of Lubieh; yet the whole surface of the valley was dotted with unenclosed fields of growing grain and carpeted with green. We continued rising until we opened on our right, a magnificent crater-like series of slopes, with a bare glimpse of the Sea of Galilee and the mountains of Bashan beyond. These slopes were covered with fields of grain in different stages of growth, and patches of flowers were scattered about, the scarlet anemone and the blue convolvulus; but the luxuriant slopes looked like mosaic, with a prevailing purple tinge, the hue of the thorny shrub merar. Ragged peasants were ploughing in the fields.

Pursuing the route along the northern ridge of this valley, we came to a fountain on the high road from Jerusalem to Damascus. The boats could come no farther than the fonntain, where the trains stopped for the night. On our route, thus far the prevailing rock was limestone; but after leaving Lubieh, we met several nodules of quartz and much trap wholly destitute of minerals. The latter first made its appearance in scattered fragments; large boulders then succeeded, and on the shore enormous masses crop out in the ravines.

Winding down the rugged road, we descended to the city seated on the western margin of the lake. Tiberias (Tûbarieh) is a walled town of some magnitude, but now in ruins, from an earthquake which in 1837 destroyed so many of its inhabitants.

We were yet in the land of Zebulon; on the opposite side of the lake are the lands of the half tribe of Manasseh.

Our instruments were uninjured, notwithstanding the ruggedness of the road, and we fitted them preparatory to a series of observations.

Saturday, April 8. Calm and warm. Took all hands up the mountain to bring the boats down. After very great difficulty we succeeded, and bearing them beyond the walls, amid a crowd of spectators, launched them on the Sea of Galilee.

We had not time to survey the lake—the advancing season and the lessening flood in the Jordan, warning us to lose no time. We therefore deferred making the necessary observations until our return. Its bottom is a concave basin,—the greatest depth ascertained is 27½ fathoms (165 feet.) But, this inland sea, alternately rising and falling, from copious rains and melting snows and rapid evaporation, is constantly fluctuating in depth. The water is cool and sweet, and the inhabitants say that it possesses medicinal properties.

We found the surface of this lake by barometrical measurement to be 653.3 feet below that of the Mediterranean.

While at Tiberias, I purchased a frame boat, the only one of any kind upon the lake—for the purpose of economy in the transportation of stores. In order that by a division of labor, our work might be well performed, I assigned to each officer and man of the expedition his appropriate duty. With the command of the Caravan Lieutenant Dale was directed to take topographical sketches of the country; Dr. Anderson to make geological observations; Mr. Bedlow to note the incidents that occurred on the march, and Mr. Francis Lynch was charged with the collection of plants and flowers.

In the water party, I took the lead in the copper boat, and assigned to myself the course, rapidity, color and depth of the river and its tributaries,—the nature of its banks and of the country through which it flowed—the vegetable productions and the birds and animals we might see—with a journal of events. To Passed Midshipman Aulick who had charge of the iron boat, was assigned the topographical sketch of the river and its banks.

As the Jordan was represented to run between high banks, I felt that our safety would materially depend upon the vigilance and alacrity of the land party. Lieutenant Dale was directed to keep as near to the river as the nature of the country would permit, and should he hear two guns fired in quick succession, to abandon the baggage and hasten with all speed to our assistance. The Sherîf and 'Akîl, all assured me that there was little danger to the Caravan, but that the great fear was an attack upon the boats when entangled among rocks and shoals.

Monday, April 10, 1848. Called all hands very early to make preparations for departure. Repaired and launched the frame boat I purchased here; named her "Uncle Sam," and engaged four Arabs as her crew.

In the morning received a visit from Emir Nassir Arar el Guzzhawy, a powerful prince of the Arabs of the Ghor. He came to welcome us, and to proffer any assistance we might require. I agreed with him for a small party to accompany our caravan as guides and scouts.

At 2, P. M., both parties started. Going through an uncultivated and unknown country, it was necessary to take a quantity of forage and provisions. Our united parties consisted, therefore, of three boats upon the water; and ten camels and about twenty horsemen upon the land, including our own officers, the dragoman, cook, and our Bedawin friends.

Our Bedawin had, many of them, exchanged their lances for more serviceable weapons, long barrelled guns and heavily mounted pistols. 'Akîl alone wore a scimitar; the priestly character of Sherîf forbade him to carry arms. With the addition of the Emir and his followers, they amounted in all, to thirty horsemen, and passing in single file, their line was long and imposing. Eleven camels stalked solemnly ahead, followed by the wild Bedawin on their blooded animals, with their abas flying in the wind, and Lieutenant Dale and his officers, in the Frank costume, brought up the rear.

Temperature of the air 82°, of the water 72°.

Until 3, P. M., we steered south, and from 3 to 3.40, southeast and east-southeast; the right or western shore of the lake descending in a slope towards the river; the left somewhat more depressed and much washed with rains, presenting a continuation of rounded bluffs, with intervening chasms; the ruins of Kerak, ancient Tarrichœa, on the southwest bend of the lake.

At 3.45, opened the river running nearly west; a hill, with the village of Semakh on the south point, and the stone foundation of a building on the right, immediately at the point of debouchure of the river. From the eastern hills, a lovely plain here sweeps down to the lake, and in the centre of the water line is the village of Semakh, behind which a wady (ravine) comes down, and due west from it the Jordan sweeps out of the lake with a short turn to the right. As we entered the river, Mount Hermon, still covered with snow, but with fissures in its cap, was thrown into view, bearing northeast.

At 4.30, course west-southwest abruptly round a ledge of small rocks; our course varied with the turns of the river from northwest, 4.35, to south at 4.45. The average breadth about 25 yards; current, 2½ knots; the banks rounded and about 30 feet high, luxuriantly clothed with grass and flowers; among them the anemone and the marigold, but there were neither trees nor shrubs. Here and there, close to the water's edge, was a drooping lily.

At 4.48 passed an inlet, about a quarter mile deep, to the north, called El Muh. Five minutes after leaving the lake, we lost sight of it entirely, and, the current carrying us with sufficient velocity, we made little use of the oars.

The scenery, as we left the lake, and descending the river, advanced into the Ghor, assumed rather a subdued than a savage character. The rough and barren mountains skirting the valley on each hand, stretched far away in the distance like walls to some gigantic fosse, their southern extremities half hidden or entirely lost in a faint purple mist.

At 4.50 heard a gun-shot from the western shore, and soon after saw some of our scouts. In a minute after, passed a low island 90 yards long, covered with shrubbery; here was an abrupt bank, 25 feet high, on the left, and a low marshy island off a point on the right, running out from the plain at the foot of the mountains. Water clear, ten feet deep; saw the shore party dismounted on the right bank. Mount Hermon glittering to the north over the level tract which sweeps between the mountains, the lake, and the river.

When the current was strong, we only used the oars to keep the boats in the channel, and floated gently down the stream, frightening in our descent, a number of wild fowl feeding in the marsh grass or on the reedy islands.

At 4.56, current increasing, swept round a bend of the shore and heard the hoarse sound of a rapid. At 4.57, came in sight of the crumbled abutments of "Jisr Semakh," (the bridge of Semakh.)

The ruins are extremely picturesque; the abutments standing in various stages of decay, and the fallen fragments obstructing the course of the river, except at one point, towards the left bank, where the pent up water finds an issue and runs in a sluice among the scattered masses of stone. After reconnoitring the rapid, we shot down the sluice. The leading boat was whirled against a rock, where she hung for a few moments, but was got off without any material damage. It was now near sunset, and we camped for the night, just below the ruined bridge. Latitude of south end of Lake Tiberias, 32° 42′ 30″ north.

Latitude of camp, 35° 35′ 19″ north.

Longitude of camp, parallel with the western shore of the lake, 35° 35′ 39″ east; variation of compass, 8° 42′ west.

The soil here is of a dark rich loam, luxuriantly clothed, three feet deep, with grass, weeds and flowers—the scarlet anemone and the yellow marigold predominating: the rock no where cropping out, but boulders of sandstone and fragments of trap are scattered over the surface. The lake was concealed although quite near, but its bold northern and eastern shores towered above the opposite bank of the river. We gathered some flowers which equalled any I have ever seen in delicacy of form and tint. Among them, were the Adonis or Pheasant's-Eye; the Briony, formerly used in medicine; the Scabiosa Stellata, in great luxuriance, and which is cultivated at home; and two kinds of clover, one with a thorny head, which I never saw before, and the other small, but beautiful, with purple flowers. Our camp was on the western shore, in the land of Zebulon; that of the tribe of Gad, lies upon the other.

Deeming it improper to advance any opinion of my own in an official report, I necessarily make this a condensed one; but in an appendix, marked B, I submit an exact transcript of my notes of the course of the Jordan, in order that others, better qualified, may judge for themselves.

Tuesday, April 11. Weather clear and pleasant. Started at 8 10, A. M. The boats down the river, the caravan by land. The current at first about 2½ knots, but increasing as we descended, until, at 8.20 we came to where the river, for more than 300 yards, was one foaming rapid; the fishing weirs and the ruins of another ancient bridge obstructing the passage. There were cultivated fields on both sides. Took every thing out of the boats, sent the men overboard to swim alongside and guide them, and shot them successively down the first rapid. The water was fortunately very deep to the first fall, where it precipitated itself over a ledge of rocks. The river becoming more shallow, we opened a channel by removing large stones, and as the current was now excessively rapid, we pulled well out into the stream, bows up, let go a grapnel, and eased each boat down in succession. Below us were yet five successive falls, with rapids between,—a perfect break-down in the bed of the river. It was very evident that the boats could not descend them.

On the right of the river, opposite to the point where the weirs and the ruined bridge blocked up the bed of the stream, was a canal or sluice, evidently made for the purpose of feeding a mill, the ruins of which were visible a short distance below. This canal, at its outlet, was sufficiently broad and deep to admit of the boats entering and proceeding a short distance, when it became too narrow to allow their further progress.

Bringing the boats thus far, we again took every thing out of them and cleared away the stones, bushes and other obstructions between the mill-sluice and the river. We then made a breach in the bank of the sluice, and as the water rushed down the artificial channel, with infinite labor, in which we were assisted by a number of Arabs, we bore them down the rocky slope and launched them in the river.

The frame boat here foundered, notwithstanding all our efforts to keep her afloat. From her construction, she was less elastic than the metallic boats, and the thumps upon the rocks which only indented them, shattered her. Thus ended all our hopes of transporting the tents from place to place on the Dead Sea, and thereby protect us from the heavy dews of night.

Shortly after leaving the last ruined bridge, we descended a cascade at an angle of six degrees, at the rate of 12 knots, and immediately after down a shoal rapid where we struck and hung for a few moments upon a rock. The course of the river was very circuitous; the soil on each side fertile, but almost wholly uncultivated.

At 5.40, P. M., passed the village of Abeidîyeh, a large collection of mud huts, on a commanding eminence on the right. The inhabitants, men, women, and children, with discordant cries, hurried down the hill towards the river when they saw us. The water, which yesterday was translucent as that of the lake, and was this morning somewhat muddy, became clear again in the evening. The mountain ranges forming the edges of the upper valley, as seen from time to time, through gaps in the foliage of the river banks, were of a light brown color surmounted with white.

The water now became clearer with a hard bottom: there were small trees in the thickets under the banks and advancing into the water—principally the oleander, the tamarisk, the willow, and tangled vines beneath. We frequeutly saw fish in the now transparent water; while ducks, storks, and a multitude of other birds rose from the reeds and osiers, or plunged into the thickets of oleander and tamarisk which fringed the banks;—beyond them, were frequent groves of the wild pistachio.

At 8, P. M., we reached the head of the falls and whirlpool of Bŭk'ah, and finding it too dark to proceed, hauled the boats to the right bank, and I clambered up a steep hill to search for the camp. About one-third up, encountered a deep dyke, cut in the flank of the hill, which had evidently been used for purposes of irrigation. After following it for some distance, succeeded in fording it, and going to the top of the hill, had to climb over briars and stone walls, the ruins of the village of Delhemîyeh. A short distance beyond, I met a mounted Bedawy who had been sent to look for us. Learned from him that the camp was below the whirlpool and abreast of the lower rapids. Sent word to Mr. Aulick to secure the boats and bring the men up as soon as they were relieved, and hastened on myself to procure the necessary guards, for our men were excessively fatigued, having been in the water and without food since breakfast.

The village of Delhemîyeh, as well as that of Bŭk'ah opposite, were destroyed, it is said, by a tribe of Bedawin, or predatory Arabs.

Many of the villages on and near the river were inhabited by Egyptians, placed there by Ibrahim Pasha, when Syria was tributary to Egypt, to repress the incursions of the Bedawin,—somewhat on our plan of the military occupation of Florida. But, since Syria has been retroceded to the Porte, they have been unprotected and fallen prey to the Bedawin. The tribes through which we had passed thus far, were the Beshâtawee, one hour above and below the bridge of Semâkh, numbering two hundred fighting men; next the 'Obeidîyeh, on both sides and one hour back from the river, mustering five hundred, and the Es Sŭkr, in whose territories we were now encamped, numbered three hundred warriors.

About three hours from the camp, on an eminence, at the foot of which flows the Yermâk, (ancient Hieromax,) was Um Keis, (the mother of ruins,) the ancient Gadara, one of the cities of the Decapolis. This place, restored by Pompey the Great, is said to contain magnificeent ruins, in an extraordinary state of preservation. In one of its wonderful tombs it is believed that the demoniac of the Gospel dwelt, when our Lord performed a miracle; and in its hot baths is laid the strange scene of incantatiou in the life of Iamblicus, when he is said to have called up the spirits of Eros and Anteros.

As the hot baths indicated the existence of volcanic characters, which might throw light upon the geological structure of that region, I gave Dr. Anderson an escort and directed him to visit Um Keis the next day, and rejoin us at the appointed place of rendezvous at night. Lake Tiberias was but four hours distant in a direct line, although we have been a day and a half on the river, so tortuous is its course, and so interrupted its channel.

We have to-day descended one cascade and seven rapids, three large and four small ones, and passed two small streams and six islands, five marshy and one wooded one. The current has been very strong.

Latitude of whirlpool of Bŭk'ah, 32° 39′ 10″ north.

Longitude of whirlpool of Bŭk'ah, 35° 35′ 40″ east.

Depth below the level of Mediterranean by barometrical measurement, 687.44 feet.

Wednesday, April 12. At day-break, examined the whirlpool and falls above and below the camp, and reconnoitred down to the River Yermâk. The banks of the Jordan were fringed with the laurestinus, the oleander, the willow, and the tamarisk, and farther inland, on the slope of the second terrace, grew a small species of oak and the cedar. The arbutus, (strawberry tree,) was mingled with the flowers of the plain. From the banks, to the elevated ridges on either side, the grass and the flowers presented a surface of luxuriant beauty.

Immediately after breakfast, we commenced preparations for bringing the boats down. With a lofty hill, the terminus of a lateral range, on each side, there was no possibility of conveying them round the falls, and our only alternative was to shoot them.

At 11.05, A. M., cast off and shot down the first rapid, and stopped near a desperate looking cascade of about eleven feet fall, to make final preparations. In the middle, was a sheer fall, with a bold, bluff rock just at the foot, which would render it necessary to turn sharp to the right, to avoid being dashed to pieces. This rock was on the outer edge of the whirlpool, which, a caldron of foam, swept round and round in circling eddies. Yet below were two fierce rapids, each about one hundred and fifty yards in length, with the points of black rocks peering above the white and agitated surface. Below them again, within a mile, were two other rapids—larger, but more shelving and less difficult.

Fortunately a large bush was growing on the left bank, about five feet up, where the wash of the water from above had formed a kind of promontory. By swimming across, some distance up the stream, one of the men carried over the end of a rope, and made it fast round the roots of the bush. The great doubt was whether the hold of the roots would be sufficient to withstand the strain, but there was no alternative. In order not to risk the men, I employed some of the most vigorous Arabs in the camp, to swim by the side of the boats, and guide them if possible, clear of danger. Landing the men therefore, and tracking the copper boat up stream, we shot her across, and gathering in the slack of the rope, let her drop to the brink of the cascade, where she fairly trembled and bent in the fierce strength of the sweeping current. It was a moment of intense anxiety. The sailors had now clambered along the banks and stood at intervals below, ready to assist us if thrown from the boat and swept towards them. One man, with me in the boat, stood by the line; a number of naked Arabs were upon the rocks and in the foaming water, gesticulating wildly, their shouts mingling with the noise of the rapids, and their dusky forms contrasting strangely with the effervescing flood,—and four on each side, in the water, were clinging on to the boat, ready to guide her clear of the threatening rock if possible.

The boat, in the meanwhile, swayed from side to side of the mad torrent, like a frightened steed, straining the line which held her. Watching the moment when her bows were brought in the right direction, I gave the signal to let go the rope. There was a rush, a plunge, an upward leap, and the rock was cleared, the pool was passed, and, half full of water, with breathless velocity, we were swept safely down the rapid. Hard work for all all hands—the thermometer standing at 90° in the shade.

At 1.45, P. M., passed down the fourth fall and a shelving rapid of one-third of a mile.

At 3.50, P. M., the iron boat came down, started again, and descended the fourth rapid, rounding back from west-southwest to southeast by south, in a distance of ninety yards.

At 4.20, passed the mouth of the Yermâk, ancient Hieromax, one hundred and thirty feet wide, with moderate current, its centre bearing east half south. Near sunset, we descended the most frightful rapid we had yet encountered, and after passing two others, arrived at Jisr Mêjami'a, (bridge of the place of meeting,) which is on the road from Nabulus, through Beisan, to Damascus, and ascended the cliff on the right, to examine the fall and rapid immediately below.

A ruined Khan (Caravansery) crowned the crest of the hill, at the foot of which, large masses of volcanic rock or lava were lying about, as if shaken from the solid mass by the spasm of an earthquake. The Khan had evidently been a solid structure and destroyed by some convulsion, so scattered were the thick and ponderous masses of masonry. The bridge gracefully spans the river at this point. It has one large and three smaller Saracenic arches below, and six smaller ones above them, four on the east and two on the west side. The river, deep, narrow and impetuous, flows through the larger arch and immediately branches,—the left arm rushing down a nearly perpendicular fall of about eight feet, and scarce a boat's length ahead encounters the bold rock of the eastern bank, which deflects it sharply to the right. The right branch, winding by an island in the centre and spreading over a great space, is shallow and breaks over a number of rocks. I decided to try the latter. Resuming the oars, we shot through the main arch and down about two hundred yards of the descent, when, it becoming too dark, hauled to the right bank and made fast for the night, a short distance above where the tents were pitched. Above and below the bridge, in the bed of the river, were huge blocks of trap and conglomerate; and almost immediately opposite was a great fissure exposing perpendicular layers of basalt, the structure distinct, black and porous. Upon the left bank, a short distance above the bridge, were twenty or thirty black Bedawin tents, with a number of camels grazing around. The men were seated in groups, smoking; the women, the drudges of the tribes, were passing to and fro, apparently busy in culinary preparations, and near them were some children playing.

Our tents were pitched upon a small promontory, commanding a view of the Khan and the bridge, with the river dashing and foaming through its central arch. Directly in front, the stream was quite wide, and separating into several channels, formed some small sedgy islands, where snipes were flying about and discordant frogs were croaking.

Early in the evening Dr. Anderson returned from his visit to the ruins of Gadara. For his observations, I respectfully refer you to his report. The trap has continued on both sides since we left Lake Tiberias, with occasional interruptions of sandstone, limestone and conglomerate. We, to-day, descended two cascades and six rapids, four large and two small ones; and passed one large tributary, the Yermâk, and one large and two small islands. The current was rarely less than four, and sometimes, down the rapids, as much as twelve to sixteen knots per hour. The water became quite discolored after passing the Yermâk.

We were in the land of Issachar, that of Gad was opposite.

Latitude of Jisr Mêjami'a, 32° 30′ 11″ north.

Level below the Mediterranean, 704.08 feet.

Thursday, April 13. Hearing that Mohammed Pasha, military governor of the district of Nabulus, was encamped in the valley of Jezrael, (a branch of the great valley of Esdraelon,) a short distance from Beisan, I sent Lieutenant Dale this morning to call upon him. I considered this a becoming mark of respect, for, except Sa'id Bey, the Turkish officers have been very civil to us. A janissary and four soldiers, sent by the Pasha of Jerusalem, I discharged at the same time, having no occasion for their services.

Succeeded in getting the boats down the rapids uninjured, except a few indentations in their bilge, and at 9.30, started at the same time with the caravan. As we would this day approach the lower Ghor, which is traversed by hostile tribes, Sherîf warned me to be prepared, and I mounted our heavy blunderbuss on the bow of the leading boat.

At 10.40, descending an ugly rapid, the leading boat struck on a rock, just beneath the surface of the water, and broaching-to, broadside on, was thrown upon her bilge, taking in a great deal of water. All hands jumping overboard, her combined strength and buoyancy carried her safely over.

At 11.02, we passed a small tributary falling in from southeast by east. A village in sight on a hill far to southeast.

There are evidently two terraces to the Jordan, and through the lowest one the river runs its serpentine course. From the stream, above the immediate banks, there is, on each side, a singulâr terrace of low hills, like truncated cones, which is the bluff terminus of an extended table land, reaching quite to the mountains of Hauran on the east, and the high hills on the western side. Their peculiarity of form is attributable, perhaps, to the washing of rain through a long series of years. The hill-sides present the appearance of chalk, without the slightest vestige of vegetation, and perfectly blinding from the reverberated sunlight.

At times, we would be perfectly becalmed, the trees and bushes which fringed the banks, intercepting the light air that came down from the mountains; when, even at this early season, the heat would be intense, and the birds ceasing to sing, hid themselves among the foliage, from which, even the noise we made in passing, could not startle them.

We have heretofore passed a number of islands, all of diminutive size; but at 11.20 to-day, there was one a quarter of a mile long. Heretofore the course of the river varied to every quarter of the compass; but to-day it preserved a more southerly direction. The prevailing growth upon the banks were the ghurrah, (like the aspen,) the turfa, (tamarisk,) sifsâf, (willow,) and difleh, (oleander.) At 11.30, entered the territory of the Emir Nassir, occupying two hours on the banks of the river, and his tribe—El Ghuzzarîyeh—numbering three hundred fighting men.

At meridian, stopped to observe for latitude; the weather very warm. We were changing our climate in a two-fold manner—by descent, and by progress southward.

At 5′, P. M., started again—the river very serpentine. In the course of an hour, the weather becoming oppressively hot, stopped to rest in a grove of tamarisk. At 2, P. M., started again: a great many Arabs on the shore running after us. They were the subjects of the Emir—and there were Arab women on a high hill to the left. The river 120 feet wide, and six feet deep,—gravelly bottom: thick canes and thistles on the margin. Water falling rapidly.

After 2, P. M., we saw no rock. At 2.15, passed down a shelving rapid, at the rate of ten knots. Soon after, passed an Arab encampment, the population in an uproar,—men and boys shouting and running down to the river-bank, and the women and children collected in groups on the flat roofs of their huts. Fifteen minutes after, came to a long reach in the river—the first straight line we had seen thus far. There were large ghurrah trees on the banks. They resemble the aspen, and are said to bear a juicy, sweet-flavored fruit. There were many birds on shore, and several fish-hawks flying about.

At 3, P. M., entered the territory of Es Sŭkr el Ghor, consisting of five hundred fighting men.

At 4.55, P. M., coming to a very tumultuous rapid, I landed, and on hands and knees clambered up a steep hill to examine it. The hill was about three hundred feet high, and the view from its summit wild and peculiar. The high alluvial terraces, on each side, were shaped by the action of the winter rains, into a number of conical hills, presenting the appearance of a giant encampment, so perfectly tent-like were their shapes. This singular configuration extended south as far as the eye could reach.

At 6.30, saw 'Akîl on the bank. Brought-to for the night, and secured the boats to the right bank, 30 feet below the summit.

The caravan found it excessively hot to-day. At one time they stopped, and were hospitably welcomed at the encampment of the Ghuzzarîyeh. The tents, numbering about forty, consisting of goat's hair cloth, dyed black, were stretched hut-fashion on poles and stakes.

Mohammed Pasha received Lieutenant Dale very kindly. He said he was about to move his command, (one thousand Turkish cavalry,) for the purpose of chastising a band of bad Arabs, but had delayed his march on our account, for fear of exasperating them to some attack upon us. He entertained him with coffee, pipes, and oranges, and insisted on sending ten horsemen to accompany us through the dangerous territory.

Mr. Dale described it as a beautiful sight, the camp and the war horses spread over this magnificent plain. On his return he passed through the ruins of Beisan, the ancient Scythopolis. There were acres of building stone, old walls, a theatre, &c., in good preservation; a few columns still stood in the valley. On the summit was a large fortress-looking building, now converted into a cow-pen by the Arabs, who have formed a village round it.

I regretted that the Pasha sent the soldiers, for I felt that their presence would tend more to endanger than to aid us; but, as it was meant in kindness, it would have been rude to send them immediately back, particularly as the march of the Turkish detachment had been delayed on our account. But their presence increased my anxiety; the sight of them might exasperate the Arabs, and I had no faith in their courage or fidelity.

The river to-day varied from thirty-five to sixty yards in width, and from five to six knots velocity of current, and five and six feet deep. Descended twelve rapids, three of them formidable ones, and passed one small tributary and five islands, one of them large and wooded.

Latitude of camp, 32° 30′ 11″ north.

We were yet in Galilee,—in the land of Issachar; opposite was Gilead, the land of Gad.

Friday, April 14. A beautiful morning, but several of us quite sick. Took leave of the caravan for the day, and with Sherîf and the Emir, descended to the boats by the aid of the gnarled and tangled roots which protruded from the bank. Launching out into the current, we were swept rapidly away before the eyes of the wondering Ghuzzarîyeh. Their astonishment at beholding our boats and our strange appearance, had in it something extremely ludicrous. On rising at an early hour this morning (for we are always up and stirring before the sun,) we found the whole bank lined with these barbarians, who were lying at full length upon the bluff with their heads projecting over, looking in amazement upon the wonders beneath.

The boats had little need of the oars to propel them; the current carrying them down at the rate of four knots per hour; the river, from its eccentric course, scarce permitting a sketch of the topography to be taken. It turned and twisted north, south, east, and west, running in the short space of half an hour to every quarter of the compass.

There was little variety in the scenery this day. The western shore was peculiar from the high calcareous limestone hills; while the left or eastern bank was low and fringed with tamarisk and willow, with here and there a thicket of lofty cane and tangled masses of shrubs and creeping plants, giving it the character of a jungle. In one place we saw the tracks of a tiger, and in another started a wild boar.

Our course down the stream was with varied rapidity. At times we were going at the rate of 3 to 4 knots per hour, and again we would be swept and hurried away, dashing and whirling onward with the furious speed of a torrent. At such moments there was excitement, for we knew not but that the next turn of the stream would plunge us down some fearful cataract, or, dash us on the sharp rocks which might lurk beneath the surface.

For the reason I have before stated, the copper-boat always took the lead, and warned the other, which followed close behind, when danger was to be shunned or encountered. When the sound of a rapid was distinct and near, the compass and the note-book were abandoned, and motioning to the other boat to check her speed, we swept into the swiftest, which is ever the deepest part of the stream. When the current caught us, the boat's-crew, and our Arab friend Jumâh, (Friday,) leaped into the stream, and clinging to the boat's sides, assisted in guiding her down the perilous descent. In this manner, she was whirled on, driving between rocks and shallows with a speed that made her quiver; then, shooting her through the foaming basin below, the men leaped in, and with oars and rudder she was brought to an eddying cove, from whence, her sister-boat was directed through the channel.

Beyond these interruptions the river flowed broad and deep, yet maintaining much of the character of a torrent. Many islands, some covered with luxuriant vegetation, others mere sand-bars and sedimentary deposits, interrupted the course of the river; but, were beautiful features in the general monotony of the shores. The regularity of high banks of alluvial deposit on the one hand, and the low swamp-like shore, covered to the water's edge with the willow, the tamarisk and the thick high cane on the other, would have been fatiguing without the occurrence of sand banks and verdant islands.

A little before 12 o'clock we stopped to take a meridian observation, but soon started again, the scenery becoming more wild as the day declined.

As the evening shadows lengthened more and more upon the stream, we repeatedly stopped to look for the caravan. The Sherîf was very uneasy. On each occasion the faithful Jumâh was our scout, but he never landed without a brace of pistols. He returned at length with the intelligence that he had seen the caravan pursuing its march in the distance, and we continued on our way.

For upwards of an hour after, we swept down the stream, and the last tints of sunset were resting on the summits of eastern mountains. Wet and weary, without a change of clothes, and with neither provisions nor tents, we began to anticipate a night upon the river, separated from our friends, when, at a turn, we beheld a horseman on the crest of a high hill, his long āba and koofeeyeh streaming in the wind, and to our delight we recognised Akíl.

The brief remainder of this day's journey was rendered more perilous by the frequency of rapids and the difficulty of navigation in the fast fading light. But, altogether the descent this day, was less difficult than those which had preceded it. The river was falling rapidly. We frequently saw sedge and drift-wood lodged high up on the branches of the overhanging trees, above the surface of the bank,—conclusive proof that the Jordan in its "swellings," still overflows the lower plain, and drives the lion from his lair, as it did in the ancient time.

For the first time, we to-day saw sand, gravel and pebbles along the shores, and the cane had become more luxuriant—all indicating an approach to the lower Ghor. The elevated plain or terrace, on each side, could be seen at intervals, and the high mountains of Ajlûn were visible in the distance.

At 4.40, P. M., hauled up just above an ugly rapid which runs by Wady Yâbes (Dry Ravine.) It looked too difficult to shoot without lightening the boats of the arms and instruments, and there being no near place of rendezvous below, we pitched our tents immediately opposite the ravine.

We this day passed through the territories of Emir Nassir, which in extent and fertility surpass many of the petty kingdoms of Europe.

The Emir and some of his people have wiry hair and very dark complexions, but no other feature of the African. His brother and several of the tribe are bright, but less so than 'Akíl.

The prevailing trees to-day have been the willow, the ghurrah and the tamarisk, the last now beginning to blossom. There were many flowers, of which the oleander was the most abundant. Where the banks were low, the cane was ever at the water's edge. The lower plain was covered with a luxuriant growth of wild oats and mustard, the last in full bloom.

In our course to-day, we passed twelve islands, all but three of diminutive size, and noted fourteen tributary streams, ten flowing in on the right and four on the left; with the exception of four, they were trickling rivulets.

We saw many fish, and a number of hawks, herons, pigeons, ducks, storks, bulbuls (or nightingales), swallows, and many others which we could not identify.

In our route of upwards of twenty miles, we saw the scouts but once, and the caravan not at all.

The course of the river varied from northeast by north and north-northwest to south. The true course from the place of departure this morning to our present camp, south-southwest. The width of the river has varied from seventy yards with two knots current, to thirty yards with ten knots current; the depth, varying with the width, has ranged from two to ten feet.

We struck three times upon sunken rocks to-day, and the last time nearly lost the leading boat; the water was slightly discolored. When we left the camp this morning the thermometer stood at 76°, but a few hours after, the weather was oppressive.

About five miles, nearly due west from the camp, is Succoth, to which Jacob came after meeting Esau.

At night, Sherîf and 'Akîl came to consult with me about the next day's journey. They gave it as their opinion that it would be impossible for the caravan to proceed that day on the western shore, and advised that early in the morning, it should cross over to the eastern side. They both said that there was not the slightest danger to the land party, but expressed great solicitude for the boats. Sherîf thought that it would be best for him to be with the caravan. I consented that the caravan should cross over, on condition that 'Akîl with his scouts should keep on the western side, in order, that as the boats would be between them, one or the other of the land parties might hear a signal and hasten to their assistance if attacked. Stationing the sentries, we then retired; some of us quite sick from frequent vomiting during the day. I thought that our Bedawin magnified the danger, to enhance their own importance. But it was well to be prepared.

Latitude by meridian observation to-day, 32° 26′ 34″ north.

Level of camp below the Mediterranean, 843.02 feet.

Latitude of camp by meridian observation of moon, 32° 24′ north.

Saturday, April 15. Leaving the place of encampment for the ford Wacabes, the caravan passed along the base of a low, conical sand-hill and traversed a small grove of oak and arbutus, and a matted undergrowth of briars with long, sharp thorns. Here, as had been arranged, 'Akîl and his scouts separated from the caravan and proceeded down the western shore, while the latter crossed over to the eastern side.

Shortly after shooting the rapid below our place of encampment, the boats were whirled along with great velocity, and barely escaped a rock near the surface, and directly in the channel. The stream was fringed with trees of the same varieties as have been heretofore noticed; and we began to meet with many false channels, which rendered the navigation more tedious and difficult.

At 9.28, A. M., passed on the right, Wady el Hammâm, (Ravine of the Bath,) with a small stream coming down. Soon after, came to an ugly rapid by Wady el Malakh, (Ravine of Salt,) with a small stream of clear, but brackish water, coming down from the west-northwest; its temperature 70°. Saw 'Akîl and some of the scouts on a hill behind it. Stopped to examine the rapid for a passage. Found here some plants of the Ghurkŭd, its leaves triangular-shaped, of a dull green color, coated with saline efflorescence. The stem and leaves were bitter to the taste. On the banks, and in the bed of the river, were many fossil rocks. The fennel was also quite abundant, of which, Jumah ate greedily.

At 11.30, stopped for the other boat, and to take meridian observation. Temperature of the air, 82°; of the water, twelve inches below the surface, 74°. The heat was oppressive for the thermometrical range; for the wind being excluded by the lofty hills and overhanging trees, it was ever a perfect calm, except, when at times, it came in squalls down the yawning ravines. The plain above was much broken, presenting abrupt mounds and sand hillocks, the former covered with varieties of the thistle, some of which were peculiar from the sabre shape of their thorns, and the rough, hairy coating of the leaves, the latter emitting a milky fluid when broken. The thorn bushes were so large and abundant as to resemble apple orchards.

At 12.05, started again, and at 12.42, saw the mountains of Belka ahead from a turn of the river. At 2.23, entered the territory of El Fâri'a, extending for one hour on each bank, the tribe numbering one hundred fighting men. We also passed through the territory of Es Sŭkr el Ghor, the tribe numbering five hundred warriors.

The eastern mountains assumed a gloomy aspect to-day and presented rough and verdureless crags of limestone. The hills to the west preserved their conical shapes with bald faces. The water was discolored, of a light mud, approaching a milk color. We gathered many flowers for preservation, and among them a plant with which we are unacquainted, resembling the castor bean. Except during the heat of the day, when every living thing but ourselves had sought refuge in the thicket, there were birds flying about in all directions.

At 2.34, P. M., we saw the caravan halted on the bank; came to, and pitched our tents at the ford of Sŭkwa, on the left or eastern bank, abreast of two small islands. The ford takes its name from a village of the Sŭkrs, about two miles distant.

'Akîl is on friendly terms with this tribe; and some of them who have come in, state that their village was last night attacked by about two hundred Bedawin, who killed several of their tribe and carried off nearly all their cattle, horses and sheep.

This has been a most solitary day's travel. We have not seen the caravan from the time of starting until now, and 'Akîl and the scouts were visible but once. With this exception we have not seen a human being.

The caravan was more fortunate. Shortly after crossing the Salt Ravine, they discovered a solitary plane tree, gnarled and twisted by the winds. Their attention was instantly drawn to it, for, within its scanty shade, they saw the glitter of a spear-head, and soon after, two mounted Bedawin came forth and hastening in another direction, were, in a few moments, lost in the thick copse-wood which lined the ravine. For an instant, our Arabs drew the rein, and consulted among themselves, when four or five started off at headlong speed in pursuit. Making a long detour to intercept the strange horsemen, they too plunged into the ravine, and like those they pursued, were soon lost to sight in the thick foliage which skirted its sides.

The strange horsemen were suspected to belong to a larger party, as there were many black tents on the eastern bank of the river; but they proved to be friendly Beni Sŭkrs on their way to Beisan.

Crossing Wady Ajlûn, down which ran a considerable stream, they met some Fellahin or Agricultural Arabs, one of whom kissed Sherîf's hand. From the southern side of the ravine, they saw an immense plain, stretching towards the Dead Sea. Far off, on a height, was the village Abu 'Obeideh, containing the tomb of one of the great followers of Mohammed.

The character of the whole of this dreary scene was singularly wild and impressive. The plain that sloped away from the bases of the hills, was broken into ridges and multitudinous cone-like mounds, presenting a wild and checkered tract, with spots of vegetation flourishing upon the frontiers of irreclaimable sterility.

In the boats, we to-day descended two moderate and six ugly rapids, and passed three tributaries to the Jordan, two quite small and one of respectable size. Also, four large and seventeen small islands. We had now reached a part of the river not visited by Franks, at least, since the time of the Crusades, except by three English sailors, who were robbed and fled from it a short distance below.

The course of the river to-day varied from northwest to east; but the prevailing direction was southwest. The velocity of the current was from three to eight knots per hour. The average width was near sixty yards, and the average depth a little over four feet.

About 18 miles east by north from the camp, were the ruins of Jerash, supposed to be the anicent Pella, to which, Eusebius states, the Christians were divinely admonished to fly, just before the siege of Jerusalem by Titus. With Gadara (Um Keis) it was one of the cities of the Decapolis. It has magnificent ruins, many of them of churches, and its situation is said to be the most beautiful, and its ruins the most interesting in all Syria.

As the attack upon the neighboring village last night showed that "bad Arabs" are about, each one slept with his weapons beside him, and the injunction was repeated to rally around the blunderbuss in the event of an alarm.

The early part of the night was pleasant, but towards morning the wind swept down coldly from the mountains.

Latitude of the camp, 32° 09′ 18″ north.

Level below the Mediterranean, 1,049.44 feet.

Sunday, April 16. A pleasant day—wind light from northeast. We were on the move early this morning. The Sherîf very uneasy, was apprehensive of an attack upon the boats to-day, but thought it advisable for him to be with the caravan to exercise his influence with the Sheikhs of tribes whose territories we might pass through. He was urgent with the Emir to accompany us on the river. The latter excused himself on the plea of head-ache.

After a cup of coffee, taken standing, we started with the boats, leaving the caravan to cross over and proceed down the western bank—yesterday's march having been made on the eastern side.

The country presented the same appearance as yesterday, except that rocks were rarely seen, but, in their stead, banks of semi-indurated clay. The lower plain was evidently narrower, and the river often swept alternately against the hills which flank the lower and mark the elevation of the upper plain.

These various ramifications of mountain ranges and intervening platforms and valleys afford, according to Humboldt, evidences of ancient volcanic eruptions undergone by the crust of the globe, these having been elevated by matter thrown up in the line of enormous cracks and fissures.

The vegetation was nearly the same as yesterday, except that it was much more luxuriant on the borders of the stream,—more parched and dull on either side beyond it. The oleander increased; there was less of the asphodel, and the acacia was rarely seen, as heretofore, a short distance inland. The tamarisk was more dense and lofty, and the canes were frequently thick and impenetrable. There was much drift wood in the stream, and bushes and branches lodged high up in the trees which lined the banks,—conclusive marks of a recent freshet. The ghurrah was also becoming more abundant, and we noticed that whenever the soil was dry, the leaves of this tree were most silvery.

About an hour after starting, we came to the place where the lamented Molyneux's boat was attacked, while he was journeying down by land. Stopped to examine. It is just above a very rapid part of the river, where the boat could not have been stopped if the crew had kept her in the stream, unless most of them had been disabled by gun shots from the shore. As they escaped, I concluded that they were surprised when asleep, or loitering on their way. Starting again, we passed under an overhanging tree, with a bush fifteen feet up in its branches, lodged there by the recent freshet, for it was deciduous, and the green leaves of the early season were upon it. The river must this year have overflowed to the foundations of the second terrace.

In many places the trees were drooping to the water's edge, and we were sometimes swept under the branches, which prevented us from carrying the awnings; in consequence of which we suffered more than heretofore from exposure to the sun.

At 11.20, the temperature of the air, 92°; of the water, 72°. Soon after taking the meridian observation, we were hailed by some Arabs from a high hill on the left, asking whether the horsemen who had passed were friends or enemies? We supposed that they referred to our scouts.

At 1, P. M., we saw tracks of wild animals upon the shore. There were many fissures in the hills, and much debris fallen into the stream.

At 2.27, came in sight of the encampment, the tents, as heretofore, already pitched; the camping place, Mukŭtta Dâmieh, (Ford of Dâmieh,) where the road from Nabulus to Salt crosses over. Nearly opposite to the camp, discovered the ruins of a Roman bridge.

Latitude at noon, 32° 06′ 39″ north.

Level below the Mediterranean, 1,096.88 feet.

In the early part of the march to-day, the caravan anticipated a skirmish. Some strange Arabs, supposed to be a marauding party, were seen in the distance. The line was immediately closed and the scouts called in, all but a few, who were sent to reconnoitre a ravine in front.

Our Bedawin felt or feigned a conviction that an engagement would take place, and all due preparations were made. The camels were halted, and the horsemen, collecting in front, waited for the reconnoitring party to return. In the mean time, our Arabs went through their feats of horsemanship, sang their war-song, and seemed to be endeavoring to work themselves into a state of frenzy, and guns were unslung and freshly capped, lances were placed in rest, and swords were loosened in their scabbards.

The other party, however, kept aloof, proving neither hostile nor friendly, and 'Akîl, as he passed, contemptuously blew his nose at them. They were believed to belong to the tribe Mīkhâil Meshakâh, whose territory was thereabouts.

Monday, April 17. A damp and chilly morning. As soon as we were up I paid the Emir and his followers for their services as guides, and discharged them.

We started at 6.25, A. M., the river forty yards wide and seven feet deep, flowing at the rate of six knots, with much drift wood in the stream. There were many large trees, some of them recently uprooted, for the green leaves were yet upon them. The banks were mostly alluvial, and we began to see the cane in blossom. Altogether, the vegetation was more tropical than heretofore.

Many birds were singing about the banks and under cover of the foliage, but we saw few of them; now and then some pigeons, doves and cranes, and occasionally a bulbul.

The bases of the hills, on each side, presented little evidences of fertility of soil, notwithstanding their proximity to the river. A few scrubby bushes were scattered here and there, exhibiting the utter sterility of the country through which we were journeying. These hills were immense masses of silicious conglomerate, with occasional limestone.

In the faces of the hills as we passed were immense caves and excavations, whether natural or artificial we could not tell.

At 1.20, P. M., came to the river Jabok, (Zerka,) flowing from east-northeast, a small stream trickling down a deep and wide torrent-bed. Stopped to examine it. The water was sweet, but the stones upon its banks were coated with salt. There was another bed, now dry, showing that in times of freshet there are two outlets to this tributary, which is incorrectly placed in the maps.

It was here that Jacob wrestled with the Angel, at whose touch, the sinew of his thigh shrunk up. In commemoration of this event, the Jews, to this day, carefully exclude that sinew from animals they kill for food.

This river too, marks the northern boundary of the land of the Ammonites.

At 4.52, we passed down wild and dangerous rapids, sweeping by the base of a perpendicular hill.

At 5.44, heard and caught glimpses of an Arab in the bushes on the left. At the same time, a number of Arabs were calling loudly to us from a hill on the right. Stopped for the boats to close in, and prepared for a skirmish. The Arabs proved friendly, having been spoken by the caravan, and they hailed to tell us that they had sent a guide for the Pilgrim's ford, the appointed place of encampment. Took the guide in and continued to descend with great rapidity.

The sun went down and the night gradually closed in upon us, and the rush of the river seemed more impetuous as the light decreased. We twice passed down rapids, taking care, each time to hug the boldest shore. Besides the transition from light to darkness, we had exchanged a heated and stifling, for a chilly atmosphere, and while the boats' crews, more fortunate, kept their blood in circulation by gently pulling with the oars, those in the stern-sheets fairly shivered with the cold.

There had been such a break-down in the bed of the stream after passing the Jabok, that I became exceedingly anxious. In the obscure gloom, we seemed to be stationary, and the shores to flit by us. With its tumultuous rush, the river hurried us onward, and we knew not what the next moment would bring forth—whether it would dash us upon a rock, or plunge us down a cataract.

The friendly Arab, although he well knew the fords of the river in his own district, was, like every one we had met, wholly unacquainted with the stream at all other points.

Under other circumstances, it would have been prudent to lie by until morning; but, we were all wet, and had neither food nor change of clothing, and apart from danger of attack in a neighborhood represented as peculiarly bad, sickness would have been the inevitable consequence of a night spent in hunger, cold and watchfulness.

At 9.30, P. M., we reached El Meshra'a, after having been fifteen hours in the boats, and found the tents already pitched.

This ford, the bathing place of the Christian pilgrims, is consecrated by tradition as the spot where the Israelites passed over with the Ark of the Covenant, and where our Blessed Saviour was baptized by John.

A short distance from the camp were the ruins of Jericho. Of that city, the first conquest of the Israelites west of the Jordan, and where Herod the Great died, but a solitary tower remains—if indeed it be the true site. The plain of Jericho is covered with olive and the nübk trees, and many shrubs and flowers. From the hills back, the Dead Sea and the grim mountains of Moab were visible to the southeast. The latter of the hue of ashes, looked as if they had been riven by thunder-bolts and scathed by lightning.

Fourteen miles distant, on the opposite side of the river, was Heshbon, "where Sihon, the King of the Amorites, dwelt."

We were in the land of Benjamin; opposite was that of Reuben on the plains of Moab.

The great secret of the depression between Lake Tiberias and the Dead Sea, is solved by the tortuous course of the Jordan. In a space of sixty miles of latitude and four or five of longitude, the Jordan traverses at least two hundred miles. The river is in the latter stage of a freshet—a few weeks earlier or later, and the descent would have been impracticable. As it is, we plunged down twenty-seven threatening rapids, besides a great many of lesser magnitude.

We passed to-day through the territories of the Beni 'Adwans and Beni Sŭkrs, and into that of the tribes of the lower Ghor.

Latitude of camp, 31° 47′ 08″ north.

Longitude of camp, 35° 35′ 16″ east.

Tuesday, April, 18. At 3, A. M., we were roused with the intelligence that the pilgrims were coming, and were obliged precipitately to move our tents a little higher up. In respect to the sanctity of the place, the boats were moored lower down on the opposite side, but kept in readiness to rescue any of the pilgrims who might be in danger of drowning.

The party which first disturbed us, was the advanced guard of the great body of the pilgrims. At the dawn of day, the latter made its appearance, coming over the crest of a high ridge in one tumultuous and eager throng. There were Copts and Russians, Poles, Armenians, Greeks and Syrians,—from all parts of Asia, from Europe, from Africa, and far-distant America,—men, women and children, of every age and hue, and in every variety of costume,—talking, screaming and shouting a medley of languages.

Mounted as variously as those who preceded them, many of the women and children were suspended in baskets or enclosed in cages, and with their eyes strained towards the river, heedless of all intervening obstacles, they hurried eagerly forward, and dismounting in haste, and disrobing with precipitation, rushed down the bank and threw themselves into the stream.

They seemed to be absorbed by one impulsive feeling and perfectly regardless of the observation of others. Each one plunged himself, or was dipped by another, three times, below the surface of the water in honor of the Trinity, and then filled a bottle or some other utensil, from the river. Most of them, as soon as they dressed, cut branches either of the agnus-castus or the willow, and dipping them into the consecrated stream, bore them away as memorials of their visit. In an hour, they began to disappear, and shortly after, the trodden surface of the bank reflected no human shadow. The pageant disappeared as rapidly as it had approached, and left to us, once more, the silence and the solitude of the wilderness.

By 8, A. M., several thousand pilgrims had arrived, bathed in the consecrated stream, and departed.

Shortly after the departure of the pilgrims, a heavy cloud settled above the western hills, and we had sharp lightning and loud thunder, and a refreshing shower of rain, the first since we left Beïrût.

In consequence of living on salt food since we left Tiberias, we were much in need of refreshment; but disappointed in the expectation of procuring provisions from Riha, (Jericho,) a few miles distant, we determined to proceed at once to the Dead Sea.

Dr. Anderson kindly volunteered to go to Jerusalem to superintend the transportation of the bread and preserved meats I had sent there, and I gladly accepted his services, and requested him to make a geological reconnoissance of his route.

At 1.45, P. M., started with the boats, the caravan making a direct line for 'Ain el Feshkhah, (Fountain of the Stride,) on the northwest shore of the Dead Sea, a few hours distant. The course of the river, at first circuitous, preserved more of a southern direction than heretofore. At 1.52, stopped to fill the India rubber water bags, and at 2.22, started again. The banks, at first lined with tamarisks and willow, became gradually fringed with the cane, and the river was wider and deeper, with a more sluggish current as it descended; passed a small stream, with a fœtid sulphureous odor, flowing in on the left.

At 3.16, the water brackish, but with no unpleasant smell. The banks, red clay and mud, becoming lower and lower and bare of all vegetation. The river eighty yards wide, seven feet deep, muddy bottom, current three knots. Saw the Dead Sea over the flat, bearing south. At the mouth of the river were three mud islands, subject to overflow.

At 3.25, P. M., passed by the extreme point where the Jordan is one hundred and eighty yards wide and three feet deep, and entered upon the Dead Sea. The river, where it enters the sea, is inclined towards the eastern shore, pretty much as represented in the map of Messrs. Robinson and Smith, which is the most exact of any we have seen.

A fresh northwest wind was blowing as we rounded the point. The wind soon freshened into a gale, and caused a heavy sea, in which the boats labored excessively. The spray was painful to the eyes and skin, and evaporating as it fell, left incrustations of salt upon our faces, hands and clothing.

At 5.40, P. M., unable to stem the sea, kept away for the northern shore, with the intention of endeavoring to beach the boats to save them. At 5.58, a gun-shot distance from the shore, the wind instantaneously abated, and with it the sea as rapidly fell, the water, from its ponderous quality, settling as soon as the agitating cause had ceased to act. The sun went down, leaving beautiful islands of rose-colored clouds over the coast of Judea; but, above the yet more sterile mountains of Moab, all was gloomy and obscure.

The northern shore is an extensive mud-flat with a sandy plain beyond, and is the very type of desolation;—branches and trunks of trees were scattered in every direction, some charred and blackened as by fire, others white with an incrustation of salt. These were collected at high-water mark, designating the line which the water had reached prior to our arrival. The northwestern shore is an unmixed bed of gravel, coming in a gradual slope from the mountains to the sea. The eastern coast is a rugged line of mountains, bare of all vegetation, coming from the north, and extending south beyond the scope of vision, and throwing out three marked and seemingly equi-distant promontories from its southeastern extremity.

At 7.58, P. M., wet and weary, reached the beach below 'Ain el Feshkhah, where the caravan had arrived and pitched the tents. The camp was in a cane-brake, beside a fœtid and brackish spring.

On their route from Meshra'a, the shore party crossed a sandy tract of damp ravines, and over a plain incrusted with salt, and sparsely covered with sour and saline bushes, where it was difficult for the camels to march without slipping. Some of the bushes were dead and withered, and snapped on the slightest touch given them in passing. They noticed many cavernous excavations in the hill-sides, the dwelling places of the Israelites, of early Christians, and of hermits during the Crusades.* They at length reached a sloping dark-brown sand, forming the beach of the Dead Sea, and followed it to 'Ain el Feshkhah.

In descending the Ghor, Mr. Dale sketched the topography of the country and took compass bearings as he proceeded. The route of the caravan was on the bank of the upper terrace, on the west side, every day, except one, when it travelled on the eastern side. That elevated plain was at first covered with fields of grain, but became more barren as they journeyed south. The terrace was strongly marked, particularly in the southern portion, where there was a continued range of perpendicular cliffs of limestone and conglomerate. This terrace averaged about 500 feet above the flat of the Jordan, the latter mostly covered with trees and grass. They descended each day to the lower plain to meet the boats.

Wednesday, April 19. The wind sprung up in the night and blew fresh from the southward. At early daylight we were awakened with the intelligence that, from the high sea running, the boats were nearly filled with water. We hastened immediately down to dry them and secure our effects. I here discharged the scouts and camel drivers, and engaged 'Akîl to go to the tribes on the Arabian shore to announce our coming and make arrangements for supplying us with provisions in the country of Moab. In the course of the day a partridge was heard up in the cliffs, and a small bird twittered in the cane-brake.

We gathered some fresh water shells and specimens of conglomerate, and noticed an entire absence of sea shells or of round pebbles upon the beach, which was covered with minute fragments of flint. There was no vegetation except the cane and some dead trees in the margin of the sea.

Thursday, April 20. Sounded over the sea in east and southeast lines towards Wady Zerka in one direction, and a little below the mouth of the Jordan in the other. Returned at 10.45, P. M., the soundings towards the chasm giving 116 fathoms (696 feet) as the greatest depth. The southeast line gave 170 fathoms, (1,020 feet,) the bottom blue mud and sand, and a number of rectangular crystals of salt. For many casts in succession there was no variation in the depth.

In the evening some of the tribe Rashâyideh came in to serve as guides, and as messengers to procure provisions.

Difference of level between the Mediterranean and the Dead Sea by barometrical measurement, 1,234.589.

Friday, April 21. A light wind from the westward; the weather clear but warm, and the sea smooth. Lofty arid mountains on both sides; a low, flat shore to the northward and to the southward; the eastern and western shores converge in the last direction, leaving only water visible between them. In that direction, too, a light veil of mist was drawn over the sea.

At 11, A. M., broke up camp; sent Sherîf to Jerusalem to assist in forwarding provisions, and embarked to make an excursion to the southward, the precipitous limestone mountains towering high above us. At 1.36, P. M., stopped at the mouth of Wady en Nar, (Ravine of Fire,) with the convent of Mar Saba midway up the ravine, and the city of Jerusalem at its head, where it takes the name of the Valley of Jehosaphat—the torrent-bed

* "And because of the Midianites, the children of Israel made them the dens which are in the mountains, and caves, and strongholds."—*Judges*, xi, 1.

"And they drove away the people of Israel into lurking holes, and the secret places of fugitives."—I *Macchabeus*, i, 56.

perfectly dry, and covered with fragments of rock. The mountain sides and summits, and the shores of the sea, are almost entirely devoid of vegetation, and the rocks are of a burnt brown color.

At 3.30, P. M., low land visible to southward. At 4.15, threw over the drag in ten fathoms water. It brought up nothing but mud. At 4.43, rounded a low gravelly point, with some drift wood upon it, and landed and pitched our tents in a small bay, by the fountain 'Ain Turâbeh—a spring of pure, clear, and comparatively cool water, issuing out upon the beach, a few rods from the sea. Near by was a thicket of canes, and a line of ghurrah and tamarisk trees skirted the shores. The temperature of the spring, 75°. The pebbles along the beach, and the stones in the torrent-beds, to-day, were coated with a saline incrustation.

We found here a pistachio in full bloom, and in the stream of the fountain were several lily-stalks. The sand bordering the fountain and stream was discolored by a sulphureous deposit, as at 'Ain el Feshkhah.

We found here also, the Yellow Henbane, with narcotic properties; the Night-Shade (Anit et dil) or Wolf Grape, supposed by Hasselquist to be the wild grape alluded to by Isaiah; the Lamb's Quarter, used in the manufacture of barilla, and a species of kale—Salicornea—Europea. This last plant is found wherever saline formations occur. It was here upon the shore of the Dead Sea, and Fremont saw it on the borders of the Great Salt Lake, west of the Mississippi. The tamarisk trees around the fountain were in full bloom. the flowers small and of a dull white color. The wood of this tree makes excellent charcoal, and in the season, the branches bear galls almost as acrid as the oak.

Soon after our arrival, one of the party fired at a duck, with a dark grey body and black head and wings, a short distance from the beach. The startled bird flew a short distance out to sea, where it alighted, and again directed its course towards the shore. We therefore inferred that its haunt was among the sedges of the the fountain.

At sunset, the temperature of the air 70°; with light variable airs. The night was clear, and passed away quietly.

Saturday, April 22. Early in the morning it was quite cold. We here gathered some flowers for preservation, and an Arab brought us several specimens of sulphur, picked up on the banks of the Jordan.

At 7.51, A. M., started from 'Ain Turâbeh, with a light wind from southeast. At 8.20, passed Wady Ta'âmirah, at the head of which is Bethlehem.

At 8.30, a thin haze over the southern sea; appearance of an island between the two shores; the sun intensely hot. At 9.50, passed through a line of foam, colored brown by floating particles of decomposed wood.

At 12.10, stopped at Wady Sudeir, below 'Ain Jidy, (Engaddi,) Fountain of the Kid, and pitched our tents upon the shore, about a mile distant from the fountain, which is four hundred feet up the cliff. Our camp was upon a broad sloping delta, its surface covered with dust and coarse pebbles, or small angular pieces of rock, mostly flint. We found here the Nŭbk (Spini Christi, of Hasselquist) and the Osher—supposed to bear the celebrated apple of Sodom. The Nŭbk has small, thick, glossy leaves; its branches are covered with sharp thorns, and it bears a berry with a large stone. The fruit has a pleasant sub-acid taste, and is much relished by the Arabs. The Osher is a small tree, its bark ribbed like that of the sassafras; the leaves are long, thick, smooth and oval shaped. The flower is delicate, white and purple, growing in clusters. The fruit is the size of a very large peach; it is very nearly hollow, is puffy and elastic to the touch, and the skin very thin, and when unripe, of a light green color. The fruit and the young branches emit a viscous, milky fluid when cut or broken. The Nŭbk is called by the Arabs the Dhom, and its fruit the Dhom-Apple. On the upper part of the plain were the remains of former terraces and a few cucumber beds, destroyed a short time since by an incursion of hostile Arabs. Also, a few patches of barley, still standing. The whole aspect of the country parched and desolate. The mountains, with caverns in their perpendicular faces, towering fifteen hundred feet above us.

Examined the boats for repairs; found them very much battered, and their keels and stem and stern posts broken.

There were tamarisk trees in the bed of the ravine, besides many pink oleanders. About the plain we found the Rock Rose, from one of the species of which the gum Ladanum is procured, also the common Pink; the Aleppo Senna, which is used in medicine; the common Mallow, and the scentless Mignonette.

Commenced a series of barometrical and thermometrical observations, and measured a base line of 3,350 feet across the plain, and angled upon all possible points. Several of the Rashâdîyeh and the Ta'âmirah Arabs came in, and we found them very useful in bringing water and procuring provisions. They were very poor, and frequently solicited charity. We established our depôt here; here we proposed to leave our tents, and every thing we could dispense with, and this would be our home while upon this sea.

The wind blew strongly from the north during the night, and brought with it a fœtid smell of sulphuretted hydrogen.

Sunday, April 23. A clear warm day, given to rest; a light breeze from the southward during the forenoon, which, towards evening, shifted to the north and blew fresh, again bringing the fœtid smell. At 3.30, P. M., Doctor Anderson and the Sherîf arrived with the provisions, and brought with them four soldiers to assist the latter in guarding the camp during our absence. Calm and sultry throughout the night; the air impregnated with a sulphureous smell, but less strong than when the north wind blew.

Monday, April 24. At 6.38, one boat started to sound diagonally across to the peninsula, and the other directly across to a black chasm on the opposite coast, while the third party remained at the camp to make observations for determining its position. The greatest depth in the diagonal line was 137 fathoms (822 feet;) of the direct one 188 fathoms (1,128 feet,) the bottom, in both cases, light colored slimy mud, with rectangular crystals of salt, some of them perfect cubes.

The peninsula is a broad promontory from forty to sixty feet high, with a sharp angular central ridge some twenty feet above it. Between it and the sea is a broad flat margin of sand. The shore was encrusted with salt and bitumen, and there were a few dead bushes at the water's edge, and much drift wood strewed upon the beach, together with myriads of dead locusts. The frequent indications of salt, sulphur, nitre, and gypsum, presented, in the opinion of Dr. Anderson, a most interesting field of investigation.

To the northward of the point is a deep bay, indenting the peninsula from the north.

The black chasm opposite to the camp is Wady Mojeb, the mouth of the river Arnon of the Old Testament.

In the afternoon we again noticed a current setting to the northward along the shore, and one farther out, setting to the southward. The last, no doubt, the impetus given by the Jordan, and the former its eddy, deflected by Usdum and the southern shore of the sea.

On our first arrival here, I despatched a messenger to the tribes along the southern coast. He returned this evening, and reported that they have all been driven away, and that the country is frequented only by robbers.

Secured a stone-colored partridge and several insects for our collection, and gathered a specimen of every variety of flower for our herbarium. There were several large fires seen on the peninsula. In the night, killed a tarantula and a scorpion.

Tuesday, April 25. A fœtid sulphurous odor in the night. At day-break, a fine invigorating breeze from the north; air over the sea very misty.

At 8, A. M., completed a set of observations and started, leaving Sherîf in charge of the camp. Weather very warm. At 9, the thermometer 89°. The limestone strata of the western mountains are horizontal. We sounded every five minutes, and occasionally pulled out in search of the northern ford laid down in the map of Messrs. Robinson & Smith, but could not find it. At 1.58, P. M., abreast of Wady Sêyâl, (Ravine of Accacias.) On the cliff above, which is that of Sebbeh, are the ruins of the fortress Massada, built by Herod. This fortress, constructed by Herod and successfully beleagured by Silva, had a commanding prospect overlooking the deep chasm of this mysterious sea. Our Arabs could give no other account of it than that there were ruins of large buildings on the summit.

The cliff is perpendicular 1,200 to 1,500 feet high, with a deep ravine breaking down on each side, so as to leave it isolated. On the level summit, visible from the sea, is a line of broken walls, pierced in one place with an arch. The cliff is removed some distance from the margin of the sea by an intervening delta of sand and detritus, of more than two miles in width. A mass of rock, regularly laminated and isolated from the surrounding hills—its aspect from the sea is one of solemn grandeur, and seems in harmony with the fearful records of its past history.

At 4.45, P. M., stopped for the night in a little cove five or six miles north of the salt mountain of Usdum. From 'Ain Jidy to this place, the patent log marked 13⅛ nautical miles, which is less than the actual distance, the log not working sometimes from the shallowness of the water.

We paid particular attention to-day to the disposition of the ancient terraces and abutments of the tertiary limestone and marls, and to the geological construction of the western shore, for which I refer you to the geological report.

There was no variety in the scenery to-day. High, barren cliffs, and dry torrent-beds, opening upon arid plains or deltas, with now and then a shrub or stunted tree, were all that the land view presented. The sea was mostly calm, and looked sluggish and greasy. The beach where we were encamped, was bordered with innumerable dead locusts. There were also incrustations of lime and salt, and bitumen in occasional lumps. The latter presented a bright, smooth surface where fractured, and looked like a consolidated fluid. The Arabs called it "Hajar Mousa," (Moses' stone.)

Near our camp were several Nŭbk and Tamarisk trees, and three kinds of shrubs and some flowers, which were gathered for preservation. On a slight eminence we discovered the ruins of a building, the foundation walls alone remaining, and a line of low wall running down to a ravine—near it was a rude canal. There were many remains of terraces. Here Costigan thought that he had found the ruins of Gomorrah.

We had seven Arabs with us, and they were of three tribes—the Rashâyîdeh, Ta'âmirah, and the Kabêneh. Being beyond the limits of their territories, they were very fearful of an attack. We found here the ruins of an aqueduct, and part of the walls of a stone building. The wind during the night blew fresh from the north, and was so hot that we could not lie with our heads under the awning which had been stretched along the shore, but crawled out and slept upon the open beach. On this, as on every other occasion, there was an officer and two men always on post, and the blunderbuss was ever mounted immediately in front.

Wednesday, April 26. At 5.30, A. M., we started and stood for Ras Hîsh, (Cape Thicket,) north point of Usdum; sounding as yesterday in quest of the ford. At 8.12, landed on the point—a broad, flat, marshy delta, of adhesive mud. There were many dead bushes encrusted with salt at the margin of the sea. At 8.30, started again. At 9, the water shoaling, hauled more off shore. Soon after, saw on the eastern side of Usdum, one-third the distance from its northern cape, a lofty, round pillar standing detached from the general mass, at the head of a deep, narrow, and abrupt chasm. It proved to be a large pillar of salt, cylindrical in front and pyramidal behind, capped with carbonate of lime. The upper, or rounded part, about forty feet high, resting on a kind of oval pedestal, from forty to sixty feet above the level of the sea. We procured specimens from it. It slightly decreases in size upwards, crumbles at the top, and is one entire mass of crystallization. A prop or buttress connects it with the mountain behind, and the whole is coated with a dust of the color of ashes. From the surrounding configuration, its peculiar shape is perhaps attributable to the action of the winter rains. The shore was soft and yielding to the foot, and the foot-prints we made on landing were, at our return, an hour after, encrusted with salt. Some of the Arabs when they came up brought an oblong, ribbed, green melon, exceedingly bitter to the taste. They had gathered it on the north spit of Usdum.

Intending to explore the southern shore of the sea, and then proceed to the eastern or Arabian side, I here dismissed all the Arabs but one, and gave them provisions and water.

At 11.28, we were unable to proceed farther south from shallowness of the water. With great difficulty landed to take a meridian altitude; but the sextant would not measure it. The southern shore of the sea presented a mud-flat, which is terminated by the hills which bound the Ghor to the southward. A very extensive plain or delta, low and marshy towards the sea, but rising gently farther back, and covered with luxuriant green, is the outlet of the Wady es Safieh, (Clear Ravine.) We coasted as close to the shore as possible, the inner oars turning up the mud, but found it impossible to land. The line of demarcation between the sea and the shore, full three-fourths of a mile distant, indistinctly traced from the stillness of the water and the shining surface of the mud.

While in full view of the peninsula, I named its northern extremity "Point Costigan," and its southern one "Point Molyneux," as a tribute to the memories of the two gallant men who lost their lives in attempting to explore this sea.

At 11.42, there was much frothy scum upon the water. Soon after, we picked up a dead bird resembling a quail. Sounding every five minutes. At 11.50, depth four feet, firmer bottom—the only ford must be about here.

At 12.21, there was a very loud reverberating noise as of thunder, and a cloud of smoke and dust on the western shore, most probably a huge rock fallen from a high cliff.

At 3.30, P. M., calm and exceedingly sultry; temperature of the air, 97°; of the water, twelve inches below the surface, 90°. The sea and shore covered with a thin purple haze. I apprehended a thunder-gust or an earthquake and took in the sail. At 3.50, we were struck with a hot, blistering hurricane, that for some time threatened to sweep us to sea.

At 4.30, reached the shore, all hands exhausted. We landed near Wady Humeir, under the mountains of Moab. The sirocco blew fiercely until midnight, during which time, we laid upon the ground with our heads wrapped up to screen them from the blistering wind. A little after midnight the wind shifted and blew lightly from the north, and the thermometer, which had stood at 106° at 8, P. M., fell to 82° before day-break.

Thursday, April 27. Wc bivouacked last night on the shore of an inlet on the south side of the peninsula.

This morning about forty Fellahin, or Agricultural Arabs, armed with swords, guns, and cudgels, came out from the thicket. I drew our men up, and then, with the interpreter, advanced to meet them. Finding us too strong to be attacked, they began to beg, and I gave food to some that seemed on the point of starvation.

At 8.45, we started, one boat sounding directly across; the other skirting the peninsula, to sketch the topography. Weather warm, air 92°, water 85° at 9, A. M.; every one oppressed by an almost overwhelming sensation of drowsiness. At 12.52, P. M., landed on the western shore at Wady Muhariwat, where a shallow salt stream ran down the bank into the sea.

At 1.15, P. M., started again, and pulled parallel with the western shore. At 3.05, encountered a very irregular, heavy swell from northwest, and at 3.20, were struck with a hot hurricane, which lasted three-quarters of an hour.

At 4.15, P. M., we stopped for the night in a spacious bay under Rŭbtat el Jâmûs, a high and desolate cliff where we could procure no water. Our provisions were also nearly exhausted, but our supper was helped out by some dhom-apples, brought by our Arab guide.

The Arabs were our guides and messengers; they brought us food when nearly famished, and water when parched with thirst. They had thus far been perfectly tractable, and I know not what we should have done without them.

Friday, April 28. Light airs from northeast, and cloudy. Took a small cup of coffee each, and started at 5.58, A. M. Steered the course for 'Ain Jidy with the intention of crossing over to Wady Mojéb if the wind should spring up favorable, but to keep on to the camp should it continue light, or prove adverse. At 7.30, the wind freshened up from northeast, which left us no alternative as we were out of water, and were we to attempt to cross the sea, we might be kept out all night or driven ashore, where, as last night, water could not be procured. Unlike on all other seas, there was no fear of drowning here, neither the boats nor those who were in them could be made to sink; but its inhospitable shores afford no food and very little wholesome water.

Notwithstanding the high wind, the sun was very hot, and the tendency to drowsiness almost irresistible. The men pulled mechanically with half closed lids, and besides them and myself, every one in my boat was fast asleep. The necessity of steering and observing all that transpired alone kept me awake.

At 1.35, P. M., arrived at the camp; Sherîf was overjoyed to see us, and we were gratified to learn that he had not been molested. In the evening we went up Wady Sudeir, and found a small stream of cool and refreshing water. We were also surprised to see evidences of former habitations in the rocks; roughly hewn caverns and natural excavations we had before seen, but none before evincing so much art. We concluded that they were the dwellings of Essenes prior to, and of hermits in the early days of Christianity.

About sunset we tried the buoyancy of the water of the sea by driving a horse and a donkey into it. When beyond their depth, the animals could with difficulty keep from turning over. A muscular man, without exertion, floated breast high out of the water. Picked up a large piece of bitumen on the shore, and some of the blossom, and green and dried fruit of the Osher were gathered for preservation.

At one time, to-day, the sea assumed an aspect peculiarly sombre; unstirred by the wind, it laid as unruffled as an inland lake. The great evaporation curtained it with a thin, transparent vapor, its purple tinge contrasting strangely with the extraordinary color of the sea beneath, and where they blended in the distance, gave it the appearance of smoke from burning sulphur. It seemed a vast cauldron of metal, fused but motionless.

A pleasant breeze from the west during the night, without unpleasant odor; but towards morning it shifted to the north and blew freshly, bringing the sulphurous smell with it.

Saturday, April 29. At day-light, despatched Lieutenant Dale, Dr. Anderson and Mr. Bedlow, with the interpreter, a Turkish soldier, and some Arab guides, to Sebbeh.

Soon after breakfast, sent Mr. Aulick in one of the boats to sound in a north and south line between the peninsula and the western shore. At 1, P. M., he returned, having sounded up a gradual ascent to 13 fathoms.

Protected by our presence, some of the Ta'âmireh to-day harvested their small patches of barley. They used their swords for reaping hooks, and the grain was trodden out by three diminutive donkeys, driven round the threshing floor in a line abreast. I purchased the grain for distribution at home.

In the afternoon, visited the fountain, which is four hundred feet up the mountain. It is shaded by a grove of the Spina Christi, and the course of its water is marked by a long line of green. At sunset the party to Sebbeh returned. Their observations confirmed the supposition of Messrs. Robinson and Smith, that the ruins are those of Masada, where nine hundred and sixty-seven Sicarii, under Eleazer, preferred self-immolation to falling alive into the hands of the Romans.

On their return, they noticed a fœtid smell in passing Berket el Khŭlîl, a pool of stagnant water.

Sunday, April 30. Weather quite warm. The forenoon given to rest. The faces of nearly all the party looked swollen and inflamed, and our bodies were covered with minute pustules. They caused me great uneasiness, although I could not tell of what they might be the symptoms, whether of improved health or coming sickness.

This was the day appointed to meet or hear from 'Akíl on the Arabian shore, and in the afternoon we sailed over to the peninsula, leaving the faithful Sherîf again in charge of the camp. On reaching the shore near Mezra'a, we met Jumâh, one of 'Akíl's followers, sent down in the morning from Kerak, where 'Akíl arrived the day before. We learned from Jumâh, that on his way from 'Ain el Feshkhah, 'Akíl and his party stopped at an encampment of Beni Sŭkrs, and that they were surprised by the hostile tribe of Beni 'Adwans, and forced to retreat, 'Akíl losing his camel with all his baggage; subsequently reinforced, they became in turn the aggressors, and after a warm engagement, came off victorious. Twelve of the Beni Sŭkrs, including Akíl's party were wounded, and twenty-two of the Beni 'Adwans were reported to have been killed. The son of the Sheikh of the latter tribe was among the slain, and his double-barrelled gun was given to the younger Sherîf, nephew of Sherîf Hazâa, for his gallantry in the action.

A little after sunset, a deputation of five Christian Arabs, headed by the son of the Christian Sheikh, brought us an invitation to visit Kerak. The town of Kerak is occupied by about two hundred Christian and one hundred Muslim families. The former are of the tribe Beni Khallas, (sons of invincible,) and number about one hundred and fifty fighting men. The latter are of the Kerakîyeh tribe, which musters about seven hundred and fifty warriors. The great body of the last named tribe live in black tents a short distance from the town. The Christians are subservient to and much tyrannized over by them.

The deputation of Christians expressed great delight in seeing fellow-Christians upon this sea. They said that we were brothers, and that however we might differ in forms, our faith was the same.

An invitation was also received from the Muslim Sheikh. I accepted it with a full sense of the risk incurred, but the whole party was so much debilitated by the sirocco we had encountered on the south side of the peninsula, and by the subsequent heat, that it became absolutely necessary to re-invigorate it at all hazards.

In the course of the evening, many of the Ghauwarîneh from Mezra'a came in. They, as well as the Christians, looked with amazement upon our boats, and were very inquisitive as to the position of their legs.

The wind was fresh from northwest during the night, the thermometer ranging from 82° down to 70°; at the latter temperature, we felt quite cold. There was a bright meteor from zenith, shooting to the northeast towards morning.

Monday, May 1. A calm and warm, but not unpleasant morning. Sent Mr. Dale and Mr. Aulick in one of the boats to complete the topographical sketch of the shore lines of the bay, verify the position of the mouth of Wady Kerak, and sound down the middle of the bay on their return.

There was much of the Nŭbk and some Osher trees upon the plain, and some patches of Dhoura or Millet, which is now a few inches high. About meridian the boat returned.

P. M. I rode out upon the plain, accompanied by two Arabs, to look for the ruins of Zoar. Saw a number of heaps of stone, but I could not tell whether they had been building stones, or collected by the Fellahin when clearing the ground for cultivation. Farther on, about the position indicated by Irby and Mangles, as the site of Zoar, there were the ruins of a large and very ancient building. The word large is used in a relative sense, as compared with most of the buildings we have seen since we left St. Jean d'Acre.

In the evening, the Christian Sheikh of Kerak, accompanied by the son of the Muslim Sheikh, arrived with horses and mules for our visit to-morrow. They brought a letter from 'Akíl, apologizing for not coming himself, in consequence of the wounds of one of his followers, and the weakness of his horses.

A little after night-fall, another party of fourteen came in, singing their war-cry, and bearing a tufted spear. There were about forty of these Arabs around us at night, and being uncertain of their disposition, we kept a more vigilant watch than usual.

The night was sultry, although the wind blew fresh; the thermometer 81°, with a heavy dew.

Tuesday, May 2. A cloudy morning; started at 5.30, A. M., with the whole party for Kerak, except one seaman, left at his own request with Jumâh, who had charge of the boats; our route was up a steep and rugged bridle path on the southern bank of the deep chasm of Wady Kerak.

We reached the town, which was seventeen miles distant, a little after noon. It is enclosed within high walls, and seated on the summit of the mountain. The country around, a high rolling plain, now brown and parched from the devastation of the locusts and the hot blasts of the sirocco. The streets are narrow, lined with low, square, mud-roofed stone huts. At the northwest angle of the wall there was a large ruined tower with a rich cornice, and at the southwest angle the ruins of an extensive castle, apparently built by the Crusaders, and subsequently repaired by the Saracens. About ten years since it was partly blown up by Ibrahim Pasha.

The Christians of Kerak received us kindly, but were too poor to furnish anything but milk and a few eggs. The Muslims from the first demanded backshish, which being refused, they became surly and disobliging.

Instead of hospitality we met with nothing but rude demands, which were invariably refused. We kept by our arms, and it was at some risk that we contrived by turns to visit the town and the ruins.

We were quartered in a room without furniture of any kind, and but for the exertions of the Christian Sheikh, could not have procured a morsel of food. This conduct of the Muslims determined me at all hazards to give them nothing whatever, and to this I steadfastly adhered.

Throughout the day our room was crowded by Arabs coming in to look at us, and the stairway was thronged with coming and returning visitors.

At night we placed a board against the door, that its fall might apprise us of an attempted entrance, and slept with our arms in our hands.

Wednesday, May 3. It was exceedingly cold during the night, the wind whistling shrill through the casements, and we were tormented by fleas. Still we were invigorated by the mountain air.

We started on our return at 6.30, A. M., with the Christian Sheikh mounted, and a few of his men on foot, leaving the Muslim Arabs in a surly mood. In about half an hour Mohammed overtook us and demanded various articles, a watch, a gun, &c., &c., intimating that if we did not give them as a backshish, there would be a hundred men in our path to compel us. Whereupon, I made him prisoner, and placing an officer and one of the most trusty men by him, with orders to shoot him on the first symptom of treachery, I held him as a hostage for the good behaviour of his tribe. This measure had the desired effect, and we reached our boats unmolested.

That evening we proceeded to Wady Môjeb, (the river Arnon,) and camped upon the southern side of its delta, on a fine, pebbly beach, in a little cove.

The Arabian shore from the peninsula to the Arnon presented a barren aspect of lofty, perpendicular cliffs of red sandstone, and here and there a ravine with patches of cane, indicating the immediate or recent presence of water.

The Arnon, now eighty-two feet wide and four feet deep, flows through a chasm with perpendicular sides of red, brown and yellow sandstone, ninety-seven feet wide; the cliffs on each side so fantastically worn as to resemble Egyptian architecture. After leaving the chasm, the river runs through a delta, in a southwesterly course, narrowing as it goes, and is ten feet deep where it debouches into the sea; on its banks were the castor bean, the tamarisk and the cane; George Overstock, seaman, had a chill to-day. Wind cool from northwest during the night.

Thursday, May 4. A warm but pleasant morning; Overstock better; sent Mr. Dale in one of the boats to sound across to 'Ain Turâbeh; just before starting heard two gun-shots, and voices in the cliffs above. Proceeded in the other boat to Wady Zerka Main, the outlet of the hot springs of Callirohoe, sketching the topography as we went; the shore the same as yesterday, except that in one place the mountain side was covered with huge boulders of trap and tufa, and every evidence of volcanic formation.

The sides of the chasm through which the Zerka flows are equally high and precipitous as those of the Arnon, but are not worn into such fantastic shapes. The chasm is one hundred and twenty-two feet wide, and the sides eighty feet high at the mouth, but much higher within. In the bed of the chasm were two streams, one eight feet wide and two deep, and the other six feet wide and two and a half deep, running down at the rate of eight knots per hour, the water at the temperature of 94°, and one mile up 95°, while that of the sea was 78°; the water not unpleasant to the taste, although a little sulphureous, and there was a saline deposit on the rocks.

It was quite cool in the night, the thermometer ranging from 70° to 68°, and there was a large fire on the Judean shore in the direction of Feshkhah.

Friday, May 5. Wind from the north; air quite chilly this morning. It is this change of temperature which makes the heat of the day so oppressive. I wished very much to have visited the ruins of Machærus, upon this singular hot water stream, and to have excavated one of the ancient tombs mentioned by Irby and Mangles; but fear for the health of the men, who are beginning to complain, warned us to lose no time in completing our reconnoisance and exploration.

At 3.40, A. M., started for 'Ain Turâbeh, sounding as we proceeded. Two furlongs from the land there were 27 fathoms, (162 feet;) the second cast five minutes after, gave 174 fathoms, (1,044 feet,) gradually deepening to 218 fathoms, (1,308 feet;) the bottom soft brown mud, with rectangular crystals of salt.

At 8, met the other boat sounding also. Put Passed Midshipman Aulick and Doctor Anderson in her, and directed them to complete the topography of the Arabian shore and determine the position of the mouth of the Jordan, while we continued on to 'Ain Turâbeh. On the way made a series of experiments with the self-registering thermometer to ascertain the temperature of the sea at various depths. That of the surface was 76°, and at 174 fathoms (1,044 feet) it was 62°, with a regular gradation between, except at ten fathoms, where we invariably found a stratum at the temperature of 59°.

In the afternoon, reconnoitred the pass over the cliffs here, to see if it be practicable to carry up the level. It proved very steep and difficult, but less so than those of 'Ain el Feshkhah and 'Ain Jidy, and I determined to attempt it; for the advancing season and the present state of the southern desert prohibited the route from near Usdum across to Gaza. Made arrangements for camels to transport the boats in sections across to Jaffa, via Jerusalem. Weather very warm through the night.

Saturday, May 6. A warm morning, the sea curtained with a mist. Commenced levelling, which duty I assigned to Lieutenant Dale, who was fully competent to the task.

At 9, A. M., the thermometer in the shade standing at 100°. At 11, Mr. Aulick and Dr. Anderson returned. The latter had collected many specimens in his department. Sent Mr. Aulick out to make experiments with the self-registering thermometer at various depths. The result the same as yesterday, both with regard to the gradual decrease of temperature and the cold stratum at ten fathoms. The increase of temperature below ten fathoms is, perhaps, attributable to heat being evolved in the process of crystallization.

Light flickering airs and very sultry during the night. Noticed, what we have often before observed, a central current of about one knot per hour setting to the southward, and another of less velocity setting to the north, along the shore; the last no doubt an eddy.

Sunday, May 7. This day given to rest. The weather exceedingly warm and oppressive. At 8.30, A. M., the thermometer stood at 106°—the clouds motionless, the sea unruffled, the rugged surface of the rocks without a shadow.

At 6, P. M., a hot hurricane, sweeping in currents from northwest to southeast, which blew down the tents and broke our last barometer. In two hours it gradually subsided to a perfect calm. All were suffering very much with languor, and prudence warned us to be gone.

The temperature of the night was lower than that of the day, and we slept soundly the sleep of exhaustion.

Monday, May 8. A cloudy, sultry morning. At 5, A. M., the levelling party proceeded to work up the pass. Constructed a large float, and carried it out and moored it, with the American flag flying, off 'Ain Ghuweir, in eighty fathoms water, too far from the shore to be molested by the Arabs.

The heat continued to increase as the day advanced, and at meridian the thermometer stood at 110° in the shade, and we were compelled to discontinue work. At 1.30, P. M., a light breeze sprung up, which gradually freshened and hauled to the northward. In the afternoon went to 'Ain Ghuweir, a short distance to the north, and found the water sweet, and not brackish, as it has been represented.

At 4, P. M., the levelling party returned, having worked up the pass, and three hundred feet beyond, into the Desert of Judea. Light airs, and sultry during the night.

Tuesday, May 9. Sent Mr. Dale at early day-light to reconnoitre the route from the pass to the Convent of Mar Saba. Sent also George Overstock and Henry Loveland, sick seamen, to the same convent to recruit. Took the boats apart, in six sections each, and sent them on camels to Jerusalem.

Tried the relative density of the water of this sea and some from the Atlantic, procured in latitude 25° north, and longitude 52° west. Distilled water being as 1—the water of the Atlantic was 1.02, and that of this sea 1.13.

The last dissolved 1-11th of its weight of muriate of soda; the water of the Atlantic 1-6th, and distilled water 5-17ths, or nearly one-third of its weight. The salt was a little damp, for which a small allowance should be made.

The exploration of this sea was now complete; we had carefully sounded its depths, determined its geographical position, taken topographical sketches of its shores, ascertained the temperature, width, depth and velocity of its tributaries, collected specimens of its own and its tributary waters, and of every kind of mineral, plant and flower; and noted the winds, currents, changes of weather, and all atmospheric phenomena. These, with a succinct account of events, exactly as they transpired, will give a correct idea of this sea as it has appeared to us. The same remarks holds with respect to the Jordan and the country through which it flows. Unless when prevented by high winds, we have on no occasion, day or night, omitted taking astronomical, barometrical and thermometrical observations.

Wednesday, May 10. At day-light sent the levelling party ahead; at 9.30, A. M., struck the tents for the last time on the shores of this sea, and at 10, started and ascended the pass. From time to time, as we slowly moved up the rugged path, we turned to look upon our flag, floating far off upon the sea.

The greatest depth we had found in the sea was 1,308 feet, directly across from 'Ain Turâbeh, and the height of the summit of its pass was 1,305.75 feet, or nearly the exact measure of its depth.

On the 17th we reached Jerusalem via Mar Saba, and found it to be 3,927.24 feet above the Dead Sea.

Resuming the level on the 22d, we proceeded slowly and laboriously to the west, until we reached the Plain of Sharon, which presented no other impediments than frequent cactus hedges, and on the 29th reached the Mediterranean Sea, a little south of Jaffa.

The results give 1,316.7 feet as the depression of the level of the Dead Sea below the Mediterranean. Jerusalem is 2,610.5 feet above the latter, and 3,927.24 feet above the former sea. Its elevation above the Dead Sea being almost exactly the multiple of its height above the Mediterranean, and the difference of level of the two seas.

On the 20th May, Dr. Anderson's engagement terminated.

Mr. Murad Serapion, our vice-consul at Jaffa, found storage for our boats, and placed his country-house at our disposal, refusing all compensation. He was zealous in his attentions, and unbounded in his hospitality—treating us more like kindred than strangers.

We remained near Jaffa, working up our previous observations, until the 7th June, when, receiving no tidings of this ship, I embarked the boats and most of our effects in a small vessel for St. Jean d'Acre; the vessel not being sufficiently large to accommodate the whole party, two officers and eight men embarked in her, and the rest proceeded to Acre by land.

On the land route, one of the men had his arm shattered by the accidental discharge of a gun; a boat that happened to be near the shore was immediately chartered to take him to Acre, and the wind being fair, she reached that place several hours before the rest of the party. On this occasion, the surgical skill and medical knowledge of Henry Bedlow, Esq., a volunteer associated in the expedition, were of invaluable service; he attended the wounded man in person to Acre, where the wound was dressed, and thence accompanied him to Beïrût, where the seaman was judiciously placed under the care of the Sisters of Charity.

For the sake alike of health and economy, I then led the party to the mountains, completing as we went the topography of the western, and the general outlines of the eastern shore of Lake Tiberias, and determining the position of the embouchure of the Jordan into it. From the northern shore of the lake we followed the Jordan up the high mountain pass, down which it rushed a foaming torrent, and through Lake Hûlêh, (Lake Mærom of the Bible,) into which and from which it flows a placid stream; and thence traced its rapid but not impetuous stream to its highest perennial source. At the foot of Mount Hermon it gushes copious, translucent and cool, from beneath a bold, perpendicular rock, and flows in two rectangular streams between banks literally fringed with flowers. The gigantic rock, all majesty above—its banks enamelled with beauty and fragrance, all loveliness beneath,—render it the fitting fountain head of a stream which was destined to lave the immaculate body of the Redeemer of the world!

Ascending to the village of Hâsbeiya, where provisions were cheap, and the air salubrious, we there waited for intelligence from the wounded seaman in Beïrût, intending, if he were in danger, to proceed thither and remain by him.

On the 22d, hearing that he was out of danger, and fearing that a sudden transition from active to inactive life might engender sickness, I led the party over the Anti-Lebanon to Damascus, taking notes, topographical sketches, and collecting specimens as we proceeded. In the latter place, we endeavored, with the boiling water apparatus, to ascertain its height above the sea, and, from the best sources, to obtain information respecting its manufactures, and its domestic and foreign trade. We found the bazaars stocked with foreign fabrics and cutlery—mostly English—paying, we were assured, a handsome profit. In the bazaars, we were shown English muslins with counterfeit American stamps—from the circumstance that American cottons are in most demand.

We thence proceeded to the ruins of Ba'albek, of which we took accurate sketches; and, crossing the plain of Bŭk'ah by the source of the Litany, (ancient Leontes,) clambered over the Lebanon, obtaining all the information we could, from reliable sources, of the products of its mountain sides and valleys, and the religious, political, and social distinctions of its various and singular population.

These subjects not being embraced in your instructions, the inquiries were made merely to add to the general stock of information respecting this interesting country; for, although it has been described by the philosophic and accurate Volney, who *did not*, and by the poetic and inaccurate Lamartine, who *did*, visit it, it has recently undergone political changes and serious social and religious modifications.

We arrived at Beïrût on the 30th June, in the fervent hope of meeting the "Supply," for the hot and sickly season was approaching, and all were debilitated, and some complaining. Two of the seamen, Mr. Dale, and myself required immediate medical attendance, and Dr. Suquét, a French physician sent to Syria by his government, was called in, and subsequently Dr. De Forest, of the American Evangelical Mission, was sent for; and Mr. Bedlow was ever present and unremitting in his attentions.

In a few days all were considered convalescent; but, unfortunately, Mr. Dale, in the hope of deriving benefit from the mountain air, rode to the village of Bhamdûn, twelve miles distant. The road was exceedingly rugged, and he reached his destination thoroughly exhausted. The next day he was somewhat recruited, but, unhappily, a sirocco set in which lasted three days, and so completely prostrated him that, I grieve to say, he expired on the 24th July.

This able and accomplished officer had been of invaluable service to the expedition; and to him the credit of levelling from the Dead Sea to the Mediterranean is justly due. By his death the profession has been shorn of one of its proudest ornaments.

In the gloom naturally created by such an event, we waited for the return of the "Supply," employing ourselves in bringing up our recent and verifying former observations.

While delayed in the neighborhood of Beïrût I procured from our consul, Mr. Chasseaud, a list of its imports and exports, for it is the sea-port of Damascus and of the central part of Syria. This, with a similar paper from Mr. Murad Serapion, our vice-consul at Jaffa, and some general information are embodied in the paper marked "C," which I respectfully submit.

I never met a more zealous consular representative than Mr. Chasseaud. Whether distant or near, we had ever proofs of his considerate kindness. He gained at once our respect and fervent good will.

To the kindness and zealous co-operation of those two gentlemen, as well as to Mr. Offley, acting United States' consul at Smyrna, we were very much indebted, and shall ever treasure their attentions in grateful remembrance. It affords me sincere pleasure to add that Colonel Rose, her Britannic Majesty's Consul-General for Syria, and Mr. Finn, her Britannic Majesty's consul at Jerusalem, practically evinced a warm interest in our labors. The former gentleman, besides the extension of courteous hospitality, wrote letters in our behalf to all his agents in our line of route, and Mr. Finn kindly took charge of our funds, and faithfully, and with much trouble, was the medium of disbursement with the Arabs. A representative of our own country could not have been more attentive and efficient than the latter. But for his kindness, I know not what we should have done; for our government has no Consular agent in Jerusalem, and it would have endangered the whole party to have taken a large sum of money within reach of grasping and unprincipled barbarians.

From this list of creditors, I must not omit the name of Mr. Finzie, her Britannic Majesty's vice-consul at St. Jean d'Acre, who did his utmost to follow the friendly directions of Colonel Rose.

It is with pleasure I add, that this liberal spirit was not confined to officials, but from travellers of all nations, the English in especial, we received the most gratifying assurances of a generous interest in the success of our undertaking.

On our first arrival at Beïrût, prior to the disembarkation of the expedition, the Rev. Eli Smith and the other gentlemen of the American Evangelical Mission in Syria, materially aided our subsequent operations by judicious advice and important information. After our return, while waiting for the ship, the reverend gentleman I have named, labored several days in furnishing correct Arabic names, with definitions, of the numerous places we had visited. Under his roof Mr. Dale breathed his last, and the pangs of sickness were much alleviated by the assiduity of every male and female member of the missionary families in the village. His own brothers and sisters could not have nursed him more tenderly. Dr. Vandyke came from a distance to see him, and Dr. De Forrest was with him at all hours, night and day. These gentlemen, content with the approval of their consciences, refused all compensation for their professional services.

Mr. Winthrop, our consul at Malta, had been very attentive to the expedition since its first landing in Syria, and from him I learned, late in July, that there could be no immediate expectation of the return of the "Supply." In the meantime, the weather had become exceedingly sultry and oppressive, and the health of every member of the expedition was more or less affected. Dr. Suquêt and our fellow-countrymen advised us to leave at once, as our only hope of renovation was in a sea voyage; the former adding that in our debilitated state we would most probably fall amongst the first victims to the cholera, which was then rapidly approaching.

Under these circumstances, I chartered a small French brig to take us, the boats, our effects, and the remains of our late companion, to Malta. These remains I had preserved in spirits, and safely deposited without the walls of the town. An unhappy accident, however, in their transportation from the shore to the vessel, and the subsequent superstitious fears of the French captain and his crew, compelled me most reluctantly to land and inter them, with all due honor, on the following day, July 30. That evening, immediately after the funeral, we embarked and set sail. After a tedious passage of thirty-eight days, during which we suffered much from sickness, debility, and scarcity of food and water, we reached Malta, where we received every possible attention from Mr. Winthrop.

The "Supply" arrived at Beïrût twenty-two days after our departure; but the cholera being in the town, she had no communication with the shore, except through the health office. On the 11th September she returned to Malta, and the next day I re-embarked the whole of the expedition, with only three of its members on the sick report.

It gratifies me to state that the boats and nearly all our effects are in almost as good a condition as when we received them, and that, besides mineralogical and botanical specimens I have brought two calves, male and female, of the royal breed of Damascus, for the improvcment of our stock, and samples of cereal grains, and the seeds of fruits and vegetables, for distribution among our farmers at home. The cattle, at my own expense, as not being authorized by law—the seed on account of the expedition. Some pigeons and pheasants, I regret to say, have perished. The former, from the Desert of Judea, above the Dead Sea, were peculiar; the latter, from the Vale of Sharon, differed little from our own.

Through fatigue, privation and sickness, the officers and men have acquitted themselves to my satisfaction. The outline maps accompanying this will bear testimony to the industry and skill of Lieutenant Dale and Passed Midshipman Aulick, and the only drawback is that the former, who shared our labors, has not been spared to participate in the gratification of our return. Mr. Aulick is not only an accomplished draftsman, but has proved himself a vigilant, intrepid and judicious officer. Mr. Bedlow I have before mentioned. Dr. Anderson's report will speak for itself, and of my son I am far from ashamed. The men of the expedition were all volunteers, and each readily pledged himself, as required, to abstain from all intoxicating drink, and to this circumstance I mainly attribute their final recovery from sickness. Continually exposed and subjected to severe labors, in the true spirit of American seamen, they never complained, and I thank God for being enabled to return such valuable men to our country.

Very respectfully,

W. F. LYNCH,

*Lieutenant United States Navy.*

Hon. J. Y. MASON,

*Secretary of the Navy.*

# APPENDIX.

## A.

CAMP, ON THE BANKS OF THE BELUS,
*Near St. Jean d'Acre, April* 3, 1848.

DEAR SIR:—Having, at your request, associated you in the expedition under my command, with the express understanding, that you are to make no communication, verbal or otherwise, of the labors or results thereof, of yourself or any member pertaining to it, save to myself officially, until relieved from the obligation by the honorable the Secretary of the Navy, I beg leave to name a few points, in the elucidation of which I believe, as well as hope, that you can materially aid us.

The geological structure and physical phenomena of the shores of the Dead Sea, and the terraces of the Jordan, and, if time permit, of the ranges of the Lebanon, also, constitute in their investigation one of the most important objects of the expedition.

The volcanic phenomena of the Dead Sea require the strictest investigation, that in connexion with a line of soundings, by the surveying party, the presumed "fault" running north and south through it may be verified or disproved.

It is desirable to obtain mineralogical specimens to ascertain if the surrounding regions be volcanic, and for the future purpose of comparing them with similar specimens from Vesuvius, or some modern active volcano, in order to ascertain whether or not modern volcanic productions differ from more ancient ones.

The nature of the soil on the eastern shore, especially as formed by disintregation, and the nature of the vegetation, as connected with it, are points of useful inquiry.

The soil in which grapes of such extraordinary size are said to grow, should be collected for analysis, to ascertain if the chemical composition has any influence on the size of the fruit.

In a minute examination for volcanic characters, parts of the eastern coast may be found to consist of basaltic rock, with a crystalline structure, perpendicular to the surface, and disintegrating in such a manner as to present perpendicular cliffs. Trap rock may be found cropping out through other rocks, more or less homogeneous in their appearance, with small disseminated crystals, sometimes magnetic. The dark basaltic rock is (said to be) frequent near Tiberias. Rocks containing fossils claim particular attention, and as many varieties of fossils should be collected as possible.

Specimens of mud from various parts of the sea, river, and lake, should be collected and placed in air-tight vessels.

It is said that the mountains of the west coast consist principally of a bituminous limestone, which inflames, smokes, and is fœtid.

Lumps of sulphur, as large as a walnut, have been found at 'Ain el Feshkhah. On the west coast, small fragments of flint, "flesh, red," and brown, have also been found; and on the banks of the Jordan, nearly opposite Jericho, rolled pebbles of white carbonate of lime with thin veins of quartz.

Although not immediately within your province, I invite your attention to cochlaæ and concheæ. Specimens of every species of crustaceæ, even the most minute, are very desirable.

It is most important to ascertain whether birds live on the shores, or fish within the depths of the Dead Sea, and not less to note carefully every stream and fissure, their direction and their depth, and to ascertain, if possible, whether the former are perpetual or only temporary torrents.

It is not my intention to limit your inquiries, or to pretend to instruct you in a branch wherein you are so much better informed than myself, but to give you an idea of the general range of investigation deemed most advisable to attain a satisfactory result. Very respectfully, your obedient servant,

WM. F. LYNCH,
*Lieutenant Commanding.*

H. J. Anderson, M. D.

---

# B.

## MINUTES TAKEN DURING THE DESCENT OF THE JORDAN.

### TIBERIAS, GALILEE.

Monday, April 10, 1848. Called all hands very early to make preparations for departure. Repaired and launched the frame boat I purchased here; named her "Uncle Sam," and engaged four Arabs as her crew.

In the morning received a visit from Emir Nassir Arar el Guzzhawy, a powerful prince of the Arabs of the Ghor. He came to welcome us, and to proffer any assistance we might require. I agreed with him for a small party to accompany our caravan as guides and scouts.

At 2, P. M., both parties start simultaneously. Going through an uncultivated and unknown country, it is necessary to take a quantity of forage and provisions. Our united parties consist, therefore, of three boats upon the water, and ten camels and about twenty horsemen upon the land, including our own officers, the dragoman, cook, and our Bedawin friends, with the Emir and his guides passing along the shore in single file. Temperature of air, 82°; of the water, 70°.

Until 3, P. M., we steer south, and from 3 to 3.40, southeast and east-southeast; the right or western shore of the lake descending in a slope towards the river; the left somewhat more depressed and much washed with rains, presenting a continuation of rounded bluffs, with intervening chasms, the ruins of Kerak, ancient Tarrichœa, on the southwest bend of the lake.

At 3.45, open the river running nearly west; a hill, with the village of Semakh on the south point, and the stone foundation of a building on the right, immediately at the point of debouchure of the river. From the eastern hills, a lovely plain here sweeps down to the lake, and in the centre of the water line is the village of Semakh, behind which a wady (ravine) comes down, and due west from it the Jordan sweeps out of the lake with a short turn to the right. As we enter the river, Mount Hermon, still covered with snow, but with fissures in its cap, is thrown into view, bearing northeast.

At 4.30, course west-southwest abruptly round a ledge of small rocks; our course varies with the turns of the river from northwest at 4.35, to south at 4.45. The average breadth about twenty-five yards; current, two and a half knots; the banks rounded and about thirty feet high, luxuriantly clothed with grass and flowers; among them the anemone and the marigold, but there are neither trees nor shrubs. Here and there, close to the water's edge, is a drooping lily.

At 4.48, pass an inlet, about quarter mile deep, to the north, called El Muh. Five minutes after leaving the lake, we lose sight of it entirely, and, the current carrying us with sufficient velocity, we make little use of the oars.

At 4.50, hear a shot from the western shore, and soon after see some of our scouts. In a minute after, pass a low island ninety yards long, covered with shrubbery; here is an abrupt bank, twenty-five feet high, on the left, and a low marshy island off a point on the right, running out from the plain at the foot of the mountains. Water clear, ten feet deep; see the shore party dismounted on the right bank. Mount Hermon glittering to the north over the level tract which sweeps between the mountains, the lake, and the river. Turning a bend immediately below where the stream is sixty yards wide, we stop to examine a rapid over the ruins of the bridge of Semakh.

At 5.05, turn the copper boat's head up stream, and let her go, stern first, down the rapid, which rushes over the rocky fragments of the bridge. She struck on a rock in mid channel, and broached broadside to, and was for some moments in danger; while in this position, the crew of the frame boat brought theirs unintentionally within the influence of the current, and she was swept down upon us with great velocity, but striking our boat at a favorable angle, she was whirled round, and sliding off the rock, drifted safely down the rapid. Taking everything out of the iron boat, she barely touched in passing; but the frame boat was extricated with difficulty. Draw the boats up on the right bank, a little below the bridge, and encamp for the night; Mount Hermon bearing northeast half north; the village of Semakh in an east-northeast direction, concealed by an intervening ridge. The soil here is a dark, rich loam, luxuriantly clothed, three feet deep, with grass, weeds, and flowers—the scarlet anemone and the yellow marigold predominating—the rocks no where cropping out, but boulders of sandstone and fragments of trap are scattered over the surface. The lake is concealed, although quite near; but its bold northern and eastern shores tower above the opposite bank of the river. The mountains behind are clothed with verdure to the summit. We here gather some flowers, which equal any I have ever seen in delicacy of form and tint; some of them are unknown to us.

Tuesday, April 11. Start at 8.10, A. M., the boats down the river, the caravan by land. 8.15, descend three rapids in quick succession, cultivated fields on both sides and ahead; whole distance through the rapids two hundred and fifty yards; everything is taken out of the boats, and the men get overboard to guide them down—the current a little below the bridge was two knots, but increased soon after to four; the water very deep at the first fall over a ledge of rocks. Below the bridge we encountered five successive falls, with rapids between; haul the boats round three of them through channels we open by removing the obstructing rocks. The frame boat sunk from repeated thumps upon the rocks, and we were compelled to abandon her. 1, P. M., we have accomplished the descent of the fifth fall and rapid, and halt to wait for the camels with our arms, instruments, sails, and awnings. The left bank in the bend sixty feet high, precipitous face, of a dark brown-colored earth; the river continues to descend with less rapidity; but still at the rate of four or five knots per hour; here and there it breaks entirely across. On the banks are thick clusters of oleander in full bloom, and some lily plants on the borders of the stream.

At 1.20, P. M., start again, the Emir in the boat with me. 1.45, descend a cascade at an angle of 6° at the rate of twelve knots, and immediately after down a shoal rapid where we strike and hang a few moments upon a rock; see our caravan on a hill in the distance; a short half-mile inland are the ruins of two mills, with a part of the canal or sluice which formerly supplied them water; haul the boats up the canal and then turning the last into the river, carry them safely round the most precipitous fall.

The soil is fertile, but the country wholly uncultivated; the surface of the banks about fifteen feet above the river, thence gradually ascending a short distance to a low range of hills, beyond which on each side the prospect is closed in by mountains.

At 4.45, stop to rest after descending the eleventh rapid; velocity of current so strong, that one of the seamen who lost his hold of the boat (they are obliged on such occasions to cling on outside) is nearly swept over the fall, and with very great difficulty gains the shore. The mountains east of Lake Tiberias visible over the left bank, summit of Mount Hermon (the summit alone is visible) northeast by north.

At 5, P. M., pass a ravine on the left in a bend between precipitous banks of sand and earth, the river winding with many turns. On the right is an extensive plain, wholly uncultivated, and a small valley between high banks on the left, where a patch of wheat is beginning to head; the river here twenty-five yards wide, two and a half feet deep, and current four knots; the water discolored; see a partridge, an owl, a large hawk, and some herons and many storks; catch a trout, of which there are many in the river. 5.10, round a high bold bluff, river deepening and widening, gravelly bottom. 5.35, abreast of Beisan, two miles distant; a solitary carob tree, about the size of a large apple tree, on the right bank. 5.45, pass two small streams on the right, a number of snipes and swallows flying about. 5.48, a bank of fuller's earth, twenty feet high, on the left, and a beautiful sloping lawn on the opposite shore, the hill side beyond covered with verdure and two trees upon its summit. Black and white martens flying about; the river eight feet deep, the water so clear that the bottom is distinctly visible; weeds becoming thick under the bank, and the sedgy grass advancing into the water. 6.49, a beautiful slope on the right or western side, terminating in a lofty hill. 5.50, Mount Hermon, north by east, a slope on the west, well set in patches of wheat. From a quarter of a mile below Beisan, river deep, with gentle descent, current four knots, the country hereabouts well cultivated. 6.15, passed a small flat island covered with grass, river 50 yards wide; started a flock of ducks and cranes; course from abreast of Beisan from west by south to south by east. 6.16, passed a small bay on the left, a path leading down to it from over the hill, evidently a watering place for cattle; canes and coarse tufted grass on the margin of the river. 6.17, a second inlet on the left. 6.18, an inlet on the right; left shore marshy, high land beyond; the water clear, of a light green hue, very much like that of the lake above and of our own Lake Ontario; many birds, particularly swallows, flying about; the river continues winding, mostly with gentle curves, but now and then turning at a sharp angle. The bends high, varying from eight to fifteen feet in height; the opposite points low and marshy; vegetation and aspect of the scenery, the same. It becoming dark, it was necessary that I should abandon the note-book and pay undivided attention to the channel, thus giving to Mr. Aulick, who followed in the iron boat, an opportunity to sketch, as well as he could, the topography of the river banks. 8, P. M., reached the falls and whirlpool of Bŭk'ah. It being too dark to attempt their descent, hauled in to the right bank and went on shore in search of the camp.

Wednesday, April 12. At 10.15, A. M., cast off and shot down the first rapid, and stop near a desperate looking cascade of about eleven feet fall, to make final preparations. In the middle is a sheer fall at an angle of about 7°, but with a bold, bluff rock just at the foot, which will render it necessary to turn sharp to the right in order to avoid being dashed to pieces. At 12 precisely, just as the meridian observations is being taken at the camp, descend the cascade and the second rapid in the copper boat. At 12.20, P. M., the iron boat follows; stop to give hot coffee to our crews, and the Arabs who had assisted us.

At 45′, P. M., descend the third fall this morning. Hard work for all hands. Pick up some quartz and lava, and two specimens of beautiful flowers. 1.45, P. M., descend a rapid with an ugly sheer, to wait for the iron boat. The course of the rapids below the fall rounds from west-southwest to southeast by east, in a distance of ninety yards.

At 4, P. M., the iron boat comes down; start again; course east-southeast. 4.25, pass an island; gravelly banks twelve feet high; the island covered with grass and weeds. 4.28, another island quite small. The river very rapid abreast of this island, with many sunken rocks in the channel, one of which we escape by about two inches. 4.35, stopped to examine a bend of the river. 4.45, round the bend, a bold, precipitous rocky cliff on the left, a flat peninsula on the right; soil fertile; grass and weeds most luxuriant. 4.55, come to a very steep and tumultuous rapid, land, and on hands and knees climb a very steep hill-side to examine it. 5.15, return, and with the aid of ropes get the boats safely down. Start again, night approaching fast; few arms in the boat, and our ammunition belts are wet. 6.15, stop just above Jisr Mêjami'a, (Bridge of Place of Meeting.) 6.25, shot through the main arch of the bridge, and stop at the head of some shelving rapids, it becoming too dark to descend them. Found the camp a short distance below.

Thursday, April 13. Started at 9.30, A. M., course south to south-southeast. 10.40, a brawling, shelving rapid; the copper boat broaches to, broadside on against the rocks, and is thrown upon her bilge, taking in a great deal of water; for some moments fear that she will go to pieces. 11.02, course southeast; a small stream from southeast by east; banks alternating, low and bushy on one side; alluvial hills of semi-indurated clay on the other. 11.17, a dangerous rapid running east by south. Again the copper boat gets broadside on. 11.28, course rounding gradually from east-southeast to south and southwest. 11.38, stop for meridian observation. 12.10, river seventy yards wide, seven feet deep; course south. 12.24, banks fifteen feet high; layers two and three feet deep, round stones. 12.28, bad rapid; course west-southwest to west-northwest; steep bank on left one hundred feet high. 12.32, course southeast by south. 12.33, southeast. 12.34, southeast by east. 12.49 to 12.51, the course southeast by south to south. 12.52, course west; many small rapids; number of drift trees in the stream; stop to rest. At 2.07, P. M., start again; course round the compass; river fifty yards wide, ten feet deep; rapid current; lofty trees on the banks. 2.36 to 2.39, a remarkably smooth but rapid current. 2.41, high bluffs on the left; beautifully variegated sand and marls; pass a small dry ravine on left. 2.46, cliffs on right; course southwest to west-southwest. 2.49, course west by south, steady descent; the river falling rapidly. 2.58, course north by west to west by south; pass a small island; land to the westward cut into square mounds; current six knots; several small birds flying about—brown body, wings white, tipped with black, and a white band round the neck and tail; large rolled stones on the bank, alternating with clay and sand; for the last hour we have seen no rocks. 3.15, a shelving rapid; descent ten knots, the river running from west to east across the valley; pass an Arab encampment on the right; population in an uproar—all rushing down to the water's edge, screaming and shouting; just below pass an island; course west-southwest to south by west, and a long reach southwest one-half south; large ghurrah trees on both banks. This tree, we are told, bears a red berry, which is juicy, sub-acid and palatable. In its branches and the powdered appearance of its leaves, it resembles the aspen. It is not here in bloom.

At 3.27, another long reach east-northeast, the course then varying from east to northeast. 3.35, course northeast by north; many birds singing; a fish-hawk (hedda) flying overhead. 3.41 to 3.46, east south-east to northeast, pass a cluster of islets. 3.49, a sharp turn by a perpendicular bluff thirty feet high on the left. 3.52 to 4.05, course west-southwest to west; long reach; see 'Akîl on summit of a hill; soon after arrive at camp.

Friday, April 14. Start at 8, A. M., course southeast, pass a small island; right bank perpendicular, ten feet high; left bank, marsh with grass and tamarisk bushes. 8.18, course south to west-northwest. 8.20, west-southwest, left bank flat and bushy; right do., eight feet high, covered with thistles. 8.21, south by west. 8.23, south, a land fall on the right, a small stream trickling down on the left. 8.29, east by north, alluvial deposit on the right, eighty feet high. 8.32, northeast, pass a low flat island covered with cane; river forty-five yards wide, four feet deep, current four and a half knots. 8.35, southeast by south, right bank covered with nettle; high hills inland. 8.37, rapid, west by south, conical hills on right; left bank low and luxuriantly covered with wild oats. 8.39, small rapid, mud bank, forty feet high on right, left low and bushy; the alluvial deposit shows many marks of separate inundations in its numerous layers. 8.40, temperature 76°, weather very pleasant. 8.42, bank on the right sloping down, covered with cane and willow, (sifsâf;) two palm trees in sight below on the left bank, much of tamarisk, (turfa,) now covered with its clustering blossom. 8.43, southeast by east, a small rapid and a rivulet, (Moya Beisan,) trickling down on the right; thick growth of weeds on each shore, the banks about twelve feet high. 8.45, an ugly rapid, the river narrowing and rushing over blocks of lava; a long thatched hut on the right bank; the leading boat struck and broached to broadside on and nearly filled with water, all hands jumping overboard; she floated off, and an Arab woman from the shore directed us to the channel. River forty-five yards wide, seven feet deep, gravelly bottom, current ten knots, water of a light milk color. 8.49, southeast by south, pass two palm trees; see many cranes and some bulbuls; river widening. 8.50, southeast, banks on each side eight to ten feet high, thickly covered with weeds; some ghurrah trees on the brink. 8.52, a small trickling stream coming in on the right. 8.54, a collection of drift wood, showing that the water has been six feet higher; it is now evidently falling about ten inches per day; on left the trees and shrubs are inclined towards the river, as if swept by high winds from the north; a mountain gorge most probably opens behind them. The river running through the lowest of two terraces, from its bed, we have but occasional glimpses of the high hills inland. 8.58, east-southeast, a small stream flowing in from the left; see wild pigeons. 9, southeast by south, banks, (mud and clay,) low on left; thirty feet high on right, with tamarisk and ghurrah trees near the water's edge. 9.03, village on the mountain height, bearing southeast; the mountains gradually sloping to the southward. 9.05, south, quite a reach of half a mile; right bank ten, left bank thirty feet, fringed with bushes, and much grass and weeds, inland; breeze from the westward. 9.10, a number of insects on the water; caught one, examined it, and let it go. 9.18, west by north, round a low point, a small rapid just below. 9.21, southwest, open Ghebel Nabulus ahead; the eastern and western ranges of mountains converging. 9.22, a stream running down on the left, a small brawling rivulet—cane and tamarisk trees on the brink—a bold triangular faced hill, eighty to one hundred feet high, on right, presenting a scarped and fortified aspect, with a slope resembling the glacis of a fort between its base and the river, luxuriantly clothed with grass and flowers; among the last much of the marigold. 9.28, west by south, a beautiful slope covered with flowers, on the right—on the left the bank low, with many bushes. 9.32, southwest, see snipes and white cranes. 9.34, a long and shelving rapid, of great force, rounding from south to east; even where its surface is perfectly smooth the river seems to flow rapidly down hill. 9.39, south-southeast, current four and a half knots, water seven feet deep, white milky color, sandy bottom; the banks alluvial deposit, in regular layers; the left six to eight feet high, with tamarisk trees; the right, low, covered with sedge. 9.42, west, round a low sand bluff. 9.44, southwest, round a low gravelly point, with tamarisks. 9.45, south, shot a bulbul for preservation. 9.55, east-southeast, round a low point of mud—perpendicular bank, ten feet high, opposite. 9.58, east by south to north, round a low mud point on left; perpendicular banks of earth on the right, ten feet high, with bushes and dead trees upon it—thistles, weeds and tamarisks on right, river seventy yards wide, four feet deep, current four knots, water clouded—a very light milk color. 10.02, northwest, round a point on right, eight feet high, thick clothed with trees and bushes; left bank bushes and dead trees. 10.05, small rapid, northeast to east by south, round a low bank with tamarisks on right; on left, large trees grounded. 10.07, east. 10.08, east by south. 10.09, southeast. 10.10, southwest, banks of bends perpendicular—of points, usually low and rounded; river seventy yards wide, six and a half feet deep; same bottom; current five knots. 10.12, west-southwest. 10.15, south by west, both banks eight to ten feet high—thick growth of wild mustard, tamarisk, and high canes; unquestionable marks of the river falling. 10.16, south, pass a willow bush growing nearly in the middle of the stream, showing that much of the bed of the river is bare at low water. 10.21, southwest to south-southeast, round a low bushy point on left, many dead tamarisks on bank. 10.22, same course; a small rapid—see a black vulture. 10.25, north by east, perpendicular bank nine feet high on left, thick high canes; tamarisk and bushes on right. 10.29, west-northwest, banks on both sides, have tall and slender tamarisks growing thickly upon them. At 10.31, west. 10.32, southeast, much drift wood in the stream. 10.35, southwest. 10.37, south, river sixty yards, five feet deep, current six knots, water light colored; pass a small stream on right. 10.38, small rapid, south by west; stop for twenty-three minutes. 11.03, southwest. 11.06, southeast. 11.07, east-northeast, high hills to the eastward; river forty-five yards, four feet deep, rocky bottom; current five knots. 11.12, west-northwest. 11.15, west half south, short rapid, eight knots velocity; perpendicular banks of blue clay, thirty feet high, on right—the left, a sandy flat. 11.16, south-southeast, six knots. 11.21, east-northeast. 11.23 to 11.26, north. 11.40, southwest, stop for meridian observation 12.05, P. M., start again; course southeast to east by northeast. 12.12, southwest. 12.14, west southwest. 12.15, southeast, river seventy yards, four and a half feet deep, current five knots.

At 12.26, small rapids west by south to north by west. 12.34, southeast by south. 12.35, a small sandy island. 12.38, south by west. 12.45, south-southeast by south, river eighty yards, four feet deep, rocky bottom, current four knots, water light colored. 12.49, west-northwest. 12.53, east-southeast, a smooth rapid descent. 12.58, west-southwest. 12.59, sharp turn to southeast by south; cane on the shores very high and thick, but few trees inland. 12.56, a small but rapid stream from northwest. 12.58, west-southwest, river sixty yards wide, eleven feet deep, sandy bottom, water milky color. 1.04, a small rivulet from the west. 1.06, a fine rapid, southwest to west. 1.08, west; bluff, bold bank on right, a small stream trickles down. 1.09, south by west, another small stream on right. 1.37, east by north, two small streams within one hundred yards of each other, flowing in on the right, a rapid but smooth descent, river seventy yards wide, five and a quarter feet deep, current four and a half knots, water same color, banks seven to ten feet high on each side, clothed with small trees, bushes and cane. 1.45, southeast to west-southwest. 1.55, south-southwest, a small stream on the right. 1.58, east by north, many prostrate trees in the river. 2, east-southeast, river fifty yards wide, six and a half feet deep, same color. 2.02, east by north, wild mustard growing very luxuriantly on the banks; start a large brown hawk. 2.03, southeast to south, banks covered with tamarisk, bushes and high grass. 2.06, west by south. 2.10, southeast by east to west-southwest, thick canes on shore, many drift trees against the left bank and upon the point on the right. 2.15, northwest to south, a brown hill with a path over it, bearing southwest by west, the hill roof-shaped with its gable on the river; stop to look for caravan. 2.35, start, south by east, a hill eighty feet high, of light clay and dark earth on the right, low growth of ghurrah on left. 2.38, southeast to east by south and east, the country unseen beyond the banks. 2.40, east-southeast to southeast, river seventy yards wide, four and a half feet deep, current four knots. 2.44, east. 2.45, southeast to southwest, high bluff, clay and light brown earth on left; low bushy point on right. 2.47, high hills on left, rounded summits covered with weeds and grass, at water's edge, on right, much of the ghurrah in blossom. 2.49, west by south to south by east, river ninety yards wide, two and a half feet deep, current three and a half knots. 2.53, a small island fifty yards long but very narrow, in the middle of the river; much of the ghurrah on both sides at the water's edge. 2.55, see an Arab on a hill in the distance, course west by south, left bank thirty to forty feet high, bold sides, with grass on top. 2.57, south, a small stream coming in on the right. 2.59, south-southwest to south by east, high washed hills on right; on the left a flat covered with grass and a few trees. 3.02, low bank on right, singular layer of alluvial at the base of a hill, resting on a stratum of pebbles about the size of the fist. 3.03, southeast by east to east-southeast, an island, two old stone huts with mud roofs on hill to the left. 3.06, ugly rapid, course west, left bank four feet high, gravel and round stones, right bank six feet, yellow clay; see a great many fish.

At 3.12, rapid; current very strong; course west. 3.15, north, another rapid, but a small one; loose stones in the river; water two feet deep; just below no bottom at eight feet. 3.18, west-northwest, chocolate colored hills, thirty feet high on left. 3.22, rapid; strike on a rock in passing. 3.25, stop to look for caravan. 3.34, start again, west by south; perpendicular bank on right; two-thirds of light colored, and the other third red clay; low on left. 3.39, southwest by west to southwest by south, and south by east to east. 3.40, a small stream coming in on the right; we seem fast closing in with the eastern mountains. 3.42, east; a bay on the right; just below, an ugly rapid, with a short turn to east round a small island. 3.45, east by south to south and southwest; left bank twenty-five feet high; light colored earth and reddish clay; dry furze on top. 3.48, a dangerous rapid; strike on a rock and broach to; nearly lose the leading boat; current running with headlong velocity; motion the iron boat the way to the channel. 3.54, southwest by west to south; high clay hills on right; left bank fifteen feet high, and bushy. 3.56, southeast by east; a small rapid by an islet; high white clay hills on right; left bank low and bushy. 3.58, south-southeast to southeast by south; high canes thirty feet on right; left bank ten to fifteen feet; grass and weeds. 4, stop to look for caravan; on the right shore, bank twenty feet high; eight feet sub-stratum; stones and gravel, and twelve feet earth and clay above. 4.18, start, southeast; banks descending on each side. 4.20, small rapid; southeast by east to southeast; high white cliffs on right, running northwest and southeast, bold and perpendicular, two hundred feet high. 4.24, south to south-southeast; low sedgy banks. 4.25, an island; (small;) course southwest. 4.26, south by west; river seventy yards, five feet deep, hard bottom, current four knots. 4.28, a small gravelly island, with several hundred cranes upon it, which take flight as we pass. 4.30, land on right bank to look for caravan; Sherîf very uneasy. 4.34, start, northeast to south-southwest; high white cliffs on left; the elevated plain begins to be seen, with high mountains in the distance; left bank detached; rounded hills coming down to the shore. 4.38, south-southeast; a long and ugly rapid by two small islands; strike twice in passing. 4.40, reach encampment, just above a slight shelving rapid.

Saturday, April 15. 8.32, A. M., start. 8.33, descending the rapid; just escape a rock near the water's edge. 8.38, a ravine coming down on the left, with a small stream lined with trees and bushes; river forty yards wide, seven feet deep, sandy bottom, current six knots. 8.40, pass an island half a mile long; a false channel on the right of it. 8.44, west by south. 8.45, northeast; low flat bend on right; high cliff with stones near summit on left. 8.48, northeast by east; an island. 8.50, north by west; a remarkable point on left, white as chalk; right bank low, with a great many pebbles. 8.52, northwest, right bank fifteen feet of stone, so closely packed as to resemble conglomerate. 8.54, northwest by west; river forty yards, five and a half feet deep; water light, or milk-color; current six knots; temperature of the air, 78°; of the water, twelve inches below the surface, 71°. 8.55, west by south and south; high conical hills to the westward; a number of doves in sight. 8.58, entangled among the trees, among which we are swept by the powerful current. 9.02, southeast; an ugly rapid.

At 9.12, south, blocks of sandstone on the right, resting on gravel. 9.15, southwest, a low island, two hundred yards long, covered with ghurrah and tamarisk trees and canes on left; a narrow channel between it and the shore; many wild pigeons and doves flying about; high hills on right, covered with brown furze and a few thorn bushes. 9.19, south by east half east, bold face of a hill to the southward and eastward—white and red clay. 9.23, east by south, shot a bird. 9.28, southwest, pass Wady el Hammâm, (Ravine of the Bath.) 9.29, west by south half south, blocks of conglomerate resting on gravel. 9.32, southwest by west, high bank of stones, gravel and sand; caves worn in the faces of the cliffs, from which many pigeons fly out. 9.34, stop to examine an ugly rapid, where a small tributary flows in from west-northwest through Wady el Malakh, (Ravine of Salt;) water brackish, but clear; its temperature 70°; on its banks find some plants of the ghurkûd; its leaves triangular shaped, of a dull light green, coated with a fine powder which is salt to the taste. The old parts of the stem purple, the younger light green; which as well as the leaves, are bitter to the taste. In and beside the stream of the river are many fossil rocks; on the banks of the tributary are some fennel plants, the aromatic flavor of which is palatable. 10.30, descend the rapid; rest awhile; start again at 10.50. 10.56, 57 and 58, three very strong rapids; course from southeast to southwest, the last by an island. 11.06, stop by an island eighty yards long, fringed with ghurrah, within covered with canes, to examine a rapid. Jumâh, (Friday,) a cousin of 'Akîl, who accompanies us, is perfectly at home in the water, and renders great service. 11.25, descend rapid and wait for the iron boat; take meridian observation; temperature, air 84°; water twelve inches down, 74°; at foot of rapid is a small islet covered with cane, and three yet smaller ones below. 12.05, P. M., start down rapids southwest half south; the washed faces of the hills present thirty or thirty-five feet volcanic looking rock, with one hundred and twenty feet earth upon them. 12.12, slight rapid south-southeast; abreast of rapid, basaltic strata midway up. 12.17, island (small) course southeast to southwest and back, rapid; stop to examine; not difficult. 12.19, south-southeast to south, a quantity of pebbles at mouth of a ravine on left; river forty-five yards wide, five and a half feet deep; water light mud color; the banks ranging from three to thirty feet, with bushes, canes and thistles on right; on left five to fifty feet; river widening seventy yards; three and a half feet deep; current six knots. 12.25, rapid; strike on a rock in mid channel; scenery the same. 12.27, south to southwest, gravelly bank on left; shoal rapid ahead; high, triangular, bald faced hills to the southward and westward, with wadys (ravines) between. 12.29, shoal rapid, west by south half south. 12.31, south-southwest to south, a low rounded bank, with a very high hill above it; on the left a small island towards the left shore; then a sharp rapid by an island two hundred and fifty yards long; current nine to ten knots. High mountains with conical summits in the distance on right; cane on both sides at the water's edge; the faces of the upper terrace, red clay and gravel; birds flying in every direction.

At 12.39, east by south, banks of stones and earth on both sides. 12.44, southeast one-half east, rapid (small) three feet deep; river below sixty yards wide, eight feet deep; bald rounded hills; east by north, mountains of Salt and Belka; southeast. 12.47, south-southwest, banks of gravel with clay above; false channel to the left round a small island; rapid; boats strike repeatedly, but thump over; current ten knots. 12.55, pigeons; an island one mile and a quarter long, well wooded; river eighty yards wide, three and a half feet deep. 12.58, northwest, high angular shaped hills; a series of shallow rapids; water two feet deep; river seventy to ninety yards wide, washing the base of very high, red clay hills. 1.03, northwest to east, a small island ten feet high; angular hills; red and white clay; strong rapid, four feet deep; bank of white pebbles on right; stop to take a sketch. 1.45, river fifty yards, seven feet deep; tamarisk and ghurrah trees on both sides, interspersed with canes; light airs from eastward. 1.52, southeast by east, river seventy yards wide, two and a half feet deep; current three knots. 1.53, river narrowing a little, three and a half feet deep; rapid, by two islands, (large and small;) strike on a rock. 1.58, south-southwest, river widening, eighty to ninety yards, three feet deep. 2.05, shallow rapid, by an island three-quarters of a mile long; river ninety yards wide, three and a half feet deep; water light mud color; three islands—two tolerably large, one quite small. 2.12, shallow rapids; strike again. 2.13, southwest, small wooded island one hundred yards long; river two and a half feet deep. 2.18, west by south, mountains visible to the westward. 2.20, west-southwest. 2.22, south by west to south by east, steep rapid four and a half feet deep; brown triangular hills to the westward, with two ravines between coming down from northwest; a low, pebbly beach on the left. 2.23, pass Wady Ajlûn; land of Fâri'a begins here; two slight shelving rapids below an island; water six feet deep, river sixty yards wide. 2.28, southeast by south to south-southeast, very strong rapids; high banks of red sand on left; right banks low and sedgy. 2.34, southeast, reach camp.

Sunday, April 16. Start at 6.35, A. M.; a clear, pleasant day; wind light from the northeast; course southwest to south by east; a cluster of conical hills to the southward. 6.41, south by west to south-southeast; banks twenty feet high—lower stratum clay, above, stones and gravel intermixed with earth; a small stream flowing in from the west; river fifty yards wide, six feet deep. 6.48, east by north round to north and northwest; pass a small island; singular conical hills to the northward; banks low, fringed mostly with the tamarisk, occasionally a willow. 6.53, north-northeast to southeast by east; slight shelving rapid; hills come down to the water's edge. 6.57, island, (small;) river seventy yards wide, three feet deep; two islands—one small, the other half a mile long; a rapid by them; strike in passing; a ledge of conglomerate on the left. 7, south, river fifty yards, five feet deep; current six knots. 7.06, south-southeast, banks of stones and earth on left; pass an island two hundred and fifty yards long, covered with trees. 7.08, low gravelly beach. 7.12, west by north to east; slight rapid; small island. 7.15, another small island. 7.17, west-northwest; river sixty yards, seven feet deep.

At 7.19, large island; below it two small islets; river seventy yards, two and a half feet deep. 7.20, south-southeast, island one hundred and twenty yards long; current very strong. 7.21, a strong rapid, southeast to southwest. 7.22, air 66°; water 70°. 7.25, south-southwest, lofty white hills, with pointed summits, to the southward and westward; a small island; depth of river two and a half feet; bushes and trees on bank—tamarisk, ghurrah and willow, with frequent thickets of canes. 7.30, southwest to south by west, round a low gravelly point on left. 7.31, slight rapid; south by west to east; a low, bare island; river three and a half feet deep. 7.36, southeast by east. 7.37, much drift wood in the river. 7.38, southeast to north-northeast, low bushes on the banks; Mountains of Salt, bearing northeast. 7.40, a long wooded island. 7.44, east-northeast; strike. 7.48, south; river forty yards wide, seven feet deep, narrow channel; Molyneux's boat attacked here; stop to examine; see tracks of a tiger. 7.50, strong rapid. 8.10, river scarce thirty yards wide, but very deep; no bottom with an eight foot pole; course north to south-southwest, pass the largest island we have seen—about one hundred and fifty acres. 8.10, vegetation the same; many drift trees in the stream. 8.14, shelving rapid, west to south; low gravelly banks. 8.20, southeast to northeast, and back to west-northwest; island about fifty acres; river forty-five yards, four feet deep; current eight knots. 8.29, southeast, small island. 8.35, air 72°; water 70°. 8.40, Castle of Ajlûn in sight to the southward and eastward; banks eight feet to ten feet high, clothed with grass; huddled brown hills, bearing east by north. 8.45, river fifty yards wide, four feet deep. 8.48, high clay hills to the eastward; two wadys, (ravines,) coming in from southwest. 8.45, slight rapid; low gravelly island, one hundred and twenty yards long. 8.59, low banks; singular high conical hills, bearing south. 9.07, island, small, covered with bushes. 9.10, river forty yards wide, five feet deep; water of a milky hue; tracks of wild animals on shore. 9.16, right bank eight feet high, with burnt bushes upon it. 9.20, island, (small,) covered with bushes; water falling fast. 9.22, small island, with a shelving rapid by it. 9.30, bold hills in shore; river fifty yards wide, three feet deep, shallow rapid; some drifted trees on left shore, and tracks of wild animals. 9.41, a small island, with drifted trees upon it; river forty yards wide, three and a half feet deep. 9.45, a small island fifty yards long; doves and pigeons numerous; alluvial banks; Castle Ajlûn, bearing ahead from a bend of the river. 9.50, southwest, shoal rapid; bald white hills, southwest to west; water in rapid two feet deep; another rapid by an island two hundred yards long; below, river forty yards wide, ten feet deep; banks covered with tamarisk and ghurrah trees; high hills; pass under a very lofty one, the lowest layer resembling conglomerate. 10.12, shoal rapid, by a small island. 10.21, gravelly banks; six feet high; drift wood on the left one. 10.30, a high hill of blue and red clay; its face bald and perpendicular; lower stratum seeming semi-indurated; river fifty yards wide, four and a half feet deep; see a crow; strike on a snag in a rapid by a small island; river fifty yards wide, two feet deep. 10.50, rapid; current very strong. 10.51, a castor bean plant on shore; banks alluvial; bushes and trees hanging over the river. 10.57, under a high cliff; start a flock of partridges; many birds flying about; temperature of air, 84°; of water, 72°.

At 11.07, river forty-five yards wide, four and a half feet deep, current five knots; see some lily plants. 11.11, shelving rapid by a large island. 11.20, a very slight rapid; see some of our party on one of the western hills; small island; a ravine coming down on the left. 11.40, low sedgy banks; stop to take meridian observation; temperature, air 92°, water 92°; weather calm, very sultry. 12.05, start again, pass a small island, banks much worn; hailed by Arabs on a high hill to the eastward; high cliffs on the right, left bank below covered with shrubs; river five feet deep, trees drooping towards the water; a piece of drift lodged in a tree eight feet above the surface of the river. 12.58, thick groves of tamarisk on the right; see some large white birds with flat heads; temperature, air 95°, water 94°; current very rapid. 1.52, a small island, thickly wooded; river fifty yards wide, seven feet deep; many drift trees in the stream. 2.04, course west by south, strong rapid; high mountains to the southeast and to the westward; strike in passing down the rapid; see tracks of a wild beast on the left shore; river widening, current three knots; number of trees increasing on the margin. 2.11, shoal rapid, by a small island, banks well wooded on both sides; current five knots; river narrowing again, four and a half feet deep. 2.22, a small island. 2.23, shoal rapid under high banks; river fifty yards wide, four and a half feet deep; current four knots. 2.27, arrive at camp; a hard day's work.

In consequence of the very great number of rapids, and the many drift trees in the stream, I was compelled to pay almost undivided attention to the management of the leading boat after 8.30, A. M., to-day; the notes of width, depth, velocity, and the nature of the banks, were written down by the interpreter as I gave them to him. In the iron boat, however, Mr. Aulick took the topography of the river.

Monday, April 17. Start 6.25, A. M., low bushy banks on both sides, river forty yards wide, six feet deep; temperature of air 61°, water 76°—remarkable looking conical hills to the southwest. 6.37, a well wooded island, half mile long. 6.42, another large island. 6.44, left bank fifteen feet high, covered with weeds and grass; much drift wood in the stream. 6.53, rapid descent. 6.57, tracks of wild beasts on the shore. 6.59, drift wood; some deposits on trees fifteen feet above the water. 7.02, note for the first time the cane in blossom; river fifty yards wide, eight feet deep; much drift. 7.34, very high red clay hills to the southward. 7.35, singular hill on right, resembling a tower; boats grounded; much drift wood in the stream, and some lodged twelve feet above us; river forty yards wide, six and a half feet deep; many birds flying about, and we hear much singing in the bushes, but do not see many birds—principally pigeons, doves and cranes. 9.17, temperature of air 73°, water 72°. 9.58, a cluster of small islands. 10.04, high perpendicular hills on left; stop to examine; took specimens of clay coated with lime. 11.10, much drift wood in the river. 11.20, some green trees floating down uprooted by the recent freshet. 11.40, stop for meridian observation, temperature of air 78°, water 74°. 12.09, start again. 1.30, P. M., see a wild boar swimming across the river. 3.30, hear many birds, but see few; weather sultry and oppressive; occasionally a stork, wild pigeon, or dove. 4.30, rapid, a dry torrent-bed on the right. 4.35, rapid, by an island; large flocks of cranes. 4.37, shoal, by a long low rapid; strike in passing; immediately after, a shelving rapid under a high cliff; pebbles below sand. 4.51, small island. 4.54, wild and dangerous rapid, by a small island. 4.58, rapid descent. 5.14, a small island, a ravine on the left. 5.34, a small tributary coming in on the left; stop to examine; find it clear and sweet. 5.40, air 78°, water 76°—see an Arab in the swamp; other Arabs hailing from a hill; false alarm. 6.43, a quantity of drift wood in the stream. 7.10, current very rapid; a perfect break-down in the river—we are swept along in the dark with headlong velocity, not knowing but the next minute we may plunge down a cataract, for the water fairly roars as it rushes tumultuously onward. 8.15, current lessening, but still quite strong; we seem to be lying motionless, while the banks, fringed with gloom, sweep by us. At 9.30, arrive at El Meshra'a, (Pilgrim's Ford,) where we find the tents pitched by the land party.

Tuesday, April 18. Start at 1.45, P. M., course southeast; river thirty yards wide, ten feet deep. 1.52, northwest round to southwest, six knots. 1.54, hailed from the right bank, stop and take in an Arab Sheikh, who knows the place of rendezvous. 1.58, pass a small island thickly wooded; stop to fill India rubber water bags; weather close and sultry. 2.22, start again; course north-northeast. 2.25, west by south. 2.27, south by west; right bank twenty-five feet high, red clay, left do.; ghurrah and high canes. 2.28, southeast. 2.30, south by east. 2.32, south-southeast. 2.34, southeast; a quantity of drift wood. 2.36, east-southeast; a camel in the river. 2.37, southeast. 2.38, south-southeast; sky becoming overcast. 2.39, south-southwest. 2.40, south-southeast; river fifty yards wide, twelve feet deep, current five knots, bottom blue mud. 2.41, southwest by south; right bank low, with thicket of canes; left, canes, with a high bank behind; another camel in the river. 2.42, south. 2.46, east-northeast. 2.47, south-southeast. 2.48, southeast. 2.53, south-southeast. 2.54, south; see a heron; a nauseous smell from a small stream on left; banks of river very low, fringed with willow, tamarisk, and high canes; river fifty yards wide, ten feet deep, muddy bottom; banks sand and clay; a few pebbles a short distance back on the right. 2.59, south-southeast; low canes on each shore; current four knots. 3, south-southeast; water very smooth, same light muddy color, and as yet sweet to the taste. 3.03, south; start a heron, a bulbul, and a snipe. 3.04, southwest; a fœtid smell. 3.07, southwest by south; see a large heron and a snipe; low sedgy banks on each side; high mountains to southwest; river widening. 3.05, a flock of ducks. 3.09, another, and two snipes; the banks on both sides look as if recently overflowed. 3.10, southwest by south; a small, round, red clay hill on right shore. 3.11, a bare channel, left by the flood. 3.12, south a long stretch; took the draught of the boats; left bank very low, with mostly dead canes on its margin; right bank fourteen to eighteen feet high, red clay, with stunted shrubs and a few tamarisk bushes at the brink. 3.13, mountains to southeast present a ragged iron-like appearance; left bank low, with canes; right bank low, also with canes, but a bank of clay about twelve feet high a short distance back. 3.16, south by east; left bank ten to twelve feet high, a short distance back; water brackish, no perceptible smell; river widening; banks becoming gradually lower and lower, red clay and mud; river fifty yards wide, seven feet deep, soft muddy bottom; see a heron. 3.21, the Dead Sea visible over the flat, bearing south; surface of water slightly ruffled; wind sweeping from northwest. 3.22, start a snipe and a white gull. 3.23, a heron; river spreading out; current decreasing. 3.25, pass one tolerably large, and two small islands at the mouth, where the river is one hundred and eighty yards wide and three feet deep, and enter upon the Dead Sea; the boats, when fairly afloat upon the latter, drawing one inch less than on the river.

# C.

## *From the United States' Consul at Beïrût.*

As I promised to give you some idea of the trade of this place, though very difficult to be correct where no records or registers are kept, yet I shall attempt to satisfy you.

As Beïrût is the port of Damascus, of Bagdad, and of all the mountains, our trade of imports is very considerable, and increasing every year. From England, we receive 20 or 30 vessels annually, laden with all sorts of cotton manufactures and colonial produce. From France, from 10 to 12 vessels annually, with coffee, sugar, Swiss manufactures of silk and cotton, &c. From Trieste, 5 or 6 vessels, with German goods; besides occasionally some vessels from Leghorn, Malta, &c.

The manufactures and cotton twist (of which the consumption is very great) sell generally for cash; and the prices, on an average, may be calculated as follows, in English yards and pounds, and in American cents.

| | | | PER PIECE. |
|---|---|---|---|
| White calicoes,......of 24 yards, | weighing | $7\frac{1}{2}$ lbs.,...... | at 172 cts. |
| Gray cloth, ........36 do. | do. | 8 lbs.,...... | at 172 cts. |
| Do. ........24 do. | do. | 4 lbs.,...... | at 90 cts. |
| Cotton, water twist,....16—24 | do. | $10\frac{1}{2}$ lbs.,...... | at 15 cts. |
| Do. do. ....12—24 | do. | $10\frac{1}{2}$ lbs.,...... | at 13 cts. |
| Madapalanes,..........36 inches wide, | fine,............ | | at 300 cts. |
| Do. ..........36 do. | middling quality, | | at 250 cts. |
| Do. ..........36 do. | common,........ | | at 210 cts. |
| Strong cotton cloth,....52 yards, | 36 inch,..... | | at 520 cts. per piece. |
| Do. do. ....52 do. | 32 inch,..... | | at 462 cts. do. |
| Do. do. ....52 do. | 27 inch,..... | | at 390 cts. do. |
| Prints, of different patterns, of 28 yards,....... | | | at 175 cts. do. |

*Articles sold on credit.*

| | | | | |
|---|---|---|---|---|
| Sugar, powdered white,...... | 6 | piastres | = 27 cts. | per oke of $2\frac{3}{4}$ lbs. |
| large loaves,.......... | 6 | do. | = 27 | do. |
| Cochineal,............ | 85 a 100 | do. | = 382 a 450 | do. |
| Pimento,.... .............. | $4\frac{3}{8}$ | do. | = $19\frac{3}{4}$ | do. |
| Pepper,.................... | $4\frac{3}{8}$ | do. | = $19\frac{3}{4}$ | do. |
| Steel,...................... | 4 | do. | = 18 | do. |
| Iron,...................... | $2\frac{1}{2}$ | do. | = $11\frac{1}{4}$ | do. |
| Coffee, small grain and green, | $5\frac{1}{4}$ | do. | = $23\frac{1}{2}$ | do. |

The duty on the above goods is 3 per cent. ad valorem, besides 2 per cent. commission, ½ per cent. brokerage, ½ per cent. warehouse rent, and some trifling porterage.

The returns from this are generally made in raw silk, (which always abounds,) in sheep's wool, madder roots, sesame seed, and in cash or bills. The silk is now 95 piastres ($4 27½) per oke, and the export duty is about 13 per cent. The other articles are procurable on the coast, and in the interior; and two or three months would be required to prepare a cargo.

J. CHASSEAUD, *U. S. Consul.*

---

## *Products of the country of which Jaffa is the sea-port.*

[The grain calculated in bushels.]

| | Kersenna. | Hamoos. | Lentils. | Sesame. | Dhoura. | Barley. | Wheat. |
|---|---|---|---|---|---|---|---|
| Gaza and villages,.......................... | ..... | 50 | 1,000 | 21,000 | 20,000 | 42,000 | 42,000 |
| Jaffa and villages,.......................... | ..... | ..... | 300 | 2,000 | 2,000 | 4,000 | 4,000 |
| Ramleh and villages,....................... | 500 | ..... | 1,000 | 16,000 | 16,000 | 33,000 | 34,000 |
| Lydd and villages,............ ........... | 1,500 | 50 | 150 | 1,000 | 8,000 | 8,000 | 8,000 |
| Nabulus and villages, (only a part given,).... | 2,000 | ..... | 1,000 | 20,000 | 10,000 | 25,000 | 20,000 |
| | 4,000 | 100 | 3,450 | 60,000 | 56,000 | 112,000 | 108,000 |

*Oil in jars, each jar containing 15 okes or $37\frac{1}{2}$ pounds.*

| | |
|---|---|
| Jerusalem and villages,......... | 60,000 jars. |
| Lydd and villages,............ | 10,000 " |
| Ramleh and villages,.......... | 5,000 " |
| Gaza and villages,............ | 3,000 " |
| Nabulus and villages,......... | 80,000 " |
| | 158,000 jars = 5,905,000 pounds. |

| | | |
|---|---|---|
| Tobacco from Ramleh, Lydd, and Gaza,........ of 300 pounds each. | | 11,000 cantars |
| Cotton from Lydd and Nabulus,.......... | 4,000 bales, each 100 okes = | 1,000,000 lbs. |
| Wool from Khâlîl, Nabulus, and Gaza,.... | 2,000 do............. = | 500,000 lbs. |
| Hides, (oxen and camel,) entering Jaffa,......No. | | 500 |
| Oranges from the gardens of Jaffa only,.......No. | | 100,000,000 |
| The foreign manufactures, (coffee and sugar,)................. | 4,000 purses, = | $100,000 |

[*Given by the American Vice-Consul at Jaffa.*]

# D.

# ORNITHOLOGICAL REPORT,

## OF BIRDS BROUGHT FROM SYRIA BY THE UNITED STATES' EXPEDITION TO THE DEAD SEA.

## CLASSIFIED BY J. CASSIN.

### FAMILY FALCONIDŒ.

#### *Genus Circaëtus.—Vieillot.*

1. Circaëtus gallicus.—(Gm.) Gould's Birds of Europe, pl. 13.
Falco gallicus.—Gmelin Syst. Nat. I. p, 259. Buffon Pl. Enl. 413.
Falco leucopsis.—Bechstein, Nat. Deut. 11, p. 572.
Falco longipes.—Nillson, Faun. Suec. p. 18.
Aquila brachydactyla.—Meyer, Tasch. Deuts. Vög. 1, p. 21.
Aquila pygargus.—Brisson.
Aquila lencomphomina.—Borkhausen, Deuts. Orn.
Circaëtus leúcopsis et anguim.—Brehm, Vög. Deuts. 1, p. 36, 37.

The well known Jean le blanc Eagle of Europe, which appears however to inhabit the greater portion of the old world. It is represented by M. Rüppel, (Syst. Ueber. Vög. Nord Ost. Afrika,) as being a common bird in northern Africa and Arabia.

This species, although presenting much of the general character of the fishing eagles, (Haliœëtus,) is also nearly related to the buzzards (Buteo.) Like many species of the latter its food consists of principally of snakes and other reptiles.

#### *Genus Falco.—Linnœus.*

2. Falco subbuteo.—Linn. Syst. Nat. 1, p. 127, Gould's Birds of Europe, pl. 22.
Falco barletta.—Daudin, Traité d'Orn, 11, p. 129.
Falco hirundinum.—Brehm, Vög. Deuts. 1, p. 65.

The hobby of English naturalists, a species, the geographical range of which is very extensive. It is described by authors as inhabiting the entire continent of Europe and the British islands, even penetrating so far north as Siberia, while on the other hand specimens have frequently been brought from India, and it is given by Dr. A. Smith as a bird of South Africa.

It is one of the species which were trained for the chase in the days of falconry, but does not appear to have been a favorite; although possessed of extreme rapidity of flight, it is said to be deficient in courage. It subsists principally upon insects.

#### *Genus Circus.—Brisson.*

3. Circus œruginosus.—(Linn.) Buffon, Pl. Enl., 424, 460.
Falco œruginosus.—Linn. Syst. Nat. 1, p. 130.
Falco rufus.—Gmelia, Syst. Nat., 1, p. 266.
Circus palustris et rufus.—Brisson, Orn., 1, p. 401, 404.

The Marsh harrier or moor buzzard, another of the species which inhabits almost the whole of the Old World. It is stated by Mr. Rüppel to be abundant in Egypt and Nubia.

### FAMILY STRIGIDŒ.

#### *Genus Otus.—Ray.*

4. Otus brachyotus.—(Gm.) Gould's Birds of Europe, pl. 40. Wilson's American Ornithology, pl. 33.
Strix brachyotus et accipitrina.—Gmelin, Syst. Nat. 1, p. 289, 295.
Strix brachyura.—Nillson, Fau. Succ., p. 62.
Strix œgolius et ulula.—Pallas.
Strix arctica.—Sparrman.
Otus palustris et agrarius.—Brehm, Vög. Deuts., p. 124.

The short eared owl of naturalists.—Except Australia, this bird inhabits the whole world; presenting, however, variations in color which may prove sufficiently constant to indicate specific distinction, The specimen in the present collection is darker in color than is usual in European or American specimens.

### FAMILY CUCULIDŒ.

#### *Genus Oxylophus.—Swainson.*

5. Oxylophus glandarius.—(Linn.) Temminck, pl. col. 414.
Cuculus glandarius.—Linn. Syst. Nat. 1, p. 169.
Cuculus pisanus.—Gm. Syst. Nat. 1, p. 416. Savigny, Hist. Nat. d'Egypt. Ois. pl. 4, fig. 2.
Cuculus Andalusia.—Brisson.

This species is common in northern Africa and Arabia. It is a rare visitor in the south of Europe; and a single individual is recorded as having been captured in Ireland in 1843; being the only instance in which it is known to have visited the British Islands. (Yarrell's British Birds, III, Sapp. p. 35.)

Although well known as a species, nothing has been ascertained of its history.

### FAMILY RALLIDŒ.

#### *Genus Ortygometra.—Ray.*

6. Ortygometra crex.—(Linn.) Gould's Birds of Europe, pl. 341.
Rallus crex.—Linn. Syst. Nat. 1, p. 261. Buffon, Pl. Enl. 750.

The land rail, or corn crake, known as a common bird of Europe, but has been considered of rare occurrence elsewhere.

The two specimens in the present collection are of much interest as demonstrating a more extensive range of locality than has usually been attributed to this bird.

### FAMILY ARDEIDŒ.

#### *Genus Butor.—Swainson.*

7. Butor minutus.—(Linn.) Gould's Birds of Europe, pl. 282.
Ardea minuta.—Linn. Syst. Nat. 1, p. 240. Selby's Brit. Orn. II, pl. 6.
Ardea danubialis et soloniensis.—Gm., Syst. Nat. II, p. 637.

This species, the lesser bittern of authors, is abundant in southern Europe, and appears also to inhabit a large portion of Asia and Africa.

# E.

# BOTANICAL REPORT.

## CATALOGUE OF THE PLANTS COLLECTED IN SYRIA AND PALESTINE, BY THE UNITED STATES' EXPEDITION, UNDER LIEUTENANT LYNCH, UNITED STATES' NAVY.

BY R. EGLESFIELD GRIFFITH, M. D.

### RANUNCULACEÆ.

This order is sparingly represented in Palestine; the greater proportion of the species belonging to it being natives of more temperate climates. The following comprise all that were found.

Anemone *coronaria.*—Near Ephesus. It was observed by Hasselquist in various parts of the country. It is the *jackaik* of the Arabs.

Clematis *orientalis.*—Sources of the Jordan and various other ocalities. Noticed by Hasselquist in 1752, and also by Pococke. A variety with narrow leaves much resembles the *C. vitalba.* Tournefort speaks of a species with a very short awn, or pappus, but no specimens were collected by the exploring party.

Adonis *autumnalis.*—This appears to be common, and to extend over the whole country; as specimens occur from Mount Carmel, Nazareth, &c., to the sources of the Jordan; yet it is not noticed by Hasselquist, Pococke, or other travellers in Palestine. Several varieties in the tint of the flowers occur among the specimens brought by Lieutenant Lynch.

Delphinium *peregrinum.*—The only specimen of this beautiful species in the collection has no locality attached to it, but is probably from some elevated situation. It was found by Hasselquist, at Jerusalem. It somewhat resembles the *D. consolida*, or common larkspur in appearance, but the flowers are smaller, of a deeper blue color, and with a longer spur.

D. *pubescens.*—Ruins of Ba'albek.—Not hitherto noticed as occuring in Palestine.

In addition to these, several other plants of this order are natives of Palestine, as *Nigella sativa* and *damascena*, the former of which is the ketzach, (Isaiah xxvii, 25, 27,) commonly translated in our version of the Old Testament as fitches. *Helleborus niger* and *foetidus* are also spoken of by Pococke as occurring, but it is probable that the first of these is not the *H. niger*, but *H. orientalis*, which is shown by Tournefort and Sibthorpe to be the melampodium of the early Greek physicians, and so much prized in the treatment of affections of the head.

### BERBERIDACEÆ.

Berberis *vulgaris.*—The common barberry is found in may places in Judea, in elevated situations, but it is not as common as in the more northern parts of Asia.

Leontice *chrysogonum* and *leontopetalon* also occur, and are considered medicinal from the pungency of their roots.

### PAPAVERACEÆ.

Papaver *rhoeas.*—Corn poppy. Wady Ali on the Jaffa road, and also, according to Hasselquist, in other places in Palestine.

P. *dubium.*—Smooth headed corn poppy. Likewise found in Wady Ali. The specimen of this is so small and imperfect, as to render it impossible to decide with certainty as to its true character, but the spreading hairs of the stem seem to point it out as *P. dubium.*

According to Pococke the glaucium *flavum* is found in many situations in Palestine, but does not appear to have been met with by Lieutenant Lynch. The same may be said of the hypecoum *procumbens*, a small procumbent plant yielding a narcotic juice.

### BRASSICACEÆ.

Many specimens of plants of this order occur in the collection, but in most cases in so mutilated a state as to prevent their identification.

Anastatica *hierochuntica*—Rose of Jericho. Common in Palestine. Although bearing the name of rose, it has no resemblance to that flower. It is a small grey-leaved plant, with short, stiff, crooked branches, which, whilst the plant is growing, spread in a radiating direction on the surface of the ground. The flowers much resemble those of the radish or rocket, and when it has perfected its seeds, the plant dies, and the branches as they dry curve upwards and inwards so as to form a kind of ball, which becoming separated from the root is blown over the sands of the desert, still retaining the seed vessels in the cavity formed by the involuted branches. When it meets with moisture, this becomes absorbed, and the branches expand and assume their natural appearance, the seed vessels burst and allow the seeds to escape, but the plant does not vivify as is generally asserted.

Sinapis *orientalis.*—This plant, which is exceedingly abundant in Syria and Palestine, is so closely allied to the *S. arvensis* of Europe as to be scarcely distinguished from it. It sometimes attains a great height, and Irby and Mangles state that they had seen it as high as their horses' heads. This is the plant usually supposed to be the mustard tree alluded to in the New Testament as having the smallest of all seeds, yet growing so tall that birds roost among its branches. Dr. Royle is of opinion that it is the charul, (Prov. xxiv, 30, 31,) translated in our version of the Scriptures as nettles.

Other species of sinapis also occur as the *S. erucoidies* and *S. hispanica*, but are not included in the collection.

Capsella *bursa pastoris* is by no means unfrequent around Jerusalem, and several species of lepidium as the *latifolium*, *perfoliatum*, *chalepense*, and *draba*, are sparingly distributed in various localities.

HUTCHINSIA *brevistyla* occurs on Mount Sion and on other elevated situations in Palestine.

KAKILE *maritima*, and CRAMBE *maritima* were found on the shores of the Dead Sea.

CHEIRANTHUS *cheiri*, or wall flower, on old walls and rocks, in various parts of the country.

### CAPPARIDACEÆ.

CAPPARIS *spinosa*.—Caper plant, from the Wady en Nahr, the ancient Kedron. It however occurs in many places, and is noticed by Hasselquist as growing at Jerusalem out of the walls and crevices of the rocks. Its unopened flower buds are familiarly known as capers. Dr. Royle is of opinion that it is the plant alluded to in Scriptures under the name of hyssop. His grounds for this are that one of its Arabic names, *asaf*, is closely allied to the Hebrew *asob*, or *esof;* that it is found in Lower Egypt, in the deserts of Sinai, and at Jerusalem growing on rocks and walls; that it possesses cleansing properties; that it grows sufficiently large to furnish a stick or rod, all which are attributed to the hyssop of Scripture, and are not found in the plant now known under that name.

CRATÆVA *gynandra*, the root of which is said to be so acrid as to blister the skin, and CLEOME *Arabica* are likewise spoken of by travellers as found in Palestine.

### CISTACEÆ.

CISTUS *incanus*.—Collected in Wady Ali, and also noticed by Pococke as frequent in many parts of the country. The specimens are without flowers or fruit. The species affording the gum ladanum (*C. creticus*) does not appear to have been met with by the party, but it is mentioned by many travellers in the Holy Land, from the time of Belon.

### VIOLACEÆ.

The only violet that is found in Palestine appears to be the *V. odorata*, so common in the more temperate climates of Europe. If introduced, it must have been so at a very early period, as Mahommed is stated to have said "the excellence of the violet is as the excellence of el Islem above all other religions." It is much used in the form of a conserve, employed in making sherbet. It is the *benefsej* of the Arabs.

### RESEDACEÆ.

RESEDA *luteola*—Dyers-weed.—Found in Wady en Nahr. The specimens are without foliage, but are distinguished by the four cleft calyx. It is used in dying yellow.

R. *lutea*.—Collected at 'Ain Jidy. These specimens, as in the last, are destitute of leaves; but the species is distinguishable by the six-toothed calyx. It was found by Hasselquist in many parts of Palestine.

### CARYOPHYLLACEÆ.

DIANTHUS *caryophyllus* appears to be very common in Palestine, as specimens are in the collection from most parts of the country. *D. superbus* and *D. armeria* were also met with in several places.

SAPONARIA *orientalis*.—Near Ephesus; and *S. vaccaria*, no locality noted.

ARENARIA *maritima*.—Shores of the Dead Sea.

GYPSOPHILA *saxifraga*.—Plains of Damascus.

SILENE *armeria, behen, cretica*, &c., were likewise found in various places on the route.

### LINACEÆ.

LINUM *usitatissimum*, or common flax, is cultivated in many places.

### MALVACEÆ.

Numerous malvaceous plants were met with, but generally of a small size; specimens of the following were collected:

ALTHEA *ficifolia*.—On the banks of the Litany.

MALVA *sylvestris*.—At 'Ain Jidy.

MALVA *rotundifolia*.—Wady en Nahr, and at the warm baths at Lake Tiberias.

SIDA *Asiatica*.—El Feshkhah.

LAVATERA *thuringiniana*.—Foot of Mount Carmel.

ABELMOSCHUS *esculentus*, or okra and GOSSYPIUM *herbaceum*, or cotton, are cultivated in many parts of this country.

### GERANIACEÆ.

The only species of geranium that were observed were *G. rotundifolium*, and *G. columbinum*.

### TILIACEÆ.

CORCHORUS *olitorius*.—This plant is cultivated in most parts of Syria and Palestine as a culinary vegetable. It is the *mulookiah* of the Arabs, and is supposed by some writers to be the malluach (Job xxx, 4) of the Old Testament, rendered in our version mallows; but the general opinion seems to be that this is the *Atriplex halimus;* but there are so many plants of a mucilaginous character used for food in the East, that it is impossible to decide with any certainty as to the species alluded to by the Hebrew writer.

### AURANTIACEÆ.

Two species of this order are cultivated in Judea, the CITRUS *aurantium*, or orange, and CITRUS *medica*, or citron, neither of which are natives, but appear to have been introduced at a very early period, especially the latter, which, if it is the tappuach of the Old Testament, (translated apple in our version,) is spoken of during the time of Solomon.

### MELIACEÆ.

MELIA *azedarach* is a common tree in Palestine, but has probably been introduced from Persia or India. It is the *eleah* of the Arabs.

### VITACEÆ.

Several varieties of the VITIS *vinifera*, or wine grape, are cultivated in Palestine, and were so from the earliest times, but it does not appear to be a native of the country; it however grows luxuriantly and bears fruit of a great size, as is noticed in the Old Testament, in the case of the spies sent to explore the Promised Land, who brought back a bunch of grapes of so great a size as to require two men to support it.

### ACERACEÆ.

But two species belonging to this order are found in the Holy Land, ACER *monspessula* and *A. creticum*, neither of them very common.

### OXALIDACEÆ.

The collection contained some fragments of a species of OXALIS, which resembled closely O. *corniculata*, which is noticed by Hasselquist as a native of Palestine; if so, it is probably an introduced plant.

ZYGOPHYLLACEÆ.

Tzygophyllum *fabago* is found in many parts of Syria and Palestine, and it is said to be an active vermifuge.

Tribulus *terrestris* is likewise abundant, and is considered to be the tribolos, (Matth. vii, 16, and Heb. vi, 8,) translated thistles and briars; but it is probable that allusion is merely made to a thorny plant in these passages, and not to any particular species.

Fagonia *cretica*.—The same may be said with regard to this plant, which, with the former, is found in dry and uncultivated soil.

RUTACEÆ.

Rutæ *graveolens*, or rue, is cultivated in Palestine in gardens, but does not appear to have been so in early times, as, although it is mentioned among the kitchen herbs in the Talmud, it is expressly stated that it is not subject to tithe, as it was not grown in gardens.

Peganum *harmala* is also found in many parts of Judea. The seeds are intoxicating and soporific.

Dictamnus *fraxinella*, once so much esteemed for its medicinal properties, occurs in the mountainous parts of the country.

CORIARIACEÆ.

Coriaria *myrtifolia* occurs near the sea-coast. The leaves are used for tanning and dyeing, and are often found mixed with Alexandrian senna.

RHAMNACEÆ.

Numerous specimens of the thorny plants appertaining to this order are abundant in Syria and Palestine.

Zizyphus *spina christi*, near Jerusalem—*nabka* of the Arabs.—This is supposed to be the plant from which the crown of thorns with which Christ was crowned, was made; but there is no certainty what is meant by the word akantha of the original text as it is used in the other passages for various thorny shrubs.

Z. *vulgaris*—common jujube, a native of Syria, Persia, &c.—The berries are ovate, red, about the size of an olive, with a central bilocular seed or nut. Belon speaks (341) of a variety with white fruit, found on Libanus. These berries are considered as pectoral, and calculated to calm a cough or irritation of the throat and chest, and form the basis of what is called jujube paste.

Paliurus *aculeatus*.—In the mountainous parts of Judea; as also

Lycium *spinosum*, and L. *afrum*.

TEREBINTHACEÆ.

Pistacia *terebinthus*.—Common in Palestine. *But'm* of the Arabs. Alah, of the Hebrew Scriptures; rendered in our version variously, as oak, terebinth, teil, elm and plain, but now generally supposed to mean terebinth, or turpentine tree in every passage. It often attains a great size, and yields the Scio turpentine.

P. *lentiscus*.—In various parts of Palestine; probably introduced from the Greek Islands. *Darn* of the Arabs. Furnishes the gum mastic.

P. *vera*.—Cultivated. *Fortuch* of the Arabs. The fruit is much used in the East under the name of pistachio nuts.

FABACEÆ.

Acacia *vera*, and A. *seyal* are found in the deserts between the Dead Sea and the Red Sea. Both furnish gum Arabic, but it is nto collected in any quantity. The shittim wood of Scripture is, in all probability, the product of these trees. It is the *karatz*, or *karad*, of the Arabs, and *sant* of the Egyptians.



A. *farnesiana* is much cultivated in gardens, on account of the fragrance of its flowers.

Alhagi *maurorum*.—In many parts of Syria. Camel's thorn—the *al-haj* of the Arabs, or *oshter khan;* affords an exudation of a sweetish juice, which concretes in small masses, and resembles manna, and is gathered by the Arabs for food, and is supposed by some writers to be the manna on which the Israelites were fed in the desert.

Anagyris *fœtida*.—Near Jerusalem. Used in medicine.

Anthyllis *Hermanniæ*.—In the mountainous parts of Palestine.

Astragalus.—A number of species are found in Syria and Palestine, as

A. *gumnifer*, A. *capitatus*,
A. *syriacus*, A. *christianus*,
A. *tragacantha*. The first three furnish gum tragacanth

Tamarindus *indica*.—Cultivated.

Cercis.—*siliquastrum*.—In various parts of Syria and Palestine, Judas tree.

Cassia *obovata*.—'Ain Jidy—blunt leaved senna. *Seneh* of the Arabs; one of the species used in medicine.

Spartium *junceum*.—Banks of the Litany, &c. Spanish broom-

Genista *monosperma*.—Various parts of Syria. *Rotem* of the Arabs. This is supposed to be the rotem of the Old Testament, translated juniper in our version. But the roots are no more fit for food (Job xxx, 4) than those of the juniper; and it may be stated that the chamarops *humilis* is also called rotem by the Arabs; and it is known that the roots of the American species furnish a kind of arrow root, used by the Indians in Florida.

Ononis *spinosa*.—Rather common. Rest harrow.

O. *viscosa*.

Lupinus.—Several species of lupine are found in Palestine and Syria, and some are cultivated.

Lupinus *varius*. Lupinus *angustifolius*.
L. *hirsutus*.

Colutea *arborescens*.—Various places in Palestine. Bladder senna.

Lablab *vulgaris*.—Cultivated.—Egyptian bean; *lablab* of Arabs.

Lathyrus *sativus*.—Cultivated. Chich pea; *giban* of the Arabs.

L. *amphicarpos*. L. *biflorus*.

Faba *vulgaris*.—Cultivated. Windsor bean; *fool* of the Arabs.

Ervum *lens*.—Cultivated. Lentiles; *addar* of the Arabs. The red pottage for which Esau sold his birthright, (Gen. xxv, 29) was made of lentiles. They are still used extensively in the East.

E. *ervillia*.—Common in Palestine. Bitter vetch. The seeds are said to be poisonous.

Cicer *arietinum*.—Cultivated. Calavanches; *hommos* of Arabs.

Pisum *arvense*.—Cultivated. Field pea; *biselleh* of the Arabs.

Phaseolus *mungos*.—Cultivated. Bean; *gishmungay-ga* of the Arabs.

Hedysarum *coronarium*. H. *caputgalli*.

Psoralea *bituminosa*.—Common. Stinking trefoil. Leaves used in medicine as a remedy for cancer.

Trifolium *alexandrinum*. Abundant in Syria and Palestine. Alexandria clover.

T. *stellatum*. T. *procumbens*.
T. *angustifolium*. T. *tomentosum*.
T. *incarnatum*. T. *resupinatum*.
T. *globosum*. T. *uniflorum*.

Trigonella *fœnum graecum*.—Not uncommon. Fenugreek; *helba* of the Arabs. Still used in medicine. The Arabs employ it in poultices and fomentations.

Medicago *radiata*. M. *citcinata*. M. *polymotpha*.

Ceratonia *siliqua*.—Common in Palestine. Carob tree; *kharoob shamee* of the Arabs. The pods and seeds are used as food for cattle, &c. It is supposed that it was the locust which, with honey, formed the food of John the Baptist, and is what is translated husks in our version of the New Testament, (Luke xv, 16,) in the parable of the prodigal son. The beans are much used in Spain at the present time to feed horses and mules.

Galega *officinalis.*—Not uncommon.—Goat's rue—used in medicine in epilepsy and convulsions.

Melilotus *officinalis.*—Common—melilot—*alchimelmeluch* of the Arabs.

Moringa *aptera.*—Cultivated—ben tree—*ben* of the Arabs. The seeds furnish much oil, which is sold in all the bazaars in the East.

### ROSACEÆ.

Rosa.—Several species of rose are found in Palestine, but the only one collected by Lieutenant Lynch was the *Rosa alba* or *biflora;* this was in abundance by sides of brooks and water-courses, as mentioned in Ecclesiasticus (xxxix, 13.) The rose cannot have been a common plant in the Holy Land, either in the wild or cultivated state, as it is not often spoken of by Jewish writers, and it is not mentioned in the canonical books of Scripture; the word translated rose in our version having reference to a bulbous plant, as will be noticed hereafter. Lane says, (notes to Arabian Nights,) "though the Arabs are far from being remarkable for exhibiting taste in the planning of their gardens, they are passionately fond of flowers, and especially of the rose.—(*Ward.*) They are announced for sale in the streets of Cairo by the cry of, 'the rose was a thorn, from the sweat of the prophet it blossomed.'"

Rubus.—The species of this genus are not common in Syria or Palestine.

R. *sanctus* is the most frequently to be met with; it closely resembles the R. *fruticosus*, judging from a specimen in the collection of M. Cohen, Esq., from Mount Sinai, where it is shown by the monks, as the bush out of which the angel of the Lord appeared to Moses in a flaming fire. (Exodus iii, 2.)

Potentilla *supina*—on the mountains.

### DRUPACEÆ.

Amygdalus *communis.*—Cultivated—almond—*lonz* of the Arabs.

A. *persica.*—Cultivated—peach—*khokh* of the Arabs.

Neither of these fruits flourish in the plains, and only attain perfection in the more temperate cliamte of the mountains.

Cydonia *vulgaris.*—Cultivated on Lebanon—quince—*safargal* of the Arabs. Celsius was of opinion that the quince is the tappuach of the Hebrew Scriptures, translated apple in our version, but as has been already stated it is more probable that it means the citron.

Sorbus *acuparia*—also found on Mount Lebanon.

Cratægus *pyracantha.*—In the cooler parts of Palestine.

C. *azarolus.*—In the same situations as the last.

### MYRTACEÆ.

Myrtus *communis*—Myrtle. This occurs in most parts of Palestine, often attaining a height of ten feet, and when in flower emitting a most delicious fragrance. It is the Hadas of the Hebrew Scriptures, correctly translated myrtle in our version, and is the *Hadas* of the Arabs. Among the Jews it was the emblem of justice. Among the Arabs it is much esteemed. "Adam," says Mahommed, "fell down from Paradise with three things, the myrtle, which is the chief of sweet scented flowers of this world."

Punica *granatum.*—Cultivated—pomegranate—*rooman* of Arabs.

### LYTHRACEÆ.

Lawsonia *inermis.*—Cultivated throughout Syria—Egyptian—privet *faghiyet*, or more commonly *el henna* of the Arabs. It is highly esteemed for the delicious fragance of its flowers. It is the copher of the Hebrews, translated camphire in our version of the Old Testament. The leaves have been used from the earliest times in the East, for the purpose of staining the nails of the hands and toes of an iron-rust color, which is considered to add to their beauty.

Lythrum *salicaria.*—In moist situations—purple loose strife.

### TAMARISCINEÆ.

Tamarix *orientalis.* T. *tetragyna.*

Common in Syria and Palestine—tamarisk tree—*Asul* or *Athul* of the Arabs—and more commonly *toorfa.* It is almost impossible to distinguish the species of this genus in a dried state. Ehrenburg states that the first is the plant of Syria, and the latter of Arabia and Persia. It is said by many botanical writers that *T. gallica* is likewise found in Syria.

### CUCURBITACEÆ.

Numerous plants of this order are found in all parts of the East.

Momordica *balsamina.*—Cultivated—balsam apple—used as a vulnerary.

Bryonia *cordifolia.*—Banks of the Jordan. The specimen in the collection is so imperfect that it is difficult to decide on it with certainty.

Cucumis *melo.*—Cultivated—musk-melon—*butikh* or *Kaun* of the Arabs.

C. *dudaim.*—Cultivated—*scheman* of the Arabs. This is a small melon, cultivated on account of the pleasant smell of the fruit, which is not eatable, and is supposed by some writers to be the same as the dudaim—mandrake of our version, (Gen. xxx, 14, 16,) but the evidence in its favor is not strong.

C. *sativus.*—Cultivated—cucumber—*kissa* or *Khiar* of the Arabs—kishuim of the Hebrew Scriptures, (Numb. xi, 5,) and correctly translated cucumbers in our version.

C. *flexuosus.*—Cultivated.

C. *citrullus.*—Cultivated—watermelon—*butikh* and *butikh hindee* of the Arabs—abattachim of the Hebrew Scriptures, (Numb. xi, 5,) translated melons in our version.

C. *colocynthus*, very common in the desert parts of Syria, covering the ground for miles in extent.—Colocynth or bitter apple, *hunzal* of the Arabs. This is probably the pakyoth of the Hebrew Scriptures, (2 Kings iv, 38, 40,) translated wild gourds in our version. It is extensively used in medicine.

C. *prophetarum*, also common in Syria.—It is smaller than the colocynth, but has the same nauseous, bitter taste; the fruit is covered with soft prickles.

Ecbalium *elaterium*, native in many places in Syria.—Wild or squirting cucumber, used in medicine as a powerful drastic purgative.

Cucurbita.—Many kinds of squash, pumpkins, and gourds are cultivated, but it is difficult to ascertain their exact species.

### PORTULACACEÆ.

Portulaca *oleracea.*—In many parts of Palestine. Purslane *Bakleancha* of the Arabs.

Glinus *lotoides.*—'Ain Jidy.

### PARONYCHIÆ.

Polycarpon *tetraphyllum.*—Maritime parts of Syria.

Paronychia *nitida.*—Near Beïrût.

### CRASSULACEÆ.

Umbilicus *pendulinus.*—On rocks.

Sedum *reflexum.*—'Ain Jidy and elsewhere.

S. *lebanoticum.*—Lebanon.

FICOIDEÆ.

MESEMBRYANTHEMUM *nodiflorum*.—Lower part of Syria—used in making morocco leather.

CACTACEÆ.

OPUNTIA *vulgaris*.—Cultivated.

APIACEÆ.

AMNI *majus*.—Bishop weed. A. *visnaga*.—Ruins of Ba'albek.

ANETHUM *graveolens*.—Cultivated. Do. *Shubit* of the Arabs. This is the anethon (Matt. xxiii, 23) erroneously translated anise in our version.

APIUM *graveolens*.—Moist places.

ANTHAMANTA *cretensis*.

BUPLEURUM *fruticosum*. B. *odontites*.

CACHRIS *libanotis*.

ARTEDIA *squamata*.

CAUCALIS *leptophylla*.

CICUTA *virosa*—Water hemlock.

CORIANDRUM *sativum*.—Cultivated.

CUMINUM *cyminum*.—Cultivated. Cummin.

ERYNGIUM *tricuspidatum*.—Near Nazareth.

LAGOECIA *cuminoides*.—Wild cummin.

LASERPITIUM *glabrum*.—Mount Tabor. Root is very purgative.

LEVISTICUM *officinale*.—Lovage.

OPOPONAX *chironium*.—Gum parsnip. Affords a fœtid gum resin, called opoponax.

PIMPINELLA *anisum* —Cultivated. Anise.

P. *saxifraga*—Burnt saxifrage.

PTYCHOTIS *coptica*.

SCANDIX *pecten*.

SMYRNIUM *perfoliatum*. S. *egyptiacum*.

TORDYLIUM *nodosum*.

Specimens of several other plants of this order are in the collection, but cannot be designated, from the want of seeds, and other imperfections.

ARALIACEÆ.

HEDERA *helix*.—Mount Tabor. Ivy.

CAPRIFOLIACEÆ.

LONICERA *caprifolium*.—Near Ba'albek. Honeysuckle.

SAMBUCUS *racemosa*.—Mountainous parts of Palestine. Mountain elder.

VILBURNUM *tinus*.—Palestine. Laurustinus.

RUBIACEÆ.

GALIUM *aparine*.—Syria and Palestine. Cleavers.

G. *verum?*—Near Ephesus.

RUBIA *tinctorum*.—Cultivated. Madder; *ferah* of the Arabs.

CRUCIANELLA *monspeliaca*.—Jerusalem.

VALERIANACEÆ.

CENTRANTHUS *ruber*—Ghebel en Shiek. Mount Hermon. Red Valerian.

VALERIANA *celtica*.—In the mountainous parts of Palestine.

V. *dioscoridis?*

DIPSACEÆ.

KNAUTIA *arvensis*.—El Feshkhah.

SCABIOSA *stellata*.—Banks of the Jordan.

S. *syriaca*.—Banks of the Litany. S. *papposa*.—Turâbeh.

ASTERACEÆ.

ACHILLEA *ageratum*. A. *nobilis*. A. *bipinnata*.

TROGOPOGON *hybridum*. T. *asperum*.

SCORNOZERA *hispanica*.

PICRIS *hieracoides*.

SONCHUS *ciliatus*—Sow thistle.

CHONDRILLA *juncea*.

LACTUCA *scariola*.

LEONTODON *lanatum?*

HIERACIUM *sanctum*.

CREPIS *vesicaria*.

SCOLYMUS *maculatus*.

CICHORIUM *endivia*. C. *spinosum*.

GRUNDELIA *tournefortii*.

EHINOPS *ritro*. E. *corymbiferus*.

CIRSIUM *laniflorum*. C. *syriacus*.

CNICUS *benedictus*.

CYNARA *cardunculus*.—Cultivated. Chardoon.

C. *scolymus*.—Cultivated. Artichoke; *khrschuf* of the Arabs.

CARTHAMUS *tinctorius*.—Cultivated. Safflower; *Kettan* of the Arabs.

BIDENS *bipartita*.—In moist places. Plant very acrid.

XERANTHEMUM *annuum*.

BACCHARIS *dioscoridis*.

ARTEMISIA *judiaca*.—Wormwood.

A. *sieberii*. A. *abrotana*.

A. *pontica*. A. *santonica*.

GRAPHALIUM *sanguineum*.—Mount of Olives.

HELYCHRYSUM *orientale*.—Mount Carmel.

ERIGERON *siculum*.

SENECIO *doria*. S. *egyptiacus*.

S. *donoricum*. S. *glaucus*.

CALENDULA *officinalis*. C. *arvensis*.

INULA *graveolens*.

DONORICUM *bellidiastrum*.

SOLIDAGO *virgaurea*.

BELLIS *annua*.

CHRYSANTHEMUM *coronarium*.

MATRICARIA *chamomilla*. M. *cretica*.

ANTHEMIS *peregrina*.

ANACYCLUS *pyrethrum*.

PALLENIS *spinosa*.

MULGEDIUM *plumieri*.

ZACINTHA *verrucosa*.

SANTOLINA *fragrantissima*.

NOTOBASIS *syriaca*.

HELIANTHUS *annuus*.—Cultivated. Sunflower.

DIOTIS *candidissima*.

CENTAUREA *beher*. C. *golactites*.

C. *calcitrapa?* C. *pumilio*.

C. *jacea*. C. *crocodilium*.

C. *stoebe*. C. *moschata*.

CAMPANULACEÆ.

CAMPANULA *speculum*. C. *laciniata*.

C. *medium*. C. *pentagona*.

### ERICACEÆ.

Erica *orientalis.*

Arbutus *unedo.*—Hills of Palestine. Strawberry tree—*Hatiladib* of the Arabs. A. *andrachne.*

Azalea *pontica.*—Upper parts of Palestine.

### STYRACACEÆ.

Styrax *officinalis.*—Common in Palestine. Storax tree—*lubne* of the Arabs. It is supposed to be the libneh of the Hebrew Scriptures, (Gen. xxx, 37, and Hosea iv, 13,) translated in our version, poplar. This seems highly probable from the similarity of the respective Hebrew and Arabic words.

### OLEACEÆ.

Olea *Europæa.*—Cultivated throughout Syria and Palestine, of which countries it appears to be a native. Olive tree—*zaitoon* of the Arabs. It is the earliest tree specifically mentioned in the Bible, except the fig.

Ornus *Europa.*—Cultivated, and probably introduced. The translation of our version of the Old Testament consider it to be the oren of the Hebrews, (Is. xliv, 14;) but in almost all others it is rendered pine.

Phyllirea *augustifolia.* P. *media.*

### JASMINEÆ.

Nyctanthes *undulata.*—Cultivated. *Sambac* of the Arabs.

Jasminum *grandiflorum.*—Cultivated.

J. *fruticans.*—Cultivated. J. *officinalis.*—Cultivated.

### APOCYNACEÆ.

Nerium *oleander.*—Sources of the Jordan, and on other streams —oleander—*diffah* of the Arabs. This beautiful shrub occurs on the banks of most of the water courses of Palestine, usually with red but sometimes with white flowers. Most travellers in that country have noticed the luxuriance and beauty of this plant. It is supposed that the wood used by Moses to sweeten the bitter waters of Marah was that of the oleander. This is said in the Targums to be the *ardiphne,* which is stated by most Hebrew interpreters to mean the same as rhodaphene of ancient Greek writers, or what is now called the oleander. In confirmation of this, it may be stated that it is still used for this purpose in some parts of India.

Vinca *minor.*—Small periwinkle.

### ASCLEPIADACEÆ.

Calotropis *procera.*—Oshoor of the Arabs—beidel assur of Alpinus.—In the vicinity of the Dead Sea, Wady el Nahr, &c. This was brought by Lieutenant Lynch as the apple of Sodom, respecting which so much difference of opinion exists among naturalists. One considering it to be the galls of the terebinth; others the fruit of a species of nightshade; others again as the colocynth. The present plant, however, answers in all respects to the accounts of Tacitus and Josephus, and was considered to be the plant alluded to by them by Seetzen.

Cynanchum *monspeliacum.* C. *creticum.*

Periploca *Graca.*

Secamone *alpini.*—The roots yield a kind of scammony.

### GENTIANACEÆ.

Erythræa *maritima.*—Sea-side centuary.

### BIGNONIACEÆ.

Sesamum *orientale.*—Cultivated. Benne—*semsem* of the Arabs. Seeds used for food.

### CONVOLVULACEÆ.

Calystegia *sepium*—binduced.

Convolvulus *althoides.*—Ghebel el Scheik.

C. *cantabricus.*—Nazareth. C. *dorychium.*

C. *batatas.*—Cultivated. Sweet potato. C. *hederaceus.*

C. *arvensis.* C. *siculum.*

C. *cneorum*—rock rose; root purgative.

C. *scammonium*—scammony. The roots afford on incision the Aleppo scammony.

Cuscuta *epithymum*—small dodder.

### BORAGINACEÆ.

Heliotropium *Europeum.*—Jaffa, Nazareth, &c.

H. *albidum.*—Opposite Feshkhah. H. *supinum.*

Anchusa *Italica.*—Bugloss.

A. *orientalis.* A. *tinctoria.*—Alkanet.

Echium *Italicum.*—Turâbeh. E. *creticum.*—Turâbeh.

E. *arenaria.*—Wady en Nahr.

Myosotis *apula.*

Cynoglossum *officinale.*

Symphytum *orientale.*

Cerinthe *orientalis.*

Onosma *echioides.*

Pulmonaria *officinalis.*

Trichodesma.

### CORDIACEÆ.

Cordia *myxa.*—Cultivated—*sebestan* of the Arabs. The fruit is excellent.

### SOLANACEÆ.

Hyoscyamus *albus*—white henbane, collected in Wady en Nahr. This species is identical in its properties with the *H. niger* or common henbane, and is used for it in the south of Europe, where it is also a native. *Bengi* of the Arabs.

H. *luteus*—yellow henbane—Turâbeh. This is closely allied to the preceding, but may be distinguished by the color of the flowers.

Another species *H. reticulatus,* is mentioned by Persoon and others as occurring in Palestine, but no specimens are in the collection.

Solanum *nigrum* var.—Turâbeh. This is one of the plants called by the Arabs *aneb-el-dib,* or wolf's grape. Several other species are noticed by travellers in Palestine, among which may be mentioned *S. incanum,* supposed by Hasselquist to be the wild grape spoken of by Isaiah, v, 4. *S. sanctum,* which is thought by Royle to be the *chedek,* translated brier and thorn in our version of the Bible, as the Arabs apply the name chedek to this plant.

Capsicum *annuum.*—Red pepper—cultivated.

Datura *metel.*—*Jouz massel* of the Arabs.

Mandragora *officinalis.* M. *autumnalis.*

Mandrake, frequent in Wady en Nahr and on Mounts Carmel and Tabor—*Jiabora* of the Arabs. The fruit of these plants is generally supposed to be mandrake or dudaim of Scripture, and they are still sought for by the inhabitants of Jerusalem on account of their supposed aphrodisiac powers.

Verbascum *sinuata.* V. *blattaria.*

Nicotiana *rustica?*—Cultivated.
Physalis *alkakengi.*

SEROPHULARIACEÆ.

Antirrhinum *majus.*—Banks of the Litany—great snap dragon.
A. *orontium.* A. *chalepense.*
Linaria *elatine.*
Scrophularie *sambucifolia.*
Trixago.
Veronica *anagallis.* V. *hederifolia.*
V. *ogrestis.* V. *filiformis.*

OROBANCHACEÆ.

Orobanche *lavis.*

LAMIACEÆ.

Amaracus *dictamnus.*—Dittany of Crete.
Hyssopus *officinalis.*—Hyssop.
Lamium *vulgatum.* L. *purpureum.* L. *orvalo.*
Lavandula *spica.*—Lavender. L. *stæchas.*—Near Ephesus.
Marrubium *peregrinum.*
Melissa *officinalis.*—Balm.
Mentha *arvensis.* M. *silvestris.*
Molucella *spinosa.*—Banks of the Jordan.
Ocymum *basilicum.*—Sweet basil.
Origanum *creticum.* O. *marjorana.* O. *heracleoticum.*
Phlomis *lychnites.* P. *fruticosa.*
P. *spica venti.*—Near Damascus.
Rosmarinus *officinalis.*—Rosemary.
Salvia *horminum.* S. *verticillata.*
S. *cretica.* S. *verbenaca.*
S. *pomifera.* S. *officinalis.*
S. *syriaca.* S. *sclarea.*
Satureja *capitata.* S. *mastichina.*
Sideritis *syriaca.*—'Ain Jidy. S. *montana.* S. *lanata.*
Stachys *spinosa.*
Teucrium *chamædrys.* T. *polium.* T. *chamæpythys.*
T. *botrys.* T. *cordium.*
T. *creticum.* T. *tenthrion*
Thymbra *juliana.* T. *spicata.*
Nepeta *pannonica.*
Betonica *officinalis.*
Prasium *majus.*

VERBENACEÆ.

Verbena *officinalis.* V. *supina.*
Vitex *agnuscastus.*

ACANTHACEÆ.

Acanthus *dioscoridis.*

PRIMULACEÆ.

Annagallis *arvensis.* A. *monelli.*
Clyclamen *hederifolium.*

PLUMBAGENACEÆ.

Stratice *limonium.*—Near Ephesus.
S. *monopetala.* S. *sinuata.*—Turâbeh.
S. *alata.* S. *flava.*
Plumbago *europea.*



Salvadora *persica.*—Banks of the Jordan, Sea of Tiberias. *Khardal romec* of the Arabs. Dr. Royle is of opinion that this is the mustard tree of Scripture, as its seeds are employed for mustard; its Arabic name is the same; the tree attains a large size, and it grows in the place in which Christ delivered the parable.

PLANTAGINACEÆ.

Plantago *major.* P. *cynops.*
P. *albicans.* P. *psyllium.*

AMARANTHACEÆ.

Achyranthes *aspera.*
Gomphera *globosa.*

CHENOPODACEÆ.

Atriplex *halimus.*—Dead Sea. A. *græca.*—Dead Sea.
Chenopodium *viride.*
C. *maritimum.*—Dead Sea. C. *scoparium.*
Anabasis *aphylla.*—Dead Sea.
Camphorosma *monspeliacum.*
Salicornia *fruticosa.*—Dead Sea.
Salsola *soda.* S. *tragus.*

PHYTOLACCACEÆ.

Phytolacca *asiatica.*

POLYGONACEÆ.

Polygonum *aviculare.*
Rheum *ribes.*
Rumex *acetosa.* R. *acutus.*
R. *roseus.* R. *vesicarius.* R. *bucephala.*
Calligonum *polygonoides.*

THYMELACEÆ.

Daphne *glomerata.*

LAURACEÆ.

Laurus *nobilis.*—Common. Bay tree—gaur or gar of the Arabs.

SANTALACEÆ.

Osyris *alba.*—Poets' rosemary.

ELEAGINACEÆ.

Eleagnus *augustifolius.*—Wild olive; zukkin or zuccoon of the Arabs. An oil made from the nuts or seeds is much esteemed among the Arabs as a vulnerary.
E. *spinosus.*

ARISTOLOCHIACEÆ.

Aristolochia *pistolochia.*

EUPHORBIACEÆ.

Ricinus *communis.*—Banks of the Jordan, &c.; castor oil bush; palma christi; *Kherwa* of the Arabs. It is now generally admitted that this is the gourd of Jonah, (W. 67, 8, 10,) the *Ki-kayon* of the Hebrew text.

Buxus *sempervirens*.—On the mountains; box tree; *shumshad* of he Arabs. This is probably the teashur of the Hebrew Scripture, and is so rendered in our version.

Crozophora *tinctoria*.—Turnsol litmus.

Euphorbia *myrsinites*. E. *portlandica*. E. *pithyusa*.
E. *peplus*. E. *serrata*.

Mercurialis *annua*.

URTICACEÆ.

Cannabis *sativa*.—Cultivated—hemp—*bust* of the Arabs. From the leaves is extracted an intoxicating drug called hashish by the Arabs, malach by the Turks, bang or gunja, in India, &c.

Urtica *dioica*. U. *pilutifera*.

Ficus *carica*.—Cultivated and wild; fig—*teen* of the Arabs; *t*eenah of the Hebrew Scriptures; always translated fig. It is the first plant specifically noticed in the Bible, when Adam and Eve are described as sewing fig leaves together to make aprons.

F. *sycomorus*.—Cultivated; sycamore fig; *jummeyz* of the Arabs. This species, which attains a very great size, is likewise spoken of in the Hebrew Scriptures under the name of shikmoth, rendered in our version by sycamore. In Egypt the wood was much used in the formation of mummy cases. It was evidently much prized for its fruit among the Jews; this fruit is sweetish, and still esteemed in the East. To ripen it, a part is cut off or scraped, which causes a more rapid maturity. This was practiced in early times, and is alluded to by the prophet Amos, (vii, 14,) for the passage where he says: "I was a gatherer of sycamore fruit," should be "a scarifier of sycamore fruit."

Morus *alba*.—Cultivated and wild; white mulberry; much grown in order to furnish food for the silk worm. It is the sycamine of the New Testament, (Luke xvii, 16.)

M. *nigra*.—Cultivated for its fruit; black mulberry; *toot* of the Arabs.

Parietaria *officinalis*. P. *judaica*. P. *lusitanica*.

JUGLANDACEÆ.

Juglans *regia*.—Cultivated; walnut; *joux* of the Arabs. This tree is a native of Persia, but was very early introduced into Judea, since it is noticed in Solomon's Song, (vi, 11;) egoz in the original, properly translated nuts.

AMENTACEÆ.

Alnus *glutinosa*.—In moist ground near streams.

Corylus *avellana*.—Hazel; *bunduk* of the Arabs.

Plantanus *orientalis*.—Oriental plane tree; *dulb* of the Arabs; sources of the Jordan. This large and noble tree is found in many parts of Palestine where the soil is rich and humid, but it cannot be ranked among the common trees of that country. It is the *armon* of the Hebrew Scriptures, which in our version is erroneously translated chestnut, but by the septuagint and the best authorities is rendered plane tree. This is confirmed by the fact that a cognate word in Arabic, *harama*, signifies to shed its bark, which is a well known characteristic of the plane, as is exemplified in the American species, known as the button wood.

Populus *dilatata*.—Moist places in the hill country; Lombardy poplar.

P. *alba*.—Moist situations; white poplar.

Salix *babylonica*.—Banks of streams; weeping willow.

S. *egyptiaca*.—Near the sea-coast; *khalaf* of the Arabs

Quercus *egilops*.—Holm or valonia oak; the acorns are used instead of galls. Q. *ilex*.

Q. *ballota*. Q. *infectoria*.
Q. *coccifera*. Q. *gramuntia*.
Q. *esculus*. Q. *crinita*.

Although many species of the oak are found in Syria and Palestine, they are principally confined to the mountain ranges, particularly to those beyond the Jordan; they are also of frequent occurrence, though of small size, about the sources of that river.

PINACEÆ.

Numerous species of this order are found in Syria and the Holy Land, but have not been fully investigated.

Pinus *cedrus*.—Lebanon; cedar of Lebanon; *arz* of the Arabs. Of these noble trees, once so numerous, not more than twelve now exist, but many young ones are springing up. In many of the passages in Scripture the Hebrew word eres is applicable to this tree only, but in others it evidently refers to the pine.

P. *sylvestris*.—Scotch fir. P. *pinea*.

Thuya *aphylla*.

Cupressus *sempervirens*.—Cypress; *suroo* and *shujurt al hyat* of the Arabs. This is thought by Rosenmuller to be the berosh of the Hebrews, but Celsius and others maintain that this word has reference to the cedar of Lebanon.

Juniperus *oxycedrus*.—*Abhul* of the Arabs; Mount Lebanon.

J. *drupacea*. J. *lycica*.

J. *phœnicea*.—*Arus* of Arabs. J. *sabina*.—*Buratee* of the Arabs.

J. *communis*.

ALISMACEÆ.

Alisma *plantago*.—Wet places; water plantain.

MUSACEÆ.

Musa *paradisiaca*.—Cultivated; plantain; *moz* of the Arabs.

IRIDACEÆ.

Crocus *sativus*.—Crocus; *zaffaran* of the Arabs.

Gladiolus *communis*.—Corn flag.

Iris *fœtidissima*. I. *tuberosa*.

I. *florentina*.—Orris. I. *susiana*.

I. *germanica*.—Common flag.

AMARYLLIDACEÆ.

Narcissus *tezetta*.—Common narcissus—*narjis* of the Arabs. It is generally admitted that the Hebrew word chabbazzeleth, translated in our version of the Old Testament as rose, has no reference to that flower, but actually is intended to designate one of the bulbous rooted plants, and very probably the narcissus.

Oporanthus *luteus*.—Common in Palestine; yellow amaryllis. This is the plant which Sir J. E. Smith thought to be the lily of the New Testament. (Matt. vi, 26.)

Ixiolirion *montanum*.—Abounds in the hilly parts of the country. It is very beautiful, with clusters of delicate violet flowers. Dr. Lindley is of opinion that the lily spoken of above was this plant, from its abundance and striking appearance.

Pancratium *illyricum*. P. *maritimum?*

DIOSCORACEÆ.

Dioscorea *alata*.—Yam; cultivated.

SMILACEÆ.

Smilax *aspera*.—Rough bind weed.

S. *excelsa*.—Tall bind weed. Both these species are frequently to be met with in the more northern parts of the country. The roots are much used in Turkey as a substitute for sarsaparilla.

### LILIACEÆ.

The species of this order are very abundant in Palestine. Kitto says: "Whoever desires views, really extensive and beautiful, of lilies, tulips, hyacinths, &c., must in the spring season visit the districts through which we passed."

ALLIUM *sativam.*—Native and cultivated; garlic.

A. *ascalonicum.*—Cultivated. Shallot—*thom* of the Arabs. Dr. Royle is of opinion that this is the garlic (shunnim) of the Old Testament; but Celsius considers it to be the last noticed species.

A. *porrum.*—Cultivated. Leek—*kaarat* and *kooras-al-bukl* of the Arabs. This species has been cultivated and esteemed from the earliest ages, and is generally considered to be one of those so much desired by the children of Israel. (Numb. xi, 5.) The Hebrew word used in this passage to designate it, (chatzin,) is variously translated in other places, by grass, herb, &c., but is generally supposed to be properly rendered leeks in the present instance.

A. *cepa.*—Cultivated. Onion—*basl* or *bassal* of the Arabs. This is without doubt the betzal of the Hebrews, spoken of in the passage just referred to. A. *subhirsutum.*

A. *veronense.*—Near Jerusalem.

A. *pallens.*

A. *paniculatum.*—These species are of a size and beauty that render them highly ornamental.

ASPARAGUS *acutifolius.*—Near Jerusalem. A. *aphyllus.*

ASPHODELUS *lutens.*—Frequent. Yellow asphodel—*erizambac* of the Arabs.

A. *ramosus.*—Foot of Mount Carmel; white asphodel.

HYACINTHUS *orientalis.*—Frequent; hyacinth.

H. *comosus.* H. *botryoides.*

LILIUM *candidum.*—Cultivated. White lily—*soosan* of the Arabs. It has usually been supposed that the white lily was a native of the Holy Land; but it is very doubtful if it was ever seen in a wild state in that country: at present it is only found in a cultivated condition.

L. *chalcedonicum.*—Environs of Lake of Tiberias, and elsewhere common—Red lily. This is now considered to be the lily of the New Testament spoken of by Christ, (Luke xii, 27.) The lily of the Old Testament (shushan) has been variously interpreted by translators as the rose, violet, lily, &c. Dr. Royle seems to incline to the belief that it is the water-lily or nelumbium; but the identity of the Arabic appellation for the lily with the Hebrew word renders it more probable that the Hebrew term applies to the same plant.

ORNITHOGALUM *umbellatum.*—Common. Star of Bethlehem.

O. *arabicum.*—Near Jerusalem.

SCILLA *bifolia.*—Near Jerusalem.

S. *amoena.*

TULIPA *gesneriana.*—Very abundant—tulip—*tulipan* of the Arabs. It presents numerous varieties of colors.

RUSCUS *hyphophyllum.* R. *aculeatus.*

### COLCHICACEÆ.

COLCHICUM *variegatum.*—Chequer flower.

C. *montanum.*—Mountain colchicum. It is supposed that one or both these species yielded the hermodactyls of the ancients.

### PALMACEÆ.

PHŒNIX *dactylifera.*—Frequent. Date tree—*tamr* of the Arabs. The most useful and important tree in Syria. By the Romans it was considered as characteristic of Judea, as is evidenced by the coins of the conquerors of that country. At the present day its fruit forms the main article of food of numerous tribes of Arabs. It is the palm tree (tamar) of Scripture.

### ARACEÆ.

ACORUS *calamus.*—Moist places—valley of Ba'albek—calamus—*vage* of the Arabs.

ARUM *dracunculus.* A. *colocasia.*—Cultivated.

A. *tenuifolium.*

### JUNCACEÆ.

JUNCUS *effusus.*

### CYPERACEÆ.

PAPYRUS *antiquorum.*—Jordan. Paper rush—*burdee* of the Arabs.

CYPERUS *esculentus.*—Jordan. Tubers used for food.

C. *rotundus.*—Moist places.

### GRAMINACEÆ.

SACCHARUM *officinale.*—Cultivated. Sugar cane—kasab es sukkar.

PHALARIS *bulbosa.* P. *aquatica.*

PANICUM *italicum.*—Seeds eatable but small. *Shadona?* of the Arabs.

P. *miliaceum*—Millet. Cultivated. P. *patens.*

P. *alopecuroides.*—Near Jerusalem.

ALOPECURUS *monspeliensis.*

AGROSTIS *spica venti.*

POA *agustifolia.* P. *vivipara.*

P. *annua.* P. *pilosa.*

P. *bulbosa.* P. *rigida.*

BRIZA *bipinnata.*

DACTYLIS *glomerata.*

CYNOSURUS *echinatus.* C. *aureus.*

FESTUCA *myuros.* F. *fusca.*

BROMUS *scoparius.* B. *madritensis.* B. *tectorum.*

B. *sterilis.* B. *distachyos.*

ARUNDO *donax.*

HORDEUM *distichon* and other species and varieties are cultivated. Barley—*Schayer* of the Arabs.

TRITICUM *vulgare* and its varieties are also cultivated.—Wheat—*henta* of the Arabs. Kitto states that these as well as other kinds of grain are naturalized in the plains of Jezreel and the heights of Galilee.

T. *spelta.*—Cultivated—spelt. This appears to be the kussemeth of the Hebrews, translated in our version of the Scriptures as rye and fitches.

AVENA *fatua.*—Banks of Jordan.

LAGURUS *ovatus.* L. *cylindricus.*

ZEA *mays.*—Cultivated. Indian corn—*karmah* of the Arabs.

ANDROPOGON *schoenanthus.*—Lemon grass.

SORGHUM *vulgare.*—Cultivated very extensively—millet. There are numerous varieties, all called by the Arabs *dhurah.*

ORYZA *sativa.*—Cultivated on the upper Jordan—rice—*aruz* of of the Arabs.

EGILOPS *ovatus.*

LOLIUM *temulentum.*—In the grain fields—darnel.

The cryptogamic plants are not numerous; among the ferns, ADIANTUM *capillus veneris*, and GRAMMITIS *ceterach*, are most frequently to be met with. As respects the mosses, the only one that is of interest is the BRYUM *truncatulum*, a minute species growing on the walls of Jerusalem, and which Hasselquist supposes may be the hyssop of Solomon, for no other reason, apparently, than its minuteness forming a striking contrast with the cedar of Lebanon.

# F.

# CHRONOMETRICAL TABLES.

TABLE OF LATITUDES AND LONGITUDES DEDUCED FROM THE ANNEXED OBSERVATIONS.

| Date. 1848. | Latitudes north | | | Longitudes east from Greenwich | | | Localities. |
|---|---|---|---|---|---|---|---|
| | ° | ′ | ″ | ° | ′ | ″ | |
| April 4, | 32 | 49 | 51 | .. | .. | .. | Wady en Neffâkh. |
| 5, | 32 | 46 | 39 | .. | .. | .. | Tur'ân. |
| 8, | 32 | 46 | 14 | .. | .. | .. | Tiberias. |
| 11, | .. | .. | .. | 35 | 35 | 39 | Bridge of Semakh. |
| 12, | 32 | 39 | 09 | 35 | 35 | 40 | Bŭk'ah. |
| 13, | 32 | 30 | 11 | .. | .. | .. | Encampment on the Jordan. |
| 16, | 32 | 16 | 27 | .. | .. | .. | do. near Wady Ajlûn. |
| 16, | 32 | 07 | 24 | .. | .. | .. | On the Jordan. |
| 18, | 31 | 47 | 08 | 35 | 35 | 16 | Ford of Meshra'a. |
| 19, | 31 | 42 | 54 | 35 | 30 | 12 | 'Ain el Feshkhah. |
| 21, | 31 | 35 | 54 | 35 | 27 | 15 | 'Ain Turâbeh. |
| 22, | 31 | 27 | 55 | 35 | 28 | 00 | 'Ain Jidy. [ghik. |
| 25, | 31 | 12 | 48 | .. | .. | .. | Mouth of Wady Mubugk- |
| 26, | 31 | 10 | 23 | .. | .. | .. | do. Wady Humeir. |
| 27, | .. | .. | .. | 35 | 35 | 18 | do. do. [mûs. |
| 27, | 31 | 15 | 05 | .. | .. | .. | do. Wady Rŭbtat el Jâ- |
| May 3, | 31 | 27 | 50 | .. | .. | .. | do. Wady Mojêb. |
| 5, | 31 | 45 | 46 | .. | .. | .. | do. of the Jordan. |
| June 12, | 32 | 42 | 30 | 35 | 35 | 19 | South end of Lake Tiberias. |
| 13, | 32 | 53 | 37 | .. | .. | .. | North do. do. |
| 18, | 33 | 25 | 13 | .. | .. | .. | Hasbeiya. |

OBSERVATIONS FOR LATITUDE, APRIL 4, 1848.—ALTITUDES OF POLARIS.

## *Wady en Neffâkh.*

| Time by Chronometer, (11422.) | | | Double Altitudes of Polaris. | | | Index error = — 35″. |
|---|---|---|---|---|---|---|
| *h.* | *m.* | *s.* | ° | ′ | ″ | Comparison of Chronometers. |
| | | | | | | *h.* *m.* *s.* |
| 6 | 45 | 59 | 63 | 23 | 5 | No. 7986 = 7 24 49.5 |
| 6 | 57 | 44 | 63 | 17 | 55 | No. 11422 = 7 13 30 |
| 7 | 2 | 32 | 63 | 15 | 20 | |

OBSERVATIONS FOR LATITUDE, APRIL 5, 1848.—ALTITUDES OF POLARIS.

## *Tur'ân.*

| Time by Chronometer, (7986.) | | | Double Altitudes of Polaris. | | | Index error = — 35″. |
|---|---|---|---|---|---|---|
| *h.* | *m.* | *s.* | ° | ′ | ″ | Comparison of Chronometers. |
| 6 | 36 | 26 | 63 | 26 | 20 | *h.* *m.* *s.* |
| | 39 | 59 | | 23 | 50 | No. 7986 = 4 30 00 |
| | 42 | 58 | | 22 | 15 | No. 11422 = 4 18 41 |
| | 44 | 50 | | 22 | 00 | |
| | 47 | 22 | | 21 | 20 | |

DETERMINATION OF TIME FOR LONGITUDE, APRIL 6, A. M.—ALTITUDES OF THE SUN.

## *Tur'ân.*

| Time by Chronometer, (7986.) | | | Double Altitude of Sun's lower limb. | | | Time by Chronometer, (7986.) | | | Double Altitude of Sun's lower limb. | | |
|---|---|---|---|---|---|---|---|---|---|---|---|
| *h.* | *m.* | *s.* | ° | ′ | ″ | *h.* | *m.* | *s.* | ° | ′ | ″ |
| 6 | 5 | 5.5 | 73 | 7 | 35 | 6 | 9 | 48 | 75 | 00 | 20 |
| | 5 | 48 | | 24 | 50 | | 10 | 20 | | 13 | 5 |
| | 6 | 30.5 | | 41 | 15 | | 10 | 52.5 | | 25 | 55 |
| | 7 | 4 | | 55 | 30 | | 11 | 16 | | 35 | 30 |
| | 7 | 35 | 74 | 7 | 5 | | 11 | 57 | | 51 | 35 |
| | 8 | 6 | | 19 | 15 | | 12 | 17 | | 59 | 15 |
| | 8 | 42.5 | | 34 | 00 | | 12 | 42 | 76 | 9 | 20 |

Index error = — 35″. { Comparison of Chronometers. No. 7986 = 5*h.* 16*m.* 10*s.* No. 11422 = 5 4 52

DETERMINATION OF TIME, APRIL 8, 1848.—EQUAL ALTITUDES OF THE SUN.

## *Tiberias.*

| Time by Chronometer, (7986.) | | | Double Altitude of Sun's lower limb. | | Time by Chronometer, (7986.) | | |
|---|---|---|---|---|---|---|---|
| *h.* | *m.* | *s.* | ° | ′ | *h.* | *m.* | *s.* |
| 6 | 11 | 17 | 77 | 00 | 12 | 36 | 12 |
| | 11 | 42 | | 10 | | 35 | 47 |
| | 12 | 8 | | 20 | | 35 | 22 |
| | 12 | 32 | | 30 | | 34 | 56 |
| | 12 | 57 | | 40 | | 34 | 32 |
| | 13 | 23 | | 50 | | 34 | 6 |
| | 13 | 48 | 78 | 00 | | 33 | 41 |
| | 14 | 14 | | 10 | | 33 | 15 |
| | 14 | 39 | | 20 | | 32 | 50 |
| | 15 | 2.5 | | 30 | | 32 | 26 |

Index error = — 35″. { Comparison of Chronometers. No. 7986 = 5*h.* 35*m.* 00*s.* No. 11422 = 5 23 46

DETERMINATION OF LATITUDE, APRIL 8, 1848.—MERIDIAN ALTITUDE OF THE SUN.

## *Tiberias.*

| Time by Chronometer, (7986.) | | | Double Altitude of Sun's lower limb. | | | Time by Chronometer, (7986.) | | | Double Altitude of Sun's lower limb. | | |
|---|---|---|---|---|---|---|---|---|---|---|---|
| *h.* | *m.* | *s.* | ° | ′ | ″ | *h.* | *m.* | *s.* | ° | ′ | ″ |
| 9 | 15 | 9 | 128 | 27 | 5 | 9 | 26 | 35 | 128 | 35 | 30 |
| | 20 | 8 | | 34 | 20 | | 28 | 1 | | 34 | 25 |
| | 22 | 47 | | 35 | 25 | | 29 | 1 | | 34 | 00 |
| | 25 | 10 | | 36 | 00 M. | Index error = — 25″. | | | | | |

DETERMINATION OF TIME, APRIL 9, 1848.—EQUAL ALTITUDES OF THE SUN.

## *Tiberias.*

| Time by Chronometer, (7986.) | | | Double Altitudes of Sun's lower limb. | | Time by Chronometer, (7986.) | | |
|---|---|---|---|---|---|---|---|
| *h.* | *m.* | *s.* | ° | ′ | *h.* | *m.* | *s.* |
| 7 | 41 | 37 | 110 | 40 | 11 | 5 | 13 |
| | 42 | 8.5 | | 50 | | 4 | 40.5 |
| | 42 | 42 | 111 | 00 | | 4 | 8 |
| | 43 | 13 | | 10 | | 3 | 38 |
| | 43 | 44 | | 20 | | 3 | 4 |
| | 44 | 16.5 | | 30 | | 2 | 33 |
| | 44 | 48 | | 40 | | 2 | 1 |
| | 45 | 23 | | 50 | | 1 | 29 |
| | 45 | 52 | 112 | 00 | | 0 | 56 |
| | 46 | 27.5 | | 10 | | 0 | 24 |

Index error = — 35″.

Comparison of Chronometers.
No. 7986 = 5*h.* 26*m.* 50*s.*
No. 11422 = 5 15 39

DETERMINATION OF LONGITUDE AND THE SUN'S AZIMUTH, APRIL 11, 1848.

## *Bridge of Semakh.*

| Time by Chronometer, (7986.) | | | Double Altitudes of Sun's lower limb. | | | Magnetic Azimuth. |
|---|---|---|---|---|---|---|
| *h.* | *m.* | *s.* | ° | ′ | ″ | ° ′ ° ′ |
| 5 | 19 | 9 | 57 | 24 | 50 | 107 00 = S. 73 00 E. |
| | 20 | 22 | 57 | 57 | 00 | |
| | 21 | 17 | 58 | 20 | 30 | |
| | 22 | 6 | 58 | 40 | 20 | 108 00 = S. 72 00 E. |
| | 23 | 1 | 59 | 2 | 20 | 109 00 = S. 71 00 E. |
| | 23 | 50 | 59 | 23 | 10 | 108 30 = S. 71 30 E. |
| | 24 | 52 | 59 | 47 | 40 | 108 30 = S. 71 30 E. |
| | 25 | 44 | 60 | 11 | 20 | 108 45 = S. 71 15 E. |
| | 26 | 30 | 60 | 29 | 10 | 109 00 = S. 71 00 E. |

Index error = — 35″.

Comparison of Chronometers.
No. 7986 = 6*h.* 7*m.* 30*s.*
No. 11422 = 5 56 25

DETERMINATION OF LATITUDE, APRIL 12, 1848.—ALTITUDES OF POLARIS.

## *Bŭk'ah.*

| Time by Chronometer, (7986.) | | | Double Altitudes of Polaris. | | |
|---|---|---|---|---|---|
| *h.* | *m.* | *s.* | ° | ′ | ″ |
| 12 | 16 | 55 | 63 | 21 | 00 |
| | 23 | 53 | | 25 | 30 |

Index error = — 35″.

Comparison of Chronometers.

| | *h.* | *m.* | *s.* |
|---|---|---|---|
| No. 7986 = | 6 | 4 | 20 |
| No. 11422 = | 5 | 53 | 17 |

DETERMINATION OF LONGITUDE, APRIL 12, 1848.—ALTITUDES OF THE SUN.

## *Bŭk'ah.*

| Time by Chronometer, (7986,) A. M. | | | Double Altitudes of Sun's lower limb. | | | Time by Chronometer, (7986,) A. M. | | | Double Altitudes of Sun's lower limb. | | |
|---|---|---|---|---|---|---|---|---|---|---|---|
| *h.* | *m.* | *s.* | ° | ′ | ″ | *h.* | *m.* | *s.* | ° | ′ | ″ |
| 7 | 8 | 20 | 101 | 22 | 20 | 7 | 10 | 34 | 102 | 11 | 10 |
| | 8 | 57 | | 35 | 30 | | 10 | 52 | | 17 | 30 |
| | 9 | 29 | | 47 | 50 | | 11 | 24 | | 28 | 30 |
| | 9 | 53 | | 58 | 20 | | 11 | 47 | | 37 | 30 |
| | 10 | 16 | 102 | 4 | 20 | | 12 | 6 | | 44 | 00 |

Index error = — 35″.

DETERMINATION OF LATITUDE, APRIL 13, 1848.—ALTITUDES OF POLARIS.

| Time by Chronometer, (7986.) | | | Double Altitudes of Polaris. | | |
|---|---|---|---|---|---|
| *h.* | *m.* | *s.* | ° | ′ | ″ |
| 8 | 18 | 50 | 62 | 6 | 30 |

Index error = — 35″.

DETERMINATION OF LATITUDE, APRIL 16, 1848.—ALTITUDES OF POLARIS.—CAMP OF 15TH.

| Time by Chronometer, (7986.) | | | Double Altitudes of Polaris. | | |
|---|---|---|---|---|---|
| *h.* | *m.* | *s.* | ° | ′ | ″ |
| 1 | 5 | 46 | 63 | 17 | 20 |
| | 8 | 50 | | 20 | 10 |
| | 13 | 00 | | 22 | 25 |
| | 16 | 5 | | 25 | 00 |
| | 19 | 56 | | 28 | 00 |

Index error = — 35″.

Comparison of Chronometers.

| | *h.* | *m.* | *s.* |
|---|---|---|---|
| No. 7986 = | 5 | 25 | 30 |
| No. 11422 = | 5 | 14 | 32 |

DETERMINATION OF LATITUDE, APRIL 16, 1848.—MERIDIAN ALTITUDES OF THE SUN.

| Time by Chronometer A. M. | | | Double Altitudes of Sun's lower limb. | | |
|---|---|---|---|---|---|
| *h.* | *m.* | *s.* | ° | ′ | ″ |
| 9 | 17 | 15 | 135 | 40 | 10 |
| | 19 | 47 | | 42 | 20 |
| | 20 | 51 | | 42 | 50 M |
| | 22 | 23 | | 42 | 40 |

Index error = — 35″.

DETERMINATION OF LATITUDE, APRIL 18, 1848.—CIRCUM-MERIDIAN ALTITUDES OF THE SUN.

## *Ford of Meshra'a.*

| Time by Chronometer, (7986,)—A. M. | | | Double Altitudes of Sun's lower limb. | | |
|---|---|---|---|---|---|
| *h.* | *m.* | *s.* | ° | ′ | ″ |
| 9 | 12 | 4 | 137 | 33 | 30 |
| | 13 | 30 | | 37 | 30 |
| | 16 | 45 | | 45 | 10 |
| | 19 | 5 | | 46 | 00 |

Index error = — 35″.

DETERMINATION OF LONGITUDE, APRIL 18, 1848.—ALTITUDES OF THE SUN.

## *Ford of Meshra'a.*

| Time by Chronometer, (7986,)—A. M. | | | Double Altitudes of Sun's lower limb. | | |
|---|---|---|---|---|---|
| *h.* | *m.* | *s.* | ° | ′ | ″ |
| 6 | 1 | 11 | 78 | 45 | 40 |
| | 2 | 16 | 79 | 12 | 20 |
| | 2 | 48 | 79 | 26 | 00 |
| | 3 | 38 | 79 | 47 | 10 |
| | 4 | 30 | 80 | 8 | 5 |
| | 5 | 3 | 80 | 21 | 30 |
| | 5 | 36 | 80 | 34 | 50 |
| | 6 | 11 | 80 | 49 | 10 |
| | 7 | 17 | 81 | 16 | 30 |
| | 8 | 45 | 81 | 53 | 20 |

Index error = — 35″.

Comparison of Chronometers.

| | *h.* | *m.* | *s.* |
|---|---|---|---|
| No. 7986 = | 6 | 2 | 00 |
| No. 11422 = | 5 | 51 | 6 |

DETERMINATION OF LONGITUDE, APRIL 19, 1848.—EQUAL ALTITUDES OF THE SUN.

### *'Ain el Feshkhah.*

| Time by Chronometer, (7986,) A.M. | | | Double Altitudes of Sun's lower limb. | | Time by Chronometer, (7986,) P.M. | | |
|---|---|---|---|---|---|---|---|
| *h.* | *m.* | *s.* | ° | ′ | *h.* | *m.* | *s.* |
| 7 | 4 | 10 | 104 | 30 | 11 | 37 | 22 |
| | 4 | 35 | | 40 | | 36 | 55 |
| | 5 | 28 | 105 | 00 | | 36 | 4 |
| | 5 | 55 | | 10 | | 35 | 38 |
| | 6 | 19.5 | | 20 | | 35 | 12 |
| | 6 | 46 | | 30 | | 34 | 45 |
| | 7 | 11 | | 40 | | 34 | 19 |
| | 7 | 39 | | 50 | | 33 | 52 |
| | 8 | 5 | 106 | 00 | | 33 | 26 |
| | 8 | 30 | | 10 | | 32 | 58 |
| | 8 | 56 | | 20 | | 32 | 33 |

Index error = —1′ 25″.

Comparison of Chronometers.

| | *h.* | *m.* | *s.* |
|---|---|---|---|
| No. 7986 = | 6 | 45 | 00 |
| No. 11422 = | 6 | 34 | 10 |

DETERMINATION OF LATITUDE, APRIL 19, 1848.—ALTITUDES OF POLARIS.

### *'Ain el Feshkhah.*

| Time by Chronometer, (7986.) | | | Double Altitudes of Polaris. | | |
|---|---|---|---|---|---|
| *h.* | *m.* | *s.* | ° | ′ | ″ |
| 6 | 45 | 14 | 60 | 47 | 30 |
| 7 | 4 | 10 | | 44 | 20 |
| | 9 | 15 | | 42 | 20 |
| | 16 | 8 | | 40 | 40 |
| | 19 | 3 | | 39 | 00 |
| | 24 | 54 | | 38 | 20 |

Index error = — 1′ 25″.

Comparison of Chronometers.

| | *h.* | *m.* | *s.* |
|---|---|---|---|
| No. 7986 = | 6 | 51 | 00 |
| No. 11422 = | 6 | 40 | 10.5 |

DETERMINATION OF LONGITUDE AND THE SUN'S AZIMUTH, APRIL 20, 1848.—ALTITUDES OF THE SUN.

### *'Ain el Feshkhah.*

| Time by Chronometer, (7986,) A.M. | | | Double Altitudes of Sun's lower limb. | | Magnetic Azimuth. | |
|---|---|---|---|---|---|---|
| *h.* | *m.* | *s.* | ° | ′ | ° | ′ |
| 6 | 2 | 7 | 80 | 10 | S. 71 | 00 E. |
| | 2 | 45 | | 20 | | |
| | 2 | 55 | | 30 | | |
| | 3 | 20 | | 40 | | |
| | 3 | 42 | | 50 | S. 70 | 30 E. |
| | 4 | 7 | 81 | 00 | | |
| | 4 | 30 | | 10 | S. 70 | 15 E. |
| | 5 | 19 | | 20 | | |
| | 5 | 43 | | 30 | | |
| | 6 | 7 | | 40 | S. 70 | 00 E. |
| | 6 | 30 | | 50 | | |

Index error = —1′ 25″.

Comparison of Chronometers.

| | *h.* | *m.* | *s.* |
|---|---|---|---|
| No. 7986 = | 6 | 41 | 00 |
| No. 11422 = | 6 | 30 | 11.5 |

DETERMINATION OF LATITUDE, APRIL 21, 1848.—ALTITUDES OF POLARIS.

### *'Ain Turâbeh.*

| Time by Chronometer, (7986.) | | | Double Altitudes of Polaris. | | |
|---|---|---|---|---|---|
| *h.* | *m.* | *s.* | ° | ′ | ″ |
| 6 | 11 | 42 | 60 | 47 | 20 |
| | 13 | 21 | | 46 | 00 |
| | 15 | 21 | | 45 | 10 |
| | 16 | 45 | | 44 | 00 |
| | 18 | 24 | | 43 | 20 |

Index error = — 1′ 25″.

Comparison of Chronometers.

| | *h.* | *m.* | *s.* |
|---|---|---|---|
| No. 7986 = | 5 | 47 | 43.5 |
| No. 11422 = | 5 | 37 | 00 |

DETERMINATION OF LATITUDE, APRIL 22, 1848.—ALTITUDES OF POLARIS.

### *'Ain Jidy.*

| Time by Chronometer, (7986.) | | | Double Altitudes of Polaris. | | |
|---|---|---|---|---|---|
| *h.* | *m.* | *s.* | ° | ′ | ″ |
| 5 | 50 | 50 | 60 | 36 | 55 |
| | 53 | 00 | | 36 | 50 |
| | 54 | 40 | | 35 | 45 |
| | 56 | 50 | | 34 | 25 |
| | 58 | 56 | | 33 | 35 |
| 6 | 1 | 16 | | 33 | 30 |
| | 3 | 29 | | 31 | 30 |
| | 5 | 12 | | 31 | 30 |
| | 7 | 3 | | 30 | 30 |
| | 8 | 28 | | 28 | 30 |

Index error = — 1′ 00″.

Comparison of Chronometers.

| | *h.* | *m.* | *s.* |
|---|---|---|---|
| No. 7986 = | 5 | 26 | 30 |
| No. 11422 = | 5 | 15 | 48.5 |

DETERMINATION OF LONGITUDE AND THE SUN'S AZIMUTH, APRIL 23, 1848.—EQUAL ALTITUDES OF THE SUN.

### *'Ain Jidy.*

| Time by Chronometer, (7986,) A. M. | | | Double Altitudes of Sun's lower limb. | | Time by Chronometer, (7986,) P. M. | | | Magnetic Azimuth. | |
|---|---|---|---|---|---|---|---|---|---|
| *h.* | *m.* | *s.* | ° | ′ | *h.* | *m.* | *s.* | ° | ′ |
| 5 | 30 | 21.5 | 68 | 00 | 1 | 12 | 4 | S. 89 | 00 W. |
| | 30 | 44 | | 10 | | 11 | 40 | | |
| | 31 | 9 | | 20 | | 11 | 16 | S. 88 | 30 W. |
| | 31 | 30.5 | | 30 | | 10 | 53 | S. 88 | 30 W. |
| | 31 | 55 | | 40 | | 10 | 28 | | |
| | 32 | 19 | | 50 | | 10 | 5 | | |
| | 32 | 42.5 | 69 | 00 | | 9 | 41 | | |
| | 33 | 6.5 | | 10 | | 9 | 17 | | |
| | 33 | 30 | | 20 | | 8 | 54 | S. 88 | 10 W. |
| | 33 | 54 | | 30 | | 8 | 30 | | |
| | 34 | 18 | | 40 | | 8 | 6 | S. 88 | 00 W. |
| | 34 | 41.5 | | 50 | | 7 | 44 | | |
| | 35 | 5 | 70 | 00 | | 7 | 19 | S. 87 | 50 W. |

Index error = — 1′ 00″.

Comparison of Chronometers.

| | | | |
|---|---|---|---|
| No. 7986 = | 5*h.* | 26*m.* | 00*s.* |
| No. 11422 = | 5 | 15 | 24 |

DETERMINATION OF LONGITUDE, APRIL 24, 1848.—EQUAL ALTITUDES OF THE SUN.

### *'Ain Jidy.*

| Time by Chronometer, (7986,)—A. M. | | | Double Altitudes of Sun's lower limb. | | Time by Chronometer, (7986,)—P. M. | | |
|---|---|---|---|---|---|---|---|
| *h.* | *m.* | *s.* | ° | ′ | *h.* | *m.* | *s.* |
| 5 | 30 | 7 | 68 | 20 | 1 | 11 | 47.5 |
| | 30 | 31 | | 30 | | 11 | 24 |
| | 30 | 54 | | 40 | | 11 | 00 |
| | 31 | 17 | | 50 | | 10 | 37 |
| | 31 | 41 | 69 | 00 | | 10 | 13 |
| | 32 | 5 | | 10 | | 9 | 49.5 |
| | 32 | 29 | | 20 | | 9 | 26 |
| | 32 | 52 | | 30 | | 9 | 2 |
| | 33 | 14 | | 40 | | 8 | 38.5 |
| | 33 | 38.5 | | 50 | | 8 | 15.5 |

Index error = — 1′ 00″.

Comparison of Chronometers.

| | | | |
|---|---|---|---|
| No. 7986 = | 6*h.* | 17*m.* | 00*s.* |
| No. 11422 = | 6 | 6 | 26 |

DETERMINATION OF LATITUDE, APRIL 25, 1848.—ALTITUDES OF POLARIS.

## *Camp at the Mouth of Wady Mubugkghik.*

| Time by Chronometer, (7986.) | | | Double Altitudes of Polaris. | | | |
|---|---|---|---|---|---|---|
| *h.* | *m.* | *s.* | ° | ′ | ″ | |
| 5 | 55 | 57 | 59 | 58 | 00 | |
| | 58 | 20 | | 58 | 30 | |
| | 59 | 40 | | 57 | 30 | Index error = — 1′ 00″. |
| 6 | 1 | 40 | | 57 | 50 | |
| | 3 | 55 | | 56 | 55 | |
| | 6 | 6 | | 55 | 40 | |
| | 8 | 20 | | 54 | 10 | |
| | 10 | 22 | | 53 | 25 | |
| | 11 | 57 | | 52 | 35 | |

DETERMINATION OF LATITUDE, APRIL 26, 1848.—ALTITUDES OF POLARIS.

## *Camp at the Mouth of Wady Humeir.*

| Time by Chronometer. | | | Double Altitudes of Polaris. | | | |
|---|---|---|---|---|---|---|
| *h.* | *m.* | *s.* | ° | ′ | ″ | |
| 5 | 22 | 55 | 60 | 6 | 30 | Index error = — 1′ 12″. |
| | 24 | 55 | | 5 | 20 | |
| | 27 | 57 | | 6 | 40 | |
| | 29 | 25 | | 5 | 45 | |
| | 31 | 11 | | 5 | 20 | |

DETERMINATION OF LONGITUDE AND THE SUN'S AZIMUTH, APRIL 27, 1848.—ALTITUDES OF THE SUN.

## *Camp at the Mouth of Wady Humeir.*

| Time by Chronometer, A. M. | | | Double Altitudes of Sun's lower limb. | | | Magnetic Azimuth. | |
|---|---|---|---|---|---|---|---|
| *h.* | *m.* | *s.* | ° | ′ | ″ | ° ′ | |
| 4 | 58 | 33.5 | 56 | 20 | 50 | N. 95 00 E. | |
| | 59 | 20 | | 40 | 30 | | |
| | 59 | 50 | | 53 | 20 | N. 96 00 E. | Index error = — 1′ 12″. |
| 5 | 00 | 19.5 | 57 | 6 | 00 | N. 95 45 E. | |
| | 00 | 51.5 | | 19 | 10 | | |
| | 1 | 27 | | 35 | 20 | | |
| | 2 | 4 | | 50 | 30 | | |
| | 2 | 57.5 | 58 | 13 | 10 | | |
| | 3 | 39 | | 32 | 10 | N. 97 00 E. | |
| | 5 | 6.5 | 59 | 10 | 10 | N. 96 30 E. | |

DETERMINATION OF LATITUDE, APRIL 27, 1848.—ALTITUDES OF POLARIS.

## *Camp at the Mouth of Wady Rŭbtat el Jâmŭs.*

| Time by Chronometer. | | | Double Altitudes of Polaris. | | | |
|---|---|---|---|---|---|---|
| *h.* | *m.* | *s.* | ° | ′ | ″ | |
| 6 | 3 | 17.5 | 59 | 57 | 20 | |
| | 5 | 22 | | 56 | 50 | Index error = — 1′ 12″. |
| | 7 | 24.5 | | 57 | 40 | |
| | 9 | 12.5 | | 56 | 00 | |
| | 11 | 55 | | 55 | 25 | |
| | 15 | 14 | | 54 | 15 | |
| | 23 | 36 | | 48 | 10 | |

DETERMINATION OF LATITUDE, MAY 3, 1848.—ALTITUDES OF POLARIS.

## *Camp at the Mouth of Wady Mojêb.*

| Time by Chronometer. | | | Double Altitudes of Polaris. | | | Time by Chronometer. | | | Double Altitudes of Polaris. | | |
|---|---|---|---|---|---|---|---|---|---|---|---|
| *h.* | *m.* | *s.* | ° | ′ | ″ | *h.* | *m.* | *s.* | ° | ′ | ″ |
| 6 | 19 | 46 | 60 | 9 | 35 | 6 | 32 | 3 | 60 | 7 | 30 |
| | 22 | 13 | | 9 | 20 | | 34 | 7 | | 6 | 20 |
| | 24 | 49 | | 8 | 20 | | 35 | 54 | | 6 | 30 |
| | 26 | 44 | | 8 | 30 | | 36 | 50.5 | | 5 | 50 |
| | 30 | 17 | | 8 | 40 | | 37 | 13 | | 5 | 20 |

Index error = — 1′ 12″.

DETERMINATION OF LATITUDE, MAY 5, 1848.—ALTITUDES OF POLARIS.

## *Mouth of the River Jordan.*

| Time by Chronometer, (7986.) | | | Double Altitudes of Polaris. | | | |
|---|---|---|---|---|---|---|
| *h.* | *m.* | *s.* | ° | ′ | ″ | |
| 6 | 6 | 25 | 60 | 48 | 45 | Index error = — 1′ 20″. |
| | 9 | 23.8 | | 46 | 20 | |
| | 12 | 25.8 | | 46 | 10 | Comparison of Chronometers. |
| | 15 | 45.5 | | 45 | 40 | |
| | 21 | 43 | | 44 | 10 | *h.* *m.* *s.* |
| | 24 | 24.8 | | 43 | 40 | No. 7986 = 5 20 00 |
| | 27 | 15 | | 42 | 40 | No. 11422 = 5 9 54 |
| | 29 | 43.6 | | 42 | 00 | |

DETERMINATION OF LATITUDE, MAY 4, 1848.—ALTITUDES OF POLARIS.

## *'Ain Turâbeh.*

| Time by Chronometer, (7986.) | | | Double Altitudes of Polaris. | | | Time by Chronometer, (7986.) | | | Double Altitudes of Polaris. | | |
|---|---|---|---|---|---|---|---|---|---|---|---|
| *h.* | *m.* | *s.* | ° | ′ | ″ | *h.* | *m.* | *s.* | ° | ′ | ″ |
| 7 | 50 | 5 | 60 | 17 | 20 | 8 | 2 | 40.5 | 60 | 17 | 30 |
| | 52 | 11 | | 17 | 20 | | 4 | 28 | | 18 | 5 |
| | 54 | 25 | | 17 | 40 | | 6 | 21 | | 18 | 25 |
| | 57 | 43 | | 18 | 10 | | 9 | 14.5 | | 18 | 30 |
| 8 | 00 | 38 | | 17 | 55 | | 11 | 44.5 | | 18 | 50 |

Index error = — 1′ 20″.

DETERMINATION OF TIME, MAY 7, 1848.—EQUAL ALTITUDES OF THE SUN.

## *'Ain Turâbeh.*

| Time by Chronometer, (7986,)—A. M. | | | Double Altitudes of Sun's lower limb. | | Time by Chronometer, (7986,)—P. M. | | |
|---|---|---|---|---|---|---|---|
| *h.* | *m.* | *s.* | ° | ′ | *h.* | *m.* | *s.* |
| 5 | 17 | 41 | 80 | 40 | 12 | 46 | 32.5 |
| | 58 | 13.5 | 85 | 00 | | 36 | 20.5 |
| | 58 | 35 5 | | 10 | | 35 | 57 |
| | 58 | 58.5 | | 20 | | 35 | 33.5 |
| | 59 | 24.5 | | 30 | | 35 | 10.5 |
| | 59 | 48 | | 40 | | 34 | 45 |
| 6 | 00 | 10 | | 50 | | 34 | 23 |
| | 00 | 36 | 86 | 00 | | 33 | 58.5 |
| | 00 | 59 | | 10 | | 33 | 35 |
| | 1 | 22 | | 20 | | 33 | 11.5 |

Index error = — 1′ 20″.

Comparison of Chronometers.
No. 7986 = 5*h.* 21*m.* 2*s.*
No. 11422 = 5 11 00

DETERMINATION OF TIME, MAY 8, 1848.—ALTITUDES OF THE SUN.

### *'Ain Turâbeh.*

| Time by Chronometer, (7986,)—A. M. | | | Double Altitudes of Sun's lower limb. | |
|---|---|---|---|---|
| *h.* | *m.* | *s.* | ° | ′ |
| 6 | 14 | 25 | 92 | 10 |
| | 14 | 50 | | 20 |
| | 15 | 16 | | 30 |
| | 15 | 37.5 | | 40 |
| | 16 | 2.5 | | 50 |
| | 16 | 49.5 | 93 | 10 |

Index error = — 1′ 20″.

Comparison of Chronometers.

| | *h.* | *m.* | *s.* |
|---|---|---|---|
| No. 7986 = | 5 | 8 | 59 |
| No. 11422 = | 4 | 59 | 00 |

DETERMINATION OF TIME, MAY 9, 1848.—ALTITUDES OF THE SUN.

### *'Ain Turâbeh.*

| Time by Chronometer, (7986,)—A. M. | | | Double Altitudes of the Sun's lower limb. | |
|---|---|---|---|---|
| *h.* | *m.* | *s.* | ° | ′ |
| 6 | 52 | 2 | 108 | 10 |
| | 52 | 25 | | 20 |
| | 52 | 49.5 | | 30 |
| | 53 | 14.5 | | 40 |
| | 53 | 38.5 | | 50 |
| | 54 | 3 | 109 | 00 |
| | 54 | 28 | | 10 |
| | 54 | 52 | | 20 |
| | 55 | 15.5 | | 30 |
| | 55 | 39.5 | | 40 |

Index error = — 1′ 20″.

Comparison of Chronometers.

| | *h.* | *m.* | *s.* |
|---|---|---|---|
| No. 7986 = | 5 | 32 | 00 |
| No. 11422 = | 5 | 22 | 3 |

DETERMINATION OF TIME MAY 11, 1848.—ALTITUDES OF THE SUN.

### *Jerusalem.*

| Time by Chronometer, (7986,)—A. M. | | | Double Altitudes of the Sun's lower limb. | | |
|---|---|---|---|---|---|
| *h.* | *m.* | *s.* | ° | ′ | ″ |
| 6 | 43 | 27.5 | 104 | 50 | 00 |
| | 43 | 51 | 105 | 00 | 00 |
| | 44 | 39 | | 20 | 00 |
| | 45 | 4.5 | | 30 | 00 |
| | 45 | 29 | | 40 | 00 |
| | 45 | 52.5 | | 50 | 00 |
| | 46 | 18.5 | 106 | 00 | 00 |

Index error = — 1′ 5″.

Comparison of Chronometers.

| | *h.* | *m.* | *s.* |
|---|---|---|---|
| No. 7986 = | 6 | 24 | 30 |
| No. 11422 = | 6 | 14 | 38 |

DETERMINATION OF TIME, MAY 12, 1848.—ALTITUDES OF THE SUN.

### *Jerusalem.*

| Time by Chronometer, (7986,)—A. M. | | | Double Altitudes of Sun's lower limb. | |
|---|---|---|---|---|
| *h.* | *m.* | *s.* | ° | ′ |
| 5 | 43 | 54.5 | 80 | 00 |
| | 47 | 26 | 81 | 30 |
| | 47 | 50 | 81 | 40 |
| | 52 | 35 | 83 | 40 |
| | 52 | 57.5 | 83 | 50 |
| | 53 | 20 | 84 | 00 |
| | 53 | 45.5 | 84 | 10 |
| | 54 | 10 | 84 | 20 |
| | 54 | 33.5 | 84 | 30 |
| | 54 | 54.5 | 84 | 40 |
| | 55 | 20 | 84 | 50 |
| | 55 | 41.5 | 85 | 00 |
| | 56 | 5 | 85 | 10 |
| | 56 | 31.5 | 85 | 20 |
| | 56 | 54 | 85 | 30 |

Index error = — 1′ 5″.

Comparison of Chronometers.

| | *h.* | *m.* | *s.* |
|---|---|---|---|
| No. 7986 = | 6 | 3 | 00 |
| No. 11422 = | 5 | 53 | 10 |

DETERMINATION OF TIME, MAY 13, 1848.—ALTITUDES OF THE SUN.

### *Jerusalem.*

| Time by Chronometer, (7986,)—A. M. | | | Double Altitudes of the Sun's lower limb. | |
|---|---|---|---|---|
| *h.* | *m.* | *s.* | ° | ′ |
| 6 | 45 | 1.5 | 106 | 00 |
| | 45 | 25 | | 10 |
| | 45 | 49.5 | | 20 |
| | 46 | 13 | | 30 |
| | 46 | 38 | | 40 |
| | 47 | 1.5 | | 50 |
| | 47 | 25 | 107 | 00 |
| | 47 | 50 | | 10 |
| | 48 | 15.5 | | 20 |
| | 48 | 39.5 | | 30 |

Index error = — 1′ 5″.

Comparison of Chronometers.

| | *h.* | *m.* | *s.* |
|---|---|---|---|
| No. 7986 = | 5 | 41 | 00 |
| No. 11422 = | 5 | 31 | 13 |

DETERMINATION OF TIME, MAY 14, 1848.—EQUAL ALTITUDES OF THE SUN.

### *Jerusalem.*

| Time by Chronometer, (7986.)—A. M. | | | Double Altitudes of Sun's lower limb. | | Time by Chronometer, (7986.)—P. M. | | |
|---|---|---|---|---|---|---|---|
| *h.* | *m.* | *s.* | ° | ′ | *h.* | *m.* | *s.* |
| 5 | 48 | 42 | 82 | 30 | 12 | 46 | 15 |
| | 49 | 8 | | 40 | | 45 | 53 |
| | 49 | 30 | | 50 | | 45 | 29.5 |
| | 49 | 55 | 83 | 00 | | 45 | 6 |
| | 50 | 20 | | 10 | | 44 | 42.5 |
| | 50 | 40.5 | | 20 | | 44 | 19.5 |
| | 51 | 5 | | 30 | | 43 | 54.5 |
| | 51 | 27.5 | | 40 | | 43 | 33.5 |
| | 51 | 52 | | 50 | | 43 | 11 |
| | 52 | 16 | 84 | 00 | | 42 | 45 |

Index error = — 1′ 5″.

Comparison of Chronometers.

| | | | |
|---|---|---|---|
| No. 7986 = | 7*h.* | 30*m.* | 00*s.* |
| No. 11422 = | 7 | 20 | 18 |

DETERMINATION OF TIME, MAY 15, 1848.—EQUAL ALTITUDES OF THE SUN.

### *Jerusalem.*

| Time by Chronometer, (7986.)—A. M. | | | Double Altitudes of Sun's lower limb. | | Time by Chronometer, (7986.)—P. M. | | |
|---|---|---|---|---|---|---|---|
| *h.* | *m.* | *s.* | ° | ′ | *h.* | *m.* | *s.* |
| 5 | 38 | 48 | 78 | 30 | 12 | 56 | 9.5 |
| | 39 | 12 | | 40 | | 55 | 46 |
| | 39 | 37 | | 50 | | 55 | 22.5 |
| | 40 | 23.5 | 79 | 00 | | 54 | 36 |
| | 40 | 46 | | 20 | | 54 | 14 |
| | 41 | 10.5 | | 30 | | 53 | 49.5 |
| | 41 | 33 | | 40 | | 53 | 25 |
| | 41 | 58 | | 50 | | 53 | 2.5 |
| | 42 | 21.5 | 80 | 00 | | 52 | 40 |

Index error = — 1′ 5″.

Comparison of Chronometers.

| | | | |
|---|---|---|---|
| No 7986 = | 6*h.* | 38*m.* | 30*s.* |
| No. 11422 = | 6 | 28 | 51 |

DETERMINATION OF TIME TO CORRECT THE WATCH, JUNE 12, 1848.—ALTITUDES OF THE SUN.

### *Encampment at south end of Lake Tiberias.*

| Time by Watch, P. M. | | | D'ble Altitude Sun's low. limb | | | Time by Watch, P. M. | | | D'ble Altitude Sun's low. limb. | | |
|---|---|---|---|---|---|---|---|---|---|---|---|
| *h.* | *m.* | *s.* | ° | ′ | ″ | *h.* | *m.* | *s.* | ° | ′ | ″ |
| 4 | 56 | 26 | 46 | 31 | 00 | 4 | 58 | 36 | 45 | 47 | 30 |
| | 57 | 06 | | 24 | 10 | | 59 | 34 | | 24 | 00 |
| | 57 | 46 | | 7 | 50 | | | | | | |

Index error = — 1′ 00″

DETERMINATION OF LATITUDE, JUNE 12, 1848.—ALTITUDES OF POLARIS.

*Encampment at south end of Lake Tiberias.*

| Time by Watch, P. M. | | | Double Altitudes of Polaris. | | |
|---|---|---|---|---|---|
| h. | m. | s. | ° | ′ | Index error = — 1′ 00″. |
| 8 | 36 | 33 | 62 | 36 | |
| | 43 | 23 | | 37 | |
| | 49 | 21 | | 37 | |

DETERMINATION OF LATITUDE, JUNE 13, 1848.—ALTITUDES OF POLARIS.

*Encampment at north end of Lake Tiberias.*

| Time by Watch, P. M. | | | Double Altitudes of Polaris. | | | |
|---|---|---|---|---|---|---|
| h. | m. | s. | ° | ′ | ″ | |
| 9 | 10 | 40 | 63 | 7 | 5 | |
| | 13 | 33 | | 8 | 50 | Index error = — 1′ 00″. |
| | 14 | 59 | | 8 | 30 | |
| | 16 | 24 | | 10 | 00 | |
| | 17 | 59 | | 10 | 35 | |
| | 21 | 1 | | 12 | 10 | |
| | 25 | 33 | | 13 | 15 | |
| | 28 | 40 | | 15 | 5 | |
| | 30 | 33 | | 15 | 10 | |
| | 32 | 00 | | 15 | 50 | |

DETERMINATION OF TIME TO CORRECT THE WATCH, JUNE 18, 1848.—ALTITUDES OF THE SUN.

*Hasbeiya.*

| Time by Watch, P. M. | | | Double Altitudes of the Sun's lower limb. | | | |
|---|---|---|---|---|---|---|
| h. | m. | s | ° | ′ | ″ | |
| 4 | 35 | 00 | 49 | 52 | 00 | Index error = — 1′ 00″. |
| | 35 | 29 | | 39 | 30 | |
| | 36 | 41 | | 10 | 30 | |
| | 37 | 37 | 48 | 47 | 20 | |
| | 38 | 23 | | 28 | 30 | |
| | 39 | 2 | | 12 | 30 | |

DETERMINATION OF LATITUDE, JUNE 18, 1848.—ALTITUDES OF POLARIS.

*Hasbeiya.*

| Time by Watch, P. M. | | | Double Altitudes of Polaris. | | | |
|---|---|---|---|---|---|---|
| h. | m. | s. | ° | ′ | ″ | |
| 8 | 7 | 23 | 63 | 59 | 55 | |
| | 9 | 40 | 64 | 1 | 10 | Index error = — 1′ 00″. |
| | 12 | 11 | | 1 | 30 | |
| | 14 | 57 | | 2 | 30 | |
| | 17 | 26 | | 3 | 30 | |
| | 21 | 39 | | 4 | 40 | |
| | 24 | 20 | | 5 | 5 | |
| | 27 | 13 | | 5 | 55 | |
| | 29 | 19 | | 6 | 20 | |
| | 30 | 39 | | 7 | 00 | |

# ANALYSIS OF THE DEAD SEA WATER.

## BY JAMES C. BOOTH AND ALEXANDER MUCKLE.

Specific gravity at 60° = 1.22742.

| | |
|---|---|
| Chloride of magnesium | 145.8971 |
| " calcium | 31.0746 |
| " sodium | 78.5537 |
| " potassium | 6.5860 |
| Bromide of potassium | 1.3741 |
| Sulphate of lime | 0.7012 |
| | 264.1867 |
| Water | 735.8133 |
| | 1000.0000 |

Total amount of solid matter found by experiment, 267.0000.

# TABLE OF METEOROLOGICAL OBSERVATIONS.

| Date. | Time. | Barometer. | Thermometer. | | Remarks. |
|---|---|---|---|---|---|
| | | | Attached. | Free. | |
| | | *Cent.* | *Centms.* | *Fahr.* | |
| 1848, April 4, | 8, P. M. | 75.19 | 10°.5 | 53° | Calm and clear; water boiled at 212°.9. |
| 4, | Midnight, | 75.275 | 9.5 | 47 | Clear. |
| 5, | 8, P. M. | 74.545 | 15.5 | 61 | Light breeze from the west; clear. |
| 6, | 8, A. M. | 74.56 | 14.75 | 58 | do do. do. |
| 7, | 8, P. M. | 78.615 | 20.35 | 70 | Clear and calm. |
| 7, | Midnight, | 78.655 | 19.75 | 68.5 | do. do. |
| 8, | 8, A. M. | 78.72 | 19.2 | 66 | Clear and pleasant. |
| 8, | Noon. | 78.705 | 21 | 70 | do. do. |
| 8, | 8, P. M. | 78.55 | 21.5 | 70.5 | do. do. |
| 9, | 8, A. M. | 78.70 | 19.7 | 69 | do. do. |
| 9, | Noon. | 78.615 | 21 | 70 | do. do. |
| 9, | Midnight, | 78.42 | 21 | 70 | do. do. |
| 10, | 8, A. M. | 78.43 | 19.75 | 69 | do. do. |
| 10, | Noon, | 78.49 | 20 | 69 | do, do. |
| 10, | 8, P. M. | 78.28 | 18.5 | 65 (?) | Cloudy. |
| 11, | 8, A. M. | 78.40 | 17.5 | 65 | Clear; with a few clouds. |
| 11, | 8, P. M. | 78.31 | 17.5 | ............ | Clear. |
| 12, | 8, A. M. | 78.59 | 20.5 | 69 | |
| 12, | Noon, | 78.485 | 26.5 | 88 | |
| 12, | 9, P. M. | 79 58 | 19 | 62 | |
| 13, | 8, A. M. | 78.65 | 21 | 69 | |
| 13, | 8, P. M. | 78.83 | 14.4 | 57 (?) | |
| 14, | 8, A. M. | 78.92 | 15 | | |
| 14, | 8, P. M. | 79.02 | 20 | 68.5 | |
| 15, | 8, P. M. | 79.63 | 20.8 | 70.2 | Clear. |
| 15, | 11, P. M. | 79.50 | 16.3 | 61 | do. |
| 16, | 6, A. M. | 79.32 | 12.5 | 54 | do. |
| 16, | 8, P. M. | 79.88 | 20 | 67 | Clear; light northeast wind. |
| 17, | 4, A. M. | 79.30 | 11.2 | 52 | Clear. |
| 17, | 10, P. M. | 79.36 | 17 | 61 | do. |
| 18, | Noon, | 79.4 | 26.8 | 82 | Squall from northeast; rain. |
| 19, | 1, P. M. | 79.82 | 28.5 | 87.5 | Cloudy. |
| 19, | 8, P. M. | 79.93 | 21.5 | 70.5 | |
| 19, | Midnight, | 80.09 | 22 | 68 | Clear and calm. |
| 20, | 9, A. M. | 80.345 | 29 | 88 | Light breeze from the south. |
| 20, | Noon, | 80.35 | 29 | 89 | Calm. |
| 20, | 8½, P. M. | 80.20 | 22 | 72 | Fresh north wind. |
| 21, | 8, A. M. | 80.30 | 30 | 88 | Clear; light westerly wind. |
| 22, | 8, P. M. | 80.01 | 25.8 | 75.8 | Clear; light variable airs. |
| 22, | 10, P. M. | 80.10 | 22.8 | 74 | Clear; strong gusts from the north. |
| 23, | 7, A. M. | 80.16 | 28 | 85 | Calm and clear. |
| 23, | Noon, | 80.14 | 28 | 86 | |
| 23, | 1, P. M. | 80.10 | 30 | 90 | Light southeast airs; few clouds; water boils at 215°. |
| 23, | Midnight, | 80.00 | 24 | 74.5 | |
| 24, | 6, A. M. | 79.89 | 24 | 78 | Light northerly wind; clouds in S. E. |
| 24, | Noon, | 79.95 | 30 | 90 | Calm and sultry. |
| 24, | 8, P. M. | 79.67 | 26 | 78.5 | Light northerly breeze. |
| 24, | Midnight, | 79.70 | 25.5 | 78 | do. do. |
| 25, | 6, A. M. | 79.74 | 25.4 | 79 | |
| May 6, | 8, A. M. | 79.83 | 31.5 | 92 | Calm and misty; oppressively sultry. |
| 6, | Noon, | 79.72 | 33 | 97 | do. do. do. do. |
| 6, | 2, P. M. | 79.60 | 34.5 | 102 | do. do. do. do. |
| 6, | Midnight, | 79.26 | 24 | 76 | do. do. |
| 7, | 8, A. M. | 79.30 | 28 | 84 | |
| 7, | 11, A. M. | 79.35 | 36 | 106 | Light airs from the east; stifling heat. |
| 7. | 4, P. M. | 79.005 | 33 | 93 | Variable winds, with passing clouds. |

May 7, at 6, P. M., a sudden and very violent gust of hot wind from the eastward overthrew all the tents, and broke the barometer.

The barometer (Bunten, No. 666,) had an error by comparison with that of the Paris Observatory, of — .016. The attached thermometer also one, = + .2.

Erratum.—Page 16, third line from bottom:—*for* "Latitude of camp," *read* "Longitude of southwest angle of the lake."

New York, *Dec.* 16*th,* 1851.

To Wm. F. Lynch, U. S. N.

*Commander of the Palestine Expedition.*

Sir:

I have the honor to transmit a copy of the Report of a Geological Reconnaissance made in Palestine during the months of April and May, 1848, conformably to your instructions.

So much of this Report as could be prepared at once was in readiness shortly after my return from Europe. The remainder was necessarily postponed until the Paleontologist and Analysts were engaged and enabled to proceed in their several departments.

The Report of Mr. Conrad, the Paleontologist, is hereto annexed. The analyses were made partly by Prof. Booth and his able assistants, Messrs. Mucklé and Hewston, and partly by myself and assistant, Mr. Schwabe.

Very respectfully,

HENRY JAS. ANDERSON.

# PREFACE.

The following pages are presented as a record of observations rapidly and imperfectly made in a land in which the observer is not always welcome, and with opportunities very limited as to time. Eight weeks with the Expedition and a short subsequent excursion could not be expected to furnish very ample or very accurate results. Such as they are however, they are now submitted with full reliance on a due appreciation of the numerous difficulties attending the first study of a region which cannot perhaps, for some time to come, be leisurely or advantageously explored.

In the geological portions of this Report the writer has endeavored to avoid theoretical explanations of phenomena, but has not always succeeded. He hopes, however, that he regards these generalisations merely as hypotheses, yet not altogether without their use in the classification of facts.

The geographical designations are believed to be correct. In some instances errors may have arisen from the difficulty of catching and recording Arabic names received in haste from temporary and uninstructed guides. For places already known, Mr. Eli Smith's list has been the standard of orthography, with the exception that by means of the letters *k* and *q* the *kêf* has been distinguished from the *qâf*, sounds never confounded in words not borrowed from the Franks. The names between Bhamdûn and the Bŭqâ' have been corrected from a manuscript journal written by Mr. Smith, and obligingly lent to me for that purpose by Dr. Edward Robinson.

The bearings are magnetic and have not been reduced for variation, which may be taken approximately as 10° W.

The chemical analyses made by my associates are marked by the initials of the makers' names. Any inaccuracies in the others are my own.

I cannot here omit my sincere acknowledgement of the courtesy and accommodation extended to me by all those gentlemen whose names are referred to as authority in the accompanying pages. Nor ought I neglect to mention the readiness with which the libraries and collections, both in this city and elsewhere, have been made accessible whenever I have found it necessary to consult them. Material assistance has been derived from an examination of some Syrian fossils belonging to Yale College, and kindly placed within my reach by Prof. Silliman; and I am bound especially to thank the Rev. Wm. M. Thomson and the Friends of Missions connected with the Second Presbyterian Church of Cincinnati for similar facilities.

It might fairly be expected that in a geological notice of the Land of the Bible something would be said of the great physical catastrophes recorded in the Sacred Volume. But with few exceptions the actual phenomena of deposit and denudation belong to a period incontestably long anterior to all annals of our race. Into the province of Scriptural Historical Geology it has therefore not been necessary to intrude. With regard to such vestiges as may be identified without irreverence, it is quite superfluous to say that nothing is found in Palestine irreconcilable with the authorized interpretation of Holy Writ. As respects the earlier vicissitudes of the terrestrial surface, the same remark applies in all its force, though no doubt they may be variously read within the limits of that liberal toleration so earnestly enjoined by high Authority in these memorable words:

"*Jam vide quam stultum sit in tantâ copiâ verissimarum sententiarum quae de illis verbis erui possunt, temere affirmare quam earum Moyses potissimum senserit, et perniciosis contentionibus ipsam offendere caritatem propter quam illa omnia dixit.*"*

* S. Aur. Augustini Conf. Lib. xii, c. xxv.

# GEOLOGICAL RECONNAISSANCE

## OF PART OF THE HOLY LAND.

## INTRODUCTORY CHAPTER.

### GENERAL GEOGRAPHICAL AND GEOLOGICAL VIEW OF THE REGION VISITED BY THE EXPEDITION.

To the Geologist, Syria appears as a much disturbed mountainous mass of secondary and later limestones, with basaltic and tertiary interruptions. The calcareous deposits form the basis and the body of the work; the Plutonic rocks are subsequent intrusions. Still later, embankments of looser texture have lodged themselves irregularly in the cavities of the re-excavated surface, and these again have been in part swept away by denuding processes of the order of our time. Of this remarkable relief the great depressions are due, without doubt, to excavating forces, partly still in action and partly extinct, modified by secular elevations and subsidences, the lines of which seldom correspond with the direction of the mountain ranges, as we now find them to exist. The whole surface of the land, after its emergence from the Oolitic ocean, was carved out and determined into basins, valleys, deep gorges and shallower ravines, not unlike those which are now respectively distinguished in the language of the country by the terms: Merj, Ghôr, Wâdy, and Ghadîr. Many of these depressions have then been brought into conditions giving rise to new eruptive and sedimentary accumulations, which have contracted, apparently by very slow degrees, the forms of basalt-lava, sandstone, conglomerate, tufa, travertine and indurated marl. The deposits, thus consolidated, have again been partially abraded by agencies of much later date, and the resulting denudations have once more in their turn been filled up and covered over by more recent embankments, until this long series of events is found to terminate at last in phenomena coëval with the first recorded notice of the spread of man upon the earth.

In the interval, whatever may have been its duration, which separates the middle Oolite from the later tertiaries, every portion of the eastern hemisphere has more than once (not simultaneously, but different parts in different periods) sunk beneath and re-emerged above the level of the sea. Syria has participated in these secular fluctuations, and shows every where more or less distinctly the usual evidences of the vertical movements of the continental surface. There must have been a time, when the summits of Libanus and Hermon, with all the vast calcareous block from which they have been cut, lay at least ten thousand feet below their present level, and were covered by the waters of the great Jurassic ocean. Since that era, what is now the eastern barrier of the Mediterranean has, in frequent alternations, been elevated to the temperature of forest vegetation, or depressed beneath the sea below the limits usually attained by the inhabitants of the deep.

The general facts of the great physical revolutions which no point of the earth's surface appears to have escaped, reappear of course in every part of the Levant. Since the epoch of the early Jurassic limestone, the orographical relief of the whole land has been repeatedly obliterated and reformed. Where water-courses and estuaries once existed, all traces of these have long since disappeared. The sands of the desert now occupy large tracts where gigantic forests once cast their shades. In the same invariable place it seems as if the long lapse of time alone had substituted insensibly one phase of nature for another, till there is scarcely an accident of topography which each locality has not witnessed in its turn. In Palestine, as elsewhere, it would be hard to name the latitude and longitude, where in ante-historic times the spot has not passed, particle by particle, into meadow, hill, head-land, bay, river-side and lake, traversing every intermediate geographical condition with each successive aspect as seemingly unchangeable as the present one is now.

In describing the leading phenomena of the geology of Syria, nothing would be gained by adhering to her present political boundaries. West of the Jordan, the limits of the Turkish Pashaliks are less familiarly known than those of the ancient provinces Phœnicia, Galilee, Samaria and Judea; while to the east, the scriptural designations, Moab, Ammon, Galaad (Gilead,) and Basan (Bashan) replace with advantage both the Roman demarcations and the straggling outline of the Pashalik of Damascus. It is only north of Beirût, that the old appellations become unsuitable, and regard must there be had in some measure to the boundaries of the Turkish districts of Tripoli and Aleppo.

Before entering upon the geological details of the country comprised within these limits, a short account of its prominent geographical features, with an outline of its geognostic boundaries, may perhaps not be out of place.

From the southern offshoots of the Taurus to the highlands of Idumea, Syria is a mountainous tract, relieved by plains of very limited extent. The ranges, like the water-courses, have a direction nearly north and south, but are frequently thrown off from the predominant bearing, and broken up in detached masses of very irregular dimensions. Hence it is that the principal rivers, the Orontes, the Leontes and the Jordan, instead of seeking their outlets in the nearest sea, run parallel to the shore of the Mediterranean, and while the two former seem to defer till the last moment the change of course which they must take to reach the coast, the latter as if conscious that it had already lost the ocean by the extraordinary depression of its channel, terminates its career in that steaming cavity, the Dead Sea, which as fast as it receives its new supplies, distils them into vapor or deposits them in dregs.

Not far from the Mediterranean, and placed there apparently to bar all further encroachments towards the East, the Libanus stretches, under various local names, from Antioch in the north to the neighborhood of St. Jean d'Acre in the south, and may even be traced beyond the Belus to the Nazarene hills, where it mingles with the spurs of its eastern competitor. Once continuous with these highlands, but now separated by a broad alluvion Mount Carmel here stands out as another fence against the sea, and while it expands south-eastwardly into the broken uplands of Samaria throws an arm along the coast far into the land of the Philistines. South of the plain of Saron (Sharon,) this offshoot may be traced as a terrace of the mountains of Judea until it finally disappears, or is scarcely recognised, in the low hills of Ascalon and Gaza. Parallel or nearly so with the Libanus of Phœnicia and east of the Coele-Syrian valley, with a range much less prolonged, runs the great Anti-Libanine wall, which after approaching the primary chain as if to prevent the escape of the Leontes, mingles with the outlying subordinates of its towering rival, and forms with them in lower Galilee the hills which overlook the noble plain of Esdrelon.

Besides these characteristic ranges, minor groups and broken masses occupy the spaces left north, south and east of the region proper of the Libanine hills. In the north, 'Aintab may be regarded as the centre of a mountainous district with valleys having more or less a southeasterly direction, while Aleppo is entered by bridle paths from various points of the compass, crossing numerous ridges, no two of which are parallel; or skirting along plains very irregularly bounded.

East of the upper Jordan and south of Damascus extends a wide basaltic tract, which in the Lejah and the Saffa is curiously cut up into a labyrinth of winding defiles, and in Jebel Haurân runs into an insulated and elevated mass of doleritic trap. Further south, the basaltic ranges run more uniformly towards the west and show the influence of the decreasing depth of the valley of the Jordan. Finally between this valley and the sea and south of the hills of Galilee, which may be considered as carved from the same formation as the relief of the junction of the Libani, we arrive, after traversing the broad valley of the Cison, (Kison, Kishon) at the northern limits of the Samaritan hills. From Mount Gelboe to the desert highlands east of Bersabee, (Beersheba) traversing the entire extent of Samaria and Judea, and midway between the sea and the Jordan, the dividing summit ridges of the Holy Land attain very unequal heights, and nowhere exhibit a long unbroken crest. The serrations are numerous and deep, and seem not to be due to the scanty rivulets which flow, for a few months in the year, eastward or westward as the narrow water-shed inclines.

Westward of the summit level, the ravines expose little else than the limestones which lie beneath the chalk, or at most occasional banks of estuary sandstone. Eastward, arenaceous rocks are of no uncommon occurrence, and the limestone assumes a character more frequently cretaceous than jurassic. Trap appears in central Galilee soon after leaving the dividing ridge, but further south it seems reserved for the east side of the Jordan. The conglomerates line for the most part the slopes of this great valley and the tufas appear confined to the vicinity of the Dead Sea and to the inferior levels of the Ghôr.

If these leading facts be kept prominently in view, there will be little difficulty in following the geological details into which a special description of the visited districts will make it necessary to enter.

One of the characteristic results of the structural vicissitudes of Syria is the number and variety of its ancient local inequalities. Long before the deposit of the chalk, the land had been excavated or broken up by the prevailing agencies of the time into hills and valleys of the same order of dimensions as those which give its surface its present configuration. To this quite as much perhaps as to the operation of dislevelling forces from beneath, are we to ascribe the great diversity of strikes and dips often exhibited by the stratification of a very limited locality. In this respect as well as in the paleontological character of the formations, the resemblance between the Syrian and the Neo-Alpine geology is continually forced upon the observer.

In another and not less important particular, the order of the Palestine superpositions, and more especially the chronological sequence of its extant organic types, confirm the general conclusion to which we are everywhere brought in the study of the teguments of the globe. Nearly all we can penetrate or inspect of the crust of the earth, presents the appearance of having been slowly deposited and consolidated long before history began, so that the geogeny of the present or historical period can scarcely be regarded as a term of the same order as the geogenies of an earlier date. It is certain, that in this interval the topographical accidents of the earth's surface, have varied by only a minute portion of what is due to the period of an entire formation. Making every allowance for the cumulative effect of secular modifications, so very slow in the production of their results, and conceding what is due to periodical forces, which though sudden and frequent, affect but points of the earth's surface and leave few traces which are not easily effaced, it may be said with some truth, that the map of the physical globe, as we now have it, would, with some few exceptions, have answered very well in all past historic time. And so particularly it may be said of Syria. Its mountains may now be a few feet higher or lower than they were, according as the uplifting or abrading forces have prevailed; its valleys and ravines may be a little more deeply engraved into their rocky beds, or cut backwards a little further as they ascend in their gradual retreat; its rivers may have gained or lost a few inches of mean depth; a bank of sandstone may have crumbled or disappeared; or a cliff of chalk may be undergoing at the base it once overlooked, the slow process of disintegration and removal; but the main landmarks and the great lines of ancient Aram and Chanaan are still there; and the last deposit of the chalk, so unmeasurably old at the birth of its successor, seems scarcely older now, for all the centuries that have elapsed. In fact, the actual progress of a formation going on before our eyes, can only be well detected at the lines of maximum activity, and these in the greater number of instances are coincident, or nearly so, with the present or recent lines of the coast. With the exception of modern conglomerates, found frequently along the sea-shore from Tripoli to el-Arîsh, and detached layers of accrescent limestone on the margin of the bay of Haïfa, Syria is not yet known as the seat of such a process. Igneous eruptions may explain the actual growth of hills and platforms of lava, and earthquakes may rend a rock, divert a water-course, or turn a level into an uneven tract; but we have no authoritative evidence from historical testimony or existing vestiges, that the Holy Land was ever visited by volcanic action properly so called, since the first history of man; and the earthquakes, though numerous and destructive, have perhaps never left traces capable of being identified with any certainty a century after their occurrence. The only inland deposits which can be said to grow at a measurable rate, are the saline incrustations, those near Jabûl for example, the subaqueous embankments at the mouth of the Jordan and the sandy encroachments in some of the deserted plains. The study of these will long be surrounded by difficulties, and the data they furnish too scanty and variable to serve as the basis of any trustworthy geological conclusion. It is for this reason that few attempts will be made in the following pages to discuss the changes which the country may have undergone since the events first recorded in its Sacred Books, nor is it proposed to enter into the question (so interesting in another field of inquiry) where or with what certainty observers may have succeeded in discovering the vestiges of those great interpositions which we know from Scripture and Tradition, once marked with their awful monuments the desecrated precincts of the Land.

If the rate of growth of the formations now in progress be so difficult to ascertain, it would be presumptuous in the extreme to venture upon a conjecture of the time required for the completion of the earlier deposits. All that the geologist can do in the present state of the science is to note the order and circumstances of the ancient accumulations. The rate at which the great work itself has proceeded, may be regarded as an unknown and even arbitrary quantity independent of the events themselves, so long as the other variables over the entire area of action are referred without exception to one and the same measure of duration.—In other words, the investigation of the chronological dependencies of the related strata may go on, quite undisturbed by the inquiry whether a given formative process was at the rate of a foot in a second or a century; that is to say whether the early structures were subject to the present laws of developement or to an action infinitely more expeditious, pervading under the Divine Rule cosmical and terrestrial phenomena alike, and accomplishing on a scale to which all velocities and forces were equally made subject, the results which we find in the order in which we find them, with due allowance for subsequent displacement and metamorphic change. In this view the preliminary facts may be collected and compared without rashly undertaking to pronounce upon any theory of Scriptural interpretation respecting the lengths of the successive acts of primeval or intermediate creation.

Even the determination of the comparatively easy matter of the *order* of deposit is still laboring under unsolved difficulties, much greater than some geologists seem willing to admit, and that too in countries subject to the constant scrutiny of the most experienced observers. In Syria the opportunities of methodical examination have been very rare indeed, and no one can feel more sensibly than the writer of the following pages, how little probable it is, that the conclusions to which he has arrived with the scanty means within his reach will be borne out by the investigations of subsequent explorers. The only importance which he attaches to these conclusions, and the principal motive which has induced the few attempts at generalisation which this paper will contain, consist in the hope that they may serve at least as provisional hypotheses, ready to take their turn in the sacrifices which must be made, before the Geology of Palestine can be considered as complete.

# SECTION I.

# REGION OF THE LIBANUS.

## CHAPTER I.

### *Reconnaissance of Route from Beirût to Jisr Bŭrghŭz.*

*Introductory Remarks.—Formations adjacent to the Coast near Beirût.—Quarries in the Ard el-Bŭrâjineh and its vicinity.—Limestones east and west of Beirût.—Sandstones south of Beirût.—Beds of Burj el-Bŭrâjineh.—Variegated Sandstones of el-Ghŭrb.—Limestone of 'Ain 'Anûb.—Fossils.—Shumlân Beds.—'Ainâb Limestone.—Casts and Fossils near Abeih.—Jebel esh-Shamûn.—Wâdy el-Qâdy (ancient Tamyras.)—Deir el-Qamr.—Bteddîn Beds.—Casts and Fossils.—Scenery and Geology of el-Mukhtârah.—Nahr el-Bârûk or el-Awaly (the ancient Bostrenus.)—Cavern of Qŭl'at en-Nîha.—Limestones and Geodic Flints of Jezzîn.—Fossils.—Ferruginous Sandstone of Kefr Hûneh.—Valley of el-Litâny (the ancient Leontes.)—Limestone Beds.—Theory of Gradual Progressive and Retrogressive Excavations of Ravines and Valleys.*

THE region of the Libanus includes the greater part of ancient Phoenicia, and extends along the coast from Tripoli to Tyre; the eastern boundary is the valley of Coele-Syria.

The mass of the main Libanus is a limestone much older than the calcareous accumulations on its flanks, and these must have preceded by a very long interval the sandstones which occupy the lateral excavations and are seldom found interstratified with the contiguous rocks. Coal is found at Kurnâyil and carboniferous shales at several other points. Trap is not altogether absent, though showing itself principally in dykes and injections of very limited extent.

A careful examination of the strikes of the Sub-libanine chalk makes it almost impossible to admit the usual hypothesis of an elevatory movement taking effect along the axis of the chain, so as to rupture and rise above the superincumbent beds. The phenomena indicute rather the gradual emergence of a submarine mountainous district from the deep waters of a cretaceous sea; the bearings of the chalky deposits being determined by the pre-existing slopes, on which the sediments have been quietly precipitated. As the dry land appeared in its aspects of reef, archipelago and continent, in geological succession, the deposits which first escaped the denudations of the emergent stage must have been retransported into new places of subaqueous equilibrium, and re-arranged on the slopes of basins, rivers, moraines and deltas, according to the laws of sedimentary distribution. Local causes, such as estuary tides and littoral peculiarities, appear during this process to have variously modified the external characters of the Superjurassic beds, so that the variety which is wanting in the species of the strata, is more than made up by contrasts of color, texture, granulation, homogeneity and compactness. The ratio of the magnesian to the calcareous ingredients, is another very variable element, as is also the greater or less abundance of organic forms, and the more or less advanced process of metamorphic change.

Taking Beirût as a starting point, we find the sea-coast occupied by a limestone of coarse texture and contorted stratification, dipping variously from 0 to 50° towards the east and east-southeast, and irregularly surmounted by marly and arenaceous beds of no very remote origin. These tertiary and quaternary deposits appear to have been subject to the ravages of the waves, in the midst of which they have acquired, from place to place, a precarious and temporary consolidation. While some of these are raised far above the present level of the Mediterranean, the lowest layers, on the contrary, may well be due to the formative agencies now at work near the water line. The recent agglutinations are loose and crumbling in their texture, except in detached blocks, which have gained a better cement by favorable circumstances, or have been longer protected from destructive interruptions. Underneath the recent coast-concretions lies a greyish or blueish white limestone, in which *Ostraeae* and *Ammonites* have occasionally been found. Alternating with this, occurs a yellowish white calc, less compact, but more readily split and dressed. Both are employed in terracing and house-building, though the latter seems the less lasting material of the two. Imperfectly conforming with these beds, and generally associated with the former, is a third limestone, quite free of molluscous fossils, and remarkable for numerous microscopic pores, the result perhaps of the disposition of the siliceous shields of constituent *foraminifera*. The relations of these deposits to the body of the Libanus, as well as their geological indications, go to prove their cretaceous character; and the abundance of chert nodules in the looser varieties of the grey limestone, confirms the presumption that the three beds belong to the upper strata of the chalk.

West of the city, between it and the promontory Râs Beirût, and less conspicuously on the east, a tufaceous and sandy limestone is found, which may be fairly ranked among the latest tertiaries. It is of a greyish white color, inclining here and there to a purpleish yellow. This tufa is made up of an intermixture of comminuted arenaceous and calcareous ingredients. The calcareous matter looks like the fragments of microscopic serpulae. The siliceous portion consists of granules of transparent quartz worn round by attrition, grains of beach-sand in fact, the largest not exceeding the twenty-fifth part of an inch in diameter. The fresh fracture presents a greater variety of colors than the weathered surface, which is a slight ochry brown, due to the presence of iron. The rock is quite porous, the pores being such as would be left after the mechanical combination of the constituent granules with the aid of very little cement. The aggregation, however, is very firm, and this conglomerate, for so it properly is, requires a smart blow to break it; an effect to be ascribed in some measure to a slight degree of flexibility and elasticity in its component parts. It is not unfrequently used as a building stone. What is not siliceous in its composition is a very pure carbonate of lime. Not the slightest trace of magnesia could be detected.

A fourth rock used in building is obtained from the quarries in the Ard el-Bŭrâjineh and its vicinity. This is a compact cretaceous limestone, white, inclining to a blueish yellow, with a chalk-white streak and uneven fracture. The planished surface is marked by many minute points, presenting under the microscope a jagged and sometimes stellated outline. Specific gravity 2.4988. A chemical analysis shows it to be a carbonate of lime, with 12 per cent. of Silex and Alumina; the latter predominating, and giving the stone when wet a strong argillaceous odor. It has some peroxide of iron, which gives a brown color to the solution in hydrochloric acid. Magnesia $1\frac{1}{2}$ per cent. This stone furnishes a very good building material; easy to hew, and hardening on exposure; many of the Beirût houses are built of it. It is much used also in the manufacture of lime. No fossils were found in it. A fifth building stone is procured from the same quarries on the right of the road from

Beirût, about 1½ hours walk from town. It is a softer chalk than the preceding, with more Magnesia and Iron, but less Alumina. The weathered surface has a dirty brown look, quite different from the cheerful whiteness of the recent fracture.

East and west of Beirût for some distance along the coast, and somewhat inland, runs a layer of compact chalk, abounding in flints; covered, where not exposed by denudations, with a mantle of tertiary marl. The hill of San Dimitri, a short league to the east of the city, consists mainly of this siliciferous limestone, which dips here contrary to the slope of the mountain side, and seems therefore to crop out from a point much lower in the Libanine series than it actually occupies. The tertiaries, if ever they covered this eminence, have long since been washed away, but the subordination may be verified northwardly near Jûneh, and southwardly in Wâdy esh-Shuweifât. This upper chalk may be regarded in fact as the characteristic rock of the coast, and the abruptness with which very frequently the change to the Eocene takes place, shows the same suddenness of transition as has been remarked elsewhere in the passage from the cretaceous to the supercretaceous rocks. This passage is however far from being always abrupt in Palestine, and the intermediate beds are often so numerous as to supply those links of continuity which are frequently found wanting in the North-European strata.

The gradual encroachment of the sea upon the land, notwithstanding the strength of its rocky rampart, may be seen with advantage at Râs Beirût, a cape four miles west of the town. The limestone is cut off abruptly by sections nearly vertical, or undermined by caverns excavated by the ceaseless action of the waves. Fissures, at first perhaps the invisible effects of contraction or percussion, have been widened from a seam's breadth into yawning chasms; and the sea once making a clear breach across the rock has not abated of its perseverance until the remnants of the former promontory have been so wasted as no longer to be recognised as once parts of the same mass. There is here as well as in every similar scene of ruin along the coast, much to tempt the imagination to accept the plausible explanation afforded by the paroxysmal theory, and it is hard to look upon the deep gorges of the mountain, or the strewn fragments of the cliff, without admitting the probability of one of those explosions which the impatience of the young geologist so often summons to the assistance of the sluggish agencies of modern time.

The rock north of the bay of Beirût is principally a compact limestone, more or less charged with flints. At least three divisions may be made of this formation, but they do not always cöexist. The general conformity of stratification is well maintained; though subject occasionally to remarkable exceptions. At the mouth of Nahr el-Kelb the stratification is indistinct with a slight dip still towards the East. North of Jûneh, around the bay of Kesrawân, the bearing of the bed is quite irregular, and from Jubeil towards Râs esh-Shŭq'ah, the strata incline towards the sea, conforming nearly the general declivity of the western flank of Jebel Libnân. The limestone here is quite compact, and the lower portion destitute of flints. An opinion has been entertained that an anticlinal ridge exists in the neighborhood of the bay of Kesrawân, but the lithological characters of the beds point to a different origin, and the diversity of dip and bearing is so common a phenomenon in this region, that if we admit of one we must admit of numberless axes of elevation, all very short and of every variety of azimuth.

West of Antûrah, lying over the compact limestones, is a series of beds, which partake of the upper cretaceous and lower tertiary character, and are very various in their geognostic and chemical constitution. The fossils are unfortunately not abundant, but as far as may be gathered from the *Hippurites*, *Cardia*, and *Ostraeae*, which distinguish several of the beds, it is here that a less abrupt transition may be traced than at several localities farther south from the upper chalk to the lower Eocene, a formation which exists incontestably on the middle and lower flanks of the Libanus.

South of Beirût and a little to the East, we find a tract of fine reddish yellow sand, running nearly in a line bisecting the angle formed by the Libanus and the coast. This tract is marked at the point where the road to Deir el-Qamr crosses it, by the Hŭrsh es-Senôber or Grove of Pines, planted more than two centuries ago by Fakher ed-Dîn. The sands as they lie exposed are loose and moveable, but imperfectly compacted beds are found beneath the surface. In their general aspect these sand-banks resemble those found higher up the Libanus, though they certainly indicate a much less complete consolidation. Even the lowest of these is raised more than 100 feet above the level of the city, and cannot be referred to any coast-line within historic time. The shore sands differ from the elevated sands in so many particulars, that the Arabs themselves will not allow that they have the same origin. They maintain gravely that the red sands come through subterraneous passages from the deserts, and refer to the region round Gaza and el-Arîsh as the probable source from which they spring. The sands are supposed to be encroaching on the suburbs; and to guard against this evil, was, it is said, one of the motives of which induced the Druse Emîr to reconstruct the old bulwark of pines. The Senôber is the *Pinus halepensis*, and is almost sure to be found on reaching the tertiary sandstones, wherever they are met with on the sides of either of the Lebanons.

From Hŭrsh es-Senôber (or Hŭrsh Beirût, as it is often called,) the plateau descends very gently towards the mountain, and after some inequalities descends again to Wâdy esh-Shahrûr. Before this, Burj el-Bŭrâjineh is passed, with the mulberries and olives of the Ard el-Bŭrâjineh on the left, and the sea about two miles distant on the right. The limestone of this district is a chalky compact rock of which two varieties have already been described. A third occurs a mile south of the quarries, and contains among other fossils two species of *Gryphaea.*

South of Burj el-Bŭrâjineh, at the Khân Bîr Werwer, the sands again appear and remain more or less conspicuous, until the village of el-Hadeth is passed on the left. The subjacent rock is here calcareous, but not far from the road the soil shows by its composition the former abundance of the yellow sand, and at B'abda there may be still found traces of its existence. About 5 miles from Beirût, Wâdy Shahrûr or Ghadhîry intersects and partially exposes the limestone of el-Bŭrâjineh, and shortly afterwards beyond the the cragged knolls of Kefr Shîma,* the convent of Sant' Antonio el Qarqafeh attracts the attention of the traveller, occupying a commanding and picturesque position on the shelves and ledges of this rock. The Deir is on the right, and a broad valley or coomb retreats far inward and up the mountain on the left, built out into a long flight of terraces, where the mulberry, the olive, the fig and the carob show, by their thriving condition, that it is not the soil which is to blame for the scantiness of productive vegetation.

Near this begins the Aklîm el-Ghŭrb. In the lower of the two subdivisions of this district (el-Ghŭrb el-Tahtâny) the limestone gradually assumes a firmer texture, and in some localities puts on a crystalline aspect with irregular and indistinct stratification.

* The Kefr Shîna of Burkhardt.

Not far from the Convent of el-Qarqafeh and between it and 'Ain 'Anûb a Hippuritic limestone shows itself and serves as a basis of the sandy patches farther south. Besides *Hippurites syriacus*, *Nerinea orientalis* and *Nerinea abbreviata* are found the casts of

Turritella congesta,

Cerithium geniculatum,

Nucula submucronata,

And the shells of Exogyra Boussingaultii (d'Orb.) with some undetermined Polyparia.

The road ascends obliquely across a spur of this limestone, until the traveller has 'Ain 'Anûb and 'Aïthâth in view, still a half hour distant, the one below, the other above him with B'abda far behind on the left, and a wide expanse of valley between. Not far from this the yellow and red sandstones reappear with the compact stone on both sides of the lane which has been in some places dug out by the hoof to the depth of several feet. The rock is a loose and almost friable aggregate of fine quartz grains, bound together by a cement consisting of lime, alumina and iron. The grains are of various sizes and shapes, many with edges very little rounded, the greater part polyhedral with well worn angles. The colors are as various as in the *grès bigarré* or *bunter Sandstein*, the red and yellow predominating with all the intermediate shades of orange, and occasionally with spots and patches of green. These colors are due mainly to the cement, and may be nearly effaced by washing in dilute acids, which leave the siliceous granules transparent and blueish or greenish white. The stratification was not easy to ascertain, but it was evident that it did not anywhere underlie the chalk. Now and then the sands arising from the disintegration of this stone lay several feet deep on each side of the road, and assume then an uniform reddish yellow hue. Where the crumbling is not so easily effected, the surface of the ground is rendered exceedingly rough by the rapid and unequal wear of the stone. This belt of variegated sandstone extends north and south nearly parallel with the Libanus, and is crossed by many of the roads running eastwardly from the coast.

It is impossible to regard this sandstone as a constituent of the Libanine chalk. Its relation to the adjacent lime-series, its meagre and subordinate dimensions, loose outline and straggling extremities, its disposition suddenly to thin out or die away abruptly against the walls of its excavated basins are evidences sufficiently convincing of its post tertiary character, without resorting to its fossils, which as yet have not been met with, if in fact they still exist.

Beyond these sandy pliocenes, not far to the right of a village called Bsâba by our Mukârîyeh, the rock though still arenaceous acquires at several points a much harder texture, and at one locality on the left of the road exhibits a singular tendency to polygonal cleavage with the opposite planes sometimes many feet apart. The mountain side again opens as the road ascends into terraced valleys, in one instance a mile across, studded with the fruits of a diligent improvement of the soil. Between 'Ain 'Anûb and Bshâmôn a Wâdy descending towards the sea, which it meets at Khân el-Ghŭfr gives a fine view of the Lebanon slope and its bold inequalities of surface. Among these, three pyramidal hills, continuous with the base on which they stand, show on their steep flanks the plunging dip of the limestone mass which has been carved, long after its last displacement, into this remarkable relief. Not far from these Mr. Thompson has as I understand found trapp in large developments, which my allotted time did not allow me to visit.

South of this Wâdy, near Shumlân, the sections near the road expose beds of indurated marl alternating with shaly limestones, variously colored. But farther on, this deposit terminates bluntly against a limestone differing in all its aspects from the chalky sediments near the coast. This is a semi-crystalline calc of the specific gravity of 2.696; the color internally a fawn or light yellowish brown mingled with a translucent greenish white, externally wood-brown, inclining to red; the weather-surface rough and almost hackly. This rock may be regarded as metamorphic travertine. Generally the yellowish ingredient takes on an orbicular, tubular or conchoidal form, leaving the interstices to be filled up with the semi-transparent and semi-crystalline paste, though the relation is sometimes reversed. These constituents are contributed like the quartz and felspar of some granites. The conchoidal forms may have been originally determined by the shells of minute mollusks, but if so, the fossils have been so changed by metamorphism that they no longer are to be regarded as organic. Treated with hydrochloric acid nothing is left, but about two per cent. of silica in the shape of very fine, white, glassy sand. Of magnesia there was found scarce a trace.

Between 'Ain 'Anûb and 'Aithâth, a limestone tract characterised by ***Hippurites plicatus*** and a ***Nerinea*** (***orientalis?***) stretches off with ill-defined limits towards the sandy embankments near Shumlân, and disappears on the southeast against an older limestone which forms the body of the high ridge west of the western fork of the Nahr el-Qâdy.

Higher up and not far from 'Ainâb we reach a compact limestone of remarkably fine and even texture, as compact and close as the inferior Solenhofen lithographic slabs, but without the slaty structure of these beds. The color of the fresh fracture is a light ash-grey, inclining to a peach blossom yellow very faintly purple, strikingly soft and agreeable to the eye. The mass is frequently intersected by thin veins of honey-yellow calcspar, frequently intersecting each other at very acute angles. It is a very pure carbonate of lime with a trace of magnesia. This limestone is a variety of that which underlies the chalk, but rises frequently above it and forms, in the entire range of the Libanus, the main body of the fossiliferous mass. Other varieties will soon be described, and its contemporary will meet us through the whole upland of Palestine and in all the deep denudations of its flanks.

Leaving now Serahmûl on the right and some distance in the rear, the road crosses a torrent intersecting the last mentioned limestone and skirting several olive groves on its left, reaches the village of 'Ainâb. Here for many miles around to the east and south and also northeasterly in the direction of Bhamdûn, the compact homogeneous limestone just described as meeting the explorer on the north of 'Ainâb occurs in full development and presents itself uncovered by the chalk and worn away in a singularly rough and jagged relief thrown upward into ridges and knolls or eaten down into gorges and ravines. Where these excavations are sufficiently deep, the double structure of this rock is well exhibited to view. The vertical sections display either a system of conforming strata, undulating with a general slope towards the sea, or unstratified masses occupying natural trough-like and sometimes valley-like cavities, apparently eroded from the stratified block. The effects of atmospheric exesion may be well seen about a mile south of the fountain. Determined probably by the shape and relative destructibility on its first subjection to the action of the corroding elements of the rock, its naked face has been long since deeply sculptured by incisions cutting vertically many feet into its substance. When these deep furrows intersect each other, as they often do, the result is a carving out of the rock into innumerable crests, pinnacles and spurs. Sometimes two parallel incisions, as the rock is unequally worn away, approach each other below, and the neighboring surfaces meeting at last, round window-like openings with curved and sharp-edged outlines unite the neighboring crevices and spread, until the whole partition wall is finally made to disappear. Where the erosion is more regular, plates and needles are sometimes thus formed, which ring very distinctly on being struck. In some places they vibrate visibly under the blow of the hammer, and yield corresponding musical sounds. The weather-surface of this limestone is a light iron-grey, the interior a very faint purplish or ash-grey yellow.

The scarcity of fossils in this remarkable formation makes it somewhat difficult to find the place of this grey limestone in the series of the Libanine rocks. I have nowhere found it covering the chalk, and yet have no reason to refer it to the Oolite. If I have called it a variety of limestone elsewhere ascertained to be undoubtedly Jurassic, it is because I wish to be understood as referring to the lithological classification, without pronouncing for the present upon its stratigraphic rank.

Provisionally this calcite may be denominated the 'Ainâb limestone. It varies very much in its liability in different places to intruding veins of spar. These are sometimes so numerous, so thick and so perpetually traversing the gangue, that the mass at last loses entirely its compact aspect, and runs finally into an impure spathic calc, that falls to pieces under a very moderate blow. The honey-yellow and white spar are often simultaneously present and intimately mingled, though each crystal retains its respective color even in veins so small as to require a lens for their inspection.

Southeast of 'Ainâb the mountain breaks into vast masses, and the scenery becomes wilder, and marked by truly Alpine contrasts and surprises. 'Ain et-Terâz is conspicuous on the left, far over a fine gorge, and 'Ain er-Rummâneh is seen below, beyond a crest of naked rock. On the right 'Abeih occupies a picturesque eminence, and between the road and the village the guide points out a rude memorial of old times, the Qabr esh-Shamûn, a burial pile in honor of a Druze, whose story the muleteers love to tell with new embellishments at every recital. Near this spot and opposite a bend in the great gorge of Nahr ed-Dâmûr, Jebel esh-Shamûn presents on the right an enormous wall of natural masonry, built up of countless strata of the solid limestone of 'Ainâb, conforming in their parallelism to the upper surface of the old rock on which they seem to rest.

The casts which prevail in the fossiliferous beds of the district of el-Ghŭrb el-Foqâny are most abundant perhaps in the vicinity of 'Abeih. Of these, well marked specimens have been found of

Exogyra Boussingaultii, *d'Orb.*
Cardium biseriatum,
  crebriechinatum,
Pholadomya decisa,
Arca indurata,
Corbula Aleihensis,
Venus indurata,
Inoceramus Lynchii?
Isocardia crenulata,
Trigonia Syriaca,
Natica Syriaca,
  indurata,
Chenopus Syriacus.

After passing Jebel esh-Shamûn (a name which, if it has not the authority of the mountaineers themselves, seems fairly enough connected with the hero of the Qabr) the road winds among passes and precipices, and plunges after various delays down a rough mountain horsepath into the Wâdy el-Qâdy, the same which nearer the sea is more generally called Wâdy ed-Dâmûr. On the sides of this steep descent the limestone has undergone a change which has converted a portion of its mass into flinty bands and nodules, not only giving rise to beds of cherty balls, as in the sea-coast chalk, but incrusting the outer surface of the hill with lambeaux of silicated calc which imparts a tempered coating to the ledges that crop out on the rocky sides of the gorge. On a careful examination of this locality, it was difficult to resist the conclusion that the silicification is due to the infiltration of water, holding at ordinary temperature either silica or some of the silicates in solution; for the proportion of silica diminishes sensibly with the depth beneath the surface, as it was easy to ascertain at several recent breaches in the rock. It is now well known that silicates, once held to be insoluble, may under various chemical conditions be dissolved even in the cold, and it ought to excite no surprise that a menstruum so charged should in the lapse of ages impregnate and *petrify* a calcareous rock, as surely, if not as readily as it turns into stone a cockle or a fern. It seems then hardly necessary to resort to the agency of volcanic or subterranean heat in cases like the present, where the hypothesis of its former instrumentality is sustained by no other evidence than the presence of the siliceous ingredient, and needed for no other purpose than to account for this presence. The petrifying process, whatever may have been its cause, has in some places eliminated every particle of carbonate of lime, and the base of the silicate also has disappeared, so that opake and even semi-crystalline quartz-crusts of more than a foot in thickness may be found, either still adhering to the subjacent flinty limestone, or broken up into fragments which have slowly worked their way down the slopes into the stream, and then with an insensible waste of substance down the stream into the sea.

The appearance of the limestone as it shows itself where it has escaped this siliceous metamorphosis, leads to the conclusion that it is continuous with the 'Ainâb beds. It has the same compactness and specific gravity, the same color and texture, the same freedom from fossils, and the same disposition to receive at times very thickly crowded spathic infiltrations.

The Nahr el-Qâdy is crossed by a stone bridge of not very ancient construction, the Jisr el-Qâdy, and was in full flow from recent rains (March 31st, 1848). On the south side as well as the north the sintered limestone is found at various altitudes above the bottom of the gorge. Numerous instances occur here, where rounded fragments of the grey limestone of 'Ainâb are found imbedded in a matrix of opake bluish-yellow quartz, with the pebbles so separated from each other as to make it difficult to conceive how this could have been effected, without supposing either that the pebbles, once in contact, have been separated by the gradual intrusion of the silica, or that they were thrown loosely into a siliceous magma of the same specific gravity, (a hardly tenable hypothesis,) or finally that they reached the siliceous receptacle after long intervals and in different stages of its growth.

From Jisr el-Qâdy to Deir el-Qamr, the road is constantly changing its level and its direction, bringing into view unexpected openings of noble scenery, and exhibiting in all the various phases of the picturesque the villages of Kefr Metta, Bshetfîn, Kefr Ja'ûd and Kefr Hatta,* with Mezra'ah on the right, and Bteddîn and B'aqlîn distant in the south. The limestone mass is deeply indented and channelled into pits and gorges separated by rough ledges and stony belts. In some of the natural terraces thus formed a loamy soil repays the labor of the mountaineer, and presents a fruitful vegetation often in striking contrast with the rugged aspect of the surrounding rock.

Between the eminence, on which the village of Deir el-Qamr is built, and the heights selected by the Emir Beshîr for the site of his palace, lies a rocky valley, which collects the scanty waters of the Nahr Bteddîn, a tributary to the Nahr el-Dâmûr. On the south side of

* There is another Kefr Hatta in the Aqlîm Jezzîn.

this valley, four distinct calcareous deposits are exposed. The inferior is the closely compacted limestone of 'Ainâb. Above this is a cretaceous stone of a hardness and color, intermediate between the 'Ainâb calc and the Mâr Sâba chalk, resembling in many respects the Hâkil limestone, but deficient in its fossils. It is traversed by numerous fissures, nearly plane and parallel, exhibiting, when exposed, a much yellower color than the mass between them. The insoluble matter amounts to six per cent., the magnesia between one and two. Covering this and near the top of the hill of Bteddîn is a compact blue limestone of somewhat slaty color and siliceous aspect. It is without fossils, and notwithstanding its flinty appearance and rather high specific gravity, gives very little residuum with hydrochloric acid, frothing violently on being so treated, and throwing out large and very tenacious bubbles. Finally, on the summit of the hill and for several miles east of the first ascent, an Ostraea limestone is found of the same age, no doubt, as the Mukhtârah and the Bhamdûn varieties. I found here besides the ***Ostraea Syriaca***, ***Exogyra Boussingaultii***, ***Strombus pervetus*** and ***Natica indurata.*** An analysis of several casts of ***Strombus pervetus*** showed no magnesia and very little insoluble residuum. Some of these contained three per cent. of peroxide of iron. The Strombus and larger Natica-casts have a greyish-purple color internally, with a straw or buff yellow without. The texture of the rock where ***Ostraea Syriaca*** predominates is very various. Some portions show the compactness of the 'Ainâb stone; generally, however, it is much coarser, sometimes marly, and in certain layers earthy and incoherent.

The ledges of this neighborhood are often covered by a very delicate film of cryptogamous vegetation, which resembles a coat of crimson paint, concealing the dull and dingy grey beneath, and affording a pleasing contrast with the shrubs which abound wherever they can find a foothold in the fissures of the rocks.

After passing es-Simeqanîyeh, the country assumes an aspect of grandeur, not surpassed in any part of the Libanus. The noble scenery of el-Mukhtârah now presents itself with its vast masses and startling contrasts, its turreted cliffs and dark defiles, its sudden barriers and winding outlets, conducting the traveller gradually down into the singular valley of the Nahr el-Bârûk. Vertical sections of the mountain side show an alternation of massive and stratified limestone, resembling at first view the successive deposits, sometimes so difficult to account for in the distribution of materials derived from the detritus of plutonic rocks. In the neighborhood of el-Judeideh the plough of the husbandman frequently turns up casts of enormous ***Strombi*** and ***Naticae.*** Between this and Mukhtârah I found in various localities ***Ostraea linguloides***, ***O. Syriaca***, ***O. Scapha***, ***Exogyra Boussingaultii***, ***Natica indurata***, ***N. Syriaca***, ***Strombus pervetus***, and several species of ***Cardia***, ***Cucullaeae***, (***Arcæ?***) ***Trigoniae*** and ***Chenopodes***, not sufficiently well preserved to admit an accurate determination.

The Nahr el-Bârûk (or el-Awaly) flows through a gorge wide enough sometimes to allow a wide belt of fertile alluvion on both sides of the stream. Further south, the vegetation near its banks is still more remarkable, and there is certainly no deficiency there of forest or fruit trees; not to speak of a profusion of wild foliage and wasted shrubbery, which the traveller would be glad to have transferred to more accessible districts.*

The older limestone, as I found it near the Jisr, resembles very much the 'Ainâb formation, but its texture is not so close, nor its color so lively. The spathic veins are less

*The whole extent of pasture land and meadow watered by the Awaly from its source to within ten miles of its mouth is designated on Carl Ritter's 15 sheet map as the Merj Besri. By some travellers, this term is restricted to the rich alluvial tract northwest of Jezzîn.

frequent and principally white. A chemical analysis shows scarcely any difference of composition, there being only one-half per cent. more of iron in the Bârûk variety, and a very little less magnesia.

Between Wâdy el-Bârûk and Wâdy el-Mukhtârah, a tributary from the northeast, a noble promontory of the same limestone presents in many of the lateral ravines fine opportunities of a proper study of its strata. Not far from the residence of Sheikh Beshîr, a lambeau of the upper chalk remains as a witness of the former proportions of this now very much diminished rock, and the remarkable quartz geodes, called sometimes Saracens' or Turks' heads, begin occasionally to appear. They are found afterwards in much greater abundance and of larger size from 'Ammatûr south through the entire Belâd esh-Shŭqîf and Belâd Beshârah. Associated with these nodules are found numerous casts of *Natica Syriaca*, *Mactra petrosa*, *Strombus pervetus*, *Ostraea Syriaca* and *Ostraea Scapha.* In several subordinate beds, partly exposed near the road ascending from the bridge, a cream-like limestone occurs of a semi-granular, subsaccharine texture, which but for its liability to contract yellow stains on exposure would answer any of the various purposes of the softer marbles.

Between B'adrân and 'Ain Qŭniyeh, the 'Ainâb limestone is again visible, and crossing a rough ravine the road climbs to 'Ain Matûr or (as it is usually pronounced) 'Ammatûr. Not far from here the cliffs on the west side of the Bârûk come magnificently into view, and display a long belt of stratified rocks running for miles, high above the stream, supported and covered over by calcareous deposits apparently of very different origin, and varying from the layered limestone in structure, color and composition. Leaving Mezra'at esh-Shûf on the right, Jebâ' esh-Shûf, Bâthir and Nîha may be visited in quick succession. From the eastern heights, which here again assume proportions nearly Alpine, many ravines come down, charged with water enough to throw off very picturesque cascades, which greatly relieve the monotonous grandeur of the scene. In spots once accessible to the influence of this moisture the limestone has undergone a very remarkable disintegration, and the more recent marls have never acquired a consolidated form.

High in the limestone cliff and apparently inaccessible from above or below is the Moghar and Qŭl'at en-Nîha, a cavern and fortress, famous as the last and long defended retreat of the heroic Fakhr ed-Dîn.

On the right of the road here, a pass descends to the Wâdy Bisra or Basrah* which extends to Meshmûshy, one of Lady Hester Stanhope's occasional residences. Crossing a stream which enters the Awaly near this, is the bridge Jisr Bhannîn where four granite columns are said to be still standing. The correspondencies here both of indentation and stratification on opposite sides of the Awaly show that the valley, deep as it is, is the result of secular erosion. In many places the broad zone of stratified limestone puts on a columnar appearance like a bed of prismatic basalt, but on nearer approach the layer-seams are visible, more so indeed than in some of the superincumbent rocks. A rocky valley separates

* Dr. Robinson was, I believe, the first who observed that the Bostrenus of Dionysius Periegetes could be no other than the Awaly. This is confirmed by the existence of a Merj Besry and a Wâdy Bisrah on this river. Bostrenus, it may be added, is given by Reland as the gentile noun of the Bosrah of Haurân. The name Basrah is not uncommon in the East. In literal Arabic, Bosrah means a brown loamy earth, and Basrah a tract of stony land. In Hebrew Botzra denotes any fortified place, and, not to speak of Beeshterah and Bosor (Betser) beyond the Jordan, there was a Bosra in Moab, and another in Edom. The fountain Ambuslee on the south side of this river, where Maundrell passed the first night of his journey from Sidon to Damascus, is evidently Ambŭsry for 'Ain Bŭsry, as 'Ammatûr, 'Andârah, 'Antûrah for 'Ain Mâtûr, 'Ain Dârah, 'Ain Tûrah, etc.

Meshmûshy from Jezzîn without marking however any change in the general phenomena of the calcareous deposits.

Throughout this district deep incisions lay bare the internal structure of the Libanine ridge. The inferior rocks may be confidently regarded as Jurassic with enormous inequalities of surface gradually corrected by the filling up of the ancient depressions through sedimentary accumulations in the estuaries, as well as by means of the mechanical precipitates of the finer materials floated out far from land into the distant waters of the chalky sea. The newer cretaceous groups lie on the slopes and fill the basins of the older ones, and a tertiary may often be found in scattered nooks, which have sheltered it from the restless destructiveness of the atmospheric agents of our own day. The fossils I found at Jezzîn were far from being as numerous as I could have wished. The few which were well preserved were ***Ostraeae*** and ***Exogyrae***, with good casts of ***Naticae***, ***Strombi*** and a ***Turritella magnicostata.***

In general it may be said of the Libanine groupes between Deir el-Qamr and Jezzîn that they possess every variety of appearance from the most porous to the most compact, from the most thoroughly silicified to the most completely disintegrated and broken down. The colors are as various as the consistence, running from a pale yellow to a dark blue and purplish black. In some strata fossils are not unfrequent, in the greater portion they cannot be found without time for a methodical search. The dips and strikes are as various as the lay of the hill sides, to which they have a tendency to conform. East of Jezzîn on a plateau above the village the beds strike N. E. and dip 25° S. E. against the general descent of the mountain side, but this bearing is not long maintained. Where the denudations in this quarter have exposed the inferior limestone, and the elements have been allowed to do their work, the rock, more especially where the magnesian ingredient abounds, seems to have lost all traces of sedimentary origin, and is often curiously eaten out into turriform and castellated inequalities, sometimes thirty feet in height. Where the erosion has gone so far, it has left lamellar and conchoidal sinuses several feet in depth, or at least a honey-comb and sponge-like cellularity, as if a powerful acid had burrowed into a stony mass having a very unequal capacity of resistance. Even the detached blocks exhibit on the sides last exposed a proportionate exesion, which appears to have been slowly effected since the separation from the parent rock.

The fresh fracture is almost always much lighter and more inclined to yellow than the weather beaten surface, which is generally a greyish blue; but occasionally though very rarely the reverse of this is found. A portion of the greyish-blue limestone east of Jezzîn has been more or less dolomitised, and an analysis of a specimen taken at random gave

| | |
|---|---|
| Carbonate of Lime, | 69.20 |
| Peroxide of Iron and Alumina, | 2.12 |
| Carbonate of Magnesia, | 27.63 |
| Undissolved, | .85 |
| | 99.80 |

The limestones on the contrary which preserve externally their chalky color contain very little or no magnesia, and still less of iron or other coloring ingredient. Besides the dolomitic and cretaceous kinds, there is a limestone alternating with them remarkable for its subcrystalline texture, but it does not occur in large proportions and is probably a metamorphic rock of very limited extent. It has scarcely a trace of magnesia, and very little iron.

In the neighborhood of Jezzîn the smaller valleys and hollows are filled with quartz balls, of the kind already spoken of, oblate spheroids from an inch to a foot in diameter. In one of these nooks, about two or three miles off the road, they have so accumulated as to form a bed of nodules and earth more than twenty feet in thickness, while the rocky sides of the valley contain within them no vestiges of any such concretions. They are evidently flints, which have long survived the entire disappearance of the chalk in which they lay, and which have been swept by the lapse of time into sheltering excavations of a much later date.

These geodes resemble in some respects the remarkable concretions found in Mount Carmel a few miles from the convent, and well known under the name of petrified melons and other fanciful designations. They differ principally in the external coat and the mode in which the innermost layer of quartz appears to be generated and applied. The Jezzîn nodules are deeply pitted and jagged on the external surface, the Carmel pebbles are round and almost smooth. In the former, the quartz incrusting the sides of the cavity is deposited in a compound mammellary form; in the latter it covers the walls of the cell with a coating of quartz crystals of small size, but evenly and beautifully laid on. Another peculiarity of the *turksheads* is the very numerous siliceous septa, forming a system of interreticulating planes diverging from the centre of the ball.

In some localities just south of Jezzîn, nodules of concentric coats of a very pure carbonate of lime are found, like hand specimens of the Egyptian alabaster. I met with it nowhere massive or in place.

About three-quarters of an hour further south, half way down a Wâdy leading to the Zaherâny, a ferruginous sandstone occurs resembling the beds of Fŭrdîs and 'Ain ez-Zehalteh. It abounds in iron and has been worked, but after a few awkward attempts at a labor which the Syrian workman looks upon with disgust, the enterprise was abandoned and is not likely to be renewed. The sides of the road are still thinly strewn with bits of the refuse slags, yielding from 40 to 70, and sometimes even 95 per cent. of iron. The ferriferous sandstone presents itself in three different forms. In the upper beds it occurs in crusty shales composed of numerous sheets of a great variety of gaily contrasted colors. Beneath the shales I found beds of loosely compacted granules, bound together by an imperfect cement consisting of lime, alumina and iron. Some of the granules were themselves calcareous, the whole of an uniform light smoky brown. Loosely scattered without any well defined place, but generally associated with the shales and forming sometimes the whole surface of a large embankment, a remarkable tuberculous conglomerate occurs, set thickly with very numerous concretionary nodules of a semi-silicated calc, containing often a little nucleus of very pure quartz. The iron in this conglomerate varies from 5 to 20 per cent. of the whole.

The sandstones continue to Kefr Hûneh and three or four miles beyond, terminating in a sandy tract partly covered with pines and marked by a lake two or three hundred yards in diameter, lying in a sort of crater of nearly circular form. At Kefr Hûneh I found the dip of the sandstone N. N. W. 45°, but it seldom attains this inclination. About a mile south of the village the ground runs off into terraces divided by vertical crevices into large polygonal figures, not unlike those which are found near 'Ain Bsâba.

On regaining the limestone the contiguous layers very frequently conform, but this seems confined only to the beds immediately beneath the sandstone and which are themselves no doubt posterior to the chalk. Near the recommencement of the limestone an elevated tract is reached presenting on the right a noble prospect of the valley of the Leontes (Qasimîyeh or Litâny.) The Wâdys descending into this from the north are excavated from the Jura platform, and but partially occupied by remnants of the upper chalk. In one of these running due north and south and traversed by a fine stream of water (Wâdy Medûn?) I found numerous small boulders of conglomerate and breccia, but they had no appearance of having been formed in the valley where they lie.

Crossing a transverse Wâdy of an earlier age, and descending gradually to the Jisr Bŭrghŭz at the Litâny, the older limestone again develops itself with its alternations of layered and unlayered beds. The Wâdy Qasimîyeh like the Bârûk and the Qâdy, is a valley of excavation. The correspondencies of structure on opposite banks are subject to variations of no higher order than those where no valleys intervene. In other words these gorges, deep as they are, and cut through a thousand feet of limestone, show no more evidence of disturbance than occurs anywhere in the intervening mass. The rocky floors of these excavations pass continuously beneath the stream-bed in unbroken layers, when these are nearly horizontal. When the dip is great, the bottom is nevertheless worn level upon the edges of the strata, which conform to the structure of the rocky wall, and may be traced on one side upward to their prolongation in the cliff. The floor of each gorge, taken as a whole, has a gradual descent, and has probably nowhere ever been deeper and then filled up; so that whatever may have at first determined the course of each new reach of the lengthening valley, the floors no longer exhibit the evidence of any other agency than the erosive and slowly displacing action of ordinary running water.

It is remarkable that the Damuras, the Bostrenus and the Leontes agree in running at first nearly north and south, and afterwards turning abruptly upon their mountain barriers and hurrying as it were directly through them westwardly into the sea. If we adopt the theory of a slow and secular vertical motion of the continents, it necessarily follows that rivers, at first mere affluents of the coast, must elongate at both extremities as long as the maritime district is an emergent one, and the source of the stream yet short of the summit level. It follows also that while each new link at the head of the river will depend for its local direction on the levels it may encounter, the general course of the whole ascending series of additional reaches will be the result of the prevailing dip of the continental surface through the entire period of this continually retrograding excavation. In the same way the mean bearing of the seaward additions to the channel's length will be determined by the general slope and sounding in each emerging zone. From the length of the interval which must separate the formation of the upper, middle and lower sections of a given river, there will have ensued new positions of the area of its ramifications, and new mean directions therefore in the accessions of a later age. That such a secular variation in the slope of the Syrian platform has actually occurred, is rendered probable by the absence of branches entering near the angles of these rivers from the south, as well as by the parallelism both in those sections which are north of the bends, and those which are west. The mountain chains are in this view what they are perhaps every where else, mainly the results of the sculpture, or what may be called the water-etching of the surface of the earth, and only exceptionally and subsequently the determining causes of the directions of the streams.

It should also be borne in mind that the bed of the river and its tributaries, when once fully excavated, is no longer liable to a material change of form from later variations of the strike and dip of the great platform into which it gradually sinks, and secondly that in consequence of a relatively rapid displacement of the line of summit levels, a wide and deep channel once occupied by the lower or middle section of a great river may, in the new position of the water-shed, collect and give passage to a stream of very insignificant dimensions. These considerations, already sufficiently important in explaining the configurations of the Mediterranean rivers will again find their application, when we come to discuss the secular changes which have probably taken place in the levels of the valley of the Jordan.

---

## CHAPTER II.

### *Reconnaissance of Route from the Bŭqâ' at 'Ain Lijjy to Beirût.*

*The summit ridge of the Lebanon.—The Jurassic limestone of 'Ain Lijjy.—Variegated sandstone of el-Fureidîs.—Sandstone and caves of Wâdy el-Kishk.—Sandstone beds of Wâdy Kŭfrah, 'Ain el-Hajel and 'Ain ez-Zehalteh.—Sandy nodules, ferruginous geodes, arenaceous ironstones and limestone of Wâdy el-Kŭfrah.—Wâdy Shâneih beds.—Iron-stained pebbles between 'Azzûnîyeh and Wâdy Beradîy.—Fossils north of 'Azzûnîyeh.—Sandstone and limestone near Khân el-Hamra.—Fossils and beds near Bhamdûn.—Sandstone north of Bhamdûn.—Cretaceous bed.—Fossils and limestones of Khân Hussein and Khân el-Meshra'ah.—Sandstones of Khân Kehâleh.—Casts and fossils of 'Aleih.—Fossils of Khân Jemhûr.—Beds west of Jemhûr.—Limestones and arenaceous embankments between Khân Jemhûr and Beirût.*

The crest of the Libanus from Jisr Bŭrghŭz north runs so much nearer to the valley of the Bŭqâ' than to the Mediterranean shore, that it may be regarded as the brink of a descent very precipitous towards the valley and comparatively gradual towards the sea. It exhibits towards the Bŭqâ' outcrops of calcareous strata dipping as a general rule towards the East, but frequently at an angle of inclination far exceeding the mean slope of the western water-shed. If therefore the whole Libanine district were brought into position by depressing the Coele-Syrian side to the level of the Mediterranean, the strata would still be very deeply and variously inclined, and would not, on the whole, represent better than at present a system of conforming and undisturbed sedimentary deposits. The summit ridge embracing the highest eminence of Jebel Jezzîn, Jebel Bârûk, Jebel er-Rîhân and Jebel Libnân is by no means so continuous or so unbroken as it seems to be when viewed from the Anti-Libanus. On the contrary, the indentations and denudations are so deep and so numerous, that no traces, or a very few at least, are now left of the comparatively level surface, which the upper Libanine region must in all probability have attained at the epoch of its last emergence from the waters of the tertiary sea.

The great mass of the more elevated portion of the chain consists of the Jurassic calc already described when speaking of the characteristic limestone of 'Ainâb and 'Ammatûr. As it occurs on the heights above 'Ain Lijjy about half way between Jisr Bŭrghŭz and Jebel Sŭnnîn, it may be regarded as a fair representation of the prevailing type of the oldest formations among the elevated outcrops of the ridge. It is seen there as a homogeneous well compacted rock with a fine wax-like texture. The color is a pure ash-grey, inclining sometimes to a shade between pearl and smoke-grey, not unfrequently with a faint tendency to purple. The fracture is subconchoidal and somewhat splintery, with sharp and well defined edges. The spathic ingredient is sometimes found only in thin seams and minute granules, scarcely visible without a lens; but as a general rule it traverses the mass in widely extended sheets attaining occasionally the thickness of an inch or more, or expanding suddenly into niduses of arragonite and calcite, both in their amorphous and their crystalline forms.

The crest of the western wall of the Coele-Syrian valley is no sooner passed than the traveller finds himself descending towards the sea. At first the calcareous strata plunge westwardly far beneath the less precipitous dip of the general slope, but by degrees the stratification conforms more closely to the mean gradient of the mountain side. It would be wrong to suppose that the inclination of the numerous beds are subject to any law yet capable of being simply or generally expressed. All that can be done is to give the prevailing dip, leaving the frequent exceptions and anomalies for the future duty of the resident observer.

Between the summit line and the village of Bârûk, north of the road from 'Ain Lijjy, a ravine opens towards 'Aghmîd, but separated from it and 'Ain ez-Zehalteh by the gorge which collects the head waters of the Awaly. Here a tendency to strikes crossing the ravines, contrary to the general rule may be occasionally observed, and the dips have a northwestwardly direction.

About two miles east of el-Fureidîs the ochrey and ferrugineous sandstone is again met with, and may be traced some miles north of the Dâmûr. This is a portion of the long belt of arenaceous embankments, which run parallel to the Libanus and lie in terraced patches and broad abutments at various altitudes on its flanks. On the eastern skirt of this sandstone tract I found the dip of 12° to 15° W. sufficiently frequent to deserve attention. The unaltered limestone is never found above the sandstone, but may be traced in various places lying unconformably beneath. The variety of colors of this arenaceous groupe is truly remarkable, but there is none, which may not be referred to the presence of iron. The sandy lambeaux have sometimes 200 yards of breadth, and then intermit and give place to ledges of a metamorphic conglomerate of minutely comminuted quartz and calc. This psammite is sometimes abutted against a wall of excavated limestone, and in a few instances seems to alternate with a coarse calcareous grit also of a comparatively recent age. The valley of Fureidîs and Bârûk is one of the most attractive combinations of trees, green fields and running water in this or any other part of Syria, and abounds in natural pictures which makes its name of "little paradise" a pardonable exaggeration. In the cliffs of Wâdy el-Kishk are several curious caves, and the perishable quality of the sandstone is shown near the junctions of the ravine by the insulated mounds that still survive the wasting action of the elements. In one of these, near the mouth of the Wâdy Kŭfrah a vertical section lays bare a singular collection of sandy nodules, (the geodes of the ancient mineralogists,) containing, within a spherical crust of ironstone from a quarter of an inch to an inch or more in thickness, a full measure of fine white sand which, on breaking the shell, runs off like a fluid. These balls vary from an inch to six inches in diameter, and do not appear, as is sometimes the case, to have been formed by concentric coats about a sandy nucleus. The various colors are not disposed around a centre, but the investing shell is built up of parellel zones apparently cut out of layers of sandstone, as if the ferruginous cement had retreated in all directions from some point within a mass of layered sand, and had consolidated the loose matter between two concentric spherical surfaces without disturbing the existing laminations.*

* An analysis of a piece broken from one of the hardest and heaviest of these crusts yielded

| | |
|---|---|
| Peroxide of Iron, | 86.85 |
| Water, | 11.50 |
| Insoluble, | 3.00 |
| With minute traces of alumina, lime and magnesia. | 101.35 M. |

The Wâdy Kŭfrah runs S. W. nearly, and the sandy belt taking a course N. N. E. soon leaves the limestone visible on the east wall of the valley, while the path on the edge of the stream over and along the arenaceous rock. The nodulose conglomerates of Kefr Hûneh reappear in this locality, and some of the other distinguishing tracts of the sandstone of that region may be followed many miles north of the main Damascus road.

The sandstone continues on the west side of Wâdy Kŭfrah, and runs up there and farther N. W. into hills of great height. Here the road to 'Ain el-Hajel crosses a remarkable junction of limestone and sandstone, and blocks of vast size of both these rocks are found scattered in great confusion. Towards 'Ain el-Hajel the sandstone runs out, but continues to develop itself in remarkable forms and phases in the direction of Sŭjerah (?) and ez-Zehalty. On approaching the latter village the cliffs exhibit a singular relation to the contiguous rocks. The subjacent limestone had evidently been exposed prior to the deposition of the sandstone to erosive forces that had acted very unequally upon the surface; and the superincumbent rock, once a sediment of loose sand, but now hardened by an infiltrated cement, fills up the inequalities of its irregular foundation, but has again in its turn been carved into gulleys and ravines leaving the separating material standing up in sharp and prominent relief.

One of the most practically interesting form into which the sands have been compacted is to be found in the large mamnillary arenaceous concretes cemented by oxides of iron, distributed throughout the district between Wâdy Kŭfrah and 'Ain ez-Zehalteh. These ironstones have a mean specific gravity of 3.02, and are made up of clusters of bulbs varying in diameter from a quarter of an inch to three inches and more. The fresh fracture has an ash-grey color, enlivened by a multitude of minute sparkling points; but when pulverized the ore becomes a yellow-brown powder which turns to black, and finally to deep red as it cools from a high heat. The iron exists in the state of hydrated oxide, one equivalent of water to one of the peroxide, and is not chemically united with the silica. The latter is easily separated by hydrochloric acid, and is quite white, being in fact mainly pulverized quartz. The composition of the entire mineral may be seen from the analysis which gave

| | |
|---|---|
| Silica, . . . . . . . . . . . . . . . . . . . . . . . . | 55.05 |
| Peroxide of Iron,. . . . . . . . . . . . . . . . . . . . | 39.35 |
| Water,. . . . . . . . . . . . . . . . . . . . . . . . | 4.00 |
| Alumina,. . . . . . . . . . . . . . . . . . . . . . . | 1.70 |
| Lime, . . . . . . . . . . . . . . . . . . . . . . . . | .30 |
| | 100.40 H. |

The dip of the sandstone is not always, as one might expect, less inclined than the dip of the older rock. On the contrary, wherever the sands appear to have been pushed under water in successive layers over a precipice of limestone, or embanked against the sides of submarine hills, they retain a steepness of stratification more allied to the accidental declivities of the surface of the underlying rock than to the position of strata out of which they were originally composed.

Near the junction in Wâdy Kŭfrah both rocks have undergone a change. The limestone loses its uniform tone of color, and exhibits numerous reddish specks on a yellow-grey ground. The spathic seams are dark-brown instead of a pearly-white, and faint indications of nearly obliterated organic forms, more especially Hippurites and corals, are here and there discernible. The corals when they occur, like the nummulites of the Anti-Libanus, are best seen where the surface has been long exposed. The weathered side of the limestone has a singularly rough and jagged look, and is sometimes pierced by minute pores which receive the roots of a microscopic cryptogamous vegetation. The sandstone near the joining surfaces involves more or less of calcareous matter which penetrates the body of the consolidated matrix, and is collected sometimes in patches of unequal thickness, at other times thinly and uniformly disseminated through the arenaceous mass. Near 'Ain ez-Zehalteh a cliff is found showing sandstone with a dip of 20° W. by N. in a basin of limestone dipping 15° N. W. Not far distant is another where the sandstone strikes N. E. and dips N. W. 40° towards limestone, of which I could not ascertain either element of position. The Wâdy Zehalteh opens towards its head in the direction of 'Ain el-Hajel, and exhibits many varieties of arenaceous conglomerates and metamorphic rocks. The whole district is eminently deserving the deliberate examination of the Geologist, and the study of the contact surfaces especially would be full of interest and instruction.

From Wâdy Zehalteh to Wâdy es-Sŭfer the paths cross a tract marked by variegated sandstones and enlivened by a cheerful vegetation. The pines are strikingly distributed, and many mulberry and fig trees diversify the scene. The streams are made available in driving mills and watering numerous patches of cultivated land, while the iron-stained rocks appear at intervals through the landscape, overhanging it in wild escarpments, or soaring far above it in the shape of turreted and battlemented peaks.

The whole of the valley above and below 'Ain ez-Zehalteh is occupied by sandstone embankments. They are crossed by most of the paths leading from this neighborhood to Wâdy Shâneih, where the deposits are found in broad developments and in characteristic forms. Near 'Azzûnîyeh, the sandstones strike and dip at angles greatly varying from each other. Farther south the strikes are various, but the dips conform very nearly to the grades of the floors of the larger ravines. On the north side of Wâdy Shâneih is a noble mural escarpment, consisting of strata varying alternately between blue-grey and greyish-yellow. The dip is towards the west or west-southwest, and does not much exceed the declivity of the bottom of the Wâdy. In Wâdy Shâneih the arenaceous and calcareous ingredients appear to have been violently intermingled in agitated waters before they were allowed to subside. The siliceous constituent generally predominates, but in many specimens the carbonate of lime amounts to 45 or 48 per cent. The two compounds are only mechanically combined, and the chalky matter is often found diffused in greyish-white specks and patches through the yellow-red sand. Traces of disintegrated corals not unfrequently occur.

The right bank of the Wâdy Shâneih is scaled here by means of a staircase partly natural and partly artificial, which may be ascended and descended by a man on horseback. Loaded mules go frequently up and down, and, difficult as the ascent appears, accidents are of very rare occurrence. The rock is sandstone, sometimes reddish-yellow, sometimes an almost chalky-white, and easily reduced to powder.* Courses of indurated marl are inter-

* One of the ledges here showed the following composition:

| | |
|---|---|
| Quartz-sand, | 81.20 |
| Iron, | 12.00 |
| Alumina, | .40 |
| Carbonate of Lime, | 4.40 |
| Carbonate of Magnesia, | .80 |
| | 98.80 S. |

stratified with the harder beds. The colors of the vertical sections are not parallel to the main planes of stratification, but inclined at various angles, as is found in all sandbanks formed by flowing water after the *accore* or bull-head is once established and the filling up has gone to the limit of still-water mark.

Between 'Azzûnîyeh and the bridge in the Wâdy Berâdi'y, a branch of Wâdy Shâneih a deposit consisting of iron-stained pebbles, partly loose, partly conglomerate, is crossed by the path leading to Bhamdûn. Not far from this locality a remarkable horse-shoe gorge gives passage to the water from 'Ain Sôfar, a stream which runs full in the wet season, and is crossed lower down by a good stone bridge. In less than an hour afterwards another Wâdy is passed, where the limestone reappears from beneath the arenaceous beds, and dislodged casts of *Naticae* and *Strombi* begin to show themselves in considerable numbers. The rock itself is made up principally of Ostraeoidal fossils, among which were found *Ostraea Scapha* and *Exogyra Boussingaultii.* Not far distant from these beds others occur containing *Echinus Syriacus* and the spines of a *Cidaris.* In its lithological aspects this calc resembles the nummulitic limestone of the Anti-Libanus, but the Nummulites themselves I did not find.

Northwest of 'Azzûnîyeh there occurs a limestone in which the metamorphic character is strikingly exhibited. The appearances presented are such as might arise from a mass of inorganic and organic fragments disseminated originally in a calcareous paste and then gradually assimilated by molecular exchanges until the very forms as well as the materials of the bodies lodged in the great bed, all but escape the closest scrutiny of the observer. From this conglomerate, for so in fact it may be regarded, an analysis produced

| | |
|---|---|
| Carbonate of Lime, | 89.25 |
| Carbonate of Magnesia, | 3.20 |
| Iron and Alumina, | 4.00 |
| Insoluble, | 2.00 |
| Error and loss, | 1.55 |
| | 100.00 S. |

At Khân el-Hamra or near it, the sandstone again presents itself followed by a remarkable limestone ledge. The strike is N. and S. with a dip about 8 degrees W. Further on, there occurs, on a limestone plateau, a curious net-work of fractures and fissures. One groupe is set in concentric polygons about a centre from which another system radiates at an average of ten degrees divergence. The limestone is, west of this, the predominating rock, and jurassic and cretaceous fossils begin here to be found in great abundance. About a mile east of Bhamdûn, forming part of a broken ridge, a locality exists, in which the *Ammonites Syriacus* occur in extraordinary numbers. They are found buried along with many other fossils, principally *Ostraeae*, *Exogyrae*, *Gryphaeae*, *Hippurites* and *Nerinææ*, together with a profusion of casts of the species here subjoined, all of which will be found described by Mr. Conrad in the Appendix to this Report.

Ammonites Syriacus, *Conrad.*
Ostraea virgata, *Goldfuss*, *Nyst.*
Syriaca, *Co.*
scapha, *Roemer.*
Exogyra Boussingaultii, *d'Orbigny.*

Nucula submucronata, *Co.*
parallela, *Co.*
Syriaca, *Co.*
perobliqua, *Co.*
Trigonia Syriaca, *Co.*

Trigonia cuneiformis.
Astarte Syriaca.
pervetus.
orientalis.
arctata.
engonata.
Corbula congesta.
Isocardia crenulata.
Arca Syriaca.
(Bhamdunensis.)
orientalis.
brevifrons.
indurata.
acclivis.
subrotunda.
obliquaria.
Cardium biseriatum.
crebriechinatum.
Syriacum.
Pholadomya decisa.
Panopaea pectorosa.
Inoceramus Lynchii.
Mactra Syriaca.
arciformis.
petrosa.
pervetus.
Cytherea Syriaca.
Venus indurata.
Syriaca.
Lucina Syriaca.
subtruncata.
Tellina Syriaca.
Orbicula subobliqua.
Turritella Syriaca.
magnicostata.
Phorus Syriacus.
Nerinaea Syriaca.
Bhamdunensis.
Strombus pervetus.
Hippurites liratus.

These casts and organic remains are found loosely accumulated in a hill or rather mound of coarse broken limestone and marl, and are washed out plentifully by the rains of the early spring. They are at that time met with in abundance in the adjacent grounds, and may be traced in the direction of the water-courses and stream-beds to a distance greater or less in proportion to the time elapsed since they were detached and the circumstances which have favored their removal.

On examining these remains it was interesting to observe that they were frequently incrusted by adhering fossils manifestly of a much later age. The Jurassic fossils, which are most frequently thus affected, are Echini, Trigoniae and Ammonites, and the adhering shells are for the most part Exogyra, more especially Exogyra Boussingaultii, a fossil characteristic of the inferior beds of the Neo-comian groupe.

Many of the casts appear to be formed originally of a mud enveloping well defined specimens of the smaller ostræoidal species, and it would seem necessary in such cases to refer these shells to the age of the imbedding casts, but the phenomena admit perhaps of another solution.

The village of Bhamdûn stands on a limestone which may be referred to the most recent Jura, and has once been commanded by eminences formed from an older rock. Near the Greek Church, and serving also as its foundation, a coarse calcareous deposit is met with, containing *Nerinaea Syriaca*, *Cytheræa Syriaca*, *Chenopus turriculoides*, and a number of casts belonging to cretaceous fossils, all united into a very loosely compacted mass by a thin cement composed of lime, clay and iron. It is clear that this rock is of an age long subsequent to the age of the casts which it contains; and these, in their turns, are posterior to the epoch of their fossils. The conglomeration of these relics of various geological æras into masses of coarse calc presents several points of interesting inquiry; and the formation may be compared in some measure to the osseous accumulations consolidated on the floors of caverns by stalagmitic infiltration. The color of this rough limestome is a chalky yellow, diversified by the greyer and browner shades of some of the constituent fossils. The cement contains 8 per cent. of insoluble matter, 87 per cent. of carbonate of lime, and from one to one and a half per cent. of magnesia. The casts differ in their chemical composition both from each other and from the binding material. A cast of ***Chenopus turriculoides*** proved on analysis to be a compound of the following ingredients:

| | |
|---|---|
| Carbonate of Lime, . . . . . . . . . . . . . . . . . . | 89.50 |
| Carbonate of Magnesia, (trace.) | |
| Peroxide of Iron, . . . . . . . . . . . . . . . . . . | 5.25 |
| Alumina, . . . . . . . . . . . . . . . . . . . . | 1.75 |
| Insoluble, . . . . . . . . . . . . . . . . . . . | 3.40 |
| | 99.90 M. |

An indurated cast of ***Tellina Syriaca*** showed a result somewhat differing from this, viz:

| | |
|---|---|
| Carbonate of Lime, . . . . . . . . . . . . . . . . . . | 81.12 |
| Carbonate of Magnesia, . . . . . . . . . . . . . . . . | 1.07 |
| Peroxide of Iron, . . . . . . . . . . . . . . . . . . | 6.78 |
| Alumina, . . . . . . . . . . . . . . . . . . . . | 2.31 |
| Insoluble, . . . . . . . . . . . . . . . . . . . | 8.17 |
| | 99.45 |

A soft cast of the same shell had the following composition:

| | |
|---|---|
| Carbonate of Lime, . . . . . . . . . . . . . . . . . . | 90.69 |
| Carbonate of Magnesia, . . . . . . . . . . . . . . . . | 2.50 |
| Peroxide of Iron, . . . . . . . . . . . . . . . . . . | 2.75 |
| Alumina, . . . . . . . . . . . . . . . . . . . . | 1.35 |
| Insoluble, (Silica, etc.) . . . . . . . . . . . . . . . | 3.50 |
| | 100.79 M. |

We may consider here two hypotheses, one which regards the casts as differing chemically from each other in and during their original construction, another looking on the difference now found as mainly superinduced. Adopting the latter view as the more probable, the question arises, are the casts growing harder or less hard? Those which are now undergoing the process of induration seem from the foregoing analysis, to owe their *petrifaction* to the gradual elimination of the alkaline earths and the simultaneous intrusion of silica and iron. In those which are growing softer (if any such there be) the reverse of this takes place.

On leaving the village of Bhamdûn, the road to Beirût strikes, with some windings a general northwesterly direction, down and across the Wâdy of the same name. In this Wâdy, a rough yellow limestone makes its appearance abounding in ***Ostraeae*** clearly referable to the chalk. A sandstone, also marked by the presence of ***Ostraeae*** of a later date, and one or two ***Exogyrae*** decidedly younger than the Neo-comian, covers in part, and in part perhaps underlies the limestone. This latter must be regarded as a reconstructed deposit, formed out of organic materials properly belonging to a far earlier age, together with fossil remains contemporary with its compact consolidation.*

Below the village a mile or more, the outcropping beds have a strike N. E. and a dip 40° N. W. The limestone laid bare at the bottom of the ravine is not dislocated, but simply excavated, without the slightest disturbance of the corresponding lines seen in the sections on opposite sides of the valley. This limestone is compact and poor in fossils, but may fairly be reckoned as included in some portion of the later Jurassic groupes. North of Wâdy Bhamdûn the coarse yellow calc again makes its appearance and is remarkable for numbers of *Strombi* and *Naticae* of very unusual size.

Combined with this is another of a red-brown iron-stone consisting of

| | |
|---|---|
| Silica, | 8.00 |
| Iron (Peroxide) | 61.20 |
| Alumina, | 4.40 |
| Carbonate of Lime, | 24.00 |
| Carbonate of Magnesia, (trace.) | |
| Water, | 1.60 |
| | 99.20 S. |

The lithological characteristic of this rock is a profusion of minute concretionary spheroidules of a sintery compound of Silica, Alumina and protoxide of Iron, not soluble in muriatic acid. These globules are black-brown, and united by a calcareous cement in which carbonate of lime and the peroxide of iron are the predominant ingredients.

This sandstone is itself however so recent in its constitution and character that there is every reason to believe, that the appearance of passing below the coarse calcareous deposits, is in a measure deceptive, and that no real alternation of concordant stratification connects the sandy and the chalky beds.

One of the limestone ledges south of the Wâdy contained involved in a more or less compact matrix a cylindrical fragment, two feet long, marked by many parallel sutures resembling, on an enormous scale, the lobes and saddles of the septa of a gigantic Baculite. The sutures penetrated the rock deeply, and even seemed to divide the fossil Ostraeae which it contained, a circumstance which almost forbids the hypothesis of an animal organization, notwithstanding the regularity of the septal digitations. The bottom of the ravine is a compact limestone much less abounding in fossils than the terraces on its sides and the ledges along its brows. This stone has the ash-yellow interior and iron-grey exterior of the 'Ainâb and 'Ammatûr variety. It has also its spathic seams and transverse laminations, but imperfect vestiges of Neo-comian and perhaps Aptian types indicate a nearer approach to the chalk.

South of Khân Hussein the ground is strewed with casts of *Cardia*, *Trigoniae*, *Arcae*, *Cythereae*, *Tellinae*, *Chenopodes*, etc. The bedding of the subjacent limestone is difficult to ascertain, and varies rapidly from place to place. Some lambeaux were found dipping N. W. 15°, others N. E. 5°. The upper surface varied generally with the dip of the underlying beds. In the deeper ravines this was less the case, and the excavation sometimes cuts

*It is due to Dr. Deforest, of the Beirût mission, to state that I owe to his kindness the opportunity of visiting these localities with advantage, and I now thank him for these and other facilities afforded during the very short time I could spend in this interesting vicinity.

directly across the strike, but even then seldom or never in a direction contrary to the dip. Farther west towards the Khân el-Meshra'ah the Ostraea limestone reappears, and still farther on each side of a high ridge-road inclining to the N. W., the fields abound in casts of *Chenopus Syriacus*, *C. Turriculoides*, *C. Induratus*, along with several species of *Cardia*, *Tellinae*, *Mactrae* and *Lucinae*.

Between Khân Hussein and Khân el-Meshra'ah, at least four distinct limestone beds are crossed in quick succession. The first is an orange-grey calc, very composite in the structure, made up of minute tufaceous granules of crystallised calcite intimately blended with these, and of microscopic specks and spangles, in which iron is the principal ingredient. There is also a notable proportion of magnesia. The second is a variety of the close-grained lithographite of 'Ainâb with thin seams of coarse and impure spar. The third is a conglomerate of very minute tuff-grains, each enveloping a nucleus which proved on examination to be either a *foraminiferum*, a mollusk or, more rarely, a rounded particle of semi-transparent quartz. The color of the fractured tuff-grains varies from straw-yellow to honey-brown. The light grains become whiter and the dark grains browner by exposure. This bed is not unlike the tufaceous conglomerate of the coast. The fourth of these deposits is a shell-limestone in which the gangue or paste is straw-colored, compact and homogeneous, while the imbedded fossils are imperfectly replaced by a dark-brown, highly crystallised calc-spar, and seldom so preserved as to admit of safe determination. Scattered over the surface of the soil covering these beds, and evidently long since dislodged from their niduses are casts of *Cardium biseriatum*, *Turritella magnicostata* and *Tellina Syriaca*.

The vicinity of 'Aleih, a village nearly in the centre of a circle passing through 'Aïthath, Khân Hussein, el-'Abâdîyeh and Khân Kehâleh, is remarkable for its reproducing, in great variety, the Bhamdûn fossils and casts. Whether they may all be met with I am not prepared to say, but the following list of such as are actually exposed is probably far from complete:

Holaster Syriacus, *Co.*
Ostræa scapha?
Exogyra Boussingaultii, *d'Orb.*
Hippurites lyratus, *Co.*
Trigonia Syriaca.
Isocardia crenulata.
Cardium biseriatum.
        crebriechinatum.
Tellina Syriaca.
Cytherea Syriaca.
Nucula abrupta.
        myiformis.
        (?)
Opis obrutus.
Inoceramus Syriacus.
Chenopus ——
Natica orientalis.

The warty granules on the Holasters of 'Aleih are sometimes very beautifully preserved, but are much more frequently effaced. In other localities, this obliteration is still more common, though the specimens are in general less compressed.

West of Khân el-Meshra'ah, the limestone north of the ravine is carved into upright buttresses and columns, so that the layer-lines are less conspicuous at a distance than the vertical flutings thus produced, giving the cliff the appearance of basaltic prisms standing on stratified rocks as observed at many points down the valley of the Dâmûr and Awaly. The fossils are less abundant here, and nearer to Khân Kehâleh the limestone shows by ferruginous stains and the yellow-red color of the beaten surface that the arenaceous beds are about to reappear. In fact the crags and ravines around Khân Kehâleh remind one of the sandstone precipices of 'Ain ez-Zehalteh presenting the same singular variety of colors, shapes, dips and terminations. Of the dips were observed, one S., one S. 40° W., one W. and one N. N. E. at no great distance from each other. At this locality a coarse limestone covers the sandstone, and has a less irregular or at least a less precipitate dip, and a strike tending gradually to a permanent N. N. E. direction. These beds are evidently among the most recent of those found at the elevation of Khân Kehâleh, and, if not the last deposited, are the last of those which have been permitted to survive the ravages of the disintegrating and denudating forces.

North or rather east of Khân Kehâleh in the neighborhood of 'Areiyeh, shells of the Trigonia Syriaca are found imperfectly retained on the casts, and numerous Terebratulæ thickly compacted in a coarse brick-red limestone which I did not fall in with elsewhere.

Near the surfaces of junction the sandstone is somewhat altered, and acquires a lateritious appearance with a large accession of iron, alumina and lime. The calcareous rocks are still more changed. The four varieties observed between Khân Hussein and Khân Meshra'ah reappear with some modifications, and in addition to these, two other beds are met with, one remarkable for a cellular texture extending several inches beneath the weathered surface, and the other an ochrey tufa with calcitic crystals scattered through a mass formed from compacted coralline sands.

At Khân Jemhûr the sandstones run out, and a shell limestone takes its place with various dips between 15° and 30° west. The Bhamdûn casts are again found in great abundance, but more frequently still imbedded in the rock than detached from it, as at the localities already mentioned. The casts are almost as various as near Bhamdûn. As in the best preservation I may mention *Chenopus induratus*, *Turritella magnicostata*, *Isocardia crenulata*, with several *Cardia*, *Panopaeae*, *Mactrae* and *Tellinae*. The rock which holds these in connection is a very coarse aggregate, and the casts and fossils are easily washed out from their adhesions. The dips are again various. One of about 10° E. is not unfrequent, followed soon by a more prevailing western inclination.

Near the Birkeh west of Khân Jemhûr, the limestone is more than usually chalky, with a dip 60° W. N. W. Beyond this the sandstone is in situ and in the hollows and ravines, rolled pebbles of sandstone and limestone in nearly equal abundance. Nearer Beirût occurs a bed of imperfectly consolidated sand, much resembling a firmly compacted rock. A chalky limestone succeeds with flint nodules and flinty seams and plates, and the series then terminates in the beds already described as characteristic of the vicinity of Beirût.

## CHAPTER III.

### *Route from Jisr Bŭrghŭz through the Merj 'Ayûn to Lake Phiala.*

*The Merj 'Ayûn.—Nummulitic limestone of el-Judeideh.—View of the 'Ard el-Hûleh.—Green-stone of Tell el-Heiyeh.—Basaltic ravines.—Jisr el-Ghŭjar.—Basalt and Limestone.—Basalt of Bâniâs.—Granite columns in a bridge in Wâdy el-Kîd.—Source of the Nahr Bâniâs (the Upper Jordan.)—Dolerite of Wâdy Kenyeh.—Limestones east of Bâniâs.—Limestones of Jubâta.—Trap-fragments.—Birket er-Râm (ancient Lake Phiala.)—Aulickite.—Paludina Phialensis.*

South of Jisr Bŭrghŭz, as soon as the traveller has gained the moderate elevation beyond the bridge, a fine rolling country is brought into view, the Merj 'Ayûn. The surface is level for Palestine, and the soil susceptible of high cultivation. Eminences of no great height separated by wide valleys and occasional plains diversify the scene. Between the hills on the west of the road a remarkable opening shows the village of Debîn, half hidden from the inhabitants of the open tract, and on the east a broken limestone ridge covered by an arable soil cuts off the view of Sûq el-Khân and Hâsbeiya. The loam of the cultivated land acquires, as we advance along the Merj, a browner and mellower look, and the influence of ingredients derived from the decomposition or detrition of volcanic rocks may be readily perceived. No trap exists to my knowledge nearer than el-Ghŭjar, not far from the southern extremity of the Merj, but I make no doubt from general indications afforded by a comparison of the beds of the Nahr el-Kharâb and the Nahr Hâsbeiya, that rocks of igneous origin will be found in various localities along the knolls and ledges which separate the Merj 'Ayûn from the Wâdy et-Teim.

At el-Judeideh, about five miles distance from Jisr Bŭrghŭz, a limestone is exposed which is much harder and heavier than the Mukhtârah stone. The color is a light brown, enlivened in the fresh fracture by a profusion of dark bluish-brown specks, which are the irregular sections of minute Nummulites or Orbiculites, varying from the hundredth to the tenth of an inch in diameter, with now and then a few much larger still.

South of el-Judeideh, the plain expands and admits within its limits several remarkable *tells*, or high broad mounds, two of which are conspicuous for their comparatively level tops, and one in particular makes it difficult to doubt that it owed its regular geometric figure to denudations of an ancient plateau that had once filled this valley to the height of the table surface of these hills.

The Jura limestone continues as the foundation rock with cretaceous interruptions throughout the whole line of wall on both sides of the dry Wâdy leading to Nahr el-Kharâb, and in this respect no material change was found at Kufeir Kely, el-Kheiyâm, el-Mutŭlleh, or Ibl el-Qamh.

About a mile south of the fountain 'Ain Berdy, the tall cliffs west of the Litâny seem to attain their greatest height, and nearly west-northwest from this position, seen high over all intervening hills, the old ruin Qŭl'at esh-Shŭqîf towers far above a wild waste of rocky cliffs and dark woodland, the northern outskirt of the Belâd Beshârah. The ravine which runs here through the middle of the plain is cut down 80 or 100 feet below its level, and a rapid stream flows along its stony bed, a tributary from the Merj 'Ayûn to the Jordan. The name given to this torrent by my guide was Neba' el-Ghŭrâr.

Between el-Mutŭlleh and Ibl el-Qamh the prospect opens southwardly towards the Ard el-Hûleh described in the book of Judges as "a spacious country, a land exceeding rich and fruitful, a place where there is no want of anything that groweth on the earth." This still fertile, but now uncultivated tract, once occupied by a people "quiet and secure, very rich, and living separated at a distance from Sidon and all men, without any fear, and with no man at all to oppose them," is now abandoned to the wandering bands of the Ghăwârineh, and at the time I passed through it, their black tents were pitched in the plain, and their buffalo herds luxuriating in its marshes. The northern portion of the Ard el-Hûleh is unequally divided by a long tongue of land, Tell el-Heiyeh, consisting principally of a grey trap closely resembling the lighter varieties of the Tŭbarîya rock. This grey green-stone is a continuation of the ridge of mixed limestone and trap, which bounds the Hâsbeiya on the west. On the southeast side of this rocky spur, about a mile from its extremity, a stream 15 feet broad flows through a narrow belt of oleanders, reeds and willows, and cuts its way deep into the basaltic platform beneath. Twelve minutes brought us to another stream less wide than the former, and not long after the path winds between one of the re-entering off-sets of the Hâsbeiya and a rough ledge of Plutonic rocks. There are two very distinct colors alternating apparently in grey-black and brick-red embankments like the trappean deposits at Delâtah. The road then continues northeast, crossing sometimes fields of wheat and barley, growing in a rich soil, gained from the detritus of the ancient lavas, whenever a sufficient space between the rock and the stream permits such an accumulation. Several other basaltic ravines are crossed, and a more northwardly course then brings the traveller to the Jisr el-Ghŭjar, a bridge across the Hâsbeiya, of three pointed arches in tolerable preservation. The disintegrated dolerite supplies the bank of the river with the means of sustaining a rich vegetation of *dilb*, *qassab*, *sifsâf*, and *difleh*. The east side of the Hâsbeiya is a stony tract of broken and weatherworn blocks of trap, but the limestone may be seen from this point overhanging the ravine about four miles towards the south. A fine view is open down the Ghôr as far as beyond Lake Merom, where it is closed by the apparent interlocking of the eastern and western promontories just north of the Jisr Benât Yakôb.

Ten minutes after leaving the Jisr el-Ghŭjar another stream is crossed, and in nine minutes more another, the Difleh,* lined with a profusion of oleanders. From this point the rich vegetation around Bâniâs appears to great advantage, and a good view is afforded in the direction of 'Ain Fît and Za'ûra across the two branches which unite to form the first or northern division of the Jordan of the Bible. Another ten minutes walk brings the traveller from the Wâdy Difleh to a brook crossing a bed of basalt, and four minutes still further east is Moyet el-Ledân, bursting in all the magnitude of a wide and full grown stream from beneath the adjacent rocks. This noble fountain fills a natural basin cut out of a basaltic plateau, Tell el-Qâdy, near the junction of the igneous and sedimentary beds. The basalt ceases suddenly and is followed by limestone and limestone pebbles, much rounded at the various places which the spring has occupied in succession. I saw no evidence of the former existence of a crater. Crossing a plain of yellow heather and leaving on both sides many *mell*-trees, with their stout and stump like trunks, two mill streams are passed in quick succession, with rounded pebbles brought down from a Wâdy on the north. We then approach a limestone cliff covered with wheat-fields and an unusual number of trees. A fifth water-course is now passed, and the road goes over a smooth and hard limestone, quite yellow

*This may have been the Difneh, or the two streams may be one.

where much beaten. Twenty-two minutes from this last brook a sixth was met with occupying the whole breadth of the road and running some distance with it. The vegetation is various and thrifty, and fine trees continue on both sides of the path a quarter of an hour longer, until the camping ground just west of Bâniâs is reached, making the distance from Jisr el-Ghŭjar to the village, a little less than two hours of a slow walking gait.

At Bâniâs (Caesarea Philippi) the igneous rocks again present themselves on both sides of the Wâdy el-Kîd, and blocks of basalt and also of limestone are found among the ruins. In the Saracenic structure at the end of the bridge, broken granite columns are laid horizontally in the piers, projecting like pieces of ordnance from the face of the wall. As no granite is found *in situ* in Palestine, these columns must have been brought from a great distance, probably at the time of the erection of Herod's temple in honor of the visit of Augustus.

The Nahr Bâniâs, like the Nahr el-Ledân issues from beneath the limestone, where it is joined by basaltic rocks. It emerges not out of the cave Moghârat er-Râs en-Neba' or Moghârah Bâniâs, but out of the strong slope in front of it, and twenty feet or more below the base of the excavation in the low cliff. I was assured that the stream might be traced from the village to Shib'a, or Sheb'a, a point six hours higher up the southern declivity of the Hermon. Of the eight ruined towers, which once defended the town, time allowed me only to visit the Burj el-Atlâs and the ravine near which it lies. The trap is easily followed on both sides of the torrent-bed, and is more varied in its aspect than at Tell el-Qâdy. Half an hour east of the town, the limestone reappears. The Wâdy 'Ain Kenyeh is on the right on ascending towards the castle Qŭl'ah Bâniâs. The direction is W. S. W., near the town, and its banks, where exposed, show layers or coulées of ancient lava and sections of dolerite in mass. Trees are numerous here, particularly the *sinjân*, the *dilb* and the *mell.* About two miles east of Bâniâs the limestone comes into view, and presents itself in three different phases. The main deposit is the light blue or purplish variety, without fossils. Then follows in order upwards a porphyroid limestone with an intermixture of dark red and purplish spots, and this is crowned by beds of a coarse ochre-yellow calc with stratified intervals of denser and looser texture and occasional red stains traceable to oxides of iron carried into the rock by infiltration. From the heights above the castle a large pond, the Birkeh Bâniâs, can be seen not far south of the town. Both here and on the level with the castle the limestone is darker in the fresh fracture than externally, and in the smaller ravines trap blocks and calcareous shales show the contiguity of the two rocks.

After an hour and three-quarters of slow ascent, near a fine sinjân grove, a little above the level of the top of the castle es-Subeibeh, the porphyroid limestones are intersected by a dry torrent-bed, and are followed not long after by trap in spheroidal aggregates partially decomposed. The rocks below are stained of a sulphur-yellow, and variegated marls in powders of different degrees of fineness appear on each side of the beaten track. Some of the fields here are enclosed by walls, and the stones of which they are made, are calcareous, with mixed colors, generally darker within than without.

At Jubâta after ten miles slow riding from Bâniâs, rugged cliffs of variegated limestone with porphyritic colors throw the road off in a southerly direction. The level spots gained among the rocks give nourishment to a multitude of mulberry trees. From here, Qŭl'ah Bâniâs bears W. S. W. distant about three miles. East of this a broad and very deep ravine or rather valley bounds the pathway on the south. The prospect southwestwardly is magnificent. Mount Thabor is visible S. 30° W., forty miles distant over the western edge of the sea of Galilee and the hills of Nazareth are seen beyond the plain of Bŭttauf, which itself is hidden by the mountains east of Safed. The limestone near Jubâta is very much eaten at the weathered surface, and the erosions leave discoidal and elongated partitions standing more or less vertically on the faces and edges of the rock. I observed a dip of S. 20° with strongly marked stratification. The valley was called Wâdy Rŭbbeh or Rŭba' by my guide. Scattered fragments of trap begin to appear about a mile and a half N. by W. from Birket er-Râm (Lake Phiala.) North of this lake is a fine meadow, the Merj es-Sa'ar nearly two miles long. Near the middle of it is a Sheikh's tomb with a noble willow, (?) *mistaiyeh*, shading it. The looser stones in the alluvion are of trap. A considerable stream crosses southwestwardly and as I understood, passed into the Hûleh south of Bâniâs. Another and smaller stream flows into the lake. What seemed the summit of Hermon bore N. 23° W. from the centre of the Birkeh. This remarkable lake occupies the bottom of a crater rather less than two miles in circumference, extinct and gradually filling up. The brim of the basin is 60 or 70 feet above the water, and the walls are of ancient lava, except at one point on the east side where the porphyry-colored limestone protrudes. The shores of the lake and the sides of the crater are covered everywhere with glistening crystals resembling a very fine hornblende of a beautiful pitch-black color with quite a high vitreous lustre. The angles of the rhomb are 136° and 44°. Powder grey-white, inclining to green. The fracture is conchoidal and very smooth. Specific gravity 3.24. Hardness 6.07. This mineral when crushed breaks up into many acicular spiculae not attracted by the magnet. The analysis gave

| | |
|---|---|
| Silica, | 49.50 |
| Peroxide of Iron, | 22.25 |
| Alumina, | 13.75 |
| Lime, | 11.40 |
| Magnesia, | 3.75 |
| | 100.65 S. |

It differs both in its angles and chemical composition from crystallised hornblende, and as a slight compliment to one of the officers of the Expedition, I would propose for it the name of *Aulickite.*

The lava in connection with which this mineral occurs, is quite unlike the dolerite of Tŭbarîya; it is of a dark-brown color and subscoriaceous fracture, filled with Olivine and minute crystals of Aulickite. The large crystals were found loose, and had probably been long detached from their gangues.

A portion of the lava selected where the small crystals appeared to constitute nearly the entire mass, was ascertained by a parallel analysis conducted by Mr. Mucklé, to be made up as follows:

| | |
|---|---|
| Silica, | 40.00 |
| Peroxide of Iron, | 22.30 |
| Alumina, | 12.85 |
| Lime, | 10.065 |
| Magnesia, | 11.205 |
| Potash, | 1.06 |
| Soda, | 2.59 |
| Oxide of Manganese, (trace.) | 100.07 M. |

Differing from the analysis of the clean crystal principally in the larger quantity of Magnesia.

The water of the lake is not deep, and is covered plentifully with the broad leaves of aquatic plants, in the midst of which the *butt*, or Syrian drake appears to enjoy himself. Just within the margin I observed great numbers of a small thin-shelled ***Paludina***, which Mr. Conrad has described as ***Paludina Phialensis.***

After crossing the Merj towards the north, and leaving on the east a Wâdy, and in the southeast Tell or Jebel es-Sa'ar, the trap-fragments cease and the variegated limestone reappears, still with a dip of 20° south. A tract covered with *sinjân*-trees then follows, and left of this is a stratified limestone with an extraordinary number of thin layers dipping, more or less, 40° south. The calcareous rocks now continue to the summit of the Hermon. They are distinctly developed in the cliffs above Mejdel, (where a compact lithographic stone, not free from fossils, crops out,) and also in a Wâdy east of it, where the limestone dips 10° south. At one point, S. E. of Mejdel, trap is found with a disposition to run into ellipsoidal masses. After a succession of ravines, green valleys and arid rocks, the road ascends and descends again into a Wâdy running west, and then striking off north-northeastwardly, emerges upon the southeastern margin of the secluded Merj Hamŭnn, an oval-shaped meadow shut in by a rocky rampart high up on the southern slope of the Hermon. The weather proved so cold here on the night of the 6th of June, that the temperature fell to freezing point even under the shelter of the tent.

Passing out of the Merj by the Wâdy el-'Asal, running west from the southern extremity of the plain, a fine view is soon presented of the Mediterranean. The limestone of the Wâdy is blue in the fresh fracture and of a dingy light yellow, or light blue externally, with much calcspar in seams and crusts. A subordinate bed occurs of a very dark limestone slightly bituminous, much intersected by spathic luminations. I could find no fossils and no very definite stratification. The Wâdy el-'Asal gives off the Wâdy Barŭftah, into which the road descends and goes up immediately S. S. W., into a calcareous tract with marly incrustations and patches of crimson moss, very profusely distributed. For about half an hour after this the road is very rough and ledges frequently occur, in which a limestone is found remarkable for its deeply sculptured indentations. I observed in several places such a relation of the stratification and the vertical fissures as the annexed figure represents.

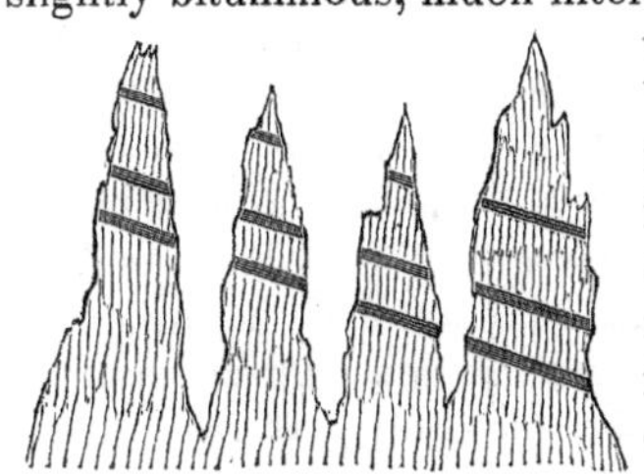

About two hours from Merj Hamŭnn in a direction varying between north-northwest and finally northeast, the road ceases to ascend, and more level spots are met with, covered with rich vegetation. Several descriptions of fruit trees are met with, among them the Injâs,* or pear. Fine patches of grass and wheat are found between the rocks. These are of limestone and furrowed vertically into pinnacles and needles. A Merj descending gently to the N. N. E. and elongated in that direction gives off here a Wâdy running northwardly. This is Wâdy 'Ain el-Felastîn, and a branch of Wâdy Shib'a. In this Wâdy is a Birkeh of bad water, and half a mile further a fountain, from which the valley gets its name, yielding water of very good quality. The limestone near 'Ain el-Felastîn is more recent than the calcareous beds south of it; it has a yellow color and characteristic texture. The entrance of Wâdy el-Felastîn into Wâdy Shib'a is at an obtuse angle on the up-hill side. Just

*Sometimes called Nejâs, and by some tribes Ijâs.

opposite the junction, the strata dip north and east with other intermediate azimuths. An hour from this brings the traveller to the village and fountains of Shib'a, of which there are several, and on the east side particularly a very large one issuing from the base of a high rock. The village may contain fifty houses, and has a very pleasing appearance from the number of fine trees about it, principally walnut, poplar, willow and mulberry. The stream turns several mills, and then descends the hill in a southwardly and southwestwardly direction. This water is represented on the best maps as falling into the Hâsbeîya; it must therefore be different from the Shib'a, or Sheb'a, to which the people of Bâniâs refer as the origin of their river, the upper branch of the Scriptural Jordan.—We procured here a good supply of bread, *dibs* and cheese, and the villagers appeared to be no way in want of the necessaries of life. This valley is entered on the east by Wâdy 'Ain el-Jôz, and the water comes mainly from that side. Ascending the western valley, Wâdy Shib'a, the limestone has the varied colors already observed, and is distinguished by a disposition to separate into masses, divided by planes nearly horizontal, but not parallel to the planes of stratification. Besides these are innumerable fissures more or less approaching the vertical direction, many of them filled with calcspar. A mile beyond this, fragments of trap with little felspar and much olivine are found strewn along the valley, and may be traced northwardly until beyond the summit level, when the Wâdy begins to descend towards Râsheiya. The origin of these I found afterwards at Tell Jehennem further north. Fragments of this rock and bits of a greenish limestone are found here, wrapped up in tufaceous and spathic incrustations. The great mass of Mt. Hermon is on the east of this depression, while a lower outlier occupies the west.

The snow lay (June 7th,) in broad patches on the western flank of the Hermon, nearly as low down as the bottom of the valley. Not far north of this spot, the Wâdy widens and is occupied by a long narrow mound, Tell Jehennem, consisting entirely of basalt. The long axis takes the direction of the valley N. N. E. and S. S. W., the north end somewhat elevated above the other. No crater is to be found, and the Tell lies insulated in the Wâdy, which receives on the east side of the mound the name of Wâdy Jehennem. There are two fountains in this valley, 'Ain Jehennem and 'Ain esh-Shôk. The water was barely drinkable, being constantly disturbed by numerous flocks of sheep and goats. West of Tell Jehennem the Wâdy is less broad, though this side more than the other is regarded as Wâdy Shib'a. On the western side of the west Wâdy, a still and rough ascent climbs up a mass of red marbled limestone, from the summit of which a fine platform or terrace on the side of Hermon may be discerned across the valley covered with good pasture and often crowded with vast numbers of sheep and goats driven up daily from Shib'a. From the same point of view the summit, as it seemed, of Mount Hermon bore E. 15° S.

The upper surface of this outlier of the Hermon is comparatively level, though very much broken up by unequal denudation and the irregular sculpture of the body of the rock. Not far west of the brow and south of the track which we struck across the summit, a remarkable effect of the long continued erosion of the limestone mass would greatly attract the attention of any traveller crossing the rocky barrier at this particular point. Numerous natural pillars of a tolerably regular form, more or less rounded and vertical, but continuous with the inclined platform on which they stand, occupying places apparently given by design. They form in this way a conclave of statue-like figures, some seeming to assume a standing and some a sitting posture. On going near, the illusion of course vanishes, and we find the result due to the unequal action of the weathering process, a series of narrow vertical ledges having first been excavated by the erosive agents which have afterwards continued their work until in the lapse of ages the limestone mass has been carved out in very high relief so as to present the appearance of an irregular platform studded with a singular variety of obelisks and pinnacles. These were found sometimes still continuous or parcelled out as it were by shallow flutings, which by gradual deepening have met from opposite sides and then by slow degrees have been worn away into wider and wider intervals until the detached pillars look as if they had never belonged to one solid and undivided block. The remarkable formation south of Wâdy Mahras and near Khashm Usdom on the western shore of the Dead Sea may be cited as similar results of the irregular erosion of what was once an extended and uninterrupted platform; in the former case, of a stratified, in the latter of an unstratified deposit. Nearly a mile west of this, about half way across the rough level of this summit area, the same process of natural sculpture has brought the upper surface of the rock into the appearance of a confused mass of architectural ruins, and on the western cliff, from which the long descent to the Hâsbeiya and the Wâdy et-Teim begins, a broad range filled with the fallen fragments of countless broken natural obelisks skirts the brow of the precipice for miles.

The dip of the limestone varies from N. to N. W. in crossing the nearly level summit of this eminence. The rock is everywhere calcareous in place, but splinters of trap are found scattered in all directions, though not plentifully, over the surface. These fragments are evidently not derived from the basaltic mound in the valley on the east, for, at present at least, the upper surface of the limestone mass is several hundred yards above the upper surface of the mound.

The view from this point of the Anti-Libanus (for so we may regard it) is truly magnificent. The more western fork of this noble wall forms the eastern side of the Leontes, and lies far below the altitude of Mount Hermon or even of its less towering attendants. Between these two branches we have the Wâdy et-Teim and its tributary valleys, into which at various points the intruding sandstones, conglomerates and traps of a long posterior age have been deposited as in vast and already excavated basins. From the brow of the precipice to the village of Hâsbeiya three hours were found barely sufficient, in a line nearly always descending. The sandstone continues for an hour and more, sometimes excessively carved out and cut up, sometimes in less angular forms with bits of mountain meadow, green valleys and fertile fields half hidden between the wild and almost savage tracts of black and barren rock.

A little below this, promontories, like enormous moraines, miles in width, overlooking the valley on three sides, shoot out from the main calcareous mass, and are found to consist of sandstone more or less consolidated* and in various stages of metamorphic change.

The number and variety of forms in which these arenaceous conglomerates present themselves are really surprising. The prevailing ones are:

No. 1. A very coarse grey-yellow grit, made up of a minute quartz gravel, partly angular and partly rounded.

* On one of these near its extremity, I passed the ruins of an ancient edifice; a number of very large hewn stones lay scattered around and among these, what seemed a door post with a well cut rabate for the door. There is also near this a room regularly excavated in the hill side, and two remarkable turret-like rocks near the road, one with seven steps nicely cut near the summit, the other with similar marks of the sculptor's tool. Five minutes distant is an oblong reservoir, 80 feet by 40. This is called Birket el-Foqâny, or the upper pool.

No. 2. An ash-purple fine grained siliceous iron-stone of much greater coherence than No. 1. This variety promised results justifying an analysis and showed the following ingredients:

I. Soluble in hydrochloric acid, 41 per cent. of the whole, consisting of

| | |
|---|---|
| Peroxide of Iron, | 87.8 |
| Alumina, | 7.3 |
| Carbonate of Lime, | 4.8 |
| | 99.9 S. |

II. Insoluble in hydrochloric acid, 58 per cent. of the whole, a combination of

| | |
|---|---|
| Silica, | 83.3 |
| Alumina, | 15.2 |
| | 98.5 S. |

Taken entire, the proportions are

| | |
|---|---|
| Silica, | 49.0 |
| Alumina, | 11.9 |
| Peroxide of Iron, | 36.0 |
| Carbonate of Lime, | 2.0 |
| | 98.9 S. |

No. 3. A coarse sandstone, yellow with red patches, the grains small and generally angular.

No. 4. A sandstone intermediate in fineness between 2 and 3, but differing from both in having layers of color not parallel to the stratification.

No. 5. A yellow ochry sandstone of powdery structure, but mixed loosely and scatteredly with granules of quartz.

No. 6. A hard iron-grey sandstone, difficult to break, bearing some resemblance to dioritic rocks, but entirely destitute of felspar; the quartz grains distinctly visible under the microscope.

The stratification is sometimes persistent, sometimes feathered and irregularly divergent as often seen in the vertical sections of alluvial or river-side embankments. The dip is almost always towards the west. These peculiarities may be best seen at the village Hâret el-Harf.* At Shuweiya something of the same kind is observable. Here on the north side of the sandy promontory, the limestone may be seen cropping out under the sandstone. From this place, Kufeir Hamâm was pointed out far in the south. Other and lower moraine-like promontories succeed, always of sandstone, but sometimes immense boulders of limestone are found lodged on these sandy embankments with no other obvious origin than the former existence of overhanging calcareous rocks, long since removed by decay, or cut off by extensive excavations.

Descending still towards Hâsbeiya, the path strikes across another moraine-terrace, on which a round reservoir, Birket el-Tahtâny, is constructed in the usual way for the reception of the water. This is near the village 'Ain Qŭniyeh. The stone fences become numerous and are sometimes built entirely of sandstone, sometimes all of limestone, but more fre-

*There is a capacious reservoir of water here of regular form and kept in very good order, (Birket Hâret el-Harf.)

quently of these materials mixed. Where the sandstone forms the platform, the scattered rocks are often calcareous; where the area is limestone, huge boulders of a ferruginous sandy grit take the place of the calcareous rocks. Still nearer Hâsbeiya colored marls and sandy patches are found along the path, and sandstone begins again to prevail. In the ravines east of the town, the manner in which the layers of sandy marl and marly sand conform to the subjacent limestone, may be seen to great advantage. Yet nearer, the ferruginous sandstone, in well-defined layers with a dip of 30° west, shows itself at several points, and might be studied with advantage in reference to the formations lower down as well as to those west of Hâsbeiya and nearer the bottom of the valley.

The town of Hâsbeiya is intersected by several ravines. North of these a stratified limestone is seen dipping west by north. From a quarry near this, slabs are obtained which are much used for roofing and other purposes. The principal ravine descends two or three miles in a direction somewhat south of west, and meets another from the north, which comes down the main Wâdy et-Teim. Both of these were well filled with water (June 8, 1848) the former especially, which was in some places 40 feet wide. Between Hâsbeiya and the junction of these streams, the limestone dips vary from 30° to 70° and even 80° N. W. The steeper strata were intermixed with siliceous and slaty beds and seem to have owed their plunging positions to the inclinations of the surface on which they were precipitated. Yet the cause may after all be the unequal action of the subterraneous uplifting forces. Fragments of weather-worn trap lay thinly strewn along the road. The torrent-beds are fringed with oleanders, willows, poplars and olive trees, and a number of mills and mill-races give some animation to the scene.

The bitumen pits, Bîyâr* el-Hummar, lie in a formation of bituminous limestone, interstratified with a limestone containing but very little of organic matter. An average specimen of the former gave on analysis, in 100 parts,

| | |
|---|---|
| Carbonate of Lime, . . . . . . . . . . . . . . . . . . . | 77.36 |
| Bituminous matter, . . . . . . . . . . . . . . . . . | 10.00 |
| Insoluble matter, . . . . . . . . . . . . . . . . . . | 6.00 |
| Alumina and Oxide of Iron, . . . . . . . . . . . . . | 5.60 |
| Carbonate of Magnesia, . . . . . . . . . . . . . . . | .88 |
| | 99.84 M. |

The other limestone was chalky with small thin-shelled *Ostraeae*, probably *Ostraea Scapha.* It contained many flinty seams. Of these some were remarkable for the abrupt discontinuance of the coloring matter without any break of molecular or chemical continuity. On analysis, these gave for the white portion distant from the junction:

| | |
|---|---|
| Silica, . . . . . . . . . . . . . . . . . . . . . . | 78.60 |
| Iron and Alumina, . . . . . . . . . . . . . . . . . . | 1.20 |
| Carbonate of Lime, . . . . . . . . . . . . . . . . . . | 18.60 |
| | 98.40 S. |

For the dark portion, also distant from the junction:

| | |
|---|---|
| Silica, . . . . . . . . . . . . . . . . . . . . . . | 75.00 |
| Iron and Alumina, . . . . . . . . . . . . . . . . . . | 17.50 |
| Carbonate of Lime, . . . . . . . . . . . . . . . . . . | 5.50 |
| | 98.00 S. |

*In literal Arabic Bi-âr, with the *Yé Hamzeh.*

Between the points selected, and between the limits of the corresponding proportionate compositions, the lime and iron varied by insensible gradation, the silica undergoing but little change. In a case somewhat similar however, the lime and silica showed this gradual penetration, the iron being there the invariable element.*

The bitumen itself is found by sinking vertical shafts through a mass of bituminous earth, mixed with small fragments of the pure material. In some of the pits the best quality is reached at the depth of 90 *drâ's*. Four hundred *qantars* have been taken out of a single pit. The shafts are disposed in a line running east and west.

This bitumen bears an exact resemblance to some species which are found on the Dead Sea shore, aud one might almost be tempted to refer these specimens to the Hâsbeiya pits. But as the material is specifically heavier than fresh water, it would never be able to pass beyond Lake Tiberias, and would probably be arrested at Lake Merom. The large masses of bitumen sometimes found floating on the Dead Sea have undoubtedly a different origin, and it is not unlikely that the bituminous limestone of Neby Mûsa and Nŭqb Qŭneitĕrah covers extensive mines of this material which in some of their outcrops may be exposed to the abrading action of the sea. The Dead Sea bitumen frequently exhibits in great perfection its vegetable origin, and the woody fibre and sap vessels are sometimes distinctly discernible, as much so as in many lignites. The Hâsbeiya asphalt is more thoroughly metamorphosed, and the traces of the woody structure are seldom to be seen. It is very little soluble in alcohol, more completely in ether, and almost entirely in oil of turpentine. The color is a jet black, and the fracture conchoidal and fimbriated, with a lustre remarkably brilliant. It softens in water at about 75°, and fuses at 250° F., burning with a yellow color and leaving a grey brittle cinder not reducible to a pure ash even in the oxydising flame of the blow-pipe.

There were eight or ten workmen (Kurds and Arabs) engaged at the pits, (June 8, 1848;) but according to the statements of the overseer the proceeds hardly paid the toil.

To return to Wâdy Jehennem. From the fountain of that name to 'Ain esh-Shôk, the valley ascends between Tell Jehennem and Jebel esh-Sheikh in a northeasterly direction. About a mile beyond, the crown of the pass is reached, and northwardly a great extent of land is visible between N. 74° W. and N. 36° E. From this point the Wâdy descends towards Râsheiya.

Continuing the ascent of Mount Hermon from the summit of this pass, a fountain, 'Ain ez-Zibîb is soon reached, and N. E. from this, twenty minutes higher, snow was found in large patches on the mountain-side, (June 9th.) At this point the limestone beds dip N. W. and the same inclination continues for several miles along the western flank. Continuing the ascent northeastwardly, the path crosses a fossiliferous limestone, and the loose fragments not unfrequently present traces of a ***Pecten***, a ***Terebratula***, a ***Nucula*** and an ***Astarte***. Among these the ***Terebratula Syriaca***, Pl. xxi, fig. 123, was found in a state sufficiently

* It would be better for the interest of geology, if the *invariability* of the chemical constitution of rocks were less readily assumed, (even for short intervals) as a postulate, whether relatively to the *era* or the *situs;* and a more methodical examination properly instituted into the laws and phases both of primitive distribution and post-formative diffusion, so that the weight of each element of composition may appear as far as possible as function both of *place* and of *time*. The influence of the latter arbitrary will always remain excessively difficult to determine by direct admeasurement in consequence of the extraordinary slowness of the corpuscular displacements, but indirect methods are at hand; and at all events the effect of *place* upon the scale of composition is fairly within the reach of the geologist if he will but accept, as he ought, the aid of chemistry in the prosecution of his tasks.

preserved to be described by Mr. Conrad, (see his report.) A climbing walk of four hours brought us to a summit, where interesting remains, probably of Roman time, now known as the Qasr esh-Shibîb, were still found in tolerable preservation. From this point or near it, there is a noble prospect northwestwardly over the whole Libanine range, eastwardly over Haurân, (Damascus bearing N. 84° E., Kelb Haurân S. 50° E.,) and southwardly over the Sea of Galilee, as far as the heights of el-Hâritheh and el-Beitâny.*

The ravines of the western slope of Mt. Hermon are scarcely to be numbered, but do not cut far into the body of the mountain. The limestone in these ravines contain frequent nests or incrustations of a coarse calcspar, imperfectly transparent with colors varying between brown, yellow and green, and exhibiting both the parallel and divergent arrangement of the principal clusters of crystals. From an unusually large mass of Arragonite in a lateral gully leading into one of these ravines, I selected a bit which was found to consist of

| | |
|---|---|
| Carbonate of Lime, . . . . . . . . . . . . . . . . . . . | 99.62 |
| Carbonate of Strontia, . . . . . . . . . . . . . . . . . | .24 |
| Iron and Alumina, . . . . . . . . . . . . . . . . . . . | .15 |
| Water, . . . . . . . . . . . . . . . . . . . . . . . | .40 |
| | 100.41 M. |

The continuation of Wâdy Jehennem forms a Wâdy or system of Wâdys, carrying scanty tributaries after the melting of the snow northwardly toward Râsheiya; but before these supplies reach that village, the greater portion disappears by evaporation or absorption.

In this descent to Râsheiya the traveller keeps on the left hand (separated from him by an irregular ridge pierced by lateral valleys) Mimîs, el-Kufeir, es-Sefîneh, Jubb Milkeh, 'Ain 'Ata, 'Ain Hersha and Tannûra. The northernmost of the main valleys is Wâdy es-Sekâyin. In this, about half an hour south of Râsheiya, the ravine is unusually straight, the course continuing steadily N. E. for some time. Steep cliffs of ragged limestone rise up on each side of the narrow gorge, showing an arrangement of conforming strata varying in dip, composition and dimensions, but presenting all appearance of having once been continued across the present excavation.

At Dahr el-Ahmar, about an hour north of Râsheiya, the limestone is found in connection with sandstone, and trap is also occasionally met with. Where the trap lies upon limestone, the layers contiguous to the igneous rocks show a gradual change in color and consistence, which may be partly due to heat, but is far more probably the slow result of molecular displacement brought about either in the moist way by infiltration or in the dry by metamorphic substitution.

Crossing the ravines, but sometimes independent of these, conglomerates of round pebbles indicate the former presence of running water, and the entire subsequent cessation of this agency, in both cases long after the sandstone had been carved into something like its actual relief. In the arenaceous rocks themselves there is a remarkable variety of color and texture. Sometimes the coloring matter has only affected the surface, sometimes it has penetrated the mass to a very great extent; sometimes the rock is quite compact and homogeneous as if a limestone had been silicified; in other places the distinct granular structure shows that the stone is a mere aggregate of well cemented sand.

*From Bîyâr el-Hummar the following bearings were taken: Sûq el-Khân S. 23° W.; Hâsbeiya S. 76° E.; the (perspectively) highest point of Jebel Sheikh S. 88° E.; a large grove was visible S. 10° W., and the termination of the valley southwardly bore S. 22° W.

In this neighborhood a very odd looking calcareous conglomerate is found, made up of bullets of a grey-black tunicated calcsinter, plentifully spread through a coarse marly gangue of a light wax-yellow color; small angular fragments of similar coated bulbs being everywhere visible in the spaces between those which remain entire. The bulbs gave on analysis:

| | |
|---|---|
| Carbonate of Lime, | 81.69 |
| Carbonate of Magnesia, | 3.66 |
| Oxide of Iron and Alumina, | 3.45 |
| Insoluble, | 9.57 |
| Bituminous matter, | .38 |
| Water, | .61 |
| | 99.36 |

One of the sandstones near Dahr el-Ahmar is strongly charged with iron. It has a dip of 10° W., with a strike N. N. E. The limestone north of the fountain strikes E. N. E., with a dip of 15°. East of this is a sandstone ledge with a parallel strike, but a dip of 40° westwardly. The outcrop of the limestone gives a horizontal measure of 500 feet between the margins, corresponding to a thickness of 321 feet, estimated perpendicularly to the planes.

In going southwardly from Dahr el-Ahmar to Hullădîyeh, I went down along the right bank of the ravine, which in this rainy season forms the upper part of the Nahr Hâsbeiya. At Bîr Zŭky and 'Ain el-Qaqubbeh* (?) the rock is still calcareous; but the limestone makes way for trap farther north, and at Hawareith both trap and limestone are found in equal abundance. Beautifully situated on a point of a low tell and looking far down the valley are the ruins of a temple apparently of Roman masonry, with some remnants of architectural embellishments, and in one part five courses of stone, each about eighteen inches thick, are still standing. From here Beit Lâhya and Khŭrbet Bahadîdy were pointed out to me, and Tanûrah beyond Wâdy Sekâyin.

From Hawareith, el-Khuladîyeh bore N. 44° W., el-Muhaidetheh N. 16° E., Dahr el-Ahmar N. 64° E., and Râsheiya S. 60° E.

The plain (Turbaz,) on the east of which Hawareith is situated, consists of trap which probably with some interruptions extends to Muhaidetheh.

Northeast from Dahr el-Ahmar is a hill which my guide called Jebel Sheikh Tŭrraj. Towards this eminence the red sandstone and variegated limestone seemed more especially to run.

In passing from Dahr el-Ahmar to Muhaidetheh† (pronounced Muhaiteh) the path crosses the limestone and sandstone in succession. The calcareous rock strikes N. E. by N. with a dip of 40°. The structure is sometimes slaty and tufaceous with a profusion of small spathic crystals intimately pervading the whole mass.

From 'Ain es-Sŭsâyin, where there are many vineyards with a limestone rock and marly soil, a straight ascent leads to an elevated tract, from which are seen Khŭrbet Rukha E. by N., and Kefr Dînis E. by S. The apparently highest point of Jebel Sheikh bore 10° east of south.

*Qu.—Quna'âby.

†From Muhaidetheh I took the following bearings: Mazŭkha N. 53° E.; Khûrbet Rukha N. 74° E.; Kefr Dînis S. 72° E.; Dahr el-Ahmar S. 24° E.; Râsheiya S. 18° E.

Near Muhaidetheh a chalky limestone presents itself, which is still better developed in the hill beyond 'Ain Sifleh. This rock contains abundant vestiges of fragments of fossilised fish, together with distinct traces of vegetable remains. It is not unlike the fish-chalk of Jûneh Bay and Hâkil, but less regularly laminated and of a more porous texture. Between 'Ain Sifleh and Jebel esh-Sheikh an eminence of volcanic origin, with a range of basaltic rocks fills up a portion of the lower valley. On the north of this, beyond 'Ain Sinneh, the ground rises and the path ascends a series of calcareous hills covered in places with broken bits of trap. Some of the rocky prominences are curiously grooved by excavations due probably to the action of rain drops, descending in lines first determined by the law of gravity and the successive shape of the exposed surface. The heights assume now a mountainous aspect, and take the name of Jebel 'Arby. The characteristic feature of pinnacled crags and turriform protuberances marks the greater part of this tract, which is intersected by a valley, Wâdy 'Arby running S. W. On the west side of this Wâdy a nummulitic limestone displays itself and extends as far as Balûl on the western slope of the Anti-Libanus, terminating in a coarse chalk. An analysis of this nummulitic limestone gave the following results:

| | |
|---|---|
| Carbonate of Lime, | 96.97 |
| Carbonate of Magnesia, | .50 |
| Iron and Alumina, | .90 |
| Insoluble, | 2.00 |
| | 100.37 S. |

Wâdy 'Arby is entered by numerous lateral ravines where the cretaceous rock as well as the nummulitic calc can be examined with advantage.

From Balûl a very extensive view is afforded down the Bŭqâ', and the villages on the eastern declivity of the Lebanon range may be easily counted from Khŭrbet Rukha to Mekseh, leaving also some hamlets in view on the western flank of the Anti-Libanus, and the distant snow-clad heights of Jebel Sunnîn rise into view beyond these a little east of north.

From Balûl a path, varying from N. by E. to N. E., leads to Lâla, behind which a noble amphitheatre of chalky hills presents in all their inconformableness the discordant strata of the outcropping rocks. The globular nodules termed Saracens' heads again make their appearance in considerable numbers.

Where the rock is last seen on descending to the alluvial floor of the valley of this part of the Leontes, a strike N. E. with a dip N. 13° may be observed. Four minutes beyond this, the stream, which on the 11th of June was here 60 feet in width, is crossed at a convenient fording place, and on the western side about half a mile from the river the limestone exhibits exactly the same strike and dip as I have already mentioned on the east.

Before reaching Kefereiya, two streams, running northwardly and then eastwardly on their way to the Litâny are crossed at the interval of a mile. One of them descends probably from Wâdy Tŭjerah, the other runs in a shallow ravine which is a branch of Wâdy Dhubbîyeh.

The ascent of the eastern flank of the Libanus from Kefereiya to 'Ain Lijjy is accomplished without toil, and traverses the same limestones as are found continuously along the middle heights of Jebel el-Bârûk. The geological features of the Libanine ranges between 'Ain Lijjy and Beirût have already been described, leaving as the next field of inquiry the highlands south of the district of Merj 'Ayûn including the hilly uplands and mountainous tracts in the northern part of Upper Galilee.

# SECTION II.

## REGION OF NORTHERN GALILEE.

---

## CHAPTER I.

### *Reconnaissance of Route from Ibel el-Qamr to Tŭbarîya.*

*Yellow limestone.—Turks-heads.—Tibnîn.—Limestone erosions.—View from Qedes, (the ancient Cades.)—Marble of Qedes.—Route from Qedes to Bijjin.—Limestone.—Eroded limestonc of Farah.—Ruins of Kefr Ber'am.—Turks-heads.—Strata near Bijjin.—Quartz balls.—Magnificent view.—Er-Râmeh.—The plain of Bŭttauf.—Meeting with Lieut. Lynch and party.—Alluvial mould and trap boulders west and east of Tur'ân. The trap of Tŭbarîya.—Limestone of Hŭmmâm, (the ancient Emmaus.)*

THIS district including the land of Nephtali is essentially calcareous, but is distinguished by a large development of igneous rocks. These latter assume a greater variety of forms and phases than the lavas of Wâdy et-Teim, where they play a very subordinate part.

If we set out from Ibel el-Qamr, we are presented shortly after crossing the stream on the west of it with a very characteristic ledge. The limestone in the north is very rough in texture, and disposed to run into vertical flutings where the weather attacks the steeper flanks. In the interior of the mass a denser structure obtains, and some portions are remarkable for their hard and compact grain. In the valley overlooked by the Qŭl'at el-Hŭnnîn, a soft yellow limestone occurs alternating with a schistose variety, which attains in some places a dip of 60 or 70°. Notwithstanding the inconformableness of these contiguous strata, there is every reason to believe that they may be both referred to the upper chalk, leaving the limestone beneath them decidedly Jurassic. There occurs from time to time associated with the yellow limestone a softer yellowish white variety in beds very nearly horizontal, some a few inches, some two feet and more in thickness. This rock yields easily to the tread of mules, and the hollows thus produced serve as characteristic marks. Corals are not unfrequent, and a few remains referable only to the chalk.

Near the point where a path turns off west to go to Bint Jubeil, (Ijbeil,) a tract begins and descends for miles, remarkable for the number of Turksheads. These quartzy nodules are stained with yellow externally, but are within of a dazzling whiteness like frozen snow. The septa converge more or less to a central axis and the form of the nodule is a very regular oblate spheroid with numerous knobs or tubers irregularly prominent from the surface. These nodules vary from the size of a cherry to the dimensions of a large human head, and I found them very frequently *in situ* fast imbedded in the rock.

In a line with Mâs and Qŭl'ah Tibnîn the limestone on the east of the former place has a very erose aspect, and this striking peculiarity continues for a mile towards the west. The rock is singularly fretted and minutely carved out in very bold relief; but the phenomena are merely superficial and nothing within would indicate that such asperities would result from exposure to ordinary atmospheric agents. Near Mâs is a yellowish-white limestone, much harder than the eastern beds. A dip west, or rather W. S. W. of about 30° occurs, which holds steadily for a distance unusual in the upper chalk of this place; but near Blîdeh on the high terrace above Qedes, and also within a quarter of an hour of Malkîyeh, ravines are found with very contorted beds, and a frequent disposition of the solid and unstratified limestone in basins excavated out of regularly stratified and long anterior deposits.

From the heights above Qedes a fine view is every now and then obtained of the Ard and Bahr el-Hûleh with the mountainous region beyond the Jordan, including the greater part of Basan as far as the probable site of Golan, a city of refuge out of the tribe of Manasses. The secondary hills and lower knolls and meadows between the mountain and the river are far from having the desert aspect that one might infer from the present depopulation of this district, but a near approach was denied me, and I was not able even to form a conjecture of the relative developments of the trap, sandstone and limestone, which in unknown proportions constitute the mass of the whole extent of Jebel Heish.

The rocks around Qedes present but little variety of aspect. There is nothing but limestone visible, and the want of fossils along with the uniformity of lithological character renders it difficult to decipher the history of the superpositions. The rock assumes in many localities a decidedly crystalline structure, and an excellent marble is found in several places, the sources probably of the materials of which the numerous and interesting ruins of ancient Cades still furnish a variety of instructive examples.

One of the best of these marbles is closely crystallized, white inclining to cream color, easy of sculpture, but retaining for ages the sharp outlines of the original relief. A beautiful Corinthian capital in fair preservation lies before the door of the easternmost temple, and shows remains of skilful chiseling on a material which has proved worthy of the work. But a formal description of the ruins found on the site of this city of refuge would hardly be in its place in this Report, and must be reserved for a more suitable occasion.

From Qedes two routes over Jebel Safed were proposed to me. One eastwardly, branching off at Mârôn, through Fârah, Râs el-Ahmar and el-Jish. The other diverging westwardly from Mârôn towards Yârôn, Kefr Ber'am, Sa'sa', through Herfîsh to Beit Jenn, or Bĭjjĭn as it is often called. The latter was selected as little known, and promising some relief from the monotonous limestones of the cliff.

At Malkîyeh, on the left of the path, the limestone breaks up into blocks, and these are sometimes still farther detached from each other by disintegrating forces, while holes and communicating channels, singular from their tortuousness, show the effects of an erosive action, now very difficult to explain. Between Malkîyeh and Mârôn a path turns off to Bint Jubeil. Near this there is a tract covered with young trees and thorny underwood, and not far beyond, a district is crossed formed of low stony hills and broad undulating valleys, with well cultivated fields of wheat, barley and *hummŭs*, wherever the surface holds out a prospect of return for the peasant's toil.

The continuity of the limestone is here broken by Wâdy Rumâsh, a valley unusually broad compared with its depth. This variable ratio of breadth and depth of excavation depends partly upon the velocity of the abrading water, and partly upon the relative destructibility of the rock. South and east of Wâdy Rumâsh, Jebel Shebâbîk en-Nimr closes the distant view with a high wall of limestone, beyond which a branch of Wâdy Mu'addimîyeh leaves the structure of the mass still more advantageously exposed to the inspection of the geologist, while 'Almeh on the north and Râs el-Ahmar on the south indicate the probable termini of the calcareous deposit.

On approaching Fârah the limestone on the east of the path shows a remarkable liability to the action of erosive agents, and the grooves and channels thus carved out assume sometimes the most fantastic shapes. I was never however, either here or elsewhere in Syria, able to trace these serpentine burrowings very deep into the substance of the rock. The very unequal wearing away must be ascribed, in part only, to a greater original hardness of the surviving features. It arises mainly from the direction which gravity gives to the descending raindrops, which by their slow and insensible etching determine at length the dimensions and proportion of each individual sinus, deepening and enlarging them all, until the surface is as curiously sculptured as a snow bank which has been irregularly wasting and dissolving under the capricious action of the elements.

Between Fârah and Yârôn a fine view is obtained of the Ard el-Khait, and the soil teems with a vegetation unusual in the hilly districts of northern Galilee. Near Yârôn on the right of our road, a sarcophagus resembling in all respects those of Qedes lay surrounded by fragments of columns and friezes of ancient workmanship, all furnishing specimens of a limestone well adapted to the various purposes of architecture. Not far from this a remarkable limestone platform, the Belât en-Nasîf (Belâtet en-Nasîf,) is intersected by the pathway. The rock is slaty and quite free from the erosions observable in the rocks farther north.

At Kefr Ber'am are to be seen two ruined temples of great interest to Jewish antiquarians, besides many scattered columns and architectural fragments, either carelessly abandoned or turned to bad account in the construction of the rudely built houses of the present day. In the principal building, four columns are still standing within the walls and some feet removed from them. Of these, two are rounded and two shaped to fill a rectangular recess. The horizontal sections of the rounded columns is of course a circle, that of the others is a figure bounded by two straight lines and two quadrants, thus:  They are apparently cut from the neighboring limestone, which here as at Qedes is well adapted for architectural effect.

Just south of Kefr Ber'am, a ravine displays on its east bank, a calcareous rock, breaking up into square blocks of great size and more or less slaty in its structure. The water grooves are not conspicuous, and are scarcely found at all on such surfaces as appear to be most recently exposed.

About two hours from Kefr Ber'am we had Sa'sa' on our right, and forty minutes later Jebel Jŭrmŭq and 'Ain el-Ghabâteh on our left. The spheroidal nodules of white quartz (Turks-heads) are found in the greatest abundance in all the cultivated fields and in every ravine likely to harbor these erratics. The lobes and lobules are of a less pure silex than the transepts and the geodic deposits lodged on the sides of the central cavity.

The ravines here are numerous and characteristic. The limestone layers are generally horizontal.

Two hours north of Beit Jenn a remarkable bright-yellow limestone crops out under the dark blue, sometimes conforming, sometimes not. Wâdy el-Milh here crosses the path in an eastwardly direction, the western portion presenting a cheerful and even rich vegetation. We found the bottom entirely dry, though it carries some water in the rainy season. From 'Ain edh-Dhebân the strata become more and more horizontal. At 'Ain en-Nôm they are quite so, and unusually thin and slaty. El-Murky is a hill, north of Bijjin, of imperfectly stratified limestone and abounds in a variety of chalcedonic flints. I see no reason to place these formations as low as the upper Jurassic groupe; but the scarcity of fossils makes it unsafe to speak with much approach to certainty.

A bye-path, winding off to the east, after leaving Bijjin, brought me to the Wâdy Khŭrbet ez-Zabŭt, where the number of quartz balls is truly surprising. So also in the Ard el-Marabîyeh, where I found upwards of a thousand covering less area than an acre. They are apparently derived by drift or slow transport from a distance, and the very beds from which they were detached have probably long since perished by denudation. The limestones of the region still contain imbedded to great depths similar quartz nodules, but they part with their contents very reluctantly and only as the mass wastes away by secular disintegration.

From an elevated point of the south face of a cliff of great height and many miles extent north and east of Râmeh, a magnificent prospect may be had over the districts of 'Akka esh-Shâghûr, Safed and el-Bŭttauf. Mount Carmel and the waters of Genesareth may be seen as two extremes, and Cana of Galilee lies far off, sought for, if not visible, between the two. My guide named to me upwards of forty places all in sight, of which I had only time to note the following: Fîq, Tŭbarîya, Hattîn, el-Mughâr, el-Mansûrah, Wâdy Tûfeh, 'Aleibûn, el-Medîneh, Mejd el-Kerûm, Kefr 'Anan, Sefûrieh, Sŭkhnîn, Deir el-Asad, Deir Hanna, Mughâr el-Hazûr, Fâradheh, Nahef, Deir el-Qâsy, Wâdy Leimôn, Ard es-Serîn, Wâdy Salâmeh, 'Ain el-Asad, 'Ain el-'Abadîyeh, er-Râmeh, 'Arîdh el-Ghûz, Shefa 'Amr and the beautiful bay from 'Akka to Cape Carmel.

A conglomerate is found near er-Râmeh, proving that a new formation is not far distant. With Deir Hanna on our left, we traversed a round plain perhaps four miles in diameter with a loamy soil capable of very productive cultivation. Near the centre of this a large reservoir of water takes the dimensions of a pretty lake, and the groups of Arab women and children gathered on its banks, told how much it was needed by the neighboring population. The number of olive trees near er-Râmeh and more to the west is very remarkable. Beyond the Birkeh I fell in with many cactuses, and several palms, fig trees, willows, sycamores and oaks. A ridge or *col*, of half an hour's breadth, divides the plain just mentioned from the larger plain of Bŭttauf. In the limestone here I found *Ostraeae* and *Gryphaeae* frequently in the rock, but was unable for want in time and suitable instruments, to effect their removal or even to note their determining features so as to pronounce now upon their age.

The plain of Bŭttauf is oblong, irregularly oval, and the long diameter which seemed to me about ten miles in length against a short diameter of three, had a bearing nearly S. W. and N. E. El-'Aseir and Rummâneh are passed here, as also el-Khŭrbeh, which is two hours distant on the right. El-'Aseir is at the foot of a hill, bounding in part the plain on the east, and is raised a little above the level of the open ground. The calcareous strata were quite distorted; no boulderstones were on the plain, which consisted of a brown crumbling marl wanting nothing but water to bring it into very fertile state. The plain is bounded on the N. W. by high hills, and on the S. W. and N. E. by very low ones, particularly on the N. E. On the southeast side a moderately high range of hills shuts up the sight of Tur'ân and Lûbieh, which are situated in fact in one of the southern offsets from the main plain, separated from it by a ridge of much disturbed limestone and (as I was told) of a black rock, which I take to be the trap of Tŭbarîya.

After the great plain a second small one is passed, and beyond this another of intermediate size, extending lengthwise E. S. E., and running on its eastern margin into a succession of mound-like inequalities, until the character of the plain has entirely disappeared. It was on descending into this part of the Bŭttauf, that quite unexpectedly (for it was the design of Captain Lynch to strike for Beisân across the plain of Esdrelon,) I saw from an eminence on the north the entrance of the train of the Expedition yet two hours journey distant on the western margin of the plain. Had I descended into the Merj a quarter of an hour earlier, I should have passed on to Nazareth and perhaps to Beisân, the message having failed to reach me of a change of the greatest advantage to our movements. Indeed, as it was, I owed the recognition entirely to the sharp optics of my Druze guide, whose incomprehensible amazement puzzled me for some time, before I could discern the least object calculated to attract the traveller's attention, or even guess from his confused description the cause of his astonishment.

West of Tur'ân the plain is covered by an alluvial mould without large stones, and the few small ones that were found were all calcareous. The earthy grains however were evidently comminuted lava, while the finer particles contained a notable proportion of carbonate of lime along with the usual constituents of the plutonic rocks.

East of Tur'ân the trap boulders begin to abound, the limestone being however the underlying rock, and after passing several Birkehs, the summit level between the Mediterranean and the Sea of Galilee is reached at a *col* between two low hills. The trap fragments have a weathered and half disintegrated look. Many of them are largely porous, the *bullulae* often regularly spheroidal and more frequently empty than filled. The cavities which were not empty contained either coatings of pearl-white calcspar very evenly laid on, or a full nucleus of the same material. Analysed this white matter gave:

| | |
|---|---|
| Carbonate of Lime, | 96.67 |
| Carbonate of Magnesia, | 2.57 |
| Silica, | 1.02 |
| Alumina, | .40 |
| | 100.66 H. |

The road now descends a broad valley bringing into view on the left ravines exposing both the limestone and the trap. The descent becomes more and more rapid, and the rock where exposed is now everywhere volcanic. The boulders are large and much weather-worn. Nearer the lake and in the cliff which overhang the gorges, a columnar structure frequently predominates. The trap of Tŭbarîya is porous, even vesicular and sometimes amygdaloïdal, the cavities not always filled or even encrusted. The color of the unweathered surface is a fine iron-grey or greyish-blue, enlivened by occasional specks of white, due to the deposits of calcareous matter in the pores, many of which however appear to have been previously filled with olivine or chrysolite long before the infiltration of the lime.

The trappean rocks around Lake Tiberias present a general resemblance to each other. At all events the difference between the dolerites of Lûbieh and Om Keis is less remarkable than the difference between two specimens which might be taken within a few feet of each other in the neighborhood of Tiberias. The relation of the trap to the limestone varies however with the locality. At Hŭmmâm (Emmaus) the limestone underlying the trap is fully displayed, and the plutonic rocks do not reach the level of the lake at any point known to me on its western shore; whereas south of the lake the rocky bed of the Jordan is plutonic. Conglomerates are not found, I believe, on the northwest or northeast shores, but occur in abundance along the paths which lead from various starting places up to the ruins of old Gadara.

---

## CHAPTER II.

### *Route from 'Akka (the ancient Ptolemaïs) to Safed and the Ard el-Hûleh.*

*Tertiary shell-tufa of 'Akka.—Limestone of Birweh.—Limestones of the Plain.—Fâradah.—The Chalk of Safed.—Fossils.—Cretaceous Silicates.—Large Ammonites.—Trap-fragments.—Lava of the crater Birket el-Jish.—Limestone of el-Jish.—Large Patella.—Volcanic vestiges.—Craters north of Teitebah and south of Delâta.—Lava of Delâta.—Birkehs.—The Merj 'Almeh.—Limestone of Wâdy Qûbâ'ah.—Limestones near Qedes.—Descent towards the Ard el-Hûleh through Wâdy 'Arûs.—Limestone.—View of the Ard el-Hûleh and Jordan.—Cretaceous limestone.—The Ard el-Hûleh.*

This district is mainly calcareous, the near approach to Jebel Safed giving the first indications of any departure from the prevailing formation. Both the Jurassic and the Cretaceous limestones are found, but in relations not easy to determine.

Near 'Akka a tertiary may be met with, not only on the sea-coast, but also on various points some miles in the interior. It consists of comminuted shells, for the most part coarsely ground and mixed sparsely with siliceous granules; but in some instances the shells are reduced to an almost impalpable powder. In both cases the materials are held together by a firm conglutination. Blocks of these are to be found in some of the walls and in scattered groupes across the plain east of the town. The coarse-grained rock yielded on analysis:

| | |
|---|---|
| Carbonate of Lime, | 91.15 |
| Carbonate of Magnesia, | 1.53 |
| Silica, etc., | 4.86 |
| Iron and Alumina, | 1.50 |
| | 99.04 S. |

An offset of this plain extends far inland amidst a groupe of circumscribed hills, and is shut off from the plain of Esdrelon by a triangular barrier more or less broken into round and tongue-like elevations. The northern hills do not begin quite as soon, and at several points before reaching these, I found fragments of weather-worn trap that I could not refer to their *situs*.

Leaving Dâmûn and Birweh or Ebraweh on the right, but yet a mile or more in advance, the road skirts the base of a groupe of low and gently sloping hills consisting of a grey-brown limestone, with occasional intrusions of tertiary beds. Not far beyond these a chalk, closely resembling the cretaceous limestones of Birkîn, begins to show itself above the harder varieties beneath, with numerous indications of small and scattered fragments of fossil fish.

Tell Birweh is remarkable for its horizontal summit and regularly sloping sides. It appeared from the point we passed it surmounted in part by a groupe of olive trees and fringed by a belt of fig trees. On the authority of my guide I have noted that there was an abundant fountain of good water at or near one of the groves.

Eastward of this, a chalky and crumbling shale crosses the path with frequent interruptions of a harder rock, and terminates with a mass of limestone dipping regularly W. S. W. Some of the Wâdys now descending from the south show a rich and fruitful vegetation.

Farther east the dip of the calcareous rock varies between south and west. Just here the inequalities of the surface diminish and die away into a beautiful and fertile plain, elevated above the larger one below. Fine crops of wheat, barley, tobacco and *hummŭs* repay the labors of the husbandman, and the plain is frequently enlivened by large herds of well fed cattle with all the marks of good breed and blood. The soil is alluvial and is laid down evenly between two ranges of hills with a width varying from the eighth to a quarter of a mile. It descends very gently towards the east all the way from its westernmost margin, and terminates near Mejd el-Kerûm. Southwardly from its eastern borders, Wâdy Qoton forms an angle with this plain, and shows itself by the abundance of its harvest well adapted to the production of tobacco, wheat, barley and oil. Trees are unusually numerous in this neighborhood; they are principally the *sinjan*, the *ghâr*, the *kharob*, the *merinîyeh*, the *qeiqab*, the *roumân*, the *lôz* and the *jôz*. The *senôber* is wanted for the threshing sledges, but has to be brought from a distance. The *souweid* is also abundant in some parts of the district, but not in the immediate vicinity of the village.

The plain continues descending almost imperceptibly from Mejd el-Kerûm towards Bâneh, Nahef and er-Râmeh. The number of olive trees is truly surprising, and the wheat-fields struck me as remarkably productive, when all the circumstances of social insecurity in eastern lands are taken into fair consideration. Near Bâneh the ground is rolling and ascends gently with a slight descent afterwards towards Nahef. The road then re-ascends towards er-Râmeh. West of this town a fine fountain, the 'Ain es-Serrârah, is made to feed a reservoir, twenty feet long by two and a half broad, which was filled with clear and pure water to the depth of a foot, an unusual and very refreshing sight in the thirsty districts of the Holy Land. Southwardly over a valley, the heights of el-Mughâr and Qul'at esh-Shûny make quite conspicuous features from the good points of view, and beyond them may be seen the lofty eastern barriers of el-Bŭttauf crowned by Qul'at Ibn Ma'an and Hattîn.

The limestone of this region is principally the hard greyish-blue variety, very much eaten out in the way so often described. Now and then a reddish color predominates, sometimes due to a very thin coating of cryptogamous vegetation, but sometimes to the actual hue of the rock; and showing in an instance submitted to analysis that iron is as usually the coloring ingredient.

Near Fărădeh (or Fărah?) a fine stream keeping alive some rude mills intersects a bed of limestone of doubtful classification. From the neighboring hills a splendid view is obtained of Lake Tiberias, and I thought I saw Jebel et-Tûr in the south. The road still ascending intersects a range of limestone dipping S. and S. S. E., that is towards the lake. This dip in some places is very great. From the heights here, I could perceive that the country west of the lake, though elevated, was sensibly depressed beneath the still higher uplands north and south, as if the subsidence that caused the Bahr Tubarîyeh had taken effect more or less through the whole region between the bay of Haifa and the lake.

A quarter of an hour before getting to Semu'y, the town of Safed is brought finely into view and may be described from many points much farther west. Just beyond Semu'y near a mill driven by a very fine stream, the limestone dips N. W. 30°, and begins to disclose the peculiar formation of the Safed hills. North of the town at the bottom of a deep ravine the path crosses a very chalky outcrop, and fragments of trap begin to be seen mixed with the numerous calcareous erratics that are sure to accumulate in all the angles of the great ravines. Between the fountain here, 'Ain ez-Zeitûn and the town, a chalky limestone with many large specimens of the Ammonites Safedensis is much exposed and cut up by extensive denudations, presenting opportunities of research that I was obliged to let pass with very sincere regret.

The hills on which Safed is built are mainly limestones with a large proportion of insoluble matter subject to alternations with layers of a silicate of lime and magnesia yielding on analysis the following result:

| | |
|---|---|
| Silica, | 74.99 |
| Carbonate of Lime, | 14.52 |
| Carbonate of Magnesia, | 6.60 |
| Bituminous matter, | 1.01 |
| Peroxide of Iron, | 1.40 |
| Alumina, | 1.60 |
| | 100.12 M. |

Another portion of the mineral was specially examined for the siliceous and bituminous matter, and was found to contain 79.42 per cent. of silica and silicates, and 1.10 of bituminous or organic matter. United with the silica was 1.4 of iron and alumina together with small quantities of lime and magnesia.

From another hill a specimen of a silicate more highly charged with lime and iron was procured, and in this there was found to be

| | |
|---|---|
| Insoluble matter, containing 95.6 per cent. of Silica, and 4 per cent. of Iron and Alumina, | 62.65 |
| Carbonate of Lime, | 27.69 |
| Carbonate of Magnesia, | 2.96 |
| Iron and Alumina, | 5.75 |
| Organic matter, | 1.35 |
| | 100.40 H. |

The limestones were two distinct epochs. The lower groupes exhibit nothing of a chalky origin, but are not easily examined from the unfrequency of their exposure. The presence of *Dentalia*, *Rostellariae* and more especially of *Chenopodes* points significantly to a Jurassic age, and is not inconsistent with the hypothesis of the existence of the inferior Oolite as the most ancient formation in this part of Palestine. The great portion of the mass south and west of the city may be assigned without hesitation to the upper chalk, and contain as fossil remains:

Ancyloceras Safedensis, *Co.*
Ammonites Safedensis, *Co.*
Corbula Syriaca, *Co.*
Pecten delumbis, *Co.*
Astarte sublineolata, *Co.*
Gryphaea vesicularis, *Lam.*

Lucina Safedensis, *Co.* Dentalium cretaceum, *Co.*

With undetermined species of *Nucula*, *Rostellaria* and *Solen*, though this last is somewhat doubtful. Of the *Ammonites* I observed one ten inches in diameter.

A peculiarity of the Safed silicates and flints is the semi-schistose semi-conchoidal fracture. The place of fissure appears to be determined by a thin film like a coat of yellow or black paint, which forms a striking contrast with the dull blue or chalky white of the unyielding interior. A closer inspection proves however that the film is a subsequent infiltration of ochrey iron, alumina and lime, and that the slaty structure, though more probably coëval with the rock, may have been caused by agents of comparatively recent date. The surface of fracture is sometimes ribbed or corrugated so regularly as to present the appearance of vegetable impressions, but I met with nothing to give rise to a reasonable conjecture that these phenomena are in any way organic.

In Wâdy Tanâhîn, which passes down on the west of Safed towards the south to join the main Wâdy Leimôn, the ravine cuts deep enough into the rocks to bring into view the order and relative thicknesses of the several sedimentary deposits. In the northwest Jebel Zebût, and below 'Akbarah Jebel Elqâb exhibit the various aspects of the Safed limestone wherever the sections are well exposed, while in Jebel Bîria (or Jews' hill, as my guide called it) and Jebel Qanân south of this, an alternation of chalky and flinty beds is rather to be inferred than asserted from actual verification. I found among the ruins of the citadel of Safed many blocks and fragments of a grey-green dolerite abounding in olivine and distinctly granulated felspar. It is hardly probable that these were brought from a very distant locality, and trap will I think be found *in situ* in the hills between Safed and the Jordan.*

It is principally between 'Ain ez-Zeitûn and the junction of the paths leading to Meirôn and el-Jish that the Ammonites were found in their beds. Not far beyond this, west of Kadîta and separated from it by an intermediate valley, boulders and numerous smaller fragments of trap begin to show themselves in all directions, scattered over the surface of the limestone hills. These disappear again shortly after and then come once more in great numbers, the limestone in the meantime acquiring the gnawn and corroded look so often mentioned before. A path strikes off here to Birket el-Jish, an oval pond about 400 feet in the longest diameter, nearly in the centre of a horizontal plain; which forms the elevated summit of a hill of remote geological antiquity, the metamorphic forms of trap and basalt together with the extensive excavations on every side leaving no doubt of this conclusion. Near the water and some distance beneath it the tops of the polygonal columns were quite visible, and in the slopes of the basin were to be observed the rounded masses not unfrequently met with, consisting of many concentric ellipsoidal coats of a disintegrated greenstone.

A valley separates this hill from that on which the village of el-Jish is placed. This latter is limestone, the dip of which at the east side was N. N. W. No trap was found here *in situ*, but the surface of the hill was covered with broken blocks of this material, increasing in size towards the summit. The terrace-walls were made of lava and limestone in nearly equal proportions. The limestone where I examined it presented two aspects. The earlier form was evidently cretaceous; the more recent had all the appearance of a tufa

*My guide brought me here to look at a snake which he had killed. It was about 4 feet in length, and answered very well the description given by Hasselquist of Coluber Haijeh.

involving to the extent of two or three per cent. a fine pyroxenic sand widely disseminated through the chalky mass. The dull white of this tertiary (for so I regard it) is spotted with yellow specks and stains hardly referable to an organic origin. The only fossil I found in this bed was one so imperfect that it left but slight chance of identification. The impression presented the radiating striae and eccentric foramen of a large *Patella*, six inches by four, but I would not venture so to consider it. On the east side of Wâdy el-Jish, where it has a northeasterly direction, the limestone has a dip of 15° north.

At 'Ain el-Jish, the cretaceous rock contains among other fossils a *Rostellaria* and a *Dentalium*. Near this spot is a bituminous limestone, probably a local deposit of very limited extent. The chalk is covered in the ravines by large and numerous boulders of trap, but where the strata were well exposed, the cretaceous bed exhibited contorted inclinations quite unusual in the limestone of this vicinity. Here and on ascending the south bank of the ravine, a moraine of trap blocks is seen prolonged from the main mass, and the walk thence to the Birkeh is over an ancient lava covered with a coat of vegetable mould varying in depth, color and composition.

The plain between the crater and Wâdy el-Jish took me nearly half an hour to walk across and was quite level. This circumstance as well as the occasional depth of the superincumbent soil would be sufficient without the evidence derived from the lithological aspects of the lava to prove a very high geological antiquity. A still more conclusive proof is found in the fact that the insulated hill on which el-Jish is built, though of cretaceous and other limestones, is covered to its very summit with the ruins of an earlier volcanic capping which we must suppose is now removed by denudation.

If we leave the Birket el-Jish and proceed eastwardly a mile or two, we find north of Teitebah another crater, like the other in all respects and about as large. No stone appears which is not volcanic. A Wâdy descends from the immediate vicinity of this Birkeh towards the Ghôr. On reaching it I found assembled a numerous concourse of Jews and Arabs, and mingling apparently in friendly intercourse.

Between this spot and Delâta a third Birkeh occurs, smaller than the other two, and marked by blocks of lava purposely, as it seems, brought into these places they now occupy. Jebel Benît is I believe limestone without basalt, but northwardly towards Delâta, after crossing several Wâdys where trap and limestone prevail alternately, the former rock reappears in its full predominance, particularly in the hill north of and a little west of the village. The limestone where it last occurs south of Delâta is of the hard, semi-silicated species, without fossils, blue externally and a yellowish-white within. Two other Birkehs are found here, the larger being the lower. The small pond which was quite at the top of the eminence was filled with very clear water.* Beside these another Birkeh, called sometimes Birket esh-Shemalîyeh in contradistinction to Birket el-Gharbîyeh (farther west) lies within an hour's walk north of the village, and is formed in a bed of lava very imperfectly covering the limestone beneath.

The Delâta lava differs much from the Tubarîya trap. It has all the aspect of a later origin and exhibits a series of *coulées* of various colors and consistence, some of them having a remarkably pumiceous and even scoriaceous look. A piece broken from the pale red pumice was analysed and gave

* I ought to observe that I cannot reconcile my observation of the distance of Delâtah from Teitebah and its position south of Wâdy Hendaj with the Delâtah of the maps.

| | |
|---|---|
| Silica, | 47.40 |
| Iron, | 32.15 |
| Alumina, | 7.50 |
| Lime, | 10.00 |
| Magnesia, | 2.45 |
| Alkalies, | .76 |
| | 100.26 S. |

Here and there the erupted rock puts on a semibasaltic character, giving the battlemented outline to the edge of the cliffs. The colors of the pumiceous lava vary from the blackness of venous blood to a light red and even reddish-white, with all the intervening shades. In some varieties the spherical cellules are as close together as they can be without communication, and have often longitudinal *bullae*, derived probably from the junction of many cells after the thinned partitions were destroyed by the continued pressure of the contained gases. In other forms the cellular structure is not apparent, and has either never existed or has disappeared by infiltration and metamorphic influences.

North of Birket esh-Shemalîyeh, a junction of lava and limestone may be seen, and before we reach the yellow-white of the normal rocks all the red hues may be met with in the calcareous that we had mentioned in the volcanic beds. The whiter limestones here have not unfrequently purple streaks and specks scattered irregularly through the mass, but disappearing altogether when the distance from the junctions exceeds a few hundred yards.

Northeast of this locality a short Wâdy terminates in a very extensive plain, raised still far above the bottom of the Ghôr. It was known to me as Merj 'Almeh. From its eastern margin you look down upon a lower terrace, both susceptible of cultivation, the upper one being in fact under good tillage, and promising, when I went through it, a fair return in wheat, vetches and barley. South of the point where we struck the eastern brow of the upper terrace, I observed another Birkeh quite drained of any water it may have held at an earlier period of the year. Merj 'Almeh lies with Wâdy Hendaj on the north and Wâdy Delâta on the south, and Wâdy Wŭqas springs from its eastern boundary, nearer I think to the latter than to the former. The ride along the brow of this elevated terrace presents a noble view of Râs el-Ahmar, the Ghôr, the Hûleh, Mt. Hermon, and the snowy peaks of some of the remotest parts of the Anti-Libanus. The strata of Mount Hermon appear from here to have an inclination of 30° towards the west, but this is not to be regarded as a reliable measure of the actual dip. On the southwest side of the last Birkeh, the basaltic columns are well developed and have a striking effect. The village of 'Almeh and the fine hill Râs el-Ahmar, are also pleasing points in the view.

The limestone reappears again in a Wâdy which, running south, terminates, I was told, in Wâdy Qŭbâ'ah. The rock north of its head is also limestone, and bounds, at its western wall, another gorge steeper in the descent, but well cultivated at the bottom. Not far from this the village of Sŭlhah was pointed out, but we did not visit it. The production of this neighborhood seemed to be principally wheat and olives. The limestone was of the chalky kind with fossils; but of these I was not able to obtain a satisfactory specimen. The prevailing dip was 30° or 40° to the west, with the western flank sloping conformably to this inclination; it being a common occurrence in Syria, to find the moderate slopes determined by the dip of the underlying rock, as if the denudations had advanced, stratum by stratum, so as not to present the transverse sections found on the precipitous sides of the great ravines.

About two miles south of Qedes the path after descending rather abruptly reaches a beautiful camping ground with abundance of fine water. I observed here two mills, quite a phenomenon in this district. Twelve minutes farther north, one of the wildest gorges of Jebel Safed comes suddenly into view, and an excellent supply of good water gushes forth here from a copious fountain which my guide called (I think at a venture) 'Ain el-Qedes, that town being still a mile on the north.

The limestone on approaching Qedes is grey externally, covered where much exposed with a coating of thin moss of various light colors. The weathered surfaces are smooth and rounded, the ordinary erosions being rather rare. Fine fields of wheat and barley follow in order, the soil being covered with large calcareous fragments, of a slightly reddish color without, but whitish-grey within. Here the erosions are more striking. The compacter portions however present no marks of unequal composition to which it might be natural to refer the relative penetration of the carving agencies, whatever these may be.

The descent from Qedes towards the Ard el-Hûleh is over a series of fine terraces which present a better cultivation than is generally met with in the unfrequented parts of the Holy Land. Wâdy 'Arûs passes downward on the north of one of these terraces between the low eminences not far from Jebel Jeld. No limestone seems here to have contracted a remarkable hardness and again puts on externally the channeled and grooved appearance so often referred to as a possible result of secular pluvial erosion. Between Bir et-Terjem and Harrâr, the soil supports a good growth of *mell* and *zarûd* trees, and the *sŭfsaf* is not absent where the springs supply sufficient moisture. In many spots a rank vegetation of weeds and nettles shows what might be done, by a better direction of the productive powers of the soil, and the traveller has to lament a waste of nutriment upon a worthless crop of *dŭrdâr*, *suweid*, *khandol*, *'aqûq* and *kŭrsa'ân*.

About a mile north of Wâdy 'Arûs the terrace plain is crossed by a rough ledge of limestone of firm texture, not abounding in fossils, but quite remarkable for the surface erosions which furrow the exposed faces of the rock into grooves running more or less in the direction of the descending raindrop. Jebel Harrâr is visible from this point nearly south, perhaps 20° east. The summit was occupied by a ruined village, overlooking the Bahr and Sahel el-Khaït.

The Jordan is from this point of view lost in the Hûleh and its course scarcely discernible except by occasional indications furnished by six or seven ponds in the great marsh, several of which however belonged, when I saw them, rather to independent confluents, and as I learned varied their place and appearance almost every year. One of these ponds was much larger than any of the others, and remained visible after they ceased to be seen in consequence of our descent into the Ghôr. The limestone dips for the most part westwardly at and near the point where I found it advisable to commence this descent. From a station here the apparent summit of Mount Hermon bore N. 56° E., and a high mountain in Jaulân S. 76° E. Two marked eminences were also seen N. 10° E. and N. 16° E. in the direction of Ibel el-Kamh and Ibel el-Hawa, though these villages of course were not in view.

North of this point and below it, the limestone reappears occasionally with cretaceous indications, and the chalky character is at least very decided. The road I pursued drops down at several turns, 50 or 60 feet rather abruptly, and then goes northwardly on the mountain side several hundred yards horizontally, till a point is reached 400 feet by estimate below the brow of the cliff. Here I found the dip of the limestone to be towards the south and west, but varying much both in direction and degree.

The path brought us gradually towards the edges of the terraces, and more and more of the Ard el-Hûleh, widely dotted with the black tents of the nomadic occupants of the plain, lay open to our observation. From this a much more rapid descent than before brought us down in twenty-five minutes fairly into the Ard, just two miles south of the southern extremity of the basaltic spur which projects from the ridge already described as Tell el-Haïyeh. A notice of the geological aspect of the country north and east of this is included in the preceding divisions of this Report.

# SECTION III.

## GEOLOGY OF THE GHOR OR VALLEY OF THE JORDAN,

### BETWEEN LAKE TIBERIAS AND THE DEAD SEA.

---

## CHAPTER I.

### *Introductory Remarks.*

*Relation of the limestone to the Plutonic rocks.—West of the Jordan no igneous rocks between el-'Abadîyeh and el-Humeirâwât.—Distribution of the Lavas west and east of the Jordan.—Auranitic and Trachonitic basalts and other igneous rocks.—Vast sandstone masses east of the Ghôr.—Age of the conglomerates.—Tertiaries and later formations.*

THE study of the Geology of this part of Palestine resolves itself into three great divisions:

1. The discussion of the geognostic constitution of the vast block of limestone and basaltic lava out of which the valley of the Jordan may be regarded as an excavation, due to the action of long continued detritory forces, such as a river-current working secularly, aided by the gradual abrasion of its banks, or other agencies more promptly efficacious to be considered in their proper places.

2. The study of the sandstones and conglomerates which line the sides and load the valleys east and west of the Ghôr, and which cannot but be regarded as formations secondary to the excavation.

3. The consideration of the accumulations and alluvions which now make up the floor of the Jordan plain, and which in their upper strata at least may be regarded as the stratified deposits drawn from the disintegration and detrition of the older rocks which were once in place at the head and higher levels of the walls of the Great Valley.

It will not, of course, be expected that a reconnaissance necessarily limited to so short a period as eight or nine days can furnish anything more than a preliminary outline of the general distributions and mutual relations of these three divisions of the inquiry, with such facts as could be collected on the spot respecting the three corresponding classes of formations.

Throughout the region traversed by the Jordan, whatever is not limestone, is deposited upon it or plays in reference to it a very subordinate part. Even the extensive tracts of Haurân basalt disclose, wherever the deep-cut valleys permit a measure of its relative predominance, a thickness far inferior to that of the calcareous mass, over which it seems to have been poured in successive ejections from centres or crevices now not easy to identify. South of el-'Abadîyeh, plutonic rocks disappear on the west of the Ghôr and are not found again on that side north of the latitude of 'Aqabah, unless we regard as an exception the low granite ridges of el-Humeirâwât. The lavas west of the Jordan, including all the varieties which occur, are comprehended in a very irregular compass of which Safed may be considered as the centre. The iron-grey basalt-lava of Tiberias represents the southerly and predominant formation, while the variegated pumices of Delâta may be cited as an average specimen of the far more recent lavas of the north, till at Tell el-Haîyeh we find again a third description of which the chronological position is more difficult to assign.

On the east of the Jordan, the plutonic rocks seem greatly to predominate. From Damascus throughout Basan, Galaad, Moab, and the land of the Madianites, as far southwardly as the mouth of the Elanitic Gulf, no great distance need to be travelled without encountering the hard, heavy, but uncompact Auranitic and Trachonitic basalts or the porphyries, melaphyres, serpentines, granites and older green-stones, which beginning in a remarkable development at the southeastern angle of the Dead Sea reappear at scattered intervals through the whole district of Mount Seir.

It is however characteristic of the Ghôr that sandstones so very rare on the west side are of frequent occurrence on the east. Yet even here they present themselves as encumbering ancient basins and valleys, and are scarcely ever found above the basalts or alternating with the chalks. The cliffs of Wâdy Môjeb and Wâdy Zerqa Ma'în are the most imposing of the arenaceous rocks, but these again are to be regarded as accumulations or outfillings very limited in extent compared with the dimensions of the limestone base.

The conglomerates of the Ghôr are probably more recent, on the whole, than the sandstones, though it is by no means difficult to distinguish at least three ages of the coarser breccias, the earliest of which may have long preceded the more modern of the consolidated sands. Nearer to us in the chronological order are the quaternaries and alluvions of the bottom oft he Ghôr, leaving the eocenes and still later tertiaries embanked in scattered beds suspended at various altitudes on both sides of the Ghôr to the height of several hundred feet above the present surface of the Dead Sea.

Keeping in view this outline of the prevailing subordinations in the Geology of the Ghôr the special descriptions will be better understood and no confusion will arise from a discussion of the rocks partly in the line of their geographical succession and partly in the more correct, but less authenticated order of their geological chronology.

## CHAPTER II.

### *Limestones and Lavas adjacent to Lake Tiberias.*

*Route from Lake Tiberias to Gadara and Jisr Mujâmi'ah.—Limestone of el-Hŭmmâm (ancient Emmaus.)—Calcareous deposits between el-Hŭmmâm and Mount Thabor.—Lavas of Lake Tiberias.—Porous lava of the town of Tiberias.—Compact variety.—Cellular lava.—Chrysolitic basalt of Jisr Om el-Qanâtir.—Marly layers.—Trap and limestone erratics near el-Bŭq'ah and Delhamîyeh.—Alluvial terraces.—Bed of the Hieromax.—Igneous rocks beyond Jordan.—Slaty chalk.—Conglomerate.—Basaltic plain.—Ruins and rocks of Om el-Keis (ancient Gadara.)—Basalt of Jisr Mujâmi'ah.*

THE great junction-surfaces where the limestone and lava are in contact deserve especial notice. These may be seen to the best advantage in the cliff just west of the hot baths (el-Hŭmmâm.) The base only of the cliff is calcareous, the crown and brow of it consisting of massive basalt. The lower strata of the limestone differ from the upper not so much in age as in color and texture. The prevailing hue is yellowish-white, with alternations of layers having a delicate flesh tinge, but rougher and more cretaceous, both in break and structure, than its compacter associate. Faint traces of organic forms are discernible in both kinds, and fossil remains would no doubt be found repaying the labor of the search. The strike I took to be nearly N. W., the dip from 15° to 20° S. W., though not far distant I found a layer dipping as many degrees decidedly east of south. Neither of these rocks are dolomitized. An analysis of the flesh-colored variety gave

| | |
|---|---|
| Alumina and Peroxide of Iron, | .570 |
| Carbonate of Lime, | 92.530 |
| Carbonate of Magnesia, | 1.862 |
| Soda, | 1.824 |
| Insoluble matter, | 1.083 |
| Loss, Water, etc., | 2.131 |
| | 100.000 S. |

The proper tests gave such marked traces of chlorine that it may be that the soda was due principally to chloride of sodium inhering after infiltration.

The harder yellowish-white variety gave less iron and more insoluble residuum. This limestone resembled its companion in the frequency of its spathic membranes which, while they penetrate the mass very deeply, are sometimes so thin that their fracture lines cannot be seen without the aid of a good lens. The coarser intrusions of calcspar are more frequently found in the yellow-white rock which shows also a semi-crystalline character with granules exceedingly minute, but spread throughout the body of the rock with a great appearance of uniformity.

Between Mount Thabor which is itself a chalky limestone with some very compact interdeposits and the somewhat analogous limestone of the Baths, a basaltic tract intervenes with occasional calcareous interruptions, leaving a probability that the limestone underlies the lava and perhaps at no very great depth. The east side of Lake Tiberias has not been geognostically explored, but there is every reason to believe that the regions about Fîk and

Qul'at el-Husn and perhaps the whole eastern shore are almost exclusively composed of the Auranitic basalt. This is certainly the case in the neighborhood of Gadara at the southeastern and of the district el-Batîheh at the northeastern extremity of the Lake.

## *Lavas of Lake Tiberias.*

The most characteristic types of the lavas of the western shore may be found in the heights just above the town. Three leading varieties may be easily distinguished. We have first, as the prevailing rock, a basalt-lava, firm in its texture, but cellular, vesicular and often amygdaloidal, with a fine angular porosity even in the apparently solid parts, such as would result from microscopic crystals irregularly thrown together, and not very closely compacted. The larger cavities are more or less rounded, lined and sometimes filled with carbonates of lime, seldom with zeolites or other silicates. The smaller cellules are often occupied by olivine, augite and felspar, the latter in very sparing proportion. When the chrysolite is found it is well imbedded and apparently congenital. The cellules are occasionally consecutive in very long trains, each little cell being then not rounded but very much elongated in the directions of the trains. The color of this variety is a dark iron-grey, the fracture quite jagged and hackly. The cellularity of the structure is not less remarkably deep in the interior of the fresh broken rock than nearer to the surface, as I was enabled to ascertain on the breaking up of a mass of this rock by a blast ordered by Capt. Lynch for the removal of a ledge which obstructed for a time the passage of the boat-trucks. The specific gravity of this rock varies from 2.6 to 2.9.

A second variety of the Tŭbarîya lava is found more superficially seated and differs from the former by a greater compactness and specific gravity, and a greater variety of imbedded minerals with which the matrix is sometimes literally studded. Olivine and spar with here and there a zeolite make up the greater part of the crystalline ingredients, enlivening by the intermixture of variously colored specks, the otherwise unattractive aspect of the rock.

A third description is found more particularly among the boulders, but not unfrequently on the edges and angles of long exposed knolls. In this case the cavities are more numerous as well as more capacious, containing, besides the usual spathic and chrysolitic contents, coatings and even casts of an impure aluminate of iron.

Near the ruined bridge, Om el-Qanâtir, fragments of basalt were obtained more charged with olivine than the trap of Tubarîya. Detached specimens were also collected of chalky and cineritious tufas, evidently the result of the pulverisation and reaggregation of the limestone and lava of the neighboring rocks. The latter of these two tufas had a laminated structure and cineritious aspect. The silica formed about 9½ per cent. of the whole; the other ingredients will appear from the following analysis:

| | |
|---|---|
| Carbonate of Lime, | 83.02 per cent. |
| Carbonate of Magnesia, | 1.85 |
| Iron and Alumina, | 2.05 |
| Silica, | 9.45 |
| Organic matter, | .55 |
| | 96.92 H. |

Between this and Wâdy Fejâz, both the calcareous and the volcanic rocks appear in place. On the west side of the Ghôr, far too high to be ascribed to any modern cause, a very extensive terrace runs along for miles with horizontal stratification, due doubtless to an earlier higher level of the whole system of the great excavation, and the detention, in quietly deposited layers, of the detritus carried to the waters. A dilapidated mill-race, with two or three mills, together with a line of ancient aqueduct, proves that the advantages of this terrace were once turned to good account. The surface of this plateau bore a rich crop of Kafûr, a long grass as tall as wheat, and furnishing a pasture much in request. The lower grounds abounded in wheat and barley, with here and there patches of oats.

A little south of Jisr Om el-Qanâtir is another bridge in ruins, with the remnants of a mill-sluice and fish-weir. The main rock is not visible, the ancient alluvions lying sometimes at least sixty feet deep, as the river-side and ravines occasionally testify. The boulders scattered over the alluvial embankment are either a very porous basalt-lava or a calc-tufa, not unlike that of 'Akka, differing from that however in the absence of comminuted *testae*. This tufa was made up principally of very small granules composed of concentric coats of carbonate of lime. Intermixed with these are larger worn globules of a fine-textured limestone, and a few microscopic grains, more or less angular, of volcanic rock. An analysis made by Mr. Hewston of two of these calc-sinters showed an unexpected difference in their composition. One of these, free from the doleritic spiculae, gave

| | |
|---|---|
| Carbonate of Lime, | 96.38 |
| Carbonate of Magnesia, | 2.19 |
| Silica, | .85 |
| Iron and Alumina, | .75 |
| Organic matter, | .15 |
| | 100.32 |

The other showed much magnesia:

| | |
|---|---|
| Carbonate of Lime, | 68.85 |
| Carbonate of Magnesia, | 26.97 |
| Iron and Alumina, | 1.10 |
| Silica, | 1.15 |
| | 98.07 |

The earth where exposed by ravines exhibits in this neighborhood a marly appearance with layers mainly horizontal and slightly differing in color. Of these sections I passed several in the course of the first ten miles, and a remarkable one was observed by Capt. Lynch on the second day of his examination of the Jordan about two miles north of Delhamîyeh.

Not far from el-Bŭq'ah, a short distance south of which we encamped for the night, erratic fragments of trap and limestone recur at distant intervals, and the basalt is itself visible on the banks of the stream.

The trap blocks are for the most part small, much worn and partially disintegrated. The vesicular cavities are sometimes quite empty, sometimes thickly coated with spathic incrustations, and more rarely entirely filled with concretionary carbonate of lime. The olivine has not withstood the encroachments of long continued atmospheric agency, and has in many instances degenerated into an ochrey or at least semi-ferruginous and amorphous material, no longer well defined in its planes, and entirely changed in color and consistence. One form of the limestone-tufas is curiously interwoven and penetrated with silicified nodules and buttons, of which the larger portions are probably metamorphs of calcareous fragments enveloped in the encrusting deposits from waters carrying at first lime and afterwards the soluble modification of silex, each to its respective receptacle.

Between el-Bŭq'ah and Delhamîyeh the Jordan breaks out into several detached rapids with a hurried and violent descent, interrupted near its head and towards the middle by formidable whirlpools and eddies. The rocky bottom is basaltic lava, which may be traced on the east side of the Jordan beyond the mouth of the Hieromax (Sheri'at el-Mandhûr.) Just above the bridge (which is still in good preservation) across this stream, the rocky platform is divided into polygonal fissures, indicative of a tendency to the prismatic or columnar separation of the mass. From the river to the eastern cliff, a distance of four miles or more, a fine terrace of ancient alluvion rises almost imperceptibly till it strikes rather abruptly the limestone of the mountain side. The soil is rich and loamy, but wasted in the support of enormous crops of idle vegetation. These weeds bear a profusion of flowers of every variety of color, red and yellow predominating. The base of the eastern cliff, where I ascended it, was limestone. Half way up I came again upon a basaltic outcrop, and before reaching the summit a rough conglomerate was crossed, the thickness and extent of which I had no means of ascertaining, as it lay exposed only at a few widely separated points.

The trap, both at the outcrop and afterwards on the summit plain, a mile beyond the edge of the descent, is a blackish brown, hard, heavy, and yet vesicularly porous rock of the same description as that which supplied the builders of Gadara with the greater part of their architectural materials.

Further south the face of the cliff exhibits many remarkable indications of a metamorphic chalk. Superincumbent upon this is a bed of slaty limestone, which breaks up readily into its constituent layers, but the secondary cleavages are difficult to detect. The exposed sides and edges of the laminæ are more or less hardened, sometimes so much so as to resist the action of an acid not too dilute to act on the interior. At mid-height the uncovered rock has a ragged, laminated and sometimes loose and even friable texture. The color is a dull chalky-white with ochre-yellow interfoliations. Higher up the same tufoidal chalk recurs with nearly the same aspect. The weather beaten edges and faces are here too not unfrequently coated or rather glazed with an insoluble silicate of lime and iron, which effectually protects the carbonate of lime against the further action of the weather.* The ascent of this cliff was made slowly and by a very winding pathway. Half an hour before reaching the summit, I passed two columns, with plain Tuscan bases, of a coarse conglomerate, the rock itself being in situ in many places between the middle of the ascent and the summit plain. This formation is probably a mere accretion derived from a tertiary detritus deposited on the flanks of the Ghôr long posteriorly to its excavation, and consolidated by a cement due to the secular infiltration of lime-charged waters. The united fragments are sometimes rounded and sometimes angular. When a breccia is formed, the smaller fragments have

*The same fine glazing covers many of the long exposed syenitic rocks of Egypt, and in those instances it has required or its formation a much longer interval of time than has elapsed since the most ancient inscriptions, the glazing in general not having been reproduced upon the surfaces laid bare by the tooling away of the highly polished film, which it thus appears must have long preceded the date of the erasures.

sharper and better defined angles than the larger ones. The pebbles are white, yellow and red limestones, and red and grey-blue flints, the limestone much predominating. Where the conglomerate is found in place, its exposed surface shows a marked prominence of the flint gravel as if the calcareous part had been more rapidly eaten away. I observed the same phenomenon (in a much slighter degree however) on the hewn surface of the blocks and columns wherever they are found, at the edge of the hills, at the ruins, or at intermediate spots.

After gaining the summit, an extensive plain goes off northwardly towards the valley of the Hieromax, and southwardly towards the Wâdy el-'Arab. A part of this plain is very level, and consists of a broad platform of basalt, covered to some depth with vegetable earth, not unfruitful of badly earned grain and unheeded thistles and weeds. The uniformity of the plain and the irregular composition of the mass of which it forms the upper surface, point to the former agency of that great geological leveller, the incessant horizontal grinding of the moveable waters of the sea acting on a rocky bottom not yet uplifted above or sunk beneath the power of this planishing process, which sooner or later must reduce to a rocky plain the most refractory asperities of the surfaces submitted to the operation.

The ruins of Gadara have been already described by those who visited them as antiquities. The materials of which the great theatre is described is exclusively Haurân basalt, very porous and cancellated in structure, but nevertheless from the toughness and iron-like hardness of the mass not badly adapted to the purposes for which it appears to have been selected. Besides its use in building, it makes an excellent mill or grindstone where coarse breaking is preferred. The chrysolitic grains are always more or less decomposed near the exposed surface of the rock, and the bullular cavities are encrusted with a thin coating of calcspar. The zeolitic portion, if such can be identified, is not discernible in distinct segregation from the rest of the gangue, but if in accordance with received views, it actually exists, it is so intimately commingled with the refractory silicates that it cannot be analysed apart.*

The basaltic formation in the lower valley of the Ghôr at this extremity of it may be seen with still greater advantage at Jisr Mujâmi'ah than at points higher up. The polygonal shrinkage is remarkably developed, and the hard, yet uncompact texture of the black augitic mass is very strongly and distinctly marked in any fragment detached at this locality. Near Om Keis is a return of the schistose and brittle limestone spoken of as on the face of the cliff bounding the Ghôr on the east. It differs from this however in several particulars, more especially in the sharpness with which the limestone in some of the valleys south of Om Keis defines its planes of easy separation.

* In passing through the main corridor of the theatre I found myself ankle-deep in an evenly spread deposit of insect exuviæ, in which with the assistance of Mr. Schafhirt, of Philadelphia, the following species have been distinguished:

Trox orientalis.
Opatrum parvulum.
Opatrum carinatum.
Sclerum contractum.
Sclerum cinereum.
Besides several species of Formica, Gryllus and Blatta.

# CHAPTER III.

## *Route from Jisr Mujâmi'ah down the Ghôr to the mouth of the Jordan.*

*Terraces of the Jordan.—Their different age and origin.—Alluvions below Jisr Mujâmi'ah.—Zôr el-Bâsha.—Rapids.—Tertiary stratifications.—Curved layers.—Ghôr Beisân.—Terraces near Beisân (ancient Scythopolis.)—Conglomerates of Tell Qûbes.—Islands in the Jordan.—Terrace of breccia.—Qurn Sŭrtŭbeh conglomerate.—Limestone and conglomerate near Mukhâdat es-Seqâ.—Cavernous rocks near Merj en-Nŭjr, (Nujh?)—Wâdy Fâri'a.—Tributaries to the Jordan from the West.—Tufas between Wâdy Seqâ and Wâdy Dâmi'a.—Chalk.—Limestone with remarkable dip.—Brown limestone south of the Nawâ'imeh.—Marls and limestones between Wâdy Kelt and Wâdy Hajla.—Analysis of the Jordan water at the Pilgrims' Baths.*

The tertiaries and alluvions, which now occupy the bottom of the Ghôr and have accumulated in some places so as to give the banks of the present Jordan a precipitous or even lofty appearance, can only be seen to adva..age by an actual descent of that stream. I availed myself of an opportunity afforded on the third day of our passage from the upper to the lower sea to examine cursorily the character of the deposits intersected by the Jordan.

There are almost everywhere in the Jordan Valley distinct traces of two independent terraces. The upper terrace extends to the basis of the rocky barriers of the Ghôr, both on the east side and the west, and appears to have been due to a geological condition long preceding the existence of the actual river, yet subsequent to the removal of the material which once occupied the space between the two opposing cliffs. In this interval the whole valley has been submerged in subordination to the great depression from which the continent (in this part at least) has been slowly re-uplifted, the sea being gradually admitted and as gradually expelled from the whole of the long valley as the process of depression and re-elevation went on, each in its unsuspected course. The last withdrawal must have left deposits which are now covered by much more recent contributions from the sides and confluents of the valley. As the land ascended, the sea retired, and the Jordan or its predecessor arose as the necessary consequence. This result is independent altogether of the theory we may adopt of the origin of the greater depression of Bahr Lût than of Wâdy el-'Arabah or of the Gulf of 'Aqabah, and is only invalidated in case of the necessity of holding that the Ghôr is either a fissure or an excavation effected subsequently to the attainment of the present level of the region of which the valley forms a feature so remarkable.

The lower terrace is due exclusively to the secular action of the Jordan posterior to its existence as a fresh water tributary either to the ocean, or to the sea which now receives it only to re-expel it by evaporation. The lateral displacement of the water-course, with the gradual widening of the eroding stream itself, is a phenomenon so frequently (it may be said so universally) attendant upon the formation of the larger river-beds, that no more adequate cause need be looked for here to account for the space now separating the banks of the upper terrace. The bank of the lower terrace follows the *receding* and gives way before the *encroaching* lateral action, but leaves continually in these incessant oscillations, the level of the abandoned side lower than the side of the attacked one, until the lapse of time has restored, by the slow arrival of deposits from the upper terrace, or from sources still more remote, some approach to the original level of the plain.

Simultaneously with this action, the curvature and depth of the stream-channel are continually varying, and any section of the river, tortuous or smooth at one era of its existence, may be straight or swift at another era earlier or later.

The talus of the lower terrace and sometimes that of the upper one are cut out by the rains and running waters into conoidal and cuneoidal knolls, which sometimes rise to the rank of actual hills, though of course they present no similar depression on the inland side of the nearly horizontal curve which constitutes the apparently very irregular outline as seen from a boat in the river. The sections thus obtained show sometimes a tertiary limestone or marl, sometimes quaternary deposits of sands, gravels, variegated clays, or unstratified detritus, all having evidently an origin far more recent than the most recent of the chalks. This conformation of the upper talus exposes sometimes an actual chalk, probably recompacted from the cretaceous wash of the rocky walls and rugged ravines of the distant limestone cliffs. The chalky terraces are generally bare of vegetation, the lower ones are often covered, especially near the rivulets, (which are not unfrequent contributors in the northern Ghôr,) with a growth sometimes luxuriant of *ghurrah*, *sŭfsâf*, *terifeh* and *difleh*.

About half an hour below the Jisr Mujâ[illegible]ah, a flat peninsula, or rather island, covered with trees, (willows, tamarisks and aspens,) shows itself on the eastern side, followed by a gravelly beach, opposing on the west shore a bed of layered alluvial clay, the general direction of the river being south. To this succeeds an indurated marl, hardened sometimes into stone, and beyond this an outcrop of basalt polygonally separated into blocks, if we may judge from the regularity of the surface-fissures at two or three places brought into view. Still further south on the left, alternating layers of rolled stones, sands and clays, form a bank fifteen feet high; and not long after, a short turn in the river-bed throws immediately before the descending navigator a steep wall a hundred feet in height, with layers inclining down the stream. To this succeeds the bank of an ancient valley-bottom, now raised 20 feet above the Jordan's level, with a dip more descending than the river itself. Banks of stratified gravel are next found, rising sometimes one hundred feet in height, succeeded by a talus of yellow pebbles and marly layers rising only to the altitude of 30 feet.

On the east side may next be seen low meadows of some extent with a river-side slope exhibiting very many thin layers of gravel and sand, each often not more than an inch thick, followed by gravelly beaches and low banks covered with tamarisks, aspens, willows, and a profusion of oleanders.

Here begins the Zôr el-Bâsha, the river-course bearing S. E. The left bank is some 15 feet in height, the right a gravelly beach to the water's edge. The stream now varies its direction through a second westerly reach, until its course is once more due south. In the short space of time comprised in this morning's navigation we had passed upwards of thirty swift descents, which were well entitled to the name of rapids. In several of these, returning eddies detained for a time entire trees and large branches, some of them brought from the country north of the Galilean Sea. Stopping for refreshment on a bank by the river-side, covered with *drekhma* and other aromatics,* I noted the rolled stones which had found a rest on this slip of land from their long wanderings down the Ghôr. Among these a fine chalk with characteristic stipplings, seemed to be particularly deserving of attention. It contains 2 per cent. of magnesia.

*In this neighborhood there was growing in great abundance the *'ausalân*, or *jizr et-tanyâs*, a plant with a root resembling a large carrot, with a coarse tough skin of a pale brown color. It was not edible, but seemed in some repute as a medicinal shrub.

Below this the immediate banks of the Jordan continue but little elevated above the water with sedgy and gravelly banks in alternate succession. Sometimes a height of only ten or twelve feet cuts off all view of the plain; at other times a higher bank leaves the still higher broken back-ground visible beyond. There are marks here of rude husbandry, and a large Arab population made its appearance on the shore, and followed us for miles with shouts intended without question as expressive of the friendliest of welcomes. The banks here again very much in height with occasional wedge-shaped ravines, through which the spring drainage of this part of the Ghôr finds a passage to the Jordan. The sections exposed are nearly vertical, and exhibit a stratification of variegated sands, sandstones, limestones and marls. Without having any fossil to assist, these deposits can only be taken as tertiary, and were probably deposited in a wider water-course than now finds its way through the valley. One of these peculiarities of the sandy beds is the suddenness with which the dips set at defiance all those gradations which are supposed to characterise a mere methodical construction. In some instances a large siliceous mass serves as a centre from which the dips and strikes shoot off in almost every direction. Another peculiarity is the curved and feathered branchings of the layer-lines, which wind away from each other in a sort of natural arabesque rendered the more striking by the variety of colors and the thinness of the sheets of sandy marl which make up the mass. Terraces now reappear wherever a view of the interior can be gained, and then low beaches succeed with reedy and thistly fringes frequently varied by the presence of the tamarisk.

The banks here showed distinctly a recent fall of two feet or more in the water of the Jordan, and we passed several islands which are covered in the height of the fresh. The land before us now appeared cut up into numerous square mounds or tells. The river is swift and rough, and wears its banks rapidly away. The background is also much broken up, and nearer the river the knolls are crowded together in cones that resemble the tents of a well arranged encampment. The sides of the western mountains beyond Beisân (Scythopolis) may be seen over and behind the neighboring mounds, while the shores of the Jordan acquire gradually a more imposing and picturesque character, with a less abrupt undulation in the outline of the indentations of the bank. This portion of the Great Valley is called the Ghôr Beisân.

Between the camping ground of April 13th and Beisân, there are three distinct terraces, the upper of which appears to have been formed since the stream has retired to its present bed. These terraces are very well watered, and are even marshy in some places. The streams are charged with bicarbonate of lime, which encrusts in deposits of the carbonate whatever can serve a suitable receptacle for the precipitated tufa. Two large Arab encampments were visited by us here, and at one of these we were very hospitably entertained. To judge by the abundance of our host's supply at quite a short notice, there seemed no great reason to doubt that the neighborhood had resources not very obvious at first sight. Certain it is that it is not for the want of water and good soil, that the labor of the husbandman is not every where apparent, though a day further south brings the traveller into a very unmanageable tract. The ground east of Beisân, two hours distant from the river, is a highly productive marl, and Mr. Dale, who visited the place, found the sloping plain well covered with wheat and intersected by a fine stream heading at the fountain 'Ain es-Sôda.

From our stopping place, Tŭbŭqah Fahil bore nearly S. E., and Sukôt (for so, and not Sukhot, our guides pronounced it) lay as far in the S. W. The plains on both sides of the depression through which the Jordan flows, are not horizontal as might be supposed, but incline towards the stream at an angle varying from five to ten degrees. As we approach the ford Mukhâdat Om el-Qubeis, the west plain of the Jordan expands and the eastern slope grows narrower and more rugged and abrupt. The upper western terrace abounds here in wheat, barley and oats, all these grains being ready (April 14th) for the harvest. One of the tracts of wheat took us 23 minutes to cross. From this we descended to the lower terrace, until a fringe of terafehs showing their tops above the edge of the land, told us that we were again near the Jordan, whose waters to an eye on the plain lie often concealed between its banks, even when these banks and their under beaches are entirely bare of vegetation.

Near the ford Om el-Qubeis, or, as some of the guides call it, Mukhâdah Tell Qŭbes, (Qubeis being merely the diminutive form,) there is an insulated hill (Tell) of compound conglomerate, very remarkable in shape, and indicative, from its structure, its height and its position, of extensive geological action in this valley long after the formation of the Ghôr. Tell Qŭbes is left as one of the most striking remnants, as it were, of an ancient bed of concretes which extended once continuously all around the fragments now remaining, and which still maintains its place (although exceedingly encroached upon and eaten out) on the east of the Jordan, for miles down the river and a mile or more inland from the bank.

The conglomerate of which Tell Qŭbes now consists, shews at various points a secondary rehandling of the old materials, some of the cemented fragments being evidently themselves but the *frusta* of an older and more metamorphosed pudding-stone. For the most part however the constituent morsels are either limestone or quartz; occasionally a black flinty pebble presents itself, which may be referred to the vulcanic silicates. But I would not venture to say that trap as such is ever found as an ingredient in this conglomerate. The limestone bits are generally rounded, and of many shades of color. Not unfrequently the pebbles are readily detached from their sockets, and in some of these I was fortunately enabled to discern on the rounded external surface, where alone they can be seen with advantage, at least two species of Nummulites, not scattered thinly through the limestone, but constituting the larger portion of the mass. The siliceous fragments are often angular, but seldom with sharp and well defined apices and edges. These flints are surviving portions of the nodules of the flinty limestone, which preceded the first conglomerate and supplied it with the most of its materials. They are now bound so intimately together that the original surfaces of separation are in many instances no longer visible, or, if visible, are rather indicated by a change of color, consistency and chemical constitution, subject to the law of continuity as we pass from one decided fragment to another. This superinduced gradation of condition is, in some of the spurs or reefs west of the main *tell*, so completely brought about, that the stone has acquired a porphyritic aspect and texture, though retaining far too much lime to be entitled to the name of porphyry. It results in other places in a mottled limestone susceptible of a good polish, and presenting a very pleasing mixture of the warmer colors.

The main Tell may be two hundred feet in height above the Jordan, and appears to have been once the site of some artificial structure, as the traces of rudely laid up walls and even of hewn stones are here and there discernible, but with difficulty, and with some liability to error as to the part which human agency may have played in shaping these blocks or bringing them together. They are moreover few and scattered and mingled with others whose presence here is more probably due to geological causes than to any form of artificial labor. On one of these detached stones three parallel grooves with a fourth at right angles to these presented strong appearances of a half worn-out sculpture; but even this may have been one of the numerous varieties of weather-scars so often met with in a certain class of rocks. In one instance only was I able to find a fossil remain, but so imperfectly exhibited that I cannot say whether it was a *Cardium* or an *Astarte.*

Encrusting the conglomerate is frequently found a tufaceous accumulation of fine gravel bound together by a calcareous cement, which has however but imperfectly filled the interstices, so that this crust though firm and hard to break is comparatively porous and uncompact.

A beautiful black conglomerate of small flinty granules consolidated in a matrix of the same color and composition has derived its materials from some not very obvious source and may be found in detached balls of which the rounded outsides give proof of long and slow attrition after the formation and subsequent metamorphosing of the parent rock. With this is associated a mass of flints of mottled color and various aspects of lamination and concretion, some quartzy, some chalcedonic, some running into hornstone, some growing into Egyptian jasper or vitrifying into prase.

Nearly opposite Tell Qŭbes, Wâdy Yâbes and Wâdy el-Hemâr, after having cleft the hills beyond, divide the lower terraces and join the immediate valley of the Jordan. The Wâdy el-Jirm lies north of the Yâbes, but I could not learn its extent or determine the rock which it has excavated, though judging from distant appearances the conglomerates begin already here after several discontinuances south of the passage to Om Keis.

An island in the Jordan opposite Tell Qŭbes is plentifully strewn with rolled quartzy pebbles and variegated flints, and beneath this coating the rock must prove to be conglomerate of which crags in place as well as large boulders occur at scattered intervals in the stream. The eastern bank is high and near the water, and consists partly of pudding-stone with beds of hardened marl, partly of a remarkably pure limestone, white and marble-like, associated with a calcareous alabaster in which the concretionary structure is nearly obliterated by metamorphic action.

The second terrace above the beach is very thickly covered with agatic and chalcedonic flints, some of them quite noticeable for the array and variety of their colors. Of these but very few fail to present marks of laminated or concretionary structure. The pebbles are rounder near the river, but exhibit nowhere a very sharp edge. The underlying rock is sometimes limestone, but principally breccia, involving the same flints as are now found loose upon its surface. These debris may be regarded as washed out of old conglomerates or ready to be consolidated in a new one. A ravine which I explored here exhibited in fine relief the two concretes already mentioned as occurring at Tell Qŭbes or two formations at least contemporary with these.

Of these the better consolidated and probably older formation is in some respects so intimately assimilated, that without close examination the boundaries of the constituent fragments cannot well be traced, as if molecular displacements taking effect through a long course of ages had at least obliterated the differences between pebble and pebble, and had given to trap, quartz and limestone, not only the appearance, but the means of having actually become very much alike. Even the colors so distinct in the second species seem to have nearly died away, and the general tone of the composition is a pale dull yellow. The newer conglomerate is much coarser, less coherent, higher colored, and far more resolvable into very distinct bits, (each retaining its original characteristic,) than the bed beneath it, which at various points shows marks of denudation before the materials of the coarser concrete were formed, deposited and finally united, after deposition, into a well cemented mass.

Between the eastern escarpment of the Ghôr and the Qurn el-Hemâr, (a long curved Tell between the road and the river,) lies a broad plain, divided by two principal valleys into three distinct slopes. The valley sides are rough and bare, and expose a coarse conglomerate more or less fractured and displaced. The stray blocks are of the same material, and the ravines are as usual more recent than the platform, and more ancient than the earliest movement of the fragments which survive.

Over this plain, with the Qurn bounding the prospect on the right, a view of the mountain range west of the Dead Sea, presents a combination of austere and dreary contours and colors, harmonising nevertheless not ungratefully into a picture well calculated to impress powerfully the traveller's imagination. Near at hand, and at various heights on the gentle declivity, below the flank of Jebel 'Ajlûn, several villages, (one or two of them in ruins,) diversify the scene, and numerous fields of barley and wheat, with the welcome recurrence of the *bŭtm*, *sidr*, (or *dôm*,) and *zaqqûm* trees, give assurance that the land is not entirely surrendered to the law of nomade rule.

The soil is thin and gravelly, but there is enough of vegetable mould to show what might be effected by a proper system of terracing and irrigation. There seems in this neighborhood no great deficiency of water. The Fajâris and the Rajeb are fed by sources that are seldom known to fail, and though the supplies do not always reach the Jordan, they are available for a great part of the plain traversed by their channels.

About two miles north of Jisr Fajâris, the remarkable peak Qurn Sŭrtŭbeh, comes distinctly into view. It bore, when I first saw it, S. 35° W., and was distant 18 or 20 miles. Three miles farther south gave a bearing S. 41° W. Between our road and the Jordan lay a fine broad plain, descending gently to the river, well covered with grain ready for the threshing floor. The rock wherever it could be found, showed, as before, conglomerates of different ages, yet probably due to causes operating under circumstances not materially unlike. Rolled stones of considerable magnitude, formed either of a flinty sandstone or of a compact and corneous chert, abound in the ravines or lurk in ancient basins and water-courses, from which the later alluvial covering has not yet been removed.

South of the Fajâris, the plains extend farther inland, and southwardly as far as Wâdy Rajeb. They were covered when we crossed them with a pale-brown grass, (es-sŭma'ah?) resembling in color and general appearance the salt-marsh grasses of the Middle States. In the midst of this grew an abundance of thistles, the *murâr*, the *dudâr*, and the *ziyeiteh*, with a proportion of the wild carrot, *'ausalân*.

While some of our Moslem attendants went off to visit the shrine of Abu 'Obeideh, our own party approached the river gradually, descending over the plain on the south side of a *tell* of conglomerate, not far distant from the Jordan. A tract of cultivated land, occupying a lower level, is then crossed, and a few minutes more bring the traveller to the ford of Seqâ.

The west side of the Jordan, south of this ford, consists of a not very broad plain of gravelly alluvion, intermixed with calcareous and conglomerate erratics. The lower cliff beyond the plain is limestone, or limestone thickly coated with conglomerate. From this an upper plain much intersected, extends with various breaks and interruptions, far inland to the proper rocky boundary of the Ghôr.

The conglomerate found in this neighborhood is remarkable at times, as well for the materials of which it consists, as for the mode in which these materials are distributed in the mass. The larger fragments are chiefly of the nummulitic limestone of the northern hills, and for the most part irregularly rounded, but sometimes angular and even pointed. These fragments seldom touch each other, and the interstices (sometimes several inches apart) are filled with a coarse mortar, harder and more difficult to break than the limestone *calculi*, to which however it does not always tenaciously adhere. The mortar is composed of a paste partly siliceous, partly calcareous, studded very thickly with angular gravel, sometimes chalky, but generally flinty, and then of a remarkable variety of colors.

From a point on the edge of a higher terrace, not far from the ford es-Seqâ, the left summit of Mount Hermon bore N. 16° 30′ E. and Abu 'Obeideh S. 74° E. Two miles south of this station, the conglomerates cease to be continuous, and shortly after the denuded limestone shows itself as the predominant rock. Near the caves and caverns, however, which in this neighborhood are not unfrequent, the conglomerate occurs in large patches, and is also found nestling, as it were, in sheltered nooks, just under the brows and along the flanks of the lateral ravines. Not long after, this formation ceases altogether, but the limestone bears the marks of metamorphic action, and its colors as well as its texture have manifestly undergone a change, not entirely the effect of atmospheric agents. The exposed surface is often singularly rough, with asperities difficult to explain, as they do not seem to be determined by a pre-existing inequality in the temper of the limestone.

Opposite the mouth of Wâdy Zerqa, stretching northwardly as well as southwardly, a white limestone occurs of a marble-like color and grain, highly charged with crystals of a disseminated calcspar. It contains corals and testaceous fossils, but not abundantly; and time did not enable me to procure any specimens on which I should rely for paleontological results. The weathered surface is ash-grey, and somewhat pitted or otherwise fretted and scarred.

A mile or more farther south brings the traveller to Merj en-Nujh, Qurn Sŭrtŭbeh bearing S. 44½° W., and Qŭl'at er-Rŭbŭd N. 35° E. This meadow is not without vegetation, and gazelles are sometimes thus invited in herds within its borders, as we found once or twice in crossing it where we did.

The cavernous disposition of the calcareous escarpment here is deserving of study, and indicates a slow and long continued waste of the body of the rock. In some instances the limestone shoots out in spurs or ridgy processes through which the exesion has quite penetrated, and as a consequence of this two or three natural arches of very picturesque construction may be remarked near the mouth of Wâdy Fâri'a.

From the north side of Wâdy Fâri'a, near its opening on the Ghôr, Qurn Sŭrtŭbeh bore S. 61° W., and Qŭl'at er-Rŭbŭd N. 50° E. From a point in the axis of the Wâdy, 40 minutes south of the former, the Qurn bore S. 65° W., the highest point of Jebel es-Salt S. 61° E., and the direction of the lowest point in the outline seen looking up the Wâdy, or what is nearly the same thing, the bearing of the last reach of the valley was N. 30° W., making a much acuter angle with the meridian or the general direction of the Ghôr, than is commonly supposed.

Nearly a mile south of the station last mentioned, a stream of water fringed with reeds and oleanders was crossed where it was running in a direction nearly due south. Shortly afterwards a southeastwardly course brought us to a lower terrace, and another quarter of an hour to the camping ground near Jisr Dâmi'a, over an alluvion formed from calcareous detritus characterised by the frequent occurrence of nests of sulphate of lime in arrow-shaped crystals.

The waters which descend to the Jordan from the unexplored mountainous district between Wâdy Fâri'a and Wâdy Nawâ'imeh are more or less charged with the salts which they have been able to elixiviate from the rocks and debris they have encountered in their course. Supplies from thermal sources meet the larger contributions from the vernal rains; and though the ingredients of the lower waters are mainly due to the warmer springs from beneath, it is nevertheless certain that the effect of the secular action of rain-water on the rocks which either filter or convey it, has not attracted the attention it deserves.

Of the wasting, burrowing, scooping energy of the streams which are insensibly but unfailingly wearing away the solid limestones and basalts on each side of the Ghôr, the best evidences are to be found in the courses and depths of the ravines already carved or etched out of the general platform of which the Jordan valley is incomparably by far the oldest excavation. But the action and reaction of the rock and its percolating waters furnish results not so obvious at first, but very remarkable in their accumulated effects. The limestones, traps and conglomerates of the Ghôr are not to be regarded in any other light, than rocks which have become by secular modification what they now are, from the unknown sediments or ejections which they have been. And the salts of the Dead Sea, that receptacle of all the extracts which the tributaries to the Jordan absorb from their rocky sides, are nothing more than what the same limestones, traps and conglomerates have yielded to the dissolving activity of the waters, which thus amply repay themselves for the deposits they leave behind.

The tufas formed on the upper and lower terraces of the Jordan, are well deserving of an attentive study. Some are strictly calcareous; others, though much more rarely, exclusively siliceous. Many are mixed in various proportions. Some are laminated, some contorted, some concretionary about granular or fibrous *nuclei*. The colors are as various as the molecular arrangements, and the range of specific gravity is from 1.5 to 3.5, and in some ferruginous tufas even as high as 4.0.

Of these tufas, I met with three between the fords of Seqâ and Dâmi'a, sufficiently distinct and characteristic to serve as specific types, if it indeed be possible to establish these in formations so arbitrary as the infinitely multiplied varieties of tufaceous deposits. The first of these is a gritty calcareous paste loosely charged with lapilli more or less broken and for the most part siliceous, often agatised, seldom chalcedonic. The second description is rather an assemblage of minute tunicated *nuclei* held together by a thin paste of lime than a tufa properly so called. The third is free from all admixture of foreign ingredients. It seems to be exclusively made up of deposits from a fluid which brought along with it in solution very dissimilar materials. Evaporation has thrown these down in an order apparently capricious, and gradually accumulated them in variegated leaf-like layers of calcites, magnesites and ochres, occasionally traversed at right angles by spathic interlaminations. A specimen of this last was found on the west of the Jordan in the meadow opposite the bridge which here still spans one of the deserted channels of the ancient stream.

Between Wâdy Fâri'a and Wâdy 'Aujeh, the rock is mainly cretaceous, coarse and of a chalky white, apparently determined in its stratification by the inequalities of the surface on which or against which it has been forced to make its beds. Several axes of intersecting dips occur, which I do not however regard as properly anticlinal, that is, superinduced upon a once unbroken dip by dislocating forces. Near an ancient cemetery (Watâyir or Qubûr el-mayyetîn) a summit level is passed so that there is a gentle descent, not only towards Erîha (Jericho,) but also just as decidedly towards the north, even as far as beyond the Merj en-Nujh. Here again blocks of conglomerate are met with though rarely, a recent limestone having in part replaced it, or having at least in some way superseded its formation.

Wâdy Fŭsâyil did not seem to be known to our guides, who pointed out however a Wâdy Wôleh or Wauleh near the cemetery, a mile or more north of Wâdy 'Aujeh. Down both of these Wâdys, but more especially the latter, a brown alluvion is washed onward by the spring rains, and, if retained by proper terracing, might cover this now barren portion of the Belâd Mashârîk with a soil of great fertility, for the means of irrigation would not be wanting.

The limestone wall of the Ghôr is here and as far as opposite Tell Qŭrŭntŭl indented by semi-elliptic bays, so that the line of march brought us several times near the points or spurs which mark the limits of the incurvations. At one of these I observed a remarkable disposition of the exterior limestone in relation to its dip. The strata were nearly vertical on the whole, but curved towards the cliff above and from it below, so as to present the lines of a frozen cataract such as is sometimes found in the glaciers of Switzerland and Norway. A similar plunging dip incrusting in like manner moderately inclined strata occurs east of the Dead Sea at the entrance of Wâdy Kerak.

The plain continues now for three or four miles as barren of vegetation as the Lybian desert. Shortly after entering it, a stone wall or rather the foundation and base of one runs along the plain for half a mile or more and turns off then at right angles towards the east. This is nearly at the middle of the chord of one of the bays formed by the promontories of the western highlands, the distance from chord to arc being here about three-quarters of a mile. Nearly opposite, but more northwardly beyond the Jordan, the mountainous district es-Salt seems to the eye to attain its greatest elevation in the direction of Rabbath Ammon and el-Fuhais. The whole extent of the Belka range appears from this point deeply indented with dark ravines penetrating far into the interior of the mountain mass.

On approaching the next projection of the western cliff, we rode over the upturned edges of the nearly vertical strata of limestone, the planes of stratification being crossed by others so as to form in the horizontal section angles of about 70°. South of this a steep precipice shows strikingly the singular contortions which the calcareous strata not unfrequently assume, contortions difficult to ascribe either to pressure in the general direction of the axis of the sinuosity or to violent dislevelling forces acting at right angles to it. Angular boulders and flinty pebbles of various colors and markings lie strewn over this part of the plain, and the road, which is much at the choice of the traveller, may again be made to form the chord of a great amphitheatre carved from the mountain's side. On the left of this line many ***sidr*** or ***dôm*** trees enliven the monotonous ***glacis*** between the road and the river, and through a gap near the middle of the western cliffs a good view of Tell Qŭrŭntŭl may be had, showing that its limestone also is laid in courses more or less curved, and sometimes violently bent.

Remains of well built structures of stone not unskilfully hewn, are passed on the left, and the road now begins to be rough and somewhat rolling as the ravines grow deeper and more numerous. Through some of these, plentiful streams of water found their way, and it was evident that we were approaching a tract capable of sustaining at least a village population.

Shortly after crossing the Nawâ'imeh, the last of the streams just mentioned, a coarse brown limestone may be observed with a dip of 15° towards the southeast. The surface irregularities continue to increase until the number of ravines and branch gulleys becomes so great that the ground is no longer a platform or undulation with occasional interruptions, but a succession of lime banks and knolls left in random relief, showing clearly with what rapidity the process of denudation may go on, when once the wasting agents are allowed to do their work.

The residuary salts left after the evaporation of the surface waters which are spread early every year over basins excavated perhaps not many years before, are found to consist chiefly of chloride of sodium, chloride of calcium and magnesium, with some of the carbonates of the earths, and, in very small proportions also, the sulphates, hyposulphites and sulphurets of the alkalies and earths with so much of pure sulphur as the evaporation must necessarily disengage.

These residua often cover the ground for many square miles in places subject to humid accumulations. The appearance they present is not unlike the hoar-frost of our early autumn; the composition of the material varying with the circumstances of the supplied fluid and the time of the year. After the deposit of the chlorides, the next rains of course dissolve and carry off these soluble ingredients, which either reappear after a fresh evaporation on the surface of a lower receptacle, or are passed onward into the Jordan to contribute to the saturation of Bahr Lût, and finally in that steaming kettle to find their way to the thickening crusts and growing banks at the bottom of its full-fed brine.

What the rains do not dissolve, (the sulphur, the carbonates of lime and magnesia, the hydrated oxides of titaniferous iron and manganese, with traces of silica in some of its insoluble combinations,) unless actually washed off in mechanical suspension, remain behind with some vestiges of undissolved chlorides, to pass into the soil and there await the ulterior transformations which incorporate them afresh with their chalky beds, or collect them by molecular affinity into separated aggregates, more or less pure, according to the opportunities of the process.

Between Wâdy Kelt and Qŭsr Hajla, the fine plain which extends westwardly towards Jericho, becomes irregularly broken up on coming nearer the Jordan, and thus gives the observer a convenient means of examining the coarse marls and limestones which piled up in nearly horizontal layers are left insulated in patches and larger tracts, with scarcely a shrub or bramble[*] to give hope of a better vegetation. These unpromising appearances are more remarkable east and north of 'Ain Hajla, until on approaching either Erîha northwestwardly or the Jordan towards the Bathing place, the ***rishrâsh***, the ***sifsâf***, the ***nŭbq*** and the ***zaqqûm***,[†] appear again to give token of the productiveness which asks, even in the desert, nothing but the presence of water to create and sustain.

[*] A lichen, a wild garlic, and an Erica, with an Asclepias, and perhaps a dwarf Tamarix make up the Flora of this neighborhood.

[†] Vitex agnus castus—Salix Sifsâf—Rhamnus nabeca—Elaeagnus angustifolius.

The examination of the immediate borders of the Jordan south of Mukhâdat el-Meshra'ah, or as it is sometimes called, Maghtas en-Nŭsârah, presents nothing very instructive for the geologist. The rock exists at an unknown depth beneath an alluvial accumulation of sand and clay, furnishing in some places abundant crops of willows and weeds, and at other points failing to develop the slightest trace of vegetable life.

### *Analysis of the Jordan Water at the Pilgrims' Baths.*

THE water contained in the bottle brought home had no smell at the time it was taken from the river, but on opening it a year afterwards, a strong odor of sulphuretted hydrogen gas was emitted, showing the decomposition of a part of the sulphates existing at the time of collection, a decomposition due most probably to the action of the carbon contained in the cork.

Five determinations on as many different days gave for the specific gravity a mean (after the requisite reductions for temperature) of 1.00183.

Total amount of fixed constituents in 2008 grains, (preventing as far as possible by the due admixture of muriate of ammonia the volatilization of any portion of the chlorine during the drying,) 3 gr. 665; that is in 1000 grains, 1.825.

In two other charges of 2008 grains each, from which the sulphuretted hydrogen had previously been expelled and the sulphurets duly estimated, there was obtained by treating with nitrate of silver (deducting for sulphuret of silver in one experiment and separating the same in another and taking the mean) chloride of silver 6 gr. 002, equivalent to chlorine 1.484.

Of the residuum after the evaporation, from 2008 grains there was found, not soluble in water, .715—consisting of:

| | |
|---|---|
| Carbonate of Lime, | .340 |
| Carbonate of Magnesia, | .292 |
| Peroxide of Iron, | .074 |
| Silica, | .005 |
| | .711 |

Of the same residuum there was found soluble in water:

| | |
|---|---|
| Precipitated by Ammonia, | .16 |
| Chloride of Calcium, | .26 |
| Chloride of Magnesium, | .89 |
| Chloride of Sodium, | 1.21 |
| Chloride of Potassium, | .07 |
| Sulphate of Lime, | .09 |
| Sulphate of Soda, | .08 |
| Various incertain combinations of sulphur with earthy and alkaline bases, | .17 |
| Crenic and hypocrenic acids, (distinct traces.) | |
| Other organic and extractive matter, (traces.) | |
| | 2.93 |
| Add insoluble portion, | .711 |
| | 3.641 |
| Remaining to be accounted for, | .024 |

I should be unwilling to convey the idea that the Jordan water, even from the same locality, will be found to present at all times the same result. Independently of errors of analysis, the water is necessarily variable in its composition. Much depends upon the season of the year, much upon the spot from which the water is drawn, and perhaps more than all upon the region visited by the winter rains and the character of the rocks and soils through which the tributary waters rise to the surface or ultimately pass. At the place from which the above water was taken, there is no reason to suppose that the Dead Sea salts have any retroactive influence, though the Jordan is brackish a quarter of a mile up a very rapid outlet. The large quantity of chloride of magnesium may be due either to the magnesian limestones or the igneous rocks traversed by the streams which feed the Jordan, and may therefore vary very much from year to year. The chloride of sodium is however much in excess, though only equal, in the Dead Sea water, to half of the chloride of magnesium. This preponderance of the latter chloride in the Great Basin, is owing without doubt to the fact that it is the most soluble of the ingredients and even, though contributed more slowly, is accepted and retained long after the alkaline chlorides are precipitated from the brine which they have saturated ages and ages ago.

The magnesia exists in the dolomites principally as carbonate. The muriate of soda is also an ingredient in all the re-emerged beds as well as in the basalts, and I found no rock in the valley of the Jordan altogether free from this admixture. How the decomposition is effected, may not be easy to make out, but that this is the result seems to be satisfactorily proved.

Bischoff has conjectured, while treating another subject, that the decomposition of carbonate of lime and chloride of sodium may take place during the process of vegetation, and may thus explain the physiology of soda plants. Should this be really the case, the chloride of calcium will find its way as a very soluble salt to the sea, and the chloride of magnesium may owe its origin and its continued increase in the Dead Sea to a process altogether similar. But it is also undeniable that the chlorides of calcium and magnesium exist already in the plutonic rocks, and the elixiviation of these ingredients is an inevitable consequence of the comminution and disintegration of nearly all basalts and traps. To either of these two sources we may refer the chlorides of the southern reaches of the Jordan, as well as their enormous accumulation in the Great Evaporating Basin, which is unceasingly receiving and condensing the tributary waters, while these in their turn are to be regarded only as temporary media of transport broken up in the act of depositing the saline supplies.

Between 'Ain es-Sultân and Jebel Qŭrŭntŭl (Quarantana) is an elevated tract which looks from the plain below like a range of rugged hills, and from the mountains above and beyond like a low flat terrace a little raised above the plain. It is out of the eastern face of this hilly tract that the Fountain of Eliseus gushes forth. The water is very agreeable to the taste, and cool enough to be acceptable even to ordinary thirst. The rocks immediately around and above the fountain are of a coarse secondary limestone, posterior to the chalks of St. Sâba and Jerusalem, buttressed with embankments of a conglomerate of small flinty pebbles resembling some of the tufas of the lower grounds, but made up much more abundantly of gravel, so that the cementing paste is a very subordinate constituent of the mass. The limestone is not deficient in fossils, but after many attempts I could bring away no specimen containing reliable impressions. Among the least obscure I remarked fragments of *Ostraeae*, *Nuculae*, *Turritellae* and *Astartae*, but I make no doubt that an examination less restricted as to time would result in the establishment of very characteristic criteria of geological age. Lithologically this limestone approaches the *calcaire grossier* and *nagelfluhe*, and is underlaid by a formation which calls to mind the *plänerkalk* and some of the calcareous beds of the *macigno*. Lower in the series than the *molasse*, but higher orographically, the *nummulitic*, *hippuritic* and *nerinaean* limestones present themselves in due succession to justify this inference. Still it would be premature to undertake to say that the 'Ain es-Sultân beds may not be referred to some of the incidents of the siliciferous chalk and the formation which supports them may perhaps be hereafter claimed as contemporary with the upper accumulations of the Jura.

One of the ingredients of the conglomerates, at least where they inclose larger fragments than usual, is a silicate which like the flint-stones of 'Ain Hôdh and Bethlehem consists of white angular splinters of silex in a brown siliceous gangue. It is hard to resist the impression that these stones are genuine concretes, though it is certainly very difficult to explain on any known principles the mode in which the materials were brought together. An hypothesis looking to molecular groupings of the coloring matter around centres of attraction does not seem entitled to a favorable reception, nor is it easy to refer these spotted flints to organic structures either of animal or vegetable origin.

# SECTION IV.

## RECONNAISSANCE OF THE DESERT OF JUDA,

### BETWEEN JERICHO, JERUSALEM AND ENGADDI.

## CHAPTER I.

### *Route from the Pilgrims' Bathing Place to Jerusalem.*

*Jeraïf er-Razn.—View from Râs el-Mukhawwifeh.—Limestones, Tufas, Sulphate of Lime, bituminous marl.—Hajar Mûsa or Moses'-stone of Neb Mûsa, its composition and fossils.—Fetid hippuritic limestone of Kekhmûm.—Tŭbŭqat el-Quneiterah.—Vertical fissures in Wâdy Rawâwah.—Chalk and flint-stones of Wâdy Hôdh.—Tertiaries.—Chalk of the Mount of Olives, the Mount of Offence and the Mount of Evil Counsel.—Its probable age.*

THE observations I was able to make within this interesting district were necessarily limited by shortness of time, one portion of it having been visited on being despatched to bring provisions from Jerusalem, the remainder while the levels were carried up to that city from the Dead Sea at 'Ain Terâbeh.

The main body of rock within the bounds of this triangle is chalk of the upper groupe overlying a limestone as ancient as the older strata of the Libanus, and referable therefore to deposits immediately succeeding the middle Jurassic. In the northeast angle of this area is found the bituminous limestone of Neby Mûsa, a formation which I was able to trace into two of the Wâdys south of this locality. Of sandstones or igneous rocks I could find no vestiges whatever.

Leaving the camp at the Pilgrims' Bathing Place, April 18th, a part of the day was employed in surveying the ground between the Jordan and Erîha, and the hills behind 'Ain es-Sultân. The results obtained have been anticipated in the pages just preceding. My escort 'Atallah and Sheikh Helû deserted me on the evening of the first day, and I gladly availed myself of the assistance of Sheikh 'Abdallah, a very intelligent guide, placed at our own joint disposal by the kindness of the Rev. Mr. Sampson, of Washington, who had secured his services at Jerusalem, and was fortunately then at Jericho with the intention of returning to the Holy City the following day.

From Erîha to the foot of Râs el-Mukhawwifeh, the ride lies over the plain ascending slowly to a convenient entrance to one of the Wâdys which disembogue upon the upper terrace of the Ghôr. This tract, which 'Abdallah called Jeraïf, or Ajrâf er-Razn, (gulleys leading to an irregular plain,) is well described by this epithet, which was probably meant by him rather as a description than a geographical appellation. The Jeraïf Razal, on the east of the Jordan, may have a similar origin.

From Râs el-Mukhawwifeh a fine view is obtained of the eastern cliffs and Wâdys. The most conspicuous eminences are Jebel Kerak, or its outliers, Jebel Môjeb, (or Jebel Shihân,) Jebel Attârûs, Jebel Kûra, Jebel Hesbân, Jebel es-Salt, and Jebel Nefrîyeh. Sheikh 'Abdallah reckoned five fords across the Jordan as within sight, Mukhâdat el-Fâyidh at the mouth, and then northwardly, Mukhâdat el-Helû, Mukhâdat el-Hajla, (probably interchanged,) Mukhâdat el-Munheidhy, Mukhâdat el-Ghurânieh. The Wâdys pointed out to us were Wâdy Môjeb, Wâdy Zerqa Ma'în, Wâdy Hesbân, Wâdy Seir, Wâdy Behâdh, Wâdy Sha'ib, Wâdy Dâmi'a. What 'Abdallah called Wâdy Behâdh appears to occupy the place generally assigned to Wâdy Keferein. The term Keferein our guide restricted to the two deserted hamlets near the valley, though the Wâdy itself may very naturally be designated by another name, derived from the circumstance of there being, or there having been, two ancient villages on its banks.

Both er-Râmeh and Keferein could be easily distinguished, the former near a Tell, or broad mound, the latter not far from the whitened cliffs south of Wâdy Behâdh. There was much woody verdure in both neighborhoods, proceeding from the abundance of *sidr* trees. On the plain beneath us, Burj er-Rîha bore N. 26° E., in the midst of wheat-fields waiting for the sickle, the barley being already gathered for the threshing floor. West of this, a squalid cluster of sheds and hedges, all that is left to mark the site of ancient Jericho, lay in a line between the castle and the cliff; and along the Kelt, till its waters were evaporated or absorbed, a green border stretched across the arid plain to tell us where the wilderness had still a conquest to achieve.

On the way to the height from which we had this prospect, I passed in quick succession, first, a coarse limestone similar to that of 'Ain es-Sultân; secondly, a calcareous bed above, but dipping beneath the other, and remarkable for its color, (a brown ground with circular and oval specks of chalk,) as well as for obscure and scattered indications of fish-teeth and scales; and thirdly, a schistose limestone, with layers of gypsum and bituminous marl.

Not far from Râs el-Mukhawwifeh, before coming to Neby Mûsa, an opening is presented down a narrow ravine, through which the head of the Lake comes finely into view. Near this the brown and white-speckled limestone, with fish remains, crops out again, and is succeeded by a pale-pink tufa, not stratified and unusually heterogenous in its parts. Crusts of sulphate of lime are thickly interwoven with the mass, but of very limited area and of unequal thickness, as if a very irregularly diffused ingredient had been replaced by imitative crystallizations of satin and calcspar. The calcareous portion of this tufa gave on analysis the following result:

| | |
|---|---|
| Carbonate of Lime, | 92.53 |
| Carbonate of Magnesia, | 1.86 |
| Iron and Alumina, | .57 |
| Chloride of Sodium, | 1.82 |
| Insoluble, | 1.08 |
| Water and Loss, | 2.14 |
| | 100.00 S. |

Next in order comes a violet-red indurated marl, succeeded by thin shales slightly bituminous, and beds of limestone, at first pure, but afterwards increasing very rapidly their respective quotas of asphaltic matter, until the Hajar Mûsa, or bitumen stone, with its black interior, and its bran or ash-colored face, shows itself fully developed in its final and permanent form.

The Hajar Mûsa, or Moses'-stone, has been long known as the material of which numberless ornaments and toys, kept for sale at the convents, are turned or carved sometimes by the Arabs, but more frequently by the inmates of the religious houses where the traveller is most likely to fall in with them. The stone has an imperfect conchoidal fracture, with occasional traces of the radiated fimbriae of the bitumen. The color varies from a fine India ink black to a dull ash-grey, according to the predominance of the calcareous ingredient. It is homogeneous in its texture, in no respect crystalline, but filled with innumerable very small shining particles, not easily visible on a first inspection. When fresh broken and especially when triturated in a mortar, it emits a strong, but not disagreeable bituminous smell. An analysis by Mr. Hewston gave:

| | |
|---|---|
| Carbonate of Lime, | 82.10 |
| Organic matter, | 13.55 |
| Iron and Alumina, | 1.95 |
| Silica, | 1.95 |
| Magnesia, (none.) | |
| | 99.55 |

This limestone is not wanting in fossils. The best determined of these are ***Inoceramus aratus***, Co., ***Pecten obrutus***, Co., ***Gryphaea vesicularis***, Lam.

At Kekhmûm (or Tshekhmûm as 'Abdallah in his local dialect pronounced it)* not far from the bituminous limestone of Wely Mûsa, a calcareous bed appears in striking contrast with its swarthy associate. This is a bright, cream-like limestone, straw-colored where exposed, with a compact texture and flat or subconchoidal break. It bears a close resemblance to some specimens from the inferior beds both at Bhamdûn and in the valley of Jehoshaphat, but differs from this in its stratigraphical relations. I found no fossils in it, except Hippuritic fragments and am unable to say whether it may safely be regarded as contemporary with its analogues in the Libanus and near Jerusalem or not. Some of the limestones of this neighborhood are remarkable for the contortions of their strata and the steepness of the general dip. Not far from this the road we took struck west of Tŭbŭqat el-Quneiterah, a high hill shaped like the frustum of a pyramid, adjoining the Nŭqb or pass of that name. Standing where we did, this vast turret-like pile appeared in projection against the glowing surface of the northern bay, our height throwing the square summit of the Tŭbŭqah against the nearer side of the watery ground on which as we passed along it lay for a time in sharply cut perspective.†

After leaving the bituminous and hippuritic limestones south and west of Neby Mûsa, the hills and gorges grow wilder and more forbiddingly sterile. The chalky cliffs seem to defy the approach of the shepherd or the husbandman, and the valleys look as if they were never visited by those waters to which they owe their birth and their growth, and which one day will find in place of the crumbling walls they are insensibly removing, an added margin to the spreading level of the Ghôr.

* This pronunciation of the *kéf* as our English *ch* may be remarked from Bethlehem as far north sometimes as Jenîn and extends across the Jordan to Haurân.

† I have a note here that the views northwardly included es-Sŭmra. Whether this is the same as the imperfectly identified Khurbet es-Sumrah near the mouth of Wâdy el-Abyad is more than I can now venture to say.

The valley west and north of us, which we kept on our right since we left the Wely was, we were told, Wâdy er-Rawâwah. Descending this obliquely the path lay over a chalky tract, and after a few winding detours brought us to two reservoirs (*hîyâdh* or *ahwâdh*) cut in the limestone rock occupying a space of about 60 feet by 45, the western division having beside its walls a square column to serve as additional support to the roof.

The rock is here split vertically, and the fissures are crossed by planes of stratification at angles not varying much from 70°, leaving 20° of dip. The limestone is, as far as it is safe to judge from a few fossils, a member of the upper cretaceous series, and the abundance of flints may perhaps be regarded as an admissible, though not very conclusive confirmation of this conjecture.

Higher in the valley is a Khân, generally deserted, but sometimes, as we found it, (it was a day of Moslem pilgrimage to the Wely) occupied for the convenience of preparing the favorite beverage of the observers of the Prophet's sober Law.*

The limestones of Wâdy Hôdh are cretaceous and among the later deposits of the series. The flint-stones which are of an endless variety are not uniformly distributed and some of the superior beds (no doubt of the upper chalk) are quite free of any such admixture. They are seldom present in globular nodules, but occur in beds of calcareous schist or of a massive indurated marl, holding the firestone imbedded in discs or digitiform *nuclei*, often coated with a thick film of silicate of lime of a color intermediate between the yellow limestone and the smoke-brown flints.

Nearer the openings upon the Ghôr, in the neighborhood of the asphaltic limestones for example, and even south of Wâdy en-Nâr, tertiaries of a character not to be mistaken are often found in a limited extent, filling ancient cavities or incrusting ancient prominences which still remain to mark the irregularities of the last secondary surface. Indeed as high as 'Ain Hôdh and even on the summit levels around Jerusalem, though more conspicuously as we descend towards the Jordan, a coarse limestone occurs assuming various phases according to locality, which cannot with any propriety be referred to a period so early as the chalk. It has all the appearance of fresh water origin, overlies the chalk, except where that has been removed by denudation and runs at times into a metamorphic travertine, a gritty conglomerate or a coarse and crumbling marl. The dips are so irregular that no inference can be drawn from them, and the suddenness with which these beds break off or thin away on one side of the hill without any reappearance on the hills immediately adjacent seems to point to a system of growths from many insulated points of origin.

Without undertaking a solution of the problem of these phenomena, which are not unusual in mountainous tracts of secondary limestone, it is not premature perhaps to say that, whatever the actual explanation may one day turn out to be, the supercretaceous deposits are arranged very much as they would be if the cretaceous surface in the course of its secular emergence had been deeply carved and channelled by water-courses into a very rugged and excessively diversified relief, and afterwards either subsequent to partial resubmergences or at least to sectional dislocations of the upraised area, detrital accumulations had taken effect in the newly formed basins, whether of the nature of smooth water, river-reaches, fens, lakes, estuaries, eddies or bays.

*This Khân was not considered by our guide as entitled to any specific appellation ; it has however been sometimes mistaken for Khân Hudhrûr, which is larger and distant from this an hour's journey northeastwardly, 'Ain Haud or Hôdh lying about as far off on the west.

The road on approaching Jerusalem lay between Bethania and Abu Dîs, and then between the Mount of Olives and the Mount of Offence. These eminences are relics left between extensive denudations from a platform of chalk with many fossils, among which were found ***Nucula crebrilineata***, ***Nucula perdita***, ***Arca parallela***, ***Pecten delumbis***, ***Astarte undulosa***, ***Opis undata***, and a ***Rostellaria***, not well defined.

The shelly chalk of Mount Olivet may likewise be traced with great advantage down the Brook Cedron, (Wâdy Kidrôn, or Wâdy er-Râhib,) into its continuation Wâdy en-Nâr, where (at least in its terminating gorges) the subcretaceous strata are brought fairly into view.

In passing between the Mount of Offence and the Hill of Evil Counsel, as well as farther north, near the village of Siloe, (Kefr Selwân,) and still higher in the Valley of Josaphat, various limestones of closer texture than the shelly chalk, is found under circumstances involving the geological relations of these calcareous beds in difficulties which future observations will no doubt remove. Either the hippuritic or nummulitic limestones must (at least in the Mediterranean basin) be regarded as essentially cretaceous, or the shelly chalk of the Wilderness of Juda must be referred to the ages of the tertiaries, a conclusion not without other fair grounds of support.

## CHAPTER II.

### *Route from Jerusalem to 'Ain Jidy.*

*Limestones of Wâdy er-Râhib, (Brook Cedron.)—Arab Encampments.—Chalk with Fossils.—Helices of the Plain South of Mird.—Kerm et-Terâd. Nŭqb el-Quneiterah, bituminous limestone.—Dolomite.—Limestones and Flints.—Sulphur balls.—Wâdys terminating in the Desert Plain.—Alluvions.—Ravines of the Plain.—Chalks of Wâdy Derejeh.—Pitted Limestones.—Prospect of the Dead Sea.—Wâdy Sudeir.—Cliff above 'Ain Jidy.*

If we enter Wâdy er-Râhib by passing out of the ravine running from the Mount of Offence in the direction of Abu Dîs and crossing the low ridge which separates this hollow from the Valley of the Cedron, we strike upon an unstratified cretaceous limestone, resting upon a dark-colored bed of semi-silicated chalk. South of the Cedron the same disposition may be traced, and though shortly after the coverings of the banks of a long reach of Wâdy er-Râhib prevent the examination of the rock, the two limestones reappear at no great distance below, in a form somewhat changed.

On the southern slope of one of these windings of the valley, two wandering tribes lay encamped, the Beni Isma'în and the Beni Hamdah, to speak on the authority of my guide, and several flocks of sheep and goats quite remarkable for their numbers, were giving evidence that good browsing had been found on the fine broad declivity that came down to us from a distant ridge on the right. Beyond this a wilder district succeeds, and the face of the limestone becomes naked and precipitous. A double ledge of flint perhaps twenty yards apart, half way up the cliffs, marks the opposite sides of the valley, as the walls of an excavation from a once unbroken platform; the hypothesis of a fissure and subsequent enlargement by dislocation instead of denudation being quite untenable, as is shown by the undisturbed continuity of the broad rocky floor with the limestone of the sides. The same remark may in fact be made of many ravines and valleys not only in Palestine but elsewhere; and a close inspection of the floors of the deepest and widest river-beds will confirm two conclusions, derived not only from the comparison of the banks, but still more satisfactorily from the regularity of the descending levels of the channel-lines in the direction of the stream: first, that these depressions are secular excavations, made in the long course of ages, insensibly and ante-historically, by the unwatched action of flowing water, which has done its unsuspected work not merely during the post-tertiary times, but already before the tertiaries were deposited and in many instances yet distinguishable before the beginning of the secondaries themselves;—secondly, that valleys once excavated and subsequently refilled during the period of a submersal, have been reopened after re-emergence in channels not materially varying from the lines of descent previously established, but subjected by dislevelling forces to an altered grading, to which the phenomenon of lakes may for the most part not unreasonably be referred.

About two miles west of Deir Mâr Sâba we pass a chalk hill, marked by two rude reservoirs in which water is rarely found. But twenty minutes nearer the convent, a capacious cistern has been excavated, 70 feet, perhaps by 30, the smaller half in the rock, the larger in the area in front of it, which at the time I passed it was very well supplied with *moyyet es-săma*, water from recent rains.

West of this Hôdh (el-Hattâbeh,) the soft chalk is visible on both sides of the valley, cropping out in corresponding dyke-heads, and rudely stratified embankments of the same material, alternate with a harder chalk of contemporary growth.

Immediately adjoining the reservoir and on both sides of it, the limestone contains the *Nuculae*, *Astartae*, *Dentalia* and *Cucullaeae* of the Mâr Sâba chalk, with spiculae and fragments of fish-bones and scales.

The dip of this limestone is quite variable. A little way beyond the Mezâr, on the left bank, not far from where the road turns off to the right towards the convent, the dip is N. W. 10°, and the layer-lines very numerous and distinct. From high ground south of our route, the convent lay immediately in sight, and the Dead Sea in the distance, Jebel Hujar being the highest peak beyond the Deir.

The plain south of Mird has a slight dip to the east. It is covered with a prodigious number of Helices, (Halazôn,) and a profusion of purple-brown flints, the fractured remnants of siliceous nodules and discs, from chalk-beds probably long since washed away.

A part of this plain is called el-Ebjâi, unless there is an error here in my note. Before passing Mird, a range of large stones is met with stretching along the plain on the right of the road and remarkable for the straightness of the alignement. Fifty or sixty years ago, it is said, the grape-vine was cultivated on this plain with much success; the plants were remarkable for their fine growth, and the fruit of very good quality; the last surviving vine was often spoken of for its size. No trace of vineyards, except the range of stones had something to do with them, is now anywhere to be found. The spot is still called Kerm et-Terâd.

There are scattered remnants of an ancient burial place in the neighborhood, with a mound or tell having a cave on its north side adjacent to the ruined cemetery, if so it really was. One of the rude heaps here (a *haurah* or *tehaur*) had the shape and air of an artificial structure, but was so much a ruin as to leave no clue to its original destination.

Not far northeast of this, succeeds the Tŭbŭqah (or high flat-topped hill) el-Quneiterah, and coming down from the N. W. between the hill and the mountains west of it, we crossed the Ghôr or rather Ghuweir el-Belâwy. East of the Tŭbŭqah is the Juft or Nŭqb, the pass into the Wâdy el-Quneiterah.

Through this ravine the low grounds at the head of the lake are strikingly exhibited and the whole length of the gorge is remarkable for its picturesque wildness as well as for the interest it affords in the study of the rocks through which it cuts its headlong and abrupt descent.

The limestone is principally, almost exclusively, the Hajar Mûsa. It is perhaps not as highly bituminised as in the neighborhood of the Wely, but it is much less interrupted by chalks or calcs not containing bitumen.

The strata are so contorted that I could make nothing out either of strike or dip. Where the layers ran more evenly, the dips varied, and time did not allow of a sufficient number of measures to get a mean. These rocks are occasionally intersected by broad beds or curved trains of flints of various shades of red, purple and brown. The fresh-broken surface and even the natural fracture perhaps long since made, are not near so darkly colored as the outside. The fragments as they lie are seldom rounded, but sometimes sharply angular and they often have the surfaces of fracture either in contact or not far apart. These siliceous banks or interdeposits have sometimes a porphyritic aspect, and are then accompanied by subordinate layers of bituminous shales and marly limestones irregularly broken up.

Lower down in a semicircular bend of the ravine, some way up a very steep escarpment on the left bank, the curvatures of the strata are again conspicuous with three or four prominent ledges maintaining their parallelism through the whole length of the contorted line. The rock on both sides consists of bituminous limestone and shale, with an unimportant exception, until the Wâdy emerges upon the *talus* leading to the plain below; but from this point, or not far from it, a fine grained dolomitised limestone, imperfectly stratified and sometimes massive, begins and continues with some modifications of color and texture as the prevailing cliff-stone of the northwest quarter of the sea.

An analysis of the Râs Feshkhah dolomite shows the following result:

| | |
|---|---|
| Carbonate of Lime, | 55.96 |
| Carbonate of Magnesia, | 40.14 |
| Iron and Alumina, | 1.10 |
| Insoluble, | 1.50 |
| Water, | .50 |
| | 99.20 M. |

The insoluble portion was principally a silicate of alumina with a little iron and magnesia. By another analysis, in which the magnesia was determined from its precipitate with phosphate of soda, there resulted:

| | |
|---|---|
| Carbonate of Lime, | 59.60 |
| Carbonate of Magnesia, | 38.24 |
| Insoluble, | 1.40 |
| | 99.24 S. |

It is instructive to compare these results with the composition of the dolomite of the cliff near 'Ain Terabeh, as will appear in the sequel.

At Râs Feshkhah and also at Mubŭghghik, far south, this stone has a grain so fine as to need the aid of a magnifier. The texture is close and firm, the color a delicate ash-grey, with the slightest tinge of purple. I had no time to look for fossils, which can only rarely be found in it, if at all. The exterior surface is jagged, full of asperities and bosses, and acquires after long exposure, an ochrey snuff-brown and rather dingy look. The sides of the cliff are covered near the base with a conglomerate of large and small fragments from the upper rocks, not very thickly laid on, but very tenaciously adherent, so as to create at first the impression that the interior base of the mountain is a solid bed of this material.

The shore is damp and even marshy, a brackish water, *moyyeh zugleh*, barely potable, oozing from the upper layers of the strand. Where the water is in sufficient quantity to flow, a crop of canebrake is the result. The beach is of small flinty pebbles, with fragments of the bituminite of Wâdy Quneiterah, and the whole neighborhood has a wild and stern look, repelling the intruder not only with its inhospitable aspect, but by the offensiveness of its sulphureous effluvia.

Not finding the party here, as I expected, instead of returning by the Nŭqb, I thought it best, at the risk of some damage to the property in my charge, to make the ascent of the cliff, which is a broken precipice of 1,000 feet in height, composed of the limestone just described. An hour of climbing was necessary to get our pack-horses up this stair-case, and this brought us to a rougher limestone having a still higher capping of great breadth, with the same dark-colored stripes that I had met with in Wâdy Quneiterah, as well as near the Deir. The prospect from the summit of the pass is a good one, and lays open the southern portion of the lake. The western head bore N. 43° E.

On reaching the summit of the ascent, our course lay W. S. W., over a plateau nearly horizontal, ploughed up at short intervals by ravines, or made undulating by shallower Ghadîrs. Not far from Wâdy en-Nâr, a watering place, or rather gulley with a rude cistern, holding rain-water for a few days after it falls, is sometimes gladly resorted to by those who have to traverse this arid tract. My guides dignified it by the name of Zirb Kharayan.

The limestone of this district is a hard gritty but very fine-grained secondary, the fragments grating under the horses' feet with a cry familiar to the ear of the geologist. The strata are nearly horizontal on the whole, but everywhere more or less undulating and sometimes quite curved.

To this succeeds, on the south, a tract of limestone less firm in texture, with nodules and ganglions not quite saturated with silicic acid, the carbonic being seldom entirely expelled from the larger flinty balls. The surface of the ground resembles an old Roman polygonal pavement; the blocks are very large and thick, and vertically fissured at angles subject to no very obvious law. The harder and purer flints lay scattered in profusion over these blocks, as if the separating agents had disintegrated and removed everything that they could pulverise or dissolve. Here again I observed that the various colors of these silicates, principally reds, yellows and browns, were strongly marked only on the outside, the interior being generally a grey.

There were picked up here by some of the attendants a number of sulphur balls varying from 1 to 3 inches in diameter. They were more or less soiled with bituminous marl.

Whether they had their origin in this neighborhood or not, is more than the facts known to me enable me to state.

A very wide depression of the desert plain receives the Wâdys west of it, and among them Wâdy er-Râhib. Properly speaking, it is not until this plain is crossed by irregular and indistinct Ghadîrs, that the lower gorges are reconstructed in all their grandeur and precipitateness. One of these then takes the name of Wâdy en-Nâr, and may fairly be regarded as continuous with Wâdy er-Râhib, though the connection is rendered obscure by the broken condition of the intermediate plateau.

Not unfrequently this plateau has ridges rising to some altitude east as well as west of it, thus leaving the appearance of a Wâdy parallel to the sea. One of these eminences was named to me as Tŭbq 'Amrîyeh, and the adjoining Nŭqb is called after it. Deir Mâr Saba could be seen from various points.

The plain is not absolutely destitute of vegetation. Large green clumbs of *suweid*, and smaller clusters of *humûdh*, (sing. *hamdh*,) of which the camel is quite fond, with occasional specimens of *drekhmeh* occur at intervals, so as to take from the chalk the look of utter barrenness; but nevertheless the whole aspect is as dreary as well can be. On the right, not far from Wâdy el-Ghuweir, some ruined walls are to be distinguished, and traces of a place of sepulture, called Maqbûrat el-'Ataiyeh. Some distance in the south lay a mass of highland, almost mountainous, and among these eminences there was pointed out to us more particularly el-Hadhrûrat es-Sîd. Wâdy et-Ta'âmirah on the west, and Wâdy Jirfân, leading to 'Ain Terâbeh, are passed in quick succession, and another, el-Qŭssâbeh, near Om el-Haymân, which seems to have been a corruption of Om el-Hummâm, a form which my guide would not recognise.*

The ravines on this route are not unfrequently the depositories of an abundant alluvion, but it shifts with the very changes which its own progress gives rise to. The hollows are gradually filled up; they then retain only the heavier gravel and flints, and finally show once more all the stony sterility of the desert.

The strata from Râs el-Ghuweir take frequently the shape of a series of arches moulded as it were on previously existing knolls of an older limestone. Near where we emerged from this tract, one of my guides gave way under the excessive heat, with the exclamation: "*amell-ni el-hedm*,"—"the burning heat has overcome me." Water was fortunately not far distant, and he revived, but continued ill for the remainder of the day.

There is here again a range of hills between the plain and the sea. The plain however can no longer be called so. It is deeply intersected by numerous ravines, of which eight were at once in sight. Of these the most considerable was Wâdy Sŭrajenâj, (qu. Serj en-Nâjy,) in a very rough shingly limestone, with Wâdy Haltemeh and Wâdy Derejeh before us. There is from here a short and steep pass re-ascending to the ground above 'Ain Jidy round Jebel 'Orf en-Naqeh; but safety to the packs required making a detour so as to cross Wâdy Derejeh much higher up.

Crossing a portion of level land relieved by patches of *zaqqûm* and *retem*, the route intersects Wâdy Haltemeh, where the limestone shows evidence of having been moulded on the rounded borders of the previously existing excavation. On the right a noble amphitheatre of chalky cliffs displays a triple row of siliceous bands, like the remnant of gigantic

*I cannot vouch for the perfect accuracy of all these names; they have the double risk of my guide's imperfect knowledge, and my own bad copying.

galleries, the whole divided by nearly vertical and parallel fissures. On the left a deep ravine, with the Ghuweir and Jubeil, Tel'at ed-Dawâri'ah, lays bare a chalky limestone containing the Mâr Sâba fossils, shells and fish-spines, much as they present themselves half way between Jerusalem and the plain of Mird.

At Wâdy Derejeh the calcareous beds resolve themselves into three classes:

First. The friable chalk of the upper strata. This is a very coarse, but uniformly constituted limestone, tolerably free of fossils, and not even abounding in flints. The exterior coating seems to be neutral carbonates, rendered so probably by exposure. Where accident or design gives a chance of examining the interior beds, the lime is found to be in excess, and the impure chalk after long exposure, exfoliates and deposits minutely upon its outer surfaces a compound of chlorides, in which the salt predominates over the bitter taste. This imperfect chalk, (if such it is, and not a tertiary,) is found to run the entire length of the western wilderness, and may be traced far south of the southern extremity of the Lake. We shall meet with it again at Wâdy Khiyâm Siyârah. It is often bituminous, and its saline ingredients are rather accidental than essential, though there are tertiaries not only in the Dead Sea district, but more especially in the Idumaean deserts, in which the salt constituents are no doubt contemporary with the deposited lime.

Secondly. Beneath this in scattered beds the fossiliferous chalk of Mâr Sâba is frequently but not invariably found.

Thirdly. Still lower in the order of superposition the prevailing limestone of the lower strata of the cliff is intersected by the ravines according to the depths to which the excavation has been carried. How far the more probable opinion, that this is the Jurassic limestone, or the view which regards it as truly contemporary with the northern chalk, and the chalk of this wilderness as a tertiary, respectively represents the facts, it would be premature to attempt positively to decide. The evidence inclines at present to the former theory, but the uncertainty which hangs over the relative ages of the African and European strata, even when petrographically, if not paleozoically equivalent, must operate as a lesson of caution, and it will be better to postpone all dogmatical conclusions until ampler collections and comparisons of fossils shall have authorized a definitive decision.

The subcretaceous beds, and sometimes the metamorphic chalk itself, exhibit on long exposed surfaces, the deep pitting which has so frequently been referred to. The long axes of these little cistern-like cavities are for the most part parallel, and not much removed from the vertical, and the cellules themselves do not occur, as well as I remember, on the inferior surfaces of the projecting ledges. The stone around these pittings is rather harder and sharper than elsewhere, but effervesces with acids quite as briskly as the remoter parts. It may serve to throw some light on the question of the origin of these little cavities to observe that something of the same kind is found to arise when the minute punctures (due it is believed to the action of a thin coating of cryptogamous vegetation) run as they sometimes do, into each other. But the full formed pittings and the punctures are seldom found on the same rock.

In all these three divisions of the calcareous beds of Wâdy Derejeh nidules of calcspar and arragonite are occasionally found. The arragonitic crystals I met with more frequently in the upper layers, disposed sometimes in parallel crusts, sometimes in radiating clusters. The dips of the superior beds are less steep than in the north, and not unfrequently the stratified stone runs for many hundred yards in strictly horizontal courses, though masses of layered chalk are never very far off.

To Wâdy Derejeh, Wâdy Hassâsah and Wâdy Muhawwimeh succeed, and across the former of these our route went just east of Jebel Hassâsah. The Wâdy of this name was broad and shallow where we passed it, contrasting with Wâdy Derefeh, which, (in places at least,) is quite deep with rugged and plunging sides.

Before crossing the Wâdy Hassâsah, a large cistern, cut in a very broad and level rock, will sometimes be found to contain water enough to meet the traveller's wants. Not far south of this, the line we followed reached in succession two or three low summit-levels, from the second of which a fine prospect was afforded of Bahr Lût from its head to 'Ain Terâbeh. The view was cut off towards the middle and south.

Passing Tell el-Merâzeh we stopped a moment at 'Ain Mu'attiq, a fountain between two projecting rocks, and descended into Wâdy Shŭqîf, and shortly afterwards into Wâdy Mudhebbih* Sa'îd 'Obeideh.

From this our route took us again into a rugged Wâdy, which was called by some of our party Wâdy Sudeir, and claimed by others to be a part of Wâdy Muhawwimeh. Arriving at 11¼, A. M., at the head of the cliff above 'Ain Jidy, the prudence of the pack-drivers secured for the protection of the beast as well as for the safety of their burdens, near an hour of cautious picking of the way, from the first steep pitch of the rocky descent to the level halting place under the ***sidr*** trees near the fountain. From 'Ain Jidy, Point Costigan bore S. 30½° E., Point Molyneux S. 1½° E. The remarkable summit of Jebel Birket el-Khŭlîl S. 26° W.

---

## CHAPTER III.

### *Route from 'Ain Terâbeh to Jerusalem.*

*Limestones of 'Ain Terâbeh.—Conglomerate.—Limestone varieties of the Cliff of 'Ain Terâbeh.—Pitted Dolomite.—Fresh Water Fountain of 'Ain Terâbeh.—Brown Dolomite.—Belted Chalk Cliffs.—Baculites Syriacus.—Caves in Wâdy Khiyâm Siyârah.—Salt chalk.—Sulphur.—Helix lithophaga.—Limestone of Wâdy Jŭrfân.—Baculites.—Glazings below Mâr Sâba.—Limestones around Mâr Sâba.—Mâr Sâba Chalk and Fossils.—Approach to Bethlehem.—Bethlehem Flints.—Fossiliferous Chalk near Jerusalem.—Jerusalem.—Limestones of the Valley of Yehôshâfât and the Tombs.—Opis Limestone.*

In order to complete the description of the triangular tract included between Jerusalem and the northern half of the western shore of the Dead Sea, it remains only to add a reconnaissance along a line from 'Ain Terâbeh near the middle of the base through Deir Mâr Sâba to the vertex at Jerusalem.

The rock at 'Ain Terâbeh is mainly a firm grey-white limestone, externally yellow or brown, sometimes quite black, much fretted and pitted, except in parts not exposed to the direct influence of the weather. It is alternately massive and stratified; the two deposits running into each other like granite and mica-slate, or more accurately like lava in blocks, and lava in sheets or coulées.

* The *h* here is radical, not servile, the root being *dhabaha*, he slaughtered.

The face of the cliff, more especially near the base, but in some places quite high up, is covered with a very thick mask of conglomerate formed of the *debris* of the neighboring limestone, detached in all probability long before the deposits of the quaternaries and alluvions of the sea margin, and gradually cemented by the infiltration and deposition of a silicate of lime. In many places this *debris* is a fine angular gravel, in others a mass of large fragments, sometimes a concrete of coarse round pebbles, and sometimes an admixture of all these forms and materials. The consequence is a variety of breccias and conglomerates so encasing and concealing the limestone, that it is not easy to believe that the higher beds of the cliff have not been deposited upon a widely spread tract of cemented fragments existing anteriorly to the limestone above it, and only exposed in its stratigraphical relations by the excavation of the Ghôr.*

The dip of the limestone is at this station southwestwardly. If we adopt here the not improbable hypothesis, that the dips of sedimentary rocks are often the result of deltary or estuary deposition, and have not, where they are arbitrary and local, been determined by dislocations subsequent to their construction, we should have to look for the origin of the estuary drifts to points in a direction crossing the great cavity, which in any hypothesis must have succeeded the limestone, though it preceded the conglomerate, and most probably the sandstone and the trap.

The limestone beds which constitute what may be called the coping of the cliff, are not uniformly chalky in the popular acceptation of the term. There may be distinguished three varieties:

1st. The pitted limestone, a decided dolomite, (not so much however as at Râs Feshkhah,) firm in texture, often subcrystalline and fine-grained, externally from light to dark-brown, internally ash-grey near the surface, but gradually whitening with the depth of the fresh fissure, free from fossils, imperfectly stratified, and subject to a natural sculpture, leaving in very high relief a rugged, craggy and turriculated fretwork, which seems destined by its hardness, to defy for ages the destroying action of the elements. Two specimens of this magnesian limestone submitted to separate analyses gave:

| | | |
|---|---|---|
| I. | Carbonate of Lime, | 64.76 |
| | Carbonate of Magnesia, | 30.28 |
| II. | Carbonate of Lime, | 59.00 |
| | Carbonate of Magnesia, | 27.00 |

With unequivocal traces of the corresponding chlorides, as well as of chloride of sodium. A third variety showed an unusual admixture of silicated earths with a large proportion of iron and alumina. But this represents rather some of the indurated seams than the dolomite itself. There were in this specimen

*This description of the conglomerate of 'Ain Terâbeh, applies with little modification to the whole extent of the cliff northwardly from 'Ain Jidy to some distance beyond 'Ain el-Feshkhah. There are unimportant interruptions, but serving only to prove the fact of the superficialness of this incrustation. Another evidence of this is to be found in the fact that the colored belts formed by groupes of layers of a peculiar limestone, running in a nearly horizontal direction on the face of the cliff, are in several places entirely cut off by the conglomerate, and the precision of the linear continuation of the strata as well as other considerations forbids the idea of a dike or other intrusion whether violent or quiet. I ought to add that the conglomerate when it takes the form of a gravelly concrete is found occasionally in very distinct beds, showing that at the era of this formation, a state of things prevailed not at all represented by the present configuration of the Ghôr. It is scarcely necessary to observe, that no geologist would think of referring this conglomerate to an epoch so modern as the alluvial or quaternary terraces between Wâdy Khŭberah and Wâdy Seiyâl, nor to a period so ancient as the older tertiaries on which these conglomerates are found sometimes, (as just north of Wâdy Sufeifeh for example,) very unequivocally to rest.

| | |
|---|---|
| Carbonate of Lime, | 63.15 |
| Carbonate of Magnesia, | 13.28 |
| Iron and Alumina, | 13.50 |
| Insoluble, | 10.10 |

With distinct traces of chloride of sodium; all the three specimens having been thoroughly washed before analysis, to remove any saline matter accidentally adherent.

For the purpose of ascertaining the solvent power of any water charged with carbonic acid gas upon this or similar limestones, I placed carefully within a clean soda water bottle, 52.81 grains of the powder of the dolomite and introduced at the same time a well defined fragment of the stone, weighing 50.20 grains. The bottle was then filled with pure water, strongly impregnated with carbonic acid gas by Mr. Roussel of Philadelphia, firmly closed and left lying on its side for the spaee of nearly six months. The powder was then found to have lost 4.19 grains, the solid lump was diminished by 0.90 grain, and the water was deprived of almost all of its fixed gas. An analysis of this 5.09 grains, resulted as follows in 100 parts:

| | |
|---|---|
| Carbonate of Lime, | 70.31 |
| Carbonate of Magnesia, | 24.16 |
| Peroxide of Iron, | .32 |
| Chloride of Sodium, | 2.10 |
| Chlorides of Magnesium and Calcium, | .87 |
| | 97.76 |

The two per cent. of chloride of sodium gives but the tenth of a grain out of the 52.81 grains; for the solid piece contributed almost nothing. In another analysis in which the chlorides were extracted by pure water alone, I found much more chlorine, but the difference must have been a local one. That the Dead Sea limestones are more or less impregnated with alkaline and earthy chlorides, has already been remarked; but it is not at present easy to say, how much of this is essential and congenital, how much superficial or superinduced.

It is obvious from the above, that if once the smallest pits are formed in the limestone, the mere action of the rain-drops on the bottoms and sides of the cavities however small, will gradually enlarge their dimensions, for the residuum left in each little cup after evaporation would soon be blown out of it, and the etching process would continue with an unequal intensity of action over the whole surface, leaving the asperities on the face of the rock very much as actually found.

2d. A compact heavy limestone, apparently not much subject to the external weather pittings, but in place of those to very minute punctures; color light buff or chalky-yellow both within and without, fracture flat and splintery, with a few indistinct indications of the Mâr Sâba fossils, and furnishing on analysis the following results:

| | |
|---|---|
| Insoluble, | .329 |
| Iron, Peroxide, | .564 |
| Carbonate of Lime, | 87.749 |
| Carbonate of Magnesia, | 8.460 |
| Chloride of Sodium, | 1.081 |
| | 98.183 |

3d. A chalky and somewhat friable limestone, subconchoidal in fracture and running into shaly ledges on the sides of the ravines which intersect it. Fossils, though not abundant are by no means rare, and approach in character the petrifactions of Mâr Sâba. A *Nucula* and an *Astarte* could be made out in some specimens, but nothing absolutely determining the the relation of this chalk to the cretaceous beds along the middle reaches of the Cedron.

Subordinate to this last, and probably not occurring any where beyond its area and thickness, is an indurated limestone in shingly and sometimes coherent layers, remarkable for its siliceous compactness, and yielding on analysis:

| | |
|---|---|
| Insoluble Matter, . . . . . . . . . . . . . . . . . . . | 16.75* |
| Iron and Alumina, . . . . . . . . . . . . . . . . . | .80 |
| Carbonate of Lime, . . . . . . . . . . . . . . . . . | 76.36 |
| Carbonate of Magnesia, . . . . . . . . . . . . . . . | 3.33 |
| Water, . . . . . . . . . . . . . . . . . . . . . | 2.50 |
| | 99.74 M. |

The fountain at the base of the cliff furnished at the time we visited it a perfectly sweet water. It is not improbable, however, that in other years this spring as well as the one at 'Ain Ghuweir, may be more or less brackish, either by a variation in the source of its upland supply, or by its having not yet received the last contribution from the annual deposit of saline matter left by the spring level of the sea upon the margin of its beech. What is remarkable in this fountain, is its nearness to the Dead Sea, being separated from it only by a narrow strip twenty or thirty feet in width. Along the fountain and in the moist ground and approaching it, the *ghŭrab* and *terafeh*, with various reeds and grasses, form a thicket of luxuriant growth, the more welcome from the barrenness every where around. The fountain at 'Ain Feshkhah was scarcely potable at the time of our visit and as far as I could learn was permanently brackish.

From the edge of the cliff the ground runs back westwardly in an irregular and broken plain. On the surface of this as a wide platform, rise up in arrangements and distributions hard to describe, numerous hills and high peaks of a limestone massive and well compacted, but very much cloven and weather-worn. The strata when such occur, dip frequently towards the lake. The brown dolomite forming the basis of its structure, is found here more or less pitted and subject to intrusions of a limestone which preserves against the elements, its inherent white color in marked contrast with the body of the rock. The general level of the plain may be assumed as not far from 1,300 feet above the surface of the Dead Sea.

From a station here, several eminences were pointed out, as Jebel Mujellah or Mujella', Jebel el-'Urf and Sîd Seqâwah, between N. N. W. and N. W. by N. The course of Wâdy Derejeh can be traced by ascending a peak south of the station. From this point may be observed a deep ravine with the strata dipping about 5° towards the west away from the lake, the upper surface of the Wâdy wall conforming to this dip.

Jebel Mujellah and Jebel el-'Urf are of chalk, white with horizontal dark colored stripes displayed in the sections obtained by the ravines. These stony stripes are, in the few places I could ascend to them, either layers of a hardened and heavy limestone, or beds of flinty nodules in a broken chalk, different from the chalk which it divides. In a large flint-stone

* Found qualitatively to consist mainly of silica, at least to the extent of fifteen-sixteenths. I may add that this limestone contains *Nucula crebrilineata* and other fossils.

found in this neighborhood I found the *Baculites Syriacus*, described by Mr. Conrad in his Report. In one of the spurs of Jebel el-'Urf, I met with a fossil chalk with the Mâr Sâba characteristics, containing in imperfect traces the fish-teeth of the locality already described near Hôdh el-Hattâbeh, and not absent I believe from the whole region east and southeast of Jerusalem.

One of the smaller hills which I ascended here, the highest however for a mile or more around me, was remarkably flat at the summit which was a circle of about 80 feet radius. The chalk was shingly and loose, of a whiteness which, though dull, glared under the intense heat of a Dead Sea mid-day sun. The surface was strewn with a few black flints, and here and there grew intrepidly a bit of *retem* or *suweid.* The flints showed that the surface had, ages before, been much higher, and the correspondencies with neighboring heights proved that the mound was but the remnant of an elevated and once unbroken tract of chalk, worn away at last by the continued encroachment of insensible excavations to a few long since separated and now widely scattered hills.*

In Sheqq el-hayyeh, a deep ravine north of 'Ain Terâbeh, the dip of the limestone is E. S. E. 10°. In other places not far distant a different inclination will be found, so that very careful and deliberate observations are required, before the circumstances which determined the calcareous accumulations can even be conjectured. The next Wâdy north is Wâdy Khiyâm Siyârah, which has cut through the brown and weather pitted dolomite, here in layers nearly horizontal.

There are two caves in this ravine, one on each side of it, and such excavations are not uncommon in the neighboring gorges. They are found more frequently in the hard rock than in the soft, as if the loose texture of the latter prevented by giving away the undermining necessary for this effect. Some of these grottoes may be natural burrowings artificially enlarged.

The rock of the adjoining hollows where no recent action can be traced, is generally magnesian limestone with the characteristic pittings, in which case the exterior brown complexion is seldom wanting. Where the rock has been more rudely dealt with, a softer stone is displayed, though the varieties of texture are very great, from a crumbling chalk to a light-brown indurated limestone, quite firm and close grained, but not liable to the external weather-pits.

The analysis of this last mentioned limestone has already been given and shows in its composition one per cent. of chloride of sodium. There are two descriptions of the softer chalk which contain a much larger proportion of this salt, and in some of these it abounds to such an extent, that the specimens in my drawer cannot be kept free from a coating of residuum, arising from the exsuding and efflorescent brine, and even after a thorough washing of the coarse splinters and flakes, the powdered remnant gives a very marked precipitate on the addition of nitrate of silver. I find on a careful analysis of one of these specimens no less than five per cent. of chlorides, of which nearly the whole is common salt. As it is difficult to ascribe the admixture of this unusual ingredient to the vicinity of the Salt Lake, it seems necessary to admit, that the limestone of the last upheaval has not yet parted with the chlorides it brought with it, but holds them measurably as it acquired them in the

* From a hill on the elevated plain above 'Ain Terâbeh and a little north of it, I found the late camping ground S. 53° E.; Râs Mersed, S. 6½° W.; Point of Usdom S. 7° W.; most projecting western beach point S. 5° W.; Point Molyneux S. 4° W.; Point Costigan S. 12° E.; mouth of Wâdy Môjeb S. 37° E.; mouth of Wâdy Zerqa Mâin S. 88° E.

*situs* of its construction, at the bottom of the estuary which washed it as the era of its emergence drew nigh; or that the rock has been impregnated with its saline contents by brine-springs no longer in existence, but set in motion by causes taking effect subsequently to the uprising of the chalk.

I ought not to omit to add that this formation in addition to its other peculiarities is characterised by a notable proportion of bitumen, so that a strong petroleous odor is perceptible immediately on the application of the hydrochloric acid and not less so after the subsidence of the effervescence. An analysis of one specimen gave over one per cent. of organic matter.

The analysis of another variety of this chalk gave, as Mr. Schwabe reports to me, 3.447 per cent. of sulphur combined with soda, partly as sulphuret, partly as hyposulphite. Some of the crumbling, thoroughly slacked pieces were specially analysed, and consisted of

| | |
|---|---|
| Water, | 3.00 |
| Insoluble, | 4.28 |
| Alumina and Iron, | 1.43 |
| Carbonate of Lime, | 73.00 |
| Chlorides, about | 1.00 |
| Hyposulphite of Soda | 16.98 |
| | 99.69 S. |

Exposed to the air for some time this chalk splits into flakes and a portion of it slacks with some vehemence and crumbles into powder, the water even when the flakes had been previously washed, giving as in the carbonated lime, proofs of the presence of chlorine in combination with the alkalies and alkaline earths.

One of the limestones intersected by Wâdy en-Nâr and some of the adjacent ravines are the favorite abode of a lapidivorous snail, the testaceous covering of which is very much like that of ***Helix planispira.*** This gasteropod, called by Mr. Conrad ***Helix lithophaga***, has the remarkable power, already known to belong to many sea-water and even fresh-water mollusks, of boring into the rock in which their instinct and appetite teaches them to dwell. The mode in which this gradual excavation is effected, is well explained by Prof. Leidy, to whom the snails, nestling in the very cavities in which they were found, were submitted for examination and description.* Two specimens of the limestone presented on analysis the results here subjoined:

| | | |
|---|---|---|
| Silica, | 1.05 | 1.14 |
| Iron ($Fe_2O_3$) and Alumina, | .10 | trace. |
| Carbonate of Lime, | 96.83 | 98.04 |
| Magnesia, (trace.) | | |
| Organic Matter, | .10 | trace. |
| | 98.08 H. | 99.18 |

The receptacles which these Helices etch out of the rock in which they live, resemble in the specimens brought home by me, the depressions that would be formed by thrusting the thumb or finger ends repeatedly and carelessly into a mass of putty or dough, supposing that the pouches thus produced ran into each other in various directions. These snail cells

* Vide Appendix, letter from Prof. Leidy.

were from one inch to two inches deep, where I observed them, but are to be met with, no doubt, of very different dimensions and extent. Not far below Deir Mâr Sâba, on an under-cliff of the Wâdy er-Râhib, the same cavernulae may be found, and I have noted them also as occurring at no great distance from 'Ain el-Harâmîyeh, between Jerusalem and Nâbulus. The cavities are smoother and the grain better filled up than one would anticipate from the porous texture of the rock, as if the sides of the burrow had been lined with some secretion from the excavating organ. The bottoms of the occupied cells are of a shape well fitted to the convexity of the testae lying within them, and the sides are occasionally marked by impressions corresponding accurately to the oval of the mouth. After lying quietly in their receptacles for upwards to fifteen months from the time of their removal, I found these snails one morning missing not only from their cells, but from the drawer in which the specimens were placed, and they were recovered by following the slimy lines which they had left the whole length of the distance they had travelled.

Between Wâdy Khiyâm es-Siyârah and Wâdy Râs el-Ghuweir the plain is gradually depressed so as to leave a range of seaward hills, the western faces of which are much chalkier in appearance than the eastern; as if the plain were a much more recent excavation than the Ghôr. These hills and more particularly the eminences parallel to them further west have rounded summits of a loose puffy chalk with many nests of black and parti-colored flints alternating with scattered patches of a cherty limestone. The fossils are not unfrequent, but the types very limited in number, being principally congeners of the Mâr Sâba petrefactions. The repulsive barrenness of this district is relieved here and there by a few scrubby bushes lost in the dreary expanse. Among these I observed a sweet scented shrub, called Haneideh by the Arabs and Eshteleh I believe by the Fellâhîn.

A pass which cuts through a low ridge of soft limestone leads from the plain just mentioned to the broader plain of Wâdy Jŭrfân. An hour's walk brings the traveller obliquely across this almost level Wâdy to another separated by a narrow barrier from a branch of Wâdy en-Nâr or rather Wâdy er-Râhib. From here to the convent or still higher up, the strata shown at the steep sides of the ravine are nearly horizontal. Occasionally however the limestone layers are very accurately arched, as if a deposit had been moulded on a series of knolls preceding them in geological order leaving a row of vault-roofs harder than the material beneath them, which is sometimes washed out so as to give rise to caves or shallow grottoes underneath the arches.

Here and there in the rocky floor of the Wâdy, traces may be seen of large fossils, probably *Baculites*, over a foot in length, two inches broad at one end, tapering to one at the other, which is slightly rounded, the color of these organic remains being much darker and their consistence harder than the enveloping rock. The outlines were very indistinct, and there were no means of removing any part for examination, so that the conjecture that they were *Baculites* must not pass for more than it is worth.

The limestone continues to increase in the number and variety of its fossils until all the forms of the Mâr Sâba species are met with. These are not confined to the upper beds, but may be found on careful search at the base of the cliffs which run from two to three hundred feet in height for some distance both above or below the Deir. The reaches of this valley are short and abrupt, so as to heighten the wildness of the scene, while the now untenanted caverns on its sides call to mind many interesting incidents in the history of this hospitable and time-honored retreat.

Just below Mâr Sâba, the strata conform to the general surface of the plain and descend nearly with the descent of the floor of the ravine. The weather pittings are remarkably distinct in the upper ledges, but less so below. Where a block has been detached from the edges of the terraces, the exposed surfaces, though the fall may and often must have been, an occurrence geologically old, do not with rare exceptions exhibit more than a few pittings and the beginning as it were of a bronzing of the face. In general the swarthy complexion of the rock and especially the pocky erosions or corrugations are measures of the antiquity of the exposure in all cases in which the material may be supposed to be the same. The conclusions derived from an examination of the colors and glazings of the Egyptian syenites are applicable to the natural limestone monuments of Syria. The earliest human obliterations of the tegumentary or cortical peculiarities of the weathered superficies are incomparably less ancient than the scales which they have removed and which are represented as they then stood, very nearly by the undefaced portions of the rock. On more perishable materials the artificially abraded surface has acquired more or less the face or epidermis of the portion not touched, but even in the least endurable sculptures it is easy to distinguish from the greater or less development of the erosions alone the surface which has been laid bare by the chisel from that where nature's slower tooling has so effectually done its work. A diligent attention to the natural and artificial *facies* of well preserved rocks in countries where the ages of very ancient sculptures may be chronologically fixed, with a comparative study of their etchings, bronzings, temperings and glazings, would greatly repay the labor thus bestowed and throw much light on that difficult and much neglected department of geology, I mean the changes superinduced by weather, water, climate and other quiet agencies upon the superficial texture and condition of long exposed rocks.

The white chalky limestone of Mâr Sâba runs into a browner chalk by insensible degrees and probably differs only in the era of the denudations. The latter is more generally stratified, at least near the Deir, and almost always of a darker color even many feet deep. It is also less rich in remains, and of the white chalk the unstratified or faintly stratified portions are more fossiliferous than the strongly marked beds. The layered part of the upper chalk is often disposed in arches determined by underlying moulds. The lamination of the siliceous deposits varies from thin slaty sheets to continuous beds a foot or more thick with parallel surfaces. These deposits take also the form of flat disks or cakes with their long axes horizontally disposed and separated from each other by the limestone in mass.

The effect of the deep and irregular excavation of the cretaceous platform is made obvious by tracing from any convenient point of view the curve shown in perspective by the intersections of the siliceous beds and the lateral surfaces of the great *frusta* left after denudation. The dark belt on the mountain flank may be seen many miles in extent running in a curve apparently variable in its dip towards the horizon, which in fact the whole line is but the outcrop of a series of nearly horizontal planes of a brown black chert and cherty limestone from ten to twenty feet in thickness. A second gallery fifty yards or more above this has an undulatory dip with a strike irregularly N. E., and consists of loose chalk, hard limestone and variegated flint-stones in their alternate beds.

From the effect of these denudations it may be readily imagined that the accidents of the surface are as varied as the texture of the block of which they constitute the sculptural relief. On the south the crest of the mountain descends from Qŭrn er-Râhib gradually to the plain of Wâdy Jŭrfân, where it is joined by Wâdy Hirmeh, (?) while southwestwardly an abrupter change of level terminates in Mezeirat el-Ghŭnâyim. West of the summit of Qŭrn er-Râhib are a series of caves called el-Hujar, each Hujrah owing its origin, at least in part, to the texture and grain of the overhanging rock, and beyond these, with a broken interval between, succeeds the hill Abu Enyâs. Northeast the fine outline of Jebel Muntâr sweeps downward until it drops perspectively so low that the Dead Sea is seen bearing a little north of east, and disappearing again from view S. 28° E. The high ground of Tŭbq es-Sŭmr is visible, but Tŭbq el-Quneiterah is hidden by Muntâr. From the same point of view Deir Mâr Sâba bore S. 49° E., Mount Olivet N. 39° W., and Jerusalem N. 45° W.

The fossils of the Mâr Sâba limestone leave it yet a matter of doubt whether the deposits belong truly to the chalk. There is in some of the species a more decided approach to the tertiary than to genuine cretaceous remains. There is a *Gryphaea*, for example, which can hardly be distinguished from another belonging to the Egyptian tertiaries in the neighborhood of Cairo, and one of the *Nuculae* may without much risk of censure be referred to an Eocene age. But other considerations, perhaps at present more conclusive in favor of the antiquity of the Mâr Sâba beds, seem to justify, on the whole, the view which considers these deposits as the latest accumulations of the long era of the chalk. At all events, whatever uncertainty attaches to the geological place of the soft white limestone of this region, rests upon the whole of the similar formation north as far as Wâdy Beisân, and southwardly until we come to the unquestionable tertiaries of the desert of et-Tîh.

The chemical elements presented in the Mâr Sâba chalk may afford perhaps some light in aid of this inquiry. They are:

| | |
|---|---|
| Carbonate of Lime, . . . . . . . . . . . . . . . . . | 96.82 |
| Carbonate of Magnesia, . . . . . . . . . . . . . . | .29 |
| Iron and Alumina, . . . . . . . . . . . . . . . . . | 1.00 |
| Insoluble, . . . . . . . . . . . . . . . . . . . . | 2.00 |
| | 100.11 M. |

I subjoin a list of the principal fossils which the short time allotted for the purpose enabled me to find and obtain in a state fit for description. For the necessary details the reader is referred to the Paleontological Report by Mr. Conrad, whose patience under the difficulties arising from the generally bad condition of the specimens I cannot too thankfully attest.

Gryphaea capuloides.
Nucula crebrilineata.
Crassatella Syriaca.
Cardium bellum.
Gryphaea?
Panopaea?
Gryphaea vesicularis.
Nucula perdita.
Pecten delumbis.
Dentalium cretaceum.
Nucula?

Between the convent and Bethlehem, afetr passing a tract of uneven and irredeemably unarable chalk lying south of the district just described, the ground begins to give token of some efforts at vegetable life. But it is not until crossing a branch of Wâdy Ta'âmirah near Deir en-Neby (so named to me) and the Wely Sheikh Khalifeh, that the evidences of the least attempt at cultivation become very apparent. Several cisterns, reservoirs and pools, are passed in succession, to which the name of el-Burâk was given generically by my guide, for the well-known el-Burâk, or Solomon's Pools, lie some distance southwest of Bethlehem.

The smaller receptacles, (bureikât,) were in a condition scarcely to be recognised, but a large *birkeh* still exists, formed by a high wall perhaps eighty feet in length, thrown across a recess in the rock, and protected by a substantial coping still in good preservation. The black tents of a detachment of the Ta'âmirah lay south of the route, and not far from there a scanty herbage and signs of water, with thin layers of a brown loam in the smaller Wâdys showed that there was something after all to account for the selection of so unpromising a site.*

Nearer Bethlehem the valleys begin to assume a cheerful look. Grape-vines, figs and olives are not wanting, and here and there the trees show a vigorous thrift. Still nearer the rise of ground, but yet in the plain, or at the lower edges of the slopes, a more fruitful vegetation is maintained. Besides corn-fields and vineyards, we met with patches of *sesame vetches* and *pulse*, and all these, along with fruit trees of various descriptions clustering in orchards and groves, form a picture as if intended to show what the powers of a protected cultivation might effect. Terracing, with suitable irrigation, and a consent on the part of the ruler that the peasant shall not be punished for the abundance of his crop, would convert Palestine once more to what it was, "a land of oil and honey," a land of "bread without want, a good land of wheat and barley, and vineyards." Under the present insecurity of property, the ungrateful toil of reclaiming the desert is seldom persevered in, and when once the hand of man is withdrawn, the coarse chalky limestone reappears wherever the meagre soil is swept away, and soon seems as if it had undergone the operation of the kiln. Silicates beautifully laminated, spotted and variously marked, begin to appear in profusion an hour from the hill; and a remarkably solid wall of these, constructed altogether of the larger fragments, stands just below the town, ready to supply the stone-fancier with a very undesirable embarrassment of choice.

The Bethlehem flints deserve more than a passing notice. As a general rule they are characterised by the frank distinctness with which the differently colored portions stand separated from each other. But in other respects there is found the usual diversity of structure, dislocation, infiltration and concretion. The shapes and arrangements of the *tessellae*, (which are sometimes dark-colored in a white matrix, but more frequently the reverse,) vary from specimen to specimen. Where cavities occur, they are always, I believe, in the dark parts, and generally lined with an impure mixture of a peroxide and carbonate of iron. The light-colored *tessellae* have often a translucent corneous appearance, and are occasionally fringed with border lines parallel to the edge. These horn-like kernels are frequently spotted with milk-white speckles, patches and stripes, and are sometimes minutely dissected and dispersed; the segments, even when pushed far asunder, being frequently recognisable as once parts of an undivided whole. In general however this connection is not very apparent, and it is hard to believe that the fragments were ever united in one undistinguishable mass. An analysis was made of both portions, and the result shows that the dark-brown material, though in the main nearly as quartzy as the white, owes its color to iron and lime, and its place to insensible secular intrusion.

| | White Portion. | Dark smoke-brown. |
|---|---|---|
| Silica, . . . . . . . . . . . . . . . . . . . . | 98.05 | 94.90 |
| Iron, (Peroxide,) and Alumina, . . . . . . . . . | .45 | 1.67 |
| Carbonate of Lime, . . . . . . . . . . . . . . | 1.26 | 3.02 |
| | 99.76 | 99.59 H. |

*An illegible note gives here as the name of a fountain in the neighborhood, Bîr Leften. The orthography is more than doubtful, though I believe is not much out of the way.

The greater part of the eminence or rather ridge on which Bethlehem is built, is quite free from flints. The limestone is chalky and coarse, resembling the beds of Wâdy er-Râhib and the looser accumulations of its upper reaches, Wâdy Yehôshâfât and Wâdy Kidrôn. Out of this soft and workable material are excavated the caverns which still frequently serve for sheep-cotes and stalls, as well as the three which the Church's pious Tradition has retained as the Cave of the Nativity, the Sepulchre of the Innocents and the Grotto of the Virgin of the Milk.

In addition to the soft white limestone there are beds of a description more compact, where the presence of *Gryphaea capuloides* leaves but little room to doubt of the proper place of the chalk. To these may be added a fine mottled red limestone or rather marble, containing from 8 to 10 per cent. of insoluble matter, principally silex. The structure is semi-crystalline and occasionally marly or tufaceous, but free from concretionary subdivisions. It does not, as far as I observed, occur in any other mass-form than in short embankments or insulated outfillings embraced by the nooks or basins of the underlying rock.

If we strike across the valley north of the Bethlehem ridge and so over the chalky hills to a point of Wâdy Kidrôn, midway between Sûr Bâhil and Abu Dîs we are brought along a tract of fossil chalk which particularly in the ledges of the Wâdy may be confidently recommended to the future explorer. Its accessibility and short distance from Jerusalem (about one hour or three-quarters below the lower pools of Gihon) present opportunities of examination not frequently attainable in Palestine. The chalk is found not only massive, but in almost every variety of bedding, from broad well-set strata to a cretaceous shingle or shale, the result perhaps of drifting deposits from water charged mechanically with the abrasures of earlier rocks. Among the fossils I may mention:

Astarte undulosa. Corbula sublineolata.
Gryphaea vesicularis. Nucula crebrilineata.
Nucula perdita.

These have all been determined and described by Mr. Conrad, to whose Report the reader is referred for technical details.

The site of Jerusalem is not without its geological importance. The ground west of the Holy City, though marked by some irregularities of surface is fairly entitled to be regarded as a summit plain, upon which the receding excavations at the heads of the opposing Wâdys have not yet fairly encroached. As such a summit level it might therefore be expected to show the usual evidences of having been raised up from the chalk-building sea long before the emergence of its flanks. One of the results would necessarily be a removal of the chalk from those parts which may have been covered by it, but which have on the other hand been far longer exposed to the denudating process. Accordingly we find in the caves and minor excavations various limestones older than the chalk, the general character of the summit being a well knit calcareous rock made a little more compact by a subsequent accession of an appreciable portion of silica. From the absence of fossils I shall not venture to pronounce upon its place in the order of geological history. But there is much to justify a reference of this limestone to the earlier chalks instead of the closing groupes of the Jura. For it is hard to conjecture how the whole of the cretaceous series should have been swept from the summit, seeing that a very large portion of the inferior chalks are still in existence low down on the eastern and western declivities and almost always where the upper chalks are found.

Among the more interesting localities, in which the relation of the stratified to the unstratified limestones may be clearly seen, I may mention the Sepulchre long known as the Tomb of the Kings. In addition to the lithological characteristics, a peculiarity may be observed here in the sudden incurvation of the superincumbent beds around the angles of the underlying rock. The layers which immediately incrust the rounded bench beneath are moulded, as might be anticipated, very nearly to the shape of the invested surface; those next in order depart more or less from this conformity, until we come to sheets of deposited limestone which have little in common with the inequalities of the lower strata or with the broken contour of the subjacent mass. This base-rock is a cream colored marble with yellowish and brownish stains and has a fracture imperfectly conchoidal. I see no room in this and similar phenomena for the hypothesis of a lateral pressure or a once semi-fluid form of the overspread matter. The undisturbed matrix and the variable curvature of the overlying strata concur to disprove such a conjecture. This marble contains 3 per cent. of magnesia, with scarcely any iron or alumina. The texture is close and even in the stratified beds which in the absence of a better evidence than I have yet to present may be regarded as an intermediate formation separating the Jura from the earlier chalks. An analysis gave

| | |
|---|---|
| Carbonate of Lime, . . . . . . . . . . . . . . . . . . | 94.60 |
| Carbonate of Magnesia, . . . . . . . . . . . . . . . | 2.88 |
| Insoluble, . . . . . . . . . . . . . . . . . . . . . . | .80 |
| | 98.28 S. |

The same limestone reappears near the Tombs in the valley of Yehôshâfât beginning a little north of the Sepulchre of the Virgin and disappearing at the bend below the Mount of Offence. At the tomb of St. James a reddish limestone occurs, which I believe to belong to the hippuritic group, and taking this point as a starting place, the chalks of Mount Olivet may be easily followed and compared.

Near the base of this mountain I found a chalk with a well-marked ***Rostellaria*** and not far from this a bed containing *Opis undata.* The higher strata are sufficiently determined by *Astarte undulosa*, *Cucullaea parallela*, *Nucula crebrilineatæ*, *Nucula perdita* and ***Pecten delumbis.***

An analysis of a specimen of the chalk found on the Jerusalem side of Mount Olivet about mid-height, gave 7.1 per cent. of insoluble matter and 92.77 of carbonate of Lime.

As my connection with the Expedition necessarily terminated on our arrival at Jerusalem, this Report will not be found to contain more than a passing notice of the prominent facts in the Geology of its immediate vicinity. Enough has been said to show, that, if the Christian traveller can find time and temper for enquiries which in the ardor of a worthier pilgrimage may well be disapproved of as frivolous, or may even be condemned as profane, he has it in his power to add to the little that we know of the Natural History of Palestine, a conjecture at least of the meaning of that Elder Chronicle which is so mysteriously written on her Sacred Hills.

# SECTION V.

## RECONNAISSANCE OF THE DEAD SEA SHORE.

### CHAPTER I.

*The West Shore of the Dead Sea.*

*Route from 'Ain Jidy to Sebbeh.—Reconnaissance between Sebbch and Khashm Usdom.—The Cliff between 'Ain Jidy and Wâdy Khŭberah.—Beds of Wâdy 'Areijeh.—Birket el-Khŭlîl.—Lynch's Strait.—Tertiaries and Quaternaries.—Tertiaries with Conglomerates of Wâdys Seiyal Sebbeh, and Sufeifeh.—Salt-pools.—Moraine South of Wâdy Kusheibeh.—Jebel Sebbeh.—Sebbeh (ancient Masada) Limestone and Ruins.—Fetid Marl of the Ruins.—Limestone of Wâdy Sennin and Rubt el-Jamûs.—Marly embankments.—Limestone Cliffs of Wâdy Mubŭghghik.—Wâdy Muhawwit.—Rock-salt of Khashm Usdom.*

The geological features and the leading stratigraphical facts characteristic of the north-west quarter of the Dead Sea shore, have already been given in this Report and stand in no need of more circumstantial detail. I shall continue therefore by resuming the narrative of the main phenomena at the southernmost point ('Ain Jidy) of the triangle just described.

Between 'Ain Jidy and Wâdy Khŭberah the cliff varying from twelve to fifteen hundred feet in height, is bold and steep, admitting nowhere of the ascent or descent of beasts of burden, and practicable only here and there to the most intrepid climber. It is divided about midway between the points just named by Wâdy el-'Areijeh, a gorge which cleaves the mountain nearly to its base. The fountain 'Ain el-'Areijeh, pours out a very copious supply of water, which however soon begins to waste itself and finally disappears altogether without reaching the western margin of the shore. Supposing this excavation to be restored, we should find as marked divisions of the great escarpment, reckoning from above: 1st, horizontal layers of limestone, from two to three hundred feet in depth: 2dly, a gallery of moraine-heads, or a series of tent-shaped embankments of debris brought down through the small ravines intersecting the upper division and lodged upon the projecting terrace below: 3dly, a sharply defined, well marked formation, less perfectly stratified than the division first named and constituting by its unbroken continuity a zone of naked rock, probably 150 feet in width, which runs like a vast frieze along the face of the cliff, and is so precipitous that the detritus pushed over the upper edge of the great architrave finds no lodgment anywhere on the almost vertical surface which marks the out-crop of this shelf-like ledge. Above this belt, I ought to add, is an interrupted bed of yellow limestone 40 feet thick. 4thly, a broad and boldly sloping talus of limestone, partly bare, partly covered by debris which show by their various colors the heights from which they have come down, descends next in order nearly to the base of the cliff. 5thly, a breast-work of fallen fragments, sometimes however swept clean away by the displacing agencies which none but the geologist either marks or suspects, separates the upper edge of the beach from the ground-line of the escarpment. 6thly, a beach of variable breadth and variable structure, sometimes sandy, sometimes gravelly or shingly, sometimes made up of loose and scattered patches of a coarse travertine or marl, falls gradually to the border of the Dead Sea, and dips at the same angle for some distance beneath the lowest level to which the Dead Sea surface has yet been known to sink.

About twenty minutes south of 'Ain 'Areijeh the ruins of a rude stone building mark a spot about midway between the 'Ain and the Birket el-Khŭlil. This Birkeh is a part of the beach more depressed and springy than the other portion, and at certain seasons wet with the exsudations of a fetid brine. We found the whole neighborhood reeking with the smells of sulphureous acid and sulphuretted hydrogen gas. The Birkeh is flooded at the time of high sea, shortly after the spring rains, and shows over its entire area, very soon after the fall of the water, a crusty residuum of impure salt, thickest at the bottom of the pans, and thinning to a mere frost-like efflorescence nearer the margin of the temporary pools. Bits of asphalt and sulphur are not unfrequently met with, the bitumen no doubt retained as one of the tributes of the overflow, the sulphur not improbably an aggregation of materials derived from the powdery deposits. Gypsum in arrow-headed crystals, as well as in amorphous patches, may be found between the Birkeh proper and the cliff, and sometimes rolled balls of scoriaceous pumice, specifically lighter than the sea water, appear after long wanderings to have floated from the lava districts of the northeastern quarter to the west side of the sea. That portion of the Birkeh where the fetid odors are most remarkable, is called Murawwihet el-Khŭlil. A pass westwardly is the Nŭqb and some remarkable mounds (the Tulûl) of the same name.

The detritus brought down Wâdy Khŭberah, and the Wâdys south of this, is delivered south of Birket el-Khŭlil, and has gradually built up a broad prominent spit or delta-like projection of the beach, contributing but in a much less degree than the peninsula directly opposite, to contract the width of the sea to the narrow sound which Carl Ritter has denominated Lynch's Channel, or Lynch's Strait, in honor of the leader of the Expedition.

The marly and gypseous tertiaries, analogous to the opposite peninsular deposits, begin distinctly to make their appearance on the west side, just south of Wâdy el-Khŭberah, though scattered benches of this material are found hanging on the lower slopes as far north as Wâdy el-'Areiyeh, and the layered heaps southeast of Jericho may be referred to the same cause.

The height of the alluvial banks at the mouths of the Wâdys here, is much less than farther south, where the tertiaries are sometimes cut through 60 feet and more, and the later alluvions in proportion. On the west a guide directed my attention to a very steep and difficult pass, Nŭqb Dhenobayerah,* and Wâdy Nĕdy, near it on the north. The marly terrace in this neighborhood is singularly cut up and carved out into blocks and pillars, so as sometimes to simulate very strikingly rows of houses with gables, chimney-stacks, and crenulated roofs. The columns, when they stand isolated, have every variety of shape, and an Oriental imagination might, one would suppose, delight in tracing all kinds of fanciful resemblances in so rich a diversity of forms. But nothing could induce my guide to dignify them by any other appellation than pillars of mud or clay, *amûd et-tîn.*

The tertiary marls and gypsites continue along the cliff between it and the sea, across Wâdy Mahras and Wâdy Khusheibeh, until they attain their principal development between

*The orthography here is somewhat doubtful. It may have been Senubeirah, the little pine-tree.

Wâdy Seiyâl and Wâdy Sebbeh. As they approach this *terminus*, they are associated with conglomerates, which are found suspended, as it were, at various heights in the recesses of the Wâdy mouths, as may be seen more particularly near Wâdy Sufeifeh.*

The salt-pools and saline basins do not terminate with Birket el-Khŭlîl, but are found for two miles along the shore, and give out nearly opposite to a fountain of brackish water on the mountain side between Wâdy Mahras and Wâdy Khusheibeh.

Not far south of the latter Wâdy the path leads up a high broad *moraine* of tertiary marl, and a ten minutes walk over the surface of this brings the traveller to the edge of the fine Wâdy Seiyâl. A descent of seventy or eighty feet leads to a terrace from which several further descents are necessary before reaching the bottom of the valley.

The term *moraine*, just employed to express the dimensions, shape and general aspect of the elevated embankments which separate the Wâdys near their mouths, would not be appropriate if it were accepted as implying that the embankments have descended in the manner of the transported debris of a Swiss or Savoyese glacier. On the contrary, these raised banks are undoubtedly the relief resulting from numerous excavations in different parts of a once continuous terrace, the altitude of which has been determined by an ancient higher level of the surface of the waters, and is indicated in some measure by the corresponding height of the tertiary embankment forming the great peninsula in the southeast quarter of the sea.

This great terrace consists for the most part of a chalky detritus spread out in layers nearly horizontal, with subordinate beds of gypsum and interlying courses of impure salt and briny clay. There is often associated with these gypseous calcites coarse conglomerates and variegated marls, and thickly scattered over the southwestern terrace-remnants, are sheets of brown flints and cherty rubble, gradually swept down from the overhanging heights.

South of the Wâdy of that name, Jebel Sebbeh, the level summit of which was the site of the ancient Masada, is detached in a measure from the general mountain-mass by a deep and extensive denudation on its west side, which does not however cut into the limestone a depth more than equal to the third of the entire altitude of the insulated block. Jebel Sebbeh is composed of the same compact limestone which has been so often mentioned before, brown or reddish-brown, where a geological antiquity has had time to bronze the exposed surface, but of a light iron or ice grey color within. Against its flanks rest in some places buttresses of the coarse carbonates of the peninsula, but on the whole the mountain is now quite free from the accessions of a later age.

A brief account of a locality so seldom visited may be interesting in more than a geological point of view.†

The rock is approached from the north by a very distinct road about 15 feet in width, marked by two parallel rows of stones which continue with interruptions for the space of a quarter of a mile. Viewed from this approach the hill is a pyramid in the upper third of its height and an offshoot of the great cliff in all that remains below. On the sea side the rock is absolutely impregnable. It rises here, in some places, almost perpendicularly to the height of 6 or 700 feet and in others where the ascent is more gradual, the access to the summit is com-

*I think that this is the same Wâdy which is sometimes called Wâdy Hefhâf, though one of the guides placed this south of Wâdy Sebbeh and north of Wâdy Sennein.

†I only know of its having been seen once since its identification with the ancient Masada by Robinson and Smith, viz. by Rev. Samuel Wolcott of Massachusetts.

45

pletely cut off by belts of natural breastworks varying from 20 to 100 feet in breadth. On the land side a military assault is possible, but would be perilous indeed in the face of any serious defence. After gaining the level of the separating gorge (which can only be done by climbing zigzag a hill closing it on the north, exposed to the fire from a round tower a little below the northern brow and from a square battlement a bowshot lower down,) there is a piece of very rough ground to cross with rocky ledges and jagged crevices. When this is passed, the climber must again descend and, turning sharp to the left, scramble up the steep side of the mountain along a line not difficult to walk when reached, but which seen at a distance with a glass gives no assurance of a foothold. Leaving at 9, A. M., the Moghârat el-Kebrît, a cave of some size just above the upper margin of the beach, we reached the summit without fatigue at a quarter before ten. A portion of the top is nearly level, and, including the broken ground at the south, there is a space of perhaps 1,000 yards by 400, which must have afforded sufficient accommodation for Eleazar and his 967 followers.

The entrance to the esplanade at the top is just below the western edge of the cliff through a gateway having a pointed Saracenic arch, after which a short turn leads to the platform forming the summit of the arch. The ruins are not very remarkable and I believe that all of them, as they now present themselves, are either of Saracenic or later origin. There are four buildings the walls of which are still partly standing, two just north of the entrance, on the west side of the plateau, another about the middle of the area and a fourth towards its northern end. The first of these is a structure of some pretension to architectural effect. The entrance door is a pointed arch on the stones of which are traced various characters, some from the Greek alphabet, others having a resemblance to the usual planetary signs. The doorway is small and set as it were in a shallow recess formed by another and larger arch pointed like the inner one. The walls are coated internally with a coarse stucco half an inch thick made of lime and fine gravel from the sea shore. The adjoining building has its walls plentifully studded in some places with Mosaic *tesserae* and covered here and there with a yellowish wash which breaks off in scales and has a very modern look. Some portions of the wall are fashioned into a network of small quadrangular cells or mullions rounded at the top, and the whole has the appearance of a building of the times of the Crusades. The ruin near the centre of the main area seems once to have been divided into several copartments and had a semi-circular recess on the eastern side, but the rough style of its construction and the fact that the loose fragments filling the joints have not yet fallen out are sufficient evidences of its modern origin.

At the northern extremity of the rock, but far below the edge of the cliff and quite inaccessible from the summit, are the ruins of a remarkable round tower with double walls of great solidity, between which, as there is reason to conjecture, once ran a staircase which ascended to the battlements. On a terrace below the tower, lies a spacious quadrangular ruin, the communication between which and the building above seems now to be cut off. The projecting ledge, on which these structures stand, recall in some degree the white promontory mentioned by Josephus, but this must have been on the south side of the rock, if that writer can be relied upon; for he tells us that when Silva had succeeded in setting fire to the wooden bulwark which the Sicarii had opposed to the tower constructed on the promontory, "a north wind that then blew brought the flames downward upon the Romans, but that after this the wind changed to the *South* and carried the flames against the wall which was now on fire through the entire thickness." Still further down other walls and breastworks can be traced, and finally surrounding the whole rock and leaving ample space within, there are outside walls running in polygonal lines marked at the several angles and elsewhere by small turrets or abutments. Beyond these walls and here and there within it, there may be observed detached enclosures or rude buildings contributing perhaps to the defence, or if we suppose the walls to be actual remains of Silva's circumvallation, the enclosures must have been accessories to the siege. A dry Wâdy now comes down from the southwest, completely separating these works into two groupes. This ravine has all the appearance of having been excavated by the waters long since the construction of the buildings near its banks.

There are three large reservoirs cut out of the solid rock and well cemented. One near the northern angle is 40 feet square and from 20 to 25 feet in height as far as a hurried measurement by the eye may be relied upon. The other two were at the southern extremity of the platform. Of these the easternmost contains an upper gallery and window with a flight of rude steps on the outside of the rock leading to a long aqueduct, the cement of which is still in good repair. The cistern at the southwestern angle was the largest of all, being twice as deep and long as the one on the north. It is entered by a descent of 30 or 40 steps from the surface of the rock and lightened by two windows opening towards the south. I found a few fragments evidently broken off from the capital of a marble column which had been cut from a white granular limestone well adapted to the sculptor's use, but fetid with a strong sulphureous smell when rubbed or broken.* Near this lay a hewn block of saccharine limestone of a different character, containing in its large pores crystals of calcspar, and scattered around were bits of ancient glass and pottery, with broken ends of implements and ornaments of bronze. Leaving the summit at half-past one and descending rapidly, we reached the Moghârat el-Kebrît in half an hour.

Wâdy Sennein is immediately south of Sebbeh. The great excavation which insulates this promontory terminates abruptly in the Wâdy, and is followed by a steep descent made craggy by the ravages which time has committed on this apparently indestructible rock. Little change of importance occurs as far as Wâdy Rubt (or Ribâtât) el-Jamûs. The limestone is less red externally than at Sebbeh, the prevailing colors being reddish-yellow, or yellow inclining to ash-grey. In the fracture, however, the appearance of the stone is hardly distinguishable from the Sebbeh limestone. Above the talus of debris at the foot of the cliff, the section-lines of the stratification are, in the main, horizontal, and the dip conforms sometimes strikingly with the existing surface, as if the rock had not been deeply abraded except in the ravines. In the Wâdy a portion of the limestone is so laid bare as to show a bed of 10 feet in thickness between horizontal surfaces, but without any evidence of stratified construction in the part thus enclosed. On the contrary, many vertical fissures divide this belt into irregular prisms, and the limestone appears to have undergone the shrinkage which is sometimes regarded as the cause of the pillaring of the columnar formations. In this limestone, amygdaloidal cavities filled, or sometimes only lined, with crystals of calcspar, not unfrequently occur, though these are occasionally replaced by a brown ochrey oxide of iron and manganese in very small spherular concretions. The debris is more angular than usual, and the edges of the limestone have sometimes even the aspect of a higher temper than the parts not so much exposed. Many of the fragments are chalcedonised, and some have a

* The *situs* of this limetone is not known to me. I have found, however, architectural remnants of it not only at Sebbeh, but at Kedes, Kefr Ber'am, Bâniâs and Lejjûn.

scoriaceous, but not a volcanic appearance, except a few bits of very porous black pumice, derived no doubt from the igneous district northeast.

Not far from this the ancient alluvions are again distinctly visible in white marly embankments of carbonate of lime, mixed with gypsum and calcspar, and marked by abundant indications of salt. The rains plough the whole of this mass into blocks, pinnacles, obelisks and other turret-like forms, with which the Arabs, when their attention is directed to them, are ready to amuse their lively fancies by all sorts of incongruous imputations of resemblance.

South of Wâdy Rubt el-Jamûs is Wâdy Melbidûn, to which succeeds the cove and Wâdy Mubŭghghik. The cliff limestone retains here the character it exhibited along the whole western shore, changing only in the comparatively unimportant particular of color. This is here darker than at Wâdy Rubt el-Jamûs, but not so red as at Sebbeh. The freshly exposed surface is a very light ash-grey, sometimes inclining to blue. The height of the cliff is certainly over 1,000 feet, and the ravines where they open into the Ghôr are deeply cut into the mass, with sides almost vertical. They exhibit, however, independently of the depth of the erosion, the usual sinuosities, as if the bends, whether originating simultaneously, or added in succession at the heads, had simply sunk into the rock as the excavation went on, preserving nearly unaltered the changes in azimuth, first impressed upon the face of the unsculptured plateaux. The upper strata lines of the cliff, as they show themselves at least in the natural section, are very nearly horizontal. The bands thus divided vary alternately in color, or seem to do so, at the distance we observed them. A part of this effect is due, I believe, to the lodgment of chalky detritus upon the projecting ledges or terraces, which range sometimes from near the cretaceous over-beds as far down as within a fourth of the whole height. The strata dip slightly towards the Lake. The debris is abundant and rather angular than rounded. I found here bits of bitumen and sulphur, with much lime-shale, together with rolled pebbles generally of flints, but sometimes of a tough and horny limestone. The rude remains of an aqueduct, and other ruins of no very ancient date, are to be observed not far within the Wâdy. There is tolerable water to be had; but the camping is made less agreeable than it might be, by the abundance of grass-hoppers, (jindib,) scorpions, flies, black ants and musquitoes. Vegetation is not absolutely wanting; I observed a number of seiyâl, hamd and ghŭraf trees. The chalks and tertiaries are not brought prominently forward here, but are more conspicuous on approaching Wâdy ez-Zuweireh. Here they begin in fact to predominate over the compact and older limestone, and a short distance west of the Wâdy mouth the masses of marl and marly gypsum with a horizontally bedded chalk, (certainly more recent than the chalks of Europe, and therefore perhaps not well entitled to the name,) assume a stern and repulsive aspect from their utter barrenness and desolation.

Into this Wâdy, a lateral valley, Wâdy en-Nejd, opens in such a way that the embouchure may be seen from the sea. Not long after this, Wâdy Muhawwit gains the upper margin of the beach, and a corresponding removal of the cliff leaves a wider interval than usual between the ancient massive limestone and the sea. This is partly unoccupied, partly encumbered by huge embankments of the post-tertiary marls; and the approach of Khashm Usdom with its enormous pile of rock-salt is almost unerringly announced by the geological indications which precede it on the north. As a striking exemplification of the magical effect of the presence of water in this chalky desert, the fine patch of verdure at the mouth of Wâdy Muhawwit may well be pointed out. Where this gives out towards Usdom, a sterile waste of white marls and bitter salt-flakes lies extended between the Khashm and the sea. The salt-mound is five miles long and less than half this in breadth. It can hardly be called a mountain, for it nowhere exceeds a few hundred feet in height. It is only the inferior portion which consists of rock-salt, and no crystallised salt was anywhere met with at a higher elevation than 100 feet above the level of the Sea. The superincumbent beds are principally carbonate of lime, but in a portion of the earthy matter capping the best specimens of salt I could find, there was more of sulphate than of carbonate, and though I am unable to state the proportion of gypsum in the overlying beds, I do not doubt that it enters in a very notable degree. A specimen taken directly from the top of the most remarkable of the tall spurs of salt carved out by the action of winter rains, (the one which our men with the harmless levity of sailors chose to call Lot's Wife,) gave on analysis the following result:

| | |
|---|---|
| Sulphate of Lime, . . . . . . . . . . . . . . . . . | 86.20 |
| Carbonate of Lime, . . . . . . . . . . . . . . . . . | 3.50 |
| Chlorides, principally of Sodium, . . . . . . . . . . . . | 6.75 |
| Magnesia and Water, . . . . . . . . . . . . . . . . | 3.15 |
| | 99.60 S. |

This deposit was seldom found where it did not take the form of a loose crumbling incrustation made up of very thin laminae, not perfectly plain and parallel, but waving and jagged, with sufficient diversity of color to make the laminated structure obvious at once. A portion of the salt in this knoll is intimately mixed with earthy matter. In one instance this was separated from the saline or soluble part and found to consist of

| | |
|---|---|
| Sulphate of Lime, . . . . . . . . . . . . . . . . . . | 33.85 |
| Carbonate of Lime, . . . . . . . . . . . . . . . . . | 3.84 |
| Carbonate of Magnesia, . . . . . . . . . . . . . . . | 19.49 |
| Alumina, . . . . . . . . . . . . . . . . . . . . . | 20.01 |
| Iron, . . . . . . . . . . . . . . . . . . . . . . . | 5.64 |
| Silica, . . . . . . . . . . . . . . . . . . . . . . | 16.66 |
| | 99.49 |

The clean and crystallised portions of this pillar show on analysis only inconsiderable traces of other ingredients than chloride of sodium.

The side of the mound facing the sea is curiously furrowed into a great number of tent-shaped knolls, and where this excavation has proceeded with unequal rapidity a singular conformation or relief is sometimes obtained. The form generally resulting is conical or rather conicuneal; the spur, which seems like a sugar-loaf when seen in front, loosing entirely this appearance when viewed from either side or from above. A considerable depression is sometimes found at the bridge of the knoll, but this is comparatively rare from the infrequency of the cases in which the material behind the triangular outline of the projecting buttress has been more destructible than the anterior portion. Where this has been so, an insulation of the mass will of course ensue, and a detached pillar is the result. Of these, there can be little doubt that some may be found at this moment in existence, though our time did not permit us even to search for them. From the soluble nature of the salt, and the crumbling looseness of the marl, it may be well imagined that while some of these needles are in the process of formation, others are being washed away, and more of them have probably been demolished than remain to be carved out of the block which is left. The nearest approach to the cylindrical form was met with in the one already spoken of, and which Captain Lynch has accurately described in his Narrative; but even that, as the description implies, was filled out behind by a low ridge connecting the apparent pillar with the general mass.

The marly capping of the rock-salt contains many rounded black flints. These are remarkable for their fragility, breaking sometimes with a slight tap of the hammer as readily as bitumen. I do not look upon them as in place, and they present little analogy with the flints of the upper chalk.

## CHAPTER II.

### *Points of Reconnaissance between Khashm Usdom and Sâfieh, and between Sâfieh and Kerak.*

*Salt Marsh south of the Dead Sea.—Wâdy el-Qurâhy, (es-Sâfieh.)—Marsh and Rocks between Wâdy el-Qurâhy and Wâdy el-Quneiyeh.—Red Sandstones of Wâdy el-Quneiyeh.—Sandstones of Wâdy Uheimir.—Large Limestone Block.—The Peninsula.—Post-tertiary Deposits.—Selenite.—Bitumen.—Limestones of the Peninsula, Sulphates, Silicates, Bituminous Marl, Sulphur, Chlorides, Rock-Salt.*

Khashm Usdom runs southeastwardly towards the salt-marsh at the south end of the lake, and which, when its level is highest, is no doubt laid completely under water. This marsh would then add some eight or ten miles to the length of the Dead Sea. The whole bay south of the Peninsula, is undergoing the same process of filling in, which has resulted in the formation of the great morass north of the Akrabim. The shoaling has already proceeded so far that it was impossible, with a boat of six inches draught of water, to approach at the season we were there, within half a mile of the southern extremity of the lake. The bottom is a very soft mud, into which the sounding-lead sank with its own weight, and the crystals of salt, so abundant in other places, appear to be wanting, either from the undersaturation of the water, or from the quantity of mud in which they lie concealed. The great marsh is intersected by six or eight drains, which carry their waters so sluggishly onward, that nothing but the lightest of suspended matter find its way to the place of deposit. At the close however of the hot season, as well as at the period of rains, a quicker current is established in these outlets, and coarser materials are brought down, with this difference, that salt is deposited in the autumn and redissolved to some extent in the spring.

East of the flat just described, Wâdy el-Qurâhy (es-Sâfieh) descending first eastwardly, then north-westwardly, pays its seldom failing tribute to the sea. Where the waters have any influence, an abundant vegetation is sure to prevail, and the Ghôr es-Sâfieh requites even the careless labor of the Ghawârineh with liberal returns of wheat, Indian corn, barley and tobacco.

Between Wâdy el-Qurâhy and Wâdy el-Quneiyeh, the marshy grounds are restricted to a much narrower belt than farther west, and are bounded by a wild mountainous tract scarcely ever trodden by the foot of the Frank. Seetzen crossed this district twice, first in

1806, then in 1807; Burkhardt pursued a parallel route ten miles inland in 1812, and Irby and Mangles on their way from Hebron to Kerak crossed the Qurâhy (their "Nahr el-Hussan") on the tenth of May 1818 near the foot of the mountains along the eastern edge of the plains. It was Captain Lynch's desire to visit this region, but he felt himself bound by his orders and was obliged reluctantly to forego the opportunity. From Irby and Mangles we learn that the mountains are of "sandstone and bad marble" and that fragments of colored granites and porphyries, with bits of serpentine, basalt and breccia are scattered in every direction, erratics as he thinks from the neighboring heights. It would be interesting to know the native *situs* of these igneous rocks, but there is as yet no evidence that it lies very near the western declivity of the mountains of Moab.

In coasting along the beach just north of Wâdy el-Qurâhy, our guides pointed out Wâdy en-Numeirah, which was not, as far as we could judge, a branch of Wâdy el-Qurâhy, but came down independently to the Sea. We observed in this neighborhood many trees and much shrubbery which indicated very distinctly the presence of abundance of water, but we could not approach the marshy shore from the great shoalness of this part of the Lake. Northwardly from the mouth of this Wâdy (be it Wâdy Numeirah or not) the swampy thicket extends for miles. Beyond the plain, a range of commanding eminences mainly of red sandstone ran parallel to the sea and were relieved on a still more lofty chain six or eight miles farther east. Between these, a valley could be partially seen through breaks in the western hills. Altogether this part of the Dead Sea exhibits a more magnificent array of towering mountain-masses and Alpine cliffs than any other portion of the Ghôr. In the lower range a short broad Wâdy comes down from a vast amphitheatre with precipitous sides, and this is deeply indented at the end by an elevated valley which ends abruptly upon the curved escarpment far above the level of the Wâdy at its feet. Up this *fer à cheval* and through the deep notch in its rear, other turreted cliffs of red sandstone appear in imposing forms, and mark by a depression in the distant range the highest and farthest portion of this triply terraced gorge.

On approaching Wâdy Uheimir* from the south, the sandstone becomes conspicuous for its variegated colors, and we enter upon a region deserving of particular attention.

The plain below the cliff is called Ard el-Hamra (red land,) the color of the soil partaking of the crimsons and vermilions of the sandstones of the neighboring hills. In the Wâdy where a fair supply of water was running when we visited it (April 26th) the arenaceous rocks are advantageously exposed. Their ruddy hue is much heightened where the cliff is exhibited in mass, the broken specimens brought away seeming rather gray than red. The component granules are of various colors, the reds predominating on the whole. Each granule is a bit of quartz, sometimes rounded, sometimes very angular, often transparent, often with an exterior ferruginous coating, easily washed off. These granules are, as might be expected, of various sizes, from 50 to 500 to the inch. The calcareous cement is sometimes visible intermingled with the siliceous particles like mortar filling up the interstitial places, sometimes only recognisable by the chemical tests for lime. The yellower sandstones are for the most part speckled with red spots and are composed of the largest grains. Interstratified with the red and yellow bands are beds of a grey-green spangly slate made of very

*This and the equivalent *Humeir* are the two diminutive forms of *Ahmar*, red. So also *Useiwid* and *Suweid* from *Aswad*, black; *Uzeiriq* and *Zureiq* from *Azraq*, blue. The trisyllabic form is derived legitimately from the masculine adjective, the dissyllable from the feminine.

minute molecules, the great number of them flattened into thin disks, talcose in their aspect and in their inelastic flexibility, giving to this schista deceptive resemblance to some of the older slates. Of this there are two varieties. In one the fissile character is not decided, in the other the laminations are very evenly and regularly laid on. An analysis of the first variety gave:

| | |
|---|---|
| I. Soluble in hydrochloric acid: | |
| Iron and Alumina, | 2.70 |
| Carbonates of Lime and Magnesia, | 7.50 |
| II. Insoluble in hydrochloric acid: | |
| Silica, etc., | 57.50 |
| Lime, Magnesia, Alkalies, | 10.37 |
| Iron and Alumina, | 20.55 |
| | 98.62 |

The Magnesia was an ingredient to a very trifling extent, and was therefore not separately determined.

I cannot regard these arenaceous accumulations, enormous as they are, as contemporary with the limestone or more ancient than it; though apparently dipping far beneath the calcareous heights beyond. They seem to me rather embanked against the limestone than underlying it, and to have been discharged over the calcareous escarpment into estuaries of the sea, when the ocean flowed as once it doubtless did high up the Ghôr then lying at a greatly lower level, from which it has been unequally upraised during the long chain of ages subsequent to the deposit of the chalk and prior to the quarternary alluvions.

The bed of Wâdy Uheimir contains angular fragments of the neighboring psammites and a few rolled limestones and erratic flints. The palm-tree finds here a congenial heat, of which we had a trial in the shape of a hot blast holding the thermometer at 106° F. through the first half of the night.

There was shown us here an unusually large limestone-block, which, if ever a mill-stone, is unaccountably far away from its post and bed-fellows; its circumference is 30 feet at least and thickness about three. It must have been brought from some distance, even if quarried from the nearest possible locality of origin. Most probably it is merely a remarkable boulder, trimmed for some purpose, not now easy to assign, into a tolerably regular shape. The guides could give no account of it, and the epithet *el-mureiseh*, by which they distinguished it, is rather a compliment to its size than a key to its history or use.

From the point of the shore corresponding to Wâdy Uheimir, the land northwardly is a depression, which if carried still lower would convert the peninsula into an island. This depression is the Ghôr or Ghuweir el-Mezra'ah, so named from a miserable collection of tents and temporary abodes, which the Ghawârineh occasionally set up in that part of it near the mouth of Wâdy el-Dera'ah.

The peninsula itself is an accumulation of post-tertiary deposits disposed horizontally, which was no doubt formed when the sea stood much higher than now, and which has followed the descending level, but at less rapid a rate, so as to be left behind, as it were, as a monument of the constructions which then were effected in its waters.

The beds of which this embankment consists are principally a friable carbonate of lime, intermixed with sand and sandy marls. Patches of sulphate of lime may be found in subordinate relations to the enveloping mass; for two of the specimens out of many which I brought away were nearly pure gypsum, though from not having remarked this on the spot, I cannot now say in what proportion the sulphate and carbonate are allied in the localities where they are found conjoined. Out of a number of fine crystals of selenite which I procured from the peninsula, one was analysed and gave:

| | |
|---|---|
| Sulphate of Lime, . . . . . . . . . . . . . . . . . . . | 78.73 |
| Water, . . . . . . . . . . . . . . . . . . . . . . . . | 21.27 |
| | 100.00 S. |

Being two atoms of water to one of sulphate of lime.

The promontory runs from 40 to 80 feet in height, and has sides so steep as only to be scalable at widely separated points. The upper surface is not so even as one might expect from the regular stratification.

A sharp ridge runs across it with the figure due to the gradual waste of the mound by drainage, both eastwardly and westwardly. The tent-shape erosion of the upper and lower bank may also be remarked, though varied, in regular alternation, by broken crags and excavated recesses which look as if ravaged by recent denudations. Flints occur in the upper beds, and balls of sulphur with stray bits of bitumen* are found in the marly beach below. Here and there may be picked up balls of a magnesian carbonate of lime, having all the appearance of quick-lime fresh from the kiln. In 100 parts these contain 90.2 of carbonate of lime and 7.5 carbonate of magnesia. Several of these balls I afterwards found on the west side of the Sea without being able to assign in either case the original locality. Some of these, though quite compact and coherent when first found, crumbled into fragments after lying a year or more in the cases to which they were consigned. In some of the specimens, taken from the inferior marly beds, a black material was observed in some abundance which turned out on analysis to be manganese. I did not succeed in finding any fossil remains, but I feel little hesitation in regarding the peninsular formations as contemporary and once continuous with those of the western shore.

The lime carbonates of the Peninsula are not very various or difficult to describe. They resolve themselves mainly into the following descriptions.

1. A soft, crumbling, chalky marl, in courses more or less horizontal. Of this the great mass of the Peninsula consists, with local differences and occasional developments of impure salt and coarse gypsum in patches and crusts.

2. A harder stone than No. 1, but still softer than ordinary Paris plaster. It is beautifully white, inclined to cream, and even straw in places much exposed. The layers are evenly laid on, but often obliterated by concretion. Even when the color distinguishes the sheets, the material is so continuous that a separation of the plane of change is sometimes not to be effected. In general, however, the layers are easily detached. The texture of this variety is remarkable for its softness and smoothness, resembling the finest prepared chalks.

* It may be observed of the specimens of bitumen that we met with around the Dead Sea, that they present all very nearly the same appearance. In fracture, texture and color, they resemble the bitumen of Biyar el-Hummar, but often show in addition very distinct marks of their vegetable origin. The following description by Prof. Booth, may answer for nearly all. "A portion is soluble in ether and alcohol with brown and yellow color; the remainder is soft, but hardens on exposure; it dissolves wholly in oil of turpentine with dark-brown color, and softens in water at 212° F. It leaves a little yellowish ash not effervescing with acid; distils almost wholly over, leaving a carbonaceous residue and a brown viscid oil." The specific gravity of the specimens examined was found to be 1.1040.

The presence of chlorine is easily detected, arising as afterwards ascertained, from chloride of sodium in the interstitial surfaces, and in some degree latent in the body of the chalk.

3. A foliated carbonate of lime much harder than No. 2, consisting of thin sheets of various colors closely packed together. In some instances I found a hundred sheets to the inch, but the crusts into which this variety is apt to run, are often less than a quarter of an inch thick, and seldom, I believe, thicker than an inch. The forms assumed are frequently conchoidal, with an external coat of honey-yellow glazing, hard enough to resist a silver pick. This description effervesces very much with acids, and is a very pure carbonate. The peculiarity of the external coats is due to the presence of a silicate of iron. These chalky shells are found principally on the beach, but a somewhat similar incrustation without the glazed coating may be met with along the base of the main mound.

4. A soft crumbling foliaceous marl, with much black powdery matter interposed, sometimes in loose sooty flakes, sometimes in well pressed leaves, alternating with the white laminations. This black powder consists of a variable quantity of carbonate of lime, much manganese, and a little iron in the state of peroxide. The folia in this variety are oftener curved than plane, and more frequently very divergent than parallel.

5. Crust-tufas composed of thin leaves of carbonate of lime, and covering with their numerous coats whatever nucleus they find within their reach. Reeds and palm-stalks seem to present to this sediment a particular attractiveness.* An analysis of one of these tufas gave:

| | |
|---|---|
| Carbonate of Lime, | 92.81 |
| Carbonate of Magnesia, | 5.01 |
| Iron and Alumina, | 1.10 |
| Organic, | .05 |
| Insoluble, | .65 |
| | 99.62 M. |

6. A pasty pulpy marl, principally carbonate of lime with some sulphate and a very notable proportion of salt and bitter chlorides. The latter ingredients I must regard as recent additions, for they abound more in the beds accessible to the present waters than in the chalks (so to term them) not far above the highest level of the periodical replenishments. The sulphates are no doubt of earlier origin than the chlorides, and are due probably to a gradual transformation of so much carbonate which in other parts of the great mound has been, as it were, altogether superseded by the gypsum. On the other hand the sulphate of lime now elevated above the opportunity of reproduction is insensibly abstracted by the solvent powers of the rains which are not wanting in the late winter and early spring months, and may be redeposited after evaporation on the low and level space between the lime-hills and the sea, to increase the bulk of what has already been gained by decomposition from the carbonate by the direct action of sulphuretted agents.

The sulphate of lime according to this view may be expected in all forms from an occasional ingredient in the marls and chalks to gypseous beds with scarcely any trace of lime, either as carbonate or as hydrate. Accordingly beside patches and banks of gypsum with little calcareous admixture, crystallised deposits of this material may be found on the

* I do not think that these incrustations originate on the Peninsula. They seem rather to be accidentally thrown upon its banks with the relics they enclose.

peninsula without a very long search. They assume for the most part the irregularly lamellated and stellated forms varying from a semi-transparent selenite to an imperfectly fibrous satin spar.

Sulphate of magnesia is subordinately associated with the sulphate of lime, and in two specimens I found sulphate of manganese present in minute proportions, the sulphate of lime being nearly or entirely away.

Of silicated rocks I found no trace except the sandy impurities distributed through the coarser gypsums and chalks, and rounded bits of green-stone so long and far from their homes that these must now be mere matters of conjecture.

Bitumen and bituminous marl are not altogether wanting, but I found nothing to lead me to suppose that the purer bitumens were anywhere native on the peninsula. Bituminous marl I found, in one instance at least, in place, though I am unable to say much of the number and dimensions of the beds.

Sulphur both as powdery intermixture with the marl and in lumps of considerable size are among the rarer productions of the peninsula. Nitre (nitrate of potash or soda) I did not find. But I infer from the presence of soda without nitric or hydrochloric acid in many of the first washings of specimens brought home, that natron (carbonate of soda) would be found to an extent which the observations made do not enable me very accurately to assign.

In addition to the preceding, rock-salt is a product of the peninsula in various shapes and in differing relations to the beds which embrace it. As a recent product of the present waters, it is found in films and flakes spread over the marly beach, each indicating, by its place and magnitude, the place and magnitude of some depression or little basin which had detained for evaporation the saturated brine. The chlorides of sodium and potassium form the bulk of these residua, the more soluble muriates of lime and magnesia often escaping with the fluid before the evaporation can force them to appear in solid form.

A second exhibition of rock-salt is in the shape of badly defined patches and misshapen ganglions imbedded in the marl. The salt in such cases is very coarse and crude, penetrated with briny carbonates and sulphates, and varying from a *sel gemme* somewhat chalky to a limestone slightly salt. In general however when the lump is tolerably large, crystallised portions of a very pure salt will not fail to make their appearance, but the existing outer surface is for the most part rather chalky and opaque than crystalline and translucent.

A third form is also known to exist, viz: of knotty packs or crooked benches, on a small scale however, of a rock-salt very uniformly pure, or rather it should be said, that whatever impurities exist in one part may by expected throughout the mass.

The two last forms are certainly not the produce of the present waters. They were in all probability already in existence, (though not as they are now,) as definite deposits contemporaneous with the constructions of the marly limestone in which they have long lain more or less concealed. There is in fact no part of the peninsular mound which does not show itself, on analysis, impregnated with salt, and it may be that the agglomerations at particular points have resulted from molecular predispositions to settle round a *nucleus*, or gather together in a *nidus*, the supply being all the time kept up by the flow of the briny fluid through the pores of the loose and permeable chalk.

# CHAPTER III.

## *East and Northeast Shore of the Dead Sea.*

*Kerak Fossils.—Limestone Cliffs.—Marls and Sandstones.—Limestone of Wâdy Beni Hamâd.—Pumices.—Limestone towards Wâdy Mojeb.—Sandstones of Wâdy Mojeb.—Limestone with Haurân Lava.—Basalt.—Fountain and Limestone of Wâdy Zerqa Ma'în.—Basalt of Wâdy Hemârah.—'Ain es-Suweimeh.—Calcareous Rocks of the Northeast Shore.—Compact Marble with Trap-cinders.—Foliated and Ramuscular Travertine.—Silicated Limestone.—Sandstones.—Volcanic Conglomerate.—Lavas.—The Jordan.—Mud and Alluvions.—Salt-Plains.—Râs Feshkhah.*

BETWEEN Kerak and the sea the mountains are principally limestone. The upper beds are cretaceous in the same sense in which the chalks of Mâr Sâba are so; but they are more compactly consolidated, and though mostly rich enough in fossils, there are masses of great extent where these remains appear to have been gradually obliterated, and metamorphic assimilations established in their places. On the other hand it is hard to resist the conclusion that the later limestones of the mountains of Moab are subsequent to the chalks of Western Europe, and may be regarded as immediately preceding the North African nummulitic groupes.

Just below Kerak, where the road skirts the south side of a deep ravine, the limestone wall is cut profoundly by deep fissures much widened by the lapse of time. Our hurried progress permitted no examination or collection of the occasional fossil specimens which a momentary absence from the party enabled me to find imbedded in these rocks. The ***Ostraeae Syriacae*** were especially large and abundant, with ***Venus perovalis***, ***Echinus Kerakensis***, and ***Exogyra densata.***

I remarked the not unusual occurrence of the Haurân basalt in the lintels of the doorways and elsewhere, and in the castle my attention was drawn to a granite column, the native place of which future explorers perhaps may be able to assign. In a short covered way cut through the rock and leading to the castle, the limestone exhibits an alternation of thin-seamed calcareous beds and layers of a shaly dark-blue flint.

About two hours west of Kerak is a spot often selected as a halting ground; the limestone looser and less compact than the strata lower down, is much richer in fossils. Among these may again be noted: ***Venus perovalis***, ***Echinus Kerakensis***, ***Exogyra densata***, ***Ostraea Syriaca.***

Detached from the cliff on the edge of which we rode, enormous blocks hang ready to drop off and precipitate themselves into the vast gorge below, as if inclined to follow the huge masses which have already been forced down. The fissures are rectangular and vertical, and sometimes singularly widened before the final launch. The strata have in general a regular descent towards the sea, keeping tolerably parallel to the upper surface, except where that runs into more than ordinary irregularity. The precipices are sometimes actually overhanging, so as to make the look down a trial to the nerves. The isolated blocks as well as the detached peaks and knobs have a cavernous structure not perhaps easy to explain, presenting pits of all sizes, from such as may harbor a few crystals of calcspar to those which give shelter to families and herds.

On descending over the edge of the eminence to pass down into the Ghôr, a remarkable disposition of the calcareous beds may be seen across the gorge. The layers which are at first nearly horizontal, plunge more and more steeply until they seem to imitate the sheets of a huge cataract of a once fluid mass. It seems not unreasonable to suppose that beds so conformable to the shape of the cliff which they cover, must have been determined in their inclinations by the configuration of the mould on which they lie. All this implies however the existence of the Ghôr as a feature of the scenery actually existing before the tertiary age.

Shortly after this descent, we meet in succession tertiary marls, argillaceous and calcareous, a recent clay slate, shaly sandstones, and a yellow limestone which I had not seen before. The arenaceous rocks are as usual mere incidents of the vicissitudes which have preceded the sandy deposits, and concur to prove the prior existence of the Ghôr. The peninsular tertiaries now begin to come in place, and hang in half consumed lambeaux or benches, on the flanks of the Wâdys near their mouths, and the traveller is then brought to the level of the isthmus, where he finds himself obliged to reascend if he still pursues a westward course, but not if he proceeds either northwardly or southwardly, these directions conducting him by very gentle slopes to the shores of the north or south bay. Unless we suppose that the sea has not yet reached its lowest level, the isthmus must inevitably one day afford a free passage to the waters, and the Peninsula, then an island, will be still more a problem than at present.

The limestone of Wâdy Beni Hamâd, on the north side of the valley at least, is firm and even tough, but is nevertheless more porous than some of the softer rocks. One of the dips observed was W. by S. towards the Peninsula. The color of this stone internally is a wax-yellow grey, the fracture splintery with very minute scales. The exposed face of the cliff is liable to acquire a thick coating or incrustation of a very rough blue and yellow tegument, which with all its strange appearance is nearly a pure carbonate of lime, with 1½ per cent. of iron. It is very thickly set with cup-like cavities, in which an olive-shaped calyx of the size of a small barley corn is sometimes contained, planted, as it were, perpendicularly to the general plane of the crust. On the shore may be found bits of the black porous pumice of the northeast coast, lumps of bitumen with external marks of long rolling and rubbing, tufaceous incrustations of reeds and other nuclei, both vegetable and mineral, with the usual variety of water-worn flints and argillaceous and cretaceous concretions. The plain is well covered with the shrub *qataf*, not, however, the same with that described under this name by Forskal. A broad and thick belt of dead locusts skirted the water's edge for a mile and more from the spot where we lay encamped.

The soundings along the axis of the North Bay increase gradually from zero to 25 fathoms at the middle of the mouth, the bottom being a grey ash-colored mud.

Between Wâdy Beni Hamâd and Wâdy Môjeb the limestone assumes a dip more or less southwardly, and is sometimes inclined as much as 20 degrees or more. But care must be taken not to regard this disposition of the strata as anything more than a prevailing one; for the remark so often made on the diversity of the limestone dip within very limited areas on the west side of the sea is not without its application on the east.

Near the shore and quite subordinate to the calcareous hills beyond, the undercliff sandstone may be traced by its color and its battlemented outline from near Wâdy Beni Hamâd northwardly beyond Wâdy el-Môjeb and even beyond Wâdy Zerqa Ma'în. Along the southern portion of this range, the section lines run nearly parallel to the horizon, but the actual dip is towards the sea and sometimes more considerable, than the view from the water would lead one to imagine.

The full development of the sandstone undercliff does not take place until a short distance south of the bay of Wâdy el-Môjeb. There is here a junction of the two formations, and just inside of the south arm of the cove there is a deposit of white sandstone upon a base of limestone which had evidently been the excavated and weather-worn rocky wall of an ancient Wâdy. The general depression of the whole country, letting in the waters of the ocean, or an alteration of level and other accessories, causing a submersion of this Wâdy-mouth beneath the waters of an inland sea, would (either one or the other) be followed by an accumulation of sandy detritus at the points where the debris would first find a resting place in quiet water, and a partial blocking up of the bay and Wâdy-mouth must necessarily ensue. The consolidation of these subaqueous moraines (which are of far more frequent occurrence than is generally supposed) may be accounted for in many ways without the charge of presumptuous conjecture. One of the easiest to imagine is an infiltration of calcareo-ferruginous cement through a bed of overlying limestone afterwards removed. The sandstone is sometimes white, sometimes beautifully variegated; yellows, reds and browns being the shades most frequently exhibited. The coloring matter appears to have come in simultaneously with the deposits of the sands, for although the tintings are far more vivid and glowing on the face of the sandstone than even a short distance within, this may well be the mere effect of long exposure, while their distribution in layers according to the nature of the sandy beds makes it impossible to suppose that the coloring was connected with the solidifying process.

In the example near Wâdy el-Môjeb the sandstone engorgement has itself been, at a long posterior epoch, subjected to the valley-making excavation, and a broad and deep ravine has been the result of unnumbered ages employed in the unsuspected disintegration and abrasion of the comparatively modern Wâdy floor and walls.

Near this spot, where the red sandstone cliffs assume a most imposing form and attitude, the rocky escarpment rises immediately from the sea, but farther north a sedgy beach between the precipice and the water permits a convenient landing and ample space for all the requisites of a far more numerous camping party than we could muster at the time. We found no rival claimants for our night's resting place, though a path well trodden passed that way, the entrance and exit of which we had no time to explore.

The chasm in the sandstone forming the passage for the Môjeb has sides varying in their first heights from 100 to 400 feet, and may be 100 feet broad or rather less. The cove at the sea side is delta-shaped and has a bar stretching along the base. The thermometer varied from 70 to 74° through the night.

The sandstones of Wâdy Môjeb and its vicinity run into the following varieties:

1. A ferruginous sandstone, composed of very minute nearly equal sized grains, tolerably well bound together, but yet coming off superficially on the ordinary pressure of the thumb. The color of the mass is a pale grey-violet with iron-grey bands or sheets, united by mutual interpenetration with the inclosing lighter colored beds.

2. A grey sandstone of rather coarser grain than No. 1, and without its parti-colored layers.

3. A fine grained schistose sandstone of much firmer texture than either 1 or 2. The color is a light blue-grey, but not decided, running into shades and faint tintings assuming more or less a parallelism with the proper surfaces of sedimentary separation.

4. A cream-white sandstone with an exfoliating yellow crust. It is mottled interiorly with insulated systems of colored layers suddenly giving out and as suddenly re-appearing These do not however seem to penetrate very far beneath the surface.

5. A sandstone resembling 4 with this difference that the alternating layers are replaced by short gangs or dykes of uniform appearance but of different colors with the mass, having however no distinguishable marks of independent deposition.

6. A firmly cohering, thoroughly assimilated sandstone of grains microscopically minute, disposed in evenly laid courses with surfaces of easy separation spread over with irregular bas-reliefs, sometimes curiously imitative of organic forms. A close examination however of several specimens brought home showed that, in these at least, the fossil-like appearances were illusory and accidental.

The limestones found near Wâdy Môjeb were either boulders from the upper cliffs or crystalline travertines in patches of very limited extent. One of the latter was quite remarkable for the number of angular *tesserae* of black Haurân lava scattered through the white mass. Some of these were strikingly exact in the rectangular disposition of their faces. They must have been thrown upon the growing tufa as its coats were successively precipitated from the thermal waters which once held the calcareous material in solution. The faces of the basaltic dice are often inclined to the larger surfaces; but this must necessarily have arisen, whenever the unequal pressure of the accrescent travertine disturbed the equilibrium of the fragments they gradually enclosed.

An analysis of these black silicates gave:

I. Oxylytic, or soluble in hydrochloric acid, 30.89 per cent. of the whole; of this in 100 parts there were:

| | |
|---|---|
| Peroxide of Iron, and protoxide converted to peroxide, . . . . | 40.72 |
| Alumina, . . . . . . . . . . . . . . . . . . . . . | 29.82 |
| Lime, . . . . . . . . . . . . . . . . . . . . . | 13.08 |
| Magnesia, . . . . . . . . . . . . . . . . . . . . | 7.99 |
| Alkalies, . . . . . . . . . . . . . . . . . . . . | 8.36 |
| | 99.97 |

II. Anoxylytic, 69.11 per cent. of the whole; it contained in 100 parts:

| | |
|---|---|
| Silica, . . . . . . . . . . . . . . . . . . . . . | 68.25 |
| Iron, Alumina and Lime, . . . . . . . . . . . . . . | 25.02 |
| Magnesia, . . . . . . . . . . . . . . . . . . . . | 2.10 |
| Alkalies, . . . . . . . . . . . . . . . . . . . . | 4.32 |
| | 99.69 |

Of igneous rocks I met with nothing but a few erratic fragments high up in the Wâdy, and many smaller bits scattered along the shore. The basalt is in such cases in an abnormal or paramorphic state, and cannot be relied upon as indicative of the present condition of the mass from which it is derived, even if the locality could be ascertained. Some of the fragments showed a slaty structure, quite unusual in this rock, others had the characteristic hackly porosity of the Tŭbarîya lava with a partial obstruction of the pores, due to spathic residua of no very ancient date, and a third description contained glands of carbonate of lime deposited in amygdaloidal cavities of a size sometimes exceeding in the long diameter three-quarters of an inch. The pumiceous variety I did not find, though it may very well be thrown upon this division of the beach.

North of Wâdy el-Môjeb the mountainous coast is less steep than farther south. It is much broken up and carved out into many small Wâdys. The limestone again comes forward, but soon after, two or three miles perhaps from Wâdy el-Môjeb, the sandstone in red and yellow bands, dipping slightly towards the north, again resumes its place, abutted on the lower flanks of the great calcareous block of which even the Haurân basalts are but subordinate dykes.

The yellow sandstone is sometimes replaced by a grey variety, and the groupes then dip gently towards the north. Still receding from Wâdy el-Môjeb the sea-side hills soon descend and leave visible above them a broad declivity decked with trees and verdure in abundance with very high cliffs far behind. The sandstones are here not of the same age. At least a very long interval has sometimes separated the yellow and the red, for the latter, which seems the older, has been deeply excavated by secular abrasion and then filled up by non-conforming beds of a sandstone of much later date. This has again been subjected to excavatory agents under circumstances altogether changed, and the new Wâdy again filled up by detritus when no longer the channel of a stream.

Further north than this, vegetation is well supported and the presence of water is easy to infer. In a Wâdy here, broader and flatter than usual, large boulders of sandstone and limestone have been brought together so as to form a spacious, but insulated groupe. Not far off were wheat-fields and high grass with palm-trees in very considerable numbers. I think we counted near a hundred.

Next succeeds a fine foaming cascade coming down between patches of cheerful vegetation, without having yet worn out the commencement of what is perhaps one day to be a frowning ravine. It looks in fact as if artificially and recently turned down the cliff. The rock over which it discharges itself is dark and scoriaceous and has a lava-like aspect, though I cannot speak with certainty as we were then some way from shore.

A fine Wâdy near this shows a western dip of the rocks with much *debris* on the hill-side. The heights now subside and show an opening towards a distant and very elevated tract. The neighboring hills have many ledges of a cindery or volcanic look. These are varied by a succession of terraces and taluses. The section dips are northwardly, the true bed dips probably N. E.

A Wâdy with fine water now succeeding, we landed and found in very close connection trap, travertine, sandstone and limestone; the sandstone green and red with dip south. From this point the arenaceous deposits increase in number and variety, and the colors are red, green, yellow and white. Marly beds appear, dipping southwest, and the delta of Wâdy Zerqa Ma'în shortly after makes its appearance with a fine stream of hot, sweet water (93° F.) issuing from the edge of a reedy beach and encountering the comparative impurity and coldness (77° F.) of the Salt and Bitter Lake. This brook, which after the Jordan is the least stinted contributor to the Lake, is at the place of its discharge about 12 feet in width and nine or ten inches in depth; making full amends by the velocity of the current (7 or 8 miles an hour) for the scantiness of its linear dimensions. It loses on its course to the lake but little of the heat with which it emerges at the baths, and nothing can be imagined more refreshing than a dip in its soft warm waters after a wash in the harsh and greasy brine of Bahr Lût. The gorge when it terminates upon the open beach is upwards of 100 feet wide, and retains this width with little variation as far up as we had time to extend our observations. The height of the rocks at the mouth of the gorge is eighty feet or more, but this altitude soon increases on ascending the ravine to 200 or 300 feet. The walls are sandstone, much resembling that of Wâdy Môjeb, the prevailing colors being red and yellow. The layers are thinner here than there, but the structure of the stone is much the same. Being unable to penetrate far into the interior, I will not attempt any description of the limestones against which the arenaceous beds are embanked, nor of the traps which overlie the calcareous deposits. From an examination of the larger erratics however, found along the floor of the Wâdy, the following varieties are ascertained, but with an unavoidable incertainty respecting their place of formation.

1. A coarse, semi-crystalline limestone with numerous longitudinal cellules or pores, flattened in the direction of the general stratification. In two specimens I found *Hamites*, in a third an *Ostraea.*

2. A chalky limestone, blueish-white, probably nummulitic. *Ostraeae* were not unfrequent in it. Perhaps differing from No. 1 only in the absence of crystalline structure.

3. An alabastrine limestone, made up of layers of white and pale-pink, the latter portion more porous and more unequally consolidated than the white. Its appearance indicates precipitation from thermal waters. An analysis of the pale-pink portion gave:

| | |
|---|---|
| Carbonate of Lime, | 96.80 |
| Carbonate of Magnesia, | .40 |
| Iron, | .65 |
| Alumina, | .55 |
| | 98.40 |

4. A white very hard chalk, slightly adhering to the tongue; fracture largely conchoidal. This limestone is thickly encrusted with a very heterogeneous concrete of small sharp fragments of flints and chalks with bits of brown bituminous marl and coarse calcspar minutely intermixed with the rest. The incrustation has all the appearance of a modern origin, long posterior however to the detachment of the boulders from its parent rock, an event certainly not very remote in the order of geological antiquity.

5. The *Exogyra densata*, pl. XVIII, fig. 106, was found detached on the edge of the Wâdy stream, less than a quarter of a mile from the mouth of the ravine. I am unable therefore to assign, from what point up the valley the fossil has been washed out.

6. In addition to the above from the Wâdy I observed on the beach below several specimens of a dark-blue limestone which I mention as a color unusual in the neighborhood of the Dead Sea. It consisted of 75 per cent. of mixed carbonate and hydrate of lime, with 25 per cent. of insoluble matter not analysed.

7. Several varieties of parti-colored flints were observed both up the Wâdy and along the shore. Among these one composed of opaquely white nuclei in a dark-blue-brown paste, is deserving of particular mention from its marked resemblance to the flints of Bethlehem and its immediate vicinity.

The district between Wâdy Zerqa Ma'în and the mouth of the Jordan may have been visited by Father Daniel of Mâr Sâba who assured the traveller Nau in 1674 that he had made the entire tour of the Dead Sea; but he has at all events left no intelligible account of what he saw. Seetzen in 1806 made nearly the complete circuit of the sea, but at some distance from the shore. In 1807 he supplied this omission by a very memorable journey of 11 days from Jericho to the Ghôr es-Sâfieh by the Baths of Calirrhoë and a return-journey of 5 days still nearer the shore, passing (as well as the rocky sea wall would permit) directly from the mouth of Wâdy el-Môjeb to the mouth of Wâdy Zerqa Ma'în and from this by the way of Tûr el-Hummarah to Jericho again. The particulars of the journey from one Wâdy mouth to the other are given by Carl Ritter from Seetzen's yet unpublished journal, but the walk from Wâdy Zerqa Ma'în to Jericho does not appear to have been recorded by Seetzen himself with corresponding fullness of dètail.

Immediately north of Wâdy Zerqa the sandstone strata run more nearly in horizontal courses. Near Wâdy Hemârah, the first valley of any magnitude north of Wâdy Zerqa, the igneous rocks make their appearance above the arenaceous beds. Several slender streams of sweet water, and one in considerable fullness in Wâdy Minshaleh, are then passed in succession, and the hills dying gradually away are still found capped with basalt-lava of different colors, consistencies and ages. An interval of mingled travertine and trap then succeeds; and finally after a combination of limestone and sandstone with every form and variety of lava, an altered sandstone, water and weather-worn, without even a straggling fragment of the other rocks upon it, takes possession of the shore, the hills receding two hours away and leaving, between them and the sea, a flat but stony and sterile waste, until the cane-brakes north of Wâdy Ghuweir show that a fountain, 'Ain es-Suweimeh, is but a short distance beyond.

The forms in which the rocks of the northeast coast present themselves, it will have already been seen from the above, are too various to admit of a full description, nor is it indeed necessary to a clear view of their principal relations. The main or predominant types may be thus classed and described.

A. *Calcareous.*

1. A course, but compact and heavy limestone,* milk-white, smooth-grained in places, and elsewhere chalky, incrusted with angular trap-cinders, or gravelly fragments, some of which are actually sunk in the matrix as if they had found it fused, and had penetrated it several inches in this state. Deeper within the substance of the limestone nothing of this is met with. From this however is not to be inferred that as the matrix wears away, the incrustation will not be continued, or rather gradually superseded by means of insensible departures of the old accretions and equally insensible additions of the new. In fact, the present exterior face is but the existing surface, to which a long and unknown denudation has reduced the limestone rock from an original bulk and form now impossible to assign.

2. A white concretionary limestone, the result doubtless of a deposit of carbonate of lime from bicarbonates held in solution in the mineral waters which have been and still are so abundant in this neighborhood. The concretion is grain to grain, and not in consecutive coatings, in which respect it differs from the following.

3. A foliated travertine, or tuff, covered with a brown incrustation; the laminae of the interior mass very thin and of alternate colors, with intermediate viscera of irregular struc-

* I found this to be a very pure carbonate of lime. Out of 21 gr. 58, the treatment by sulphuric acid gave 28 gr. 60 sulphate of lime. This is equivalent to 21 gr. 02 of carbonate of lime, and I found in fact 0 gr. 47 insoluble matter, principally silica, iron and alumina.

ture. Effervesces very strongly with acids. This travertine seemed to me not undeserving of analysis; I removed the outer crust carefully, and this I found to consist of:

| | |
|---|---|
| Carbonate of Lime, . . . . . . . . . . . . . . . . . . . | 79.0 |
| Carbonate of Magnesia, . . . . . . . . . . . . . . . . | 8.4 |
| Alumina, . . . . . . . . . . . . . . . . . . . . . . | 10.1 |
| Iron, . . . . . . . . . . . . . . . . . . . . . . . | 3.0 |
| Alkalies, (trace.) | |
| | 100.5 |

Of the main portion of the travertine, about 3 per cent. proved to be soluble in water, and consisted principally of chlorides and a minute admixture of soluble sulphates. The remaining 97 per cent. gave on analysis:

| | |
|---|---|
| Carbonate of Lime, . . . . . . . . . . . . . . . | 83.9 per cent of the 97. |
| Carbonate of Magnesia,. . . . . . . . . . . . . . | 1.7 |
| Iron, Alumina and some Lime, . . . . . . . . . . | 5.9 |
| Alkalies and Water, . . . . . . . . . . . . . . | 3.5 |
| Insoluble, . . . . . . . . . . . . . . . . . . . | 4.8 |

4. A mammillary, or ramuscular travertine, the teats as usual composed of fibres radiating from a central axis. These processes become in time amalgamated and consolidated, and the resulting mass has a crystalline subsaccharoidal appearance, in which the radiating fibres are only faintly discernible. Constituents as follows:

| | |
|---|---|
| I. Dissolved by hydrochloric acid. | |
| Carbonate of Lime, . . . . . . . . . . . . . . . . . . | 39.40 |
| Carbonate of Magnesia, . . . . . . . . . . . . . . . . | .90 |
| Alumina, . . . . . . . . . . . . . . . . . . . . . . | .70 |
| Peroxide of Iron, . . . . . . . . . . . . . . . . . . | .10 |
| II. Not dissolved by hydrochloric acid: | |
| Silica, . . . . . . . . . . . . . . . . . . . . . . . | .71 |
| Alumina, . . . . . . . . . . . . . . . . . . . . . . | .24 |
| Lime, . . . . . . . . . . . . . . . . . . . . . . . | .20 |
| Magnesia, . . . . . . . . . . . . . . . . . . . . . | .01 |
| Potassa and Soda, . . . . . . . . . . . . . . . . . . | .15 |
| | 42.41 |

In addition I ought to mention, that 0 gr. 36 of chlorides, (or about 0.8 per cent. of the whole weight,) was obtained in another experiment, by washing the powder in water before the application of the acid. This was mainly chloride of sodium. I have already mentioned that there is scarcely a rock in the valley of the Jordan, which does not give very distinct traces of chlorine.

5. A ferruginous silicated limestone, much resembling the red lavas of Delâta, but quite different in composition. It consists of:

| | |
|---|---|
| Carbonate of Lime, | 85.35 |
| Carbonate of Magnesia, | 2.61 |
| Peroxide of Iron, | 4.90 |
| Silica, | 7.15 |
| | 100.01 |

This limestone has a brick-red color, and a burnt and even slaggy look. It is traversed by numberless capillary passages leading from one cellule to another, these cavities for the most part filled with a very fine drusy carbonate of lime, nearly white and introduced long after the instillation of the iron.

6. A blood-brown limestone allied to the former. Composition:

| | |
|---|---|
| Silica, | 7.36 |
| Alumina, | 3.60 |
| Iron, Peroxide, | 10.24 |
| Manganese, oxide, (trace.) | |
| Carbonate of Lime, | 75.20 |
| Carbonate of Magnesia, (trace.) | |
| Water, | 3.20 |
| | 99.60 S. |

The drusy cavities in this description are much larger than in the former, amounting sometimes to well-formed geodes. On the contrary the capillary ducts are very rare. Parts of this rock are very ochry and others hematitic, but alumina is very seldom present.

B. *Arenaceous or Siliceous.*

1. A white sandstone, consisting of translucent pearl-blue grains, generally small and uniform, but with some admixture of larger kernels, all however of homogeneous aspect and origin.

2. A yellow sandstone of minute sparkling grains, in general close packed, but subject to little cavities or cellules, widely set apart; some of these thinly coated with films of carbonated lime. This was analysed, and gave:

| | |
|---|---|
| Silica, | 15.30 |
| Carbonate of Lime, | 7.70 |
| Carbonate of Magnesia, | .40 |
| Iron and Alumina, | .44 |
| Alkalies, | .41 |
| | 24.25 |

3. A red sandstone, strongly impregnated with iron. Texture more even than the preceding, and free from its cellular porosities.

C. *Calcareo-Siliceous.*

A volcanic conglomerate of very heterogeneous composition. The materials seem at first sight partly agglutinated, partly interfused. They have every shade of color, and almost every variety of hardness and chemical composition found in the volcanic slags. An analysis of a portion large enough to embrace nearly all the different ingredients, and representing very fairly the general character of the bed gave:

| | |
|---|---|
| Insoluble in hydrochloric acid, (mostly Silica,) . . . . . . . . | 31.0 |
| Carbonate of Lime, . . . . . . . . . . . . . . . . . . . | 53.9 |
| Peroxide of Iron, . . . . . . . . . . . . . . . . . . . | 10.1 |
| Alumina, . . . . . . . . . . . . . . . . . . . . . . | 2.7 |
| Magnesia, . . . . . . . . . . . . . . . . . . . . . | 1.3 |
| | 99.0 |

D. *Igneous.*

1. A tough compact basalt without pores, those which existed being now filled up by various intrusory materials. The fracture is not hackly like the dolerite of Tiberias, or some of the basalt-lavas of Haurân, but yet very harsh and somewhat splintery. Color blue-green, running into a very dark ash-grey.

2. A more recent lava, showing in some specimens the contortions still retained in the crested coulées of the volcanic ejections, ascribable to the post-tertiary or last extinguished fires.

3. An exceedingly porous and spherically cancellated pumice, ochry brown, verging to black. Fragments from these rocks, which are thinly scattered among the other lavas, when detached and washed into the sea, may float to the other end of the lake, and are often found on the western shore.

4. A volcanic slag less impregnated with lime than C 1, and not conglomerate (properly so called) in its structure. As the analysis of this was not likely to lead to any practical result, from the great variability of its character, even within the distance of a dozen yards, it was not deemed worth while to undertake it. A qualitative analysis of a few specimens showed very variable proportions of silica, alumina and lime, the latter ingredient, however, not exceeding ten or eleven per cent., when most abundant, and sometimes being altogether wanting except as insoluble silicate of lime, and then in a degree only just appreciable; magnesia being on such occasions almost as conspicuous as lime.

From 'Ain es-Suweimeh, as it was pointed out to us, to the mouth of the Jordan, we passed on our right a constant succession of cane-brakes and muddy beaches, the course we took varying from N. W. ½° N. at first, to W. by S. near the outlet of the river. After pulling up the Jordan against a strong current for the space of a quarter of an hour, we still found the water quite salt, and we then landed at a point 400 yards distant from the southern extremity of the western bank.

The mud of the flat here is very tenaceous and adhesive, the whole being an alluvial formation, covered by the sea at high water. Beyond the alluvial flat the banks proper consist of a white chalky travertine, worn into tent-shape knolls, and are now probably never overflowed. Far off, the mountains on both sides rise quite abruptly from the tertiary beds, and rear their far more ancient masses of Jura-lime and chalk in broken piles from 12 to 15 hundred feet on the west side, and from 15 to 20 hundred feet on the east side of the Ghôr, leaving a space between the opposing walls at least four miles greater at the head of the lake than at Râs Feshkhah, a few miles farther south.

From the extremity of the triangular spit forming the termination of the western bank of the Jordan, round the northwestern bay, the walk would require a delay to the middle of

June, as the marshy ground is not firm and dry in all places until then. Three streams were passed by us, the last being one fed by 'Ain Jehâyir. Cane-breaks appear at intervals, and especially near the middle and the largest of these rivulets. The water they contribute is very brackish, if not quite salt, being little else than the return of the Dead Sea waters after they have parted with a portion of their contents. The muriates which the evaporating process had already won from the retreating waters, had begun (May 6th) to whiten the neighboring planes, and toward the close of the summer a thick deposit of impure salt is observable in those parts of the flat which assume more or less the basin form.

As the higher ground running off from Râs Feshkhah northwardly is approached, the alluvial tract narrows its dimensions, but grows more varied in its vegetation. In addition to the reeds and canes of the brakes, the *terafeh* and the *rishrâsh* begin to make their appearance again, and the monotony of the *Ard el-müqsabeh* is much less difficult to endure. At first there is a tract of marshy tertiaries between the low ground and the hills; but these finally disappear, and the foot of Râs Feshkhah then touches the inner margin of the beach. The limestone mass of the great cliff is thickly coated with the conglomerate already described, which is not merely confined to the sea side, but invests the lower flanks of the hills, where they recede most widely from the Jordan. The return to this promontory completed the reconnaissance of the Dead Sea shore in its entire circumference; for the portion between 'Ain Feshkhah and 'Ain Terâbeh presents little that has not already been anticipated.

I cannot close this Report without once more stating very distinctly the conviction which I entertain of the essentially unsettled character of all conclusions drawn from phenomena so imperfectly studied as the depositions and denudations described in the foregoing pages. With this understanding they are respectfully submitted, and will be cheerfully and promptly varied as new evidence comes in.

I beg to be allowed too, in conclusion, to express my many obligations to the Commander of the Expedition for the interest he took in the prosecution of the work, and the solicitude he showed, in the midst of our rapid march, to leave nothing unattempted that could contribute to a favorable result. To him, under the protection of that Providence who had already done so much to endear His chosen land to every Christian heart, we were indebted for our comparative success, and in making this acknowledgment of what I personally owe to the chief of the Expedition, I know that I but say what has been felt by every member of the little party which was allowed to share in his toils.

# APPENDIX.

### *Analysis of the basalt-lava of Tŭbarîya.*

For the purpose of removing the crusts of carbonate of lime in the beds and pores of the lava, the pulverised mineral was left in a very dilute solution of hydrochloric acid. Notwithstanding the precautions taken, the iron and alumina were attacked by the acid liquor, and a slight decomposition of the soluble silicate had also taken place. On analysing the matter dissolved by the acidulated water I found

| | |
|---|---|
| Iron, principally peroxide, . . . . . . . . . . . | 36.11 |
| Alumina, . . . . . . . . . . . . . . . | 23.94 |
| Lime, carbonate, . . . . . . . . . . . . . | 32.12 |
| Magnesia, . . . . . . . . . . . . . . . | 6.07 |
| Silica, (trace.) | |
| Alkalies, (trace.) | |
| | 98.24 |

The remainder (97.6 per cent. of the whole) was then carefully digested in strong hydrochloric acid. No silica was detached in either a flocculent or gelatinous state, but a small portion was held in solution and separated from the precipitates as they were obtained. The proportion of silicic acid thus abstracted would not have exceeded one per cent. Under these circumstances I cannot regard the basaltic lava of Tŭbarîya as a compound of zeolitic and feldspathic silicates. Nor can it be decomposed as some volcanic silicates into two definite constituents, one soluble in hydrochloric acid and the other not. It is true that a portion of the powdered silicate is much more easily dissolved than the rest, but this depends mainly upon the degree of comminution of the particles; and the result of repeated experiments showed that by careful levigation and continual elutriation the whole of the silicate might eventually be dissolved. Six experiments made with a view of determining the relative solubility of the tractable and refractory portions gave the following results, after reducing the strengths of the acid and the times of digestion to a common mean.

| Experiment. | Dissolved, per cent. | Undissolved, per cent. |
|---|---|---|
| 1 | 28.7 | 71.8 |
| 2 | 23.2 | 75.8 |
| 3 | 26.8 | 72.6 |
| 4 | 25.6 | 73.3 |
| 5 | 29.1 | 69.7 |
| 6 | 20.9 | 79.3 |

A part of this discrepancy is due undoubtedly to the different proportions in which the bases are combined in different specimens from the same rock; but another portion is ascribable to the different degrees of comminution.

Instead therefore of distinguishing as usual the portions differently affected by the acid as zeolitic and feldspathic, I prefer to designate these simply as easily and difficultly soluble, or rather as dissolved and undissolved, leaving other analysts to pronounce upon the causes of this indefinite separation. On the whole it may be assumed that about 26 per cent. may be readily dissolved, leaving 74 per cent. of residuum. Prolonged digestion in weak acid produced the same effect as stronger acid in shorter time; but the law of this relation I cannot state with any certainty.

As the silica separated by the action of the acid was never found suspended in the solution and was held dissolved in it in a very small proportion, it follows that whatever quantity was liberated by the hydrochloric acid went to augment, pro tanto, the undissolved residuum. The analysis of the acid solution will give therefore the bases only, and a mean of several experiments gave

| | |
|---|---|
| Oxides of Iron, ($Fe\,O + Fe_2\,O_3$*) | 52.27 |
| Alumina, | 19.17 |
| Carbonate of Lime, | 11.53 |
| Magnesia, | 14.18 |
| Alkalies, | 2.41 |
| | 99.56 |

Each of the precipitates contained a trace of silicic acid, but the whole amount was inconsiderable, certainly not exceeding two per cent. The proportion of iron here given is so much more than is usually found in the soluble parts of basalts or basaltic lavas, that I should not be disposed to assert that the preceding analysis represents the prevailing composition of the Tŭbarîya trap.

After the treatment with hydrochloric acid the yet insoluble residuum was boiled for some time in a strong solution of caustic potassa. The part dissolved amounted to 10.4 per cent. of the original powder and consisted of

| | |
|---|---|
| Silica, | 76.4 |
| Iron and Alumina, | 8.3 |
| Carbonate of Lime, | 6.4 |
| Magnesia, | 9.4 |
| | 100.5 |

In one of the three analyses, what remained after the action of the caustic potassa constituted 63.6 per cent. of the whole mineral and was divided into two equal portions, one of which was fused in four times its weight of carbonate of soda, the other decomposed by Brunner's apparatus. The first portion gave on analysis:

| | |
|---|---|
| Silica, | 49.3 |
| Iron, | 12.7 |
| Alumina, with some Iron, | 15.8 |
| Lime, | 14.0 |
| Magnesia, | 3.6 |
| | 95.4 |

The remainder consisted of the fixed alkalies, as appears from the analysis of the second portion; this gave

| | |
|---|---|
| Silica, | 50.3 |
| Iron, | 14.1 |
| Alumina, | 13.8 |
| Lime, | 13.1 |
| Magnesia, | 4.3 |
| Potassa, | 3.0 |
| Soda, | 1.6 |
| | 100.2 |

The preceding numbers checked by another analysis of the entire mineral, made directly by the usual process, and corrected by a separate analysis for the alkalies, give as the composition of this rock regarded as an aggregate, the following result:

*With some Titanium and Manganese.

| | |
|---|---|
| Silica, | 38.41 |
| Oxides of Iron, | 23.15 |
| Alumina, | 14.62 |
| Carbonate of Lime, | 12.70 |
| Magnesia, | 7.01 |
| Potassa, | 2.14 |
| Soda, | 1.28 |
| | 99.31 |

For the purpose of comparison I subjoin several analysis of German basalts not very dissimilar.

1. Basalt from Aschaffenburg, by von Bibra.
2. Basalt from Ober-Cassel, near Bonn, by Bergemann.
3. Basalt from Siegburg, by Bergemann.

| | Tŭbarîya. | 1 | 2 | 3 |
|---|---|---|---|---|
| Silica, | 38.41 | 37.0 | 37.43 | 35.01 |
| Alumina, | 14.62 | 18.1 | 13.16 | 12.10 |
| Iron, (oxides,) | 23.15 | *23.0 | *23.33 | *28.58 |
| Lime, Carbonate, | 12.70 | 10.9 | 15.10 | 17.75 |
| Magnesia, do. | 7.01 | 4.8 | 3.47 | 4.78 |
| Alkalies, | 3.42 | 3.9 | 2.06 | 1.36 |

As the rocks in the Jordan valley are principally either basalt-lavas or limestones, and as the ingredients of the Dead Sea water are derived in part at least from such materials as are washed or elixiviated out of these rocks, it became an interesting subject of inquiry, what action has water either pure or charged with carbonic acid gas upon lava or limestone, long submitted to the solvent. To determine this, 50 gr. 53 of the Tŭbarîya lava, very carefully weighed at a given temperature, was enclosed in a clean soda water bottle, which was then charged by Mr. Roussel, of Philadelphia, with his carbonated water to the extent permitted by his excellent apparatus. After five months the bottle was opened, the powder gathered on a filter and the weight again obtained at a temperature and desiccation as before. There was now found 48 gr. 90, showing an absence of 1 gr. 63; being a little over three per cent. of the original amount. And in fact a residuum very nearly equal to this (deducting first the inconsiderable portion already existing in the water) was recovered by evaporating the menstruum to dryness. An analysis of this showed the following result:

| | |
|---|---|
| Carbonate of Lime, | 82.5 |
| Carbonate of Iron, | 10.3 |
| Carbonate of Magnesia, | 3.4 |
| Chlorides of Sodium and other Chlorides, | 3.1 |
| Traces of a soluble Silicate. | |
| | 99.3 |

The presence of sulphuric acid was also faintly discernible in this residuum, but the amount was regarded as too minute to be quantitatively ascertained.

After making every allowance for the great difference which must be expected between the action of concentrated carbonic acid gas upon finely pulverised materials and the secular action of rain or spring water (very lightly charged with this reagent) upon a solid unbroken bottom, it cannot be denied that in the long run all the soluble constituents of the washed rocks will be conveyed by the solvents flowing through them, or along them, into the last basin into which these solvents are discharged. The insoluble or undissolved particles after being mechanically suspended and transported for a time, will settle sooner or later, as the current may permit, but the dissolved ingredients of the upland deposits must be looked for, unless previously decomposed, in their ultimate receptacles; whether these be the ocean or inland seas, or (what is best adapted to exhibit them) a lake without

*Carbonate and Magnetic oxide.

outlet, like the Dead Sea, the Caspian, or the Great Salt-Lake of the West. It is true that the earthy carbonates and metallic oxides, dissolved by carbonic acid, are frequently and sometimes very promptly reprecipitated, and thus seldom cross the lower brims of intermediate receptacles until redissolved; but the chlorides and even the sulphates are for the most part soluble in water, and rarely fail to accompany the fluid menstruum as far as it flows. How the sulphates eventually all but disappear, remains perhaps to be clearly accounted for: but the preponderance of the chlorides in the terminal basins is a result which chemistry was almost bound to foretell.

## *Analysis of the Hot Springs of Emmaus.*

THESE *thermae* have been so often described that I purposely omit every thing not immediately bearing upon their geological relations.

The temperature on a mean of three trials (two on one day, the third on another) was found to be 143.3° F. The smell of sulphuretted hydrogen is very distinct, and after long standing yellow-white deposits of sulphur make their appearance, but in very inconsiderable proportions, mixed with some carbonates of lime and magnesia, which had existed previously in solution as bicarbonates of these bases. The sulphur also exists in part in the form of alkaline sulphurets and sulphates, but altogether this ingredient does not exceed two per cent. of the solid matter contained by the water. Its principal combinations have been assumed to be sulphate of lime and sulphuretted hydrogen gas. The proportion in which the latter ingredient enters can only safely be relied upon, when determined from waters just collected, and will therefore not appear in the following analysis.

Gmelin had already in 1840, found the water of the Hŭmmâm to consist of:

| | |
|---|---|
| Chloride of Sodium, | 1.702 |
| Chloride of Potassium, | .043 |
| Chloride of Calcium, | .819 |
| Chloride of Magnesium, | .229 |
| Sulphate of Lime, | .124 |
| | 2.914 |
| Water, etc. | 97.986 |
| | 100.000 |

An analysis of the chlorides contained in this water was carefully made by Prof. Booth and Mr. Mucklé. They found in 100 parts:

| | |
|---|---|
| Chloride of Sodium, | 1.727 |
| Chloride of Calcium, | .896 |
| Chloride of Magnesium, | .195 |
| Sulphate of Lime, | .108 |
| | 2.926 |

The quantity of solid matter found on evaporation was 3.056. A part of this difference may have been due to the difficulty of dehydrating the chlorides even after prolonged drying at 300°; but there remained nevertheless indications of other ingredients than those above given. In fact there were traces of bromine, organic matter, and several other constituents in proportions too minute to be determined in a preliminary analysis.

Subsequent examinations of this water have led me to the following results, reckoning the bicarbonates as carbonates, and taking no account of the organic matter or the possible bromides which must be left to further inquiry.

| | |
|---|---|
| Chloride of Sodium, | 1.715 |
| Chloride of Potassium, | .016 |
| Chloride of Calcium, | .887 |
| Chloride of Magnesium, | .203 |
| Sulphate of Lime, | .072 |
| Sulphate of Soda, | .062 |
| Carbonate of Lime, | .036 |
| Carbonate of Magnesia, | .009 |
| Sulphate of Magnesia, | .016 |
| Alkaline and earthy Sulphurets, uncertain. | |
| | 3.016 |

The existence of sulphuric acid in combination with soda and magnesia, as well as with limestone, was inferred from the fact that the precipitate obtained by treating with alcohol the concentrated water was much more soluble than gypsum, while at the same time a soda salt other than a muriate was sufficiently indicated. I ought to add that the water analysed by Gmelin had a specific gravity of 1.022375. That which was brought home by the Expedition gave on a mean of four trials (temperature reduced to 60°) 1.02336.

Although sulphate of soda and chloride of calcium may co-exist without immediate mutual decomposition in the same mineral water, there is every reason to believe that in the lapse of time the less soluble sulphate will make its appearance and will be precipitated, at least in the condensed contents of the Dead Sea Basin. It will not then be as sulphate of soda that we are to look for the constituents of this salt in the water of Bahr Lût, nor even in Lake Tiberias or along the Jordan; and the decomposition may perhaps be effected while the menstruum is yet too dilute for the precipitation of the sulphate of lime.

## *Analysis of Sediment from the Bottom of the Dead Sea.*

The sediments were obtained at various depths and distances from the shore. The specimen selected for analysis was procured from a spot where the water had a depth of 116 fathoms, and was not far from the centre of the Sea. For greater precaution against any adventitious matter derived from the vessel in which it had been brought home (a small well-tinned and closed box), the portion submitted to analysis was carefully cut out of the interior of the mass which in the course of the time elapsed (a twelve month) had contracted some degree of hardness. But if there be reason for supposing that the slight metallic addition due to the oxidation of the vessel had already diffused itself through the mud, there could not have been over one per cent. of iron ascribable to this source.

A preliminary experiment showed the following results, due to the moisture yet adherent:

| | |
|---|---|
| Of 86.2 gr. submitted to a sand-bath heat of 200, after two hours there remained | 76.0 |
| " five hours " " | 69.5 |
| The next day, after free exposure in the laboratory, | 68.9 |
| After four hours more of sand-bath, | 68.7 |

It then ceased to lose weight.

Of what remained after expelling the retained humidity of this mud, I found soluble in water 20.5 per cent. This was analysed qualitatively and consisted mainly of chloride of sodium, with minute crystals of which the sediment was plentifully studded. The other chlorides existed nearly as in the Dead Sea Water, the chloride of magnesium being largely in excess.

Of that portion which was not soluble in water there was 57.5 per cent. soluble in hydrochloric acid. An analysis of this gave

| | |
|---|---|
| Carbonate of Lime, | 74.7 per cent. |
| Carbonate of Magnesia, | .4 |
| Peroxide of Iron, | 12.6 |
| Alumina, | 12.1 |

The remaining portion (42.5 per cent. of that part which water did not dissolve) was not soluble in hydrochloric acid, and consisted of

| | |
|---|---|
| Silica, | 85.1 per cent. |
| Alumina, | 4.9 |
| Peroxide of Iron, | 2.5 |
| Magnesia, | 3.9 |
| Lime, | 3.3 |
| Alkalies, (traces.) | |

This portion, as already observed, consisted mainly of a very fine quartz sand with about one-fourth more of minutely triturated silicate powder, derived partly from the basalts of the Valley of the Jordan and partly from the flints of the chalk.

As this specimen was obtained from a part of the Lake not very distant from the focus of the detrital deposits, it may be regarded as exhibiting the maximum of the most transportable matter and the minimum of the least. Yet the carbonate of lime exceeds the silica only in the ratio of 7 to 6. As the ratio of the lime to the silex in the detritus as first detached must far exceed this, it would seem to follow that, notwithstanding the large quantity of carbonate of lime in the Dead Sea sediment (far exceeding that of any marine delta,) a great deal of it has nevertheless disappeared, and must have undergone decomposition before reaching the sea, and probably before arriving at the Jordan.

Another conclusion (and one eminently deserving attention) to which we are brought by this result, if confirmed by further analyses, is that the magnesia so largely incorporated with the lime in the sources of the descending debris is nearly exhausted on reaching the final resting place of the transported material. Most of the limestones in the Jordan Valley contain at least 2.30 per cent. of magnesia, and the dolomites of the western shore show even 23 per cent. Whereas we find but one-half of one per cent. in the oxylytic portion of the sediment, the only portion probably which has been derived from the calci-magnesian rocks. It would seem then that the magnesia in the Dead Sea water is extracted from the rock-powder by some other process than vegetable reaction, though this undoubtedly contributes; but I confess myself at a loss to suggest a *rationale* which can satisfactorily explain the extent of this disappearance. If the sediment contained a larger proportion of magnesia, there would be no difficulty in looking to the magnesian chlorides in the lavas as competent to the effect, allowing time to do its work; but the carbonates have also contributed their share, and the decomposing process is yet to be detected.

## *Analysis of the Dead Sea Water.*

The quantity submitted to analysis was drawn up by Capt. Lynch himself from a depth of 185 fathoms. The determination of its constituents was very carefully made by Professor Booth, of Philadelphia, assisted by Mr. Alexander Mucklé. I subjoin the results as already given in Captain Lynch's Official Report, submitted February 3, 1849.

Specific gravity = 1.22742.

| | |
|---|---|
| Chloride of Sodium, | 78.554 |
| Chloride of Potassium, | 6.586 |
| Chloride of Magnesium, | 145.897 |
| Chloride of Calcium, | 31.075 |
| Bromine Salts, | 1.374 |
| Sulphate of Lime, | .701 |
| | 264.187 |
| Water, | 735.813 |
| | 1000.000 |

It may be remarked that the great specific gravity of this water does not indicate full saturation with any of the chlorides, for the water is still capable of holding much chloride of sodium, and of course still more chloride of magnesium, in solution. Since, however, crystals of chloride of sodium remain undissolved at the depth of 116 fathoms,* it follows that the water of the Dead Sea is very unequally charged with its constituents, and that no safe inference can be drawn from an analysis of the surface water, and still less of any specimen in which the depth is not given. I will also add, that in two analyses of Dead Sea water for chloride of calcium alone, I have found more of this salt than in the analysis above given, in one instance 48 gr. 47 in 1000; but the water was in these cases taken from another part of the Sea.

## *On the great depression of the Dead Sea Basin.*

No sooner was it ascertained that the surface of the Dead Sea lay very much depressed below the level of the ocean, than various hypotheses were proposed to account geologically for this remarkable phenomenon. It was not long before it was perceived that, whatever may have been the origin of the depression of the cavity itself, the explanation of the very low level of the surface of the water contained in it lay not merely in the depression of the basin, but quite as much in the evaporating power of a tropical sun operating upon a fluid mass limited in its supply. That there would be a certain quantity of this fluid remaining over unevaporated, variable in its volume and ranging between a variable *maximum* and a variable *minimum*, is nothing more than might have been expected. If the level of the Dead Sea were much raised by a more rapid contribution, the area exposed to evaporation would expand until the rate of expenditure thus augmented would equal the rate of supply, and the lake would then cease to rise. If on the contrary the level were depressed by a lessened contribution, the area would be correspondingly contracted, the rate of replenishment would come to be equal to the rate of waste, and the lake would after this cease to fall. In this respect the Dead Sea does not in fact differ from any shut lake whether it lies above the ocean level or not. It is only remarkable in this that from the shape and depth of the cavity and the very high temperature compared with the limited supply, the bowl cannot (in the present relation of replenishment and waste) be filled to overflowing, or even to the extent of the twentieth part of its capacity. The saltness of the sea is an inevitable consequence of these conditions. The saline ingredients being continually introduced and never running out, the brine is of course brought at length to a state of saturation. It requires in fact nothing but a higher temperature to dry up or to convert into salt seas the contents of any great inland basin, the North American lakes for example; and the fresh-water portion of the St. Lawrence itself would in that case dwindle to an insignificant river falling into the estuary connected with the present gulf; so that the upper valley would be an intervening dry Ghôr intercepting the communication between the shrunken Lake Ontario and the ocean, and consisting of two parts, one tending towards the lake, the other towards the sea, with the water-shed near the present outlet of the lake.

Were such a result actually brought about and exhibited to our senses, it is plain that the depression of the surface of the then salt lake Ontario and of the bottom of its basin, though more striking in its appearance, would in reality be no harder to explain than the deep excavation of the lake cavity is now.

To account for such depressions we are reduced at present to two hypotheses neither of them very promising. The first assumes a fissure or series of fissures to have taken place in one of the early geological eras, and unequal denudations or partial accumulations subsequent to these to have imparted gradually the present relief. The second supposes the *carina* to have been once one of continuous descent, so that no lakes in the course of the river existed at that time. The dislevelling agencies have then in the course of geological ages disturbed the line of the *carina* by their effects on the whole embracing platform, depressing and uplifting its various sections according to the laws of the disturbing forces. The depressed areas become the cavities which hold lakes, the elevated portions separate these completely or not, according to the depths of the connecting valleys and the still deeper subsequent excavation.

The fissure theory is favored in the Jordan case, by the volcanic character of some of the neighboring districts, by the straightness of the Ghôr and by that diversity of structure, on opposite sides of the valley, which might be expected where a *fissure* is modified into a *fault*. On the other hand it is liable to the serious objection that it cannot explain the origin of curvilinearly winding valleys which are far more numerous than the rectilinear excavations.

*They were found at this depth a little above 'Ain el-Feshkhah. It is very probable, however, that they may be met with much nearer the surface.

The theory of a pre-existing continuity of descending water discharging itself at some remote era of geological antiquity into the gulf of 'Aqabeh, if that gulf itself and even the Red Sea were not then a continuation of the Ghôr, is met by the usual difficulty of accounting for the change *since* made in the levels of the stream-bed, and by the still more formidable objection that to admit of a subsidence of three thousand feet at the latitude of the Dead Sea, we must accept a corresponding depression of the whole platform east and west of it; whereas the land on both sides is just as elevated opposite to the deepest part of the sea, as north of its northern, or south of its southern extremities. The objection is strengthened at first sight by the fact that this comparative horizontality of lake districts is found to prevail with few exceptions wherever these very remarkable cavities are found.

Another consideration pressing with equal force against the theory of a once continuous descent from Wâdy et-Teim to the Red Sea is the absence of all south-tending valleys south of the point now at least of the great depression; showing very conclusively that the present system of Wâdys had their origin subsequently to the sinking of the area which embraces the Dead Sea. But the disappearance of the more ancient valleys would still remain to be explained.

To these objections the only answer appears to be that as the lake districts have been depressed beneath the sea subsequently to the first excavation of the river-beds, their disturbed re-emergence has subjected the whole area in which they were destined to lie to the levelling detrition due to the incessant grinding of the upper or moveable stratum of the ocean which in instances innumerable has by its long continued and unsparing planing down of local unevennesses quite worn away the principal undulations of the re-emerging lands. Without such an hypothesis indeed, it would seem impossible to account for the remarkable horizontality to which the upturned edges of plunging strata are sometimes worn away for many hundred miles. And with such an hypothesis the disappearance of the valleys formed before the submergence and the growth of new ones with different directions subsequent to the re-emergence become a portion of the changes to be expected on the freshly exposed plane, even supposing no other forces to concur than those which are now allowed to subsist.

One fact appears well established:—that whether we ascribe the formation of the Ghôr to a fissure or a water-current excavation with subsequent disturbance, the necessity exists equally in both cases of supposing that the Ghôr and some of its tributary Wâdys already existed long before the tertiary era, a fact which is but an instance of a general law and corroborated by the frequent occurrence of tertiary accumulations in the broader and deeper valleys of every part of the globe. In the Jordan-'Aqabeh Ghôr, these tertiaries have taken possession of the whole valley-bottom, and line the hill sides from Hâsbeiya to Wâdy Wetîr.

In the event of the adoption of the hypothesis of a secular excavation of the Jurassic platform followed by a gradual submarine depression of the whole district of which the Jordan is the axis and ending in an imperfect re-emergence with a water-shed far south of the Dead Sea, we are to suppose that the destructive process which has obliterated the secondary tributaries to the river-bed now ascending towards the south, began as soon as the first submersal and was repeated long afterwards, when the emerging district had brought its still remaining inequalities successively in subjection to the levelling operation of the upper and moveable stratum of the tertiary seas.

The effect of this obliteration of valleys existing before the submersion, would not extend to their entire destruction, but would leave a portion near the mouths of these excavations still much depressed below the partially abraded platform; but the upper valleys would have disappeared, and would in time be replaced by others having directions determined by the new order of levels.

## *Letter from* Dr. Joseph Leidy *to* Dr. H. J. Anderson.

May 8th, 1850.

Dear Sir:

The two specimens of *Helix lithophaga* which you presented to me for examination, and which you informed me you had had in your possession for upwards of eighteen months, I found alive and in good preservation for dissection. The very great length of time which they lived without food or water, exhibits a beautiful instance of the adaptation of an animal to the circumstances in which it exists in nature. During the long periods of heat and drought to which this animal is exposed in its native country, it may hibernate without detriment to life, and upon the recurrence of moist matter it assumes its usual degree of activity. Evaporation is prevented by its retiring very far into the shell, making one or two thick diaphragms of mucus and carbonate of lime over the aperture of the latter, and by retreating into rounded cavities in the limestone rocks, which you inform me it has the extraordinary power of boring for itself.

The fact of many aquatic mollusca, as the *Pholades, Teredines, Patellæ,* etc., being capable of boring into rocks and other hard substances, is a very familiar one to naturalists, but this is the first instance of which I have heard of a terrestrial gasteropod possessing the same power. In reflecting upon the subject, I am inclined to think that the instrument by which it is accomplished is the tongue. This organ in all *Helices* is covered by a lamina upon which are arranged in transverse rows several thousand minute, hard, usually conical, carinated teeth. A drawing of a part and lateral view of one of these teeth, magnified, from near the middle of the lingual lamina of *Helix lithophaga,* Fig. 1 and 2, will give you some idea of their appearance. When viewed from above, the lingual laminæ resemble a rasp and form an instrument well adapted to triturating the food. Its posterior part is contained in a cul-de-sac projecting from the buccal body behind, in which the teeth are being constantly renewed as the anterior ones are wearing away. Here then we have an instrument which if hard enough would answer the purpose of boring. To test this I tried to scratch a piece of marble with the lingual laminæ of one of the specimens of *Helix lithophaga,* which succeeded in so doing. Strong sulphuric and nitric acid had no effect upon the teeth, except to separate them from one another. Submitted to a strong heat, they turned black, and after the organic elements were consumed, nitric and chlorohydric acid still left an insoluble residue, from which we perceive, silex enters into their composition. Probably then the mode in which the animal operates upon the rock is to moisten the surface with the mucus of its body and then to rasp with the tongue until a convenient place of shelter is formed.

1

2

The internal anatomy of this *Helix* resembles that of *H. pomatia,* and more the European species generally than the American, for it is a curious fact that while the multifid vesicles, dartsac and flagellum to the penis, are so common in the former, they are rare in the latter. The more important points may be stated in a few words. The ovary is long and doubled upon itself. The generative bladder is round and situated near the ovary; its duct is long and midway receives a long blind duct as in *Helix adspersa* and *Pupa incana.* The dartsac is large and cylindrical. The multifid vesicles consist of a pair of cœcal tubes, three or four lines long, joined together at their base, and terminating at the bottom of the vagina. The epididymis is moderately tortuous; the vas deferens more than usually so. The penis is long and conicocylindrical, its retractor muscle is inserted just above the middle; its flagellum is short and tortuous.

With respect,

I subscribe myself,

JOSEPH LEIDY.

To Dr. Anderson.

PHILADELPHIA, *June* 3, 1852.

DEAR SIR:

Having been requested to describe an interesting series of organic remains, collected by you while connected with the Expedition to Palestine, I submit the result of my examination, hoping you will not expect too much from one so little qualified as myself to do justice to the subject. Many of the species may have been described in European Journals to which I have not access, but longer delay in order to verify this supposition, is not permitted me. In the introduction I have alluded to the stratigraphical relations of these fossils, which I hope you will find correct. They are nearly all casts, except the specimens of *Ostrea* and *Exogyra*, all the species of which retain the shell mineralised. It is worthy of remark, that some species of this family and of *Pectenidæ* are widely distributed throughout the globe. Thus *Pecten quinquecostatus* and *Ostrea vesicularis* occur in Syria, Europe and America. *Ostrea falcata* and *Gryphæa vomer* of Morton, originally discovered in the Cretaceous beds of New Jersey, occur in Europe also, where they have since been described under other names, and I have elsewhere stated, that *Exogyra Boussingaultii* is found in Syria, Europe and America.

Respectfully submitted,

T. A. CONRAD.

DR. HENRY JAMES ANDERSON.

# DESCRIPTION OF THE FOSSILS OF SYRIA,

## COLLECTED IN THE PALESTINE EXPEDITION.

## INTRODUCTION.

The White Chalk of Syria appears to me to correspond in age with the Upper Chalk of Europe; but I am unable to determine by the fossils whether any difference in age occurs between the rocks of the various localities.

The Jurassic fossils of Syria are chiefly casts. One of them nearly resembles *Nerinea Gosæ*, a species of the European Oolite. Several other fossils have a general resemblance to species of the same age, occurring in Germany and England; but there is sufficient variation to warrant a separation in distinct species. I believe all the fossils of Syria described in the following pages to be Jurassic, except those indicated as Cretaceous species. The bivalves in this collection predominate over the univalves, though a few of the latter, as *Nerinea* and a species of *Turritella* are very abundant. Nearly all have been more or less distorted by pressure. In almost every instance they represent the entire shell, as though it lived and died undisturbed in the bed of a sea remote from shore. This bed of the Ocean, probably after ages of revolutions, lifting the strata above water and sinking them in repeated oscillations, became finally the floor of a far later sea, tenanted with animal life wholly different in all its external forms from those whose mineralised remains were scattered among them. Thus we find well preserved shells of *Exogyra* adhering to the Jurassic casts of various species of shells and Echinoderms, but as the other bivalves of the Cretaceous period are generally casts, they can only be separated from Jurassic forms by their general resemblance to cretaceous species; but, excepting the *Exogyra Boussingaultii, d'Orb.*, if it really be that species, I do not observe any undoubtedly Cretaceous fossils in any other state than in Chalk and a limestone evidently of the same age. The *Cardium biseriatum* is certainly nearly allied to *C. peregrinorsum* of d'Orbigny; but it appears to be sufficiently distinct, and is no doubt a Jurassic species, as the mineral character of the casts is the same as in the undoubted Jurassic fossils. The Oolite shells, which I cannot distinguish from published species, are *Ostræa scapha*, Roemer, and *Ostræa virgata*, Goldfuss.

THE fossils of Syria described in the following pages are chiefly casts or internal moulds, and consequently it is difficult to refer them correctly to appropriate genera, and not less so to define a species by specific characters. It is therefore upon the figures that I rely for conveying a knowledge of the different species. In every instance, when not otherwise noted, the figures and descriptions represent casts.

## ECHINODERMATA.

### ECHINUS.—*Lin.*, *Lam.*

*Echinus Syriacus*, Pl. 1, fig. 1, and Pl. 22, fig 127. Depressed hemi-spherical; plates very small; pores pentagonal, minute, in vertical series; upper surface minutely granulated; primary tubercles small, arranged in series of four vertical lines; tubercles of the base comparatively large, the surface minutely granulated between them.

Local.: The Lebanon, Mountains of Moab.

### HOLASTER.—*Agassiz.*

*Holaster Syriacus*, Pl. 1, fig. 2. Cordate, widely truncated posteriorly; anterior side of disk very oblique; canal wide and profound; ambulacral areas deeply impressed; posterior pair of ambulacra short and obtuse; posterior side of disk carinated in the middle; anus large, suboval, distant from the basal line; mouth transverse, suboval.

Local.: Mount Lebanon.

### CIDARIS.—*Lam.*

*Spines of Cidaris*, Pl. 1, fig. 3, 4, 5. These are apparently identical with European specimens in the Collection of the Academy of Natural Sciences of Philadelphia.

Local.: Bhamdûn.

## TESTACEA.—BIVALVES.

### OSTRÆA.—*Lin.*, *Lam.*

1. *Ostræa virgata*, Goldfuss, Nyst., Pl. 1, fig. 6, 7, 8. Ovate or obliquely cuneiform; superior valve flat, concentrically striated; inferior valve convex, affixed at the umbo, furnished with numerous narrow dichotomous ribs.

OSTRÆA VIRGATA, Goldfuss, Petrifacten, vol. II, t. lxxvi, fig. 34.

Local.: The Lebanon, Bhamdûn.

I have with some doubt referred this to the Belgian species, a fossil of the Oolitic period.

2. *Ostræa Syriaca*, Pl. 2, fig. 12. Dilated, depressed, having concentric undulations and rugose lines; superior valve flattened, widely undulated; beaks small, not prominent.

Local.: Mukhtârah, Mount Lebanon.

3. *Ostræa linguloides*, Pl. 2, fig. 13. Subcuneiform, depressed; anterior and posterior margins straight; beak narrow, not prominent.

Local.: Mukhtârah, Mount Lebanon.

A single valve only was obtained, and it may be a young shell or variety of Ostræa scapha. It has a striking resemblance to *Ostræa cretacea*, Morton, but it is evidently a Jurassic species.

4. ***Ostræa scapha***, Roemer, Pl. 15, fig. 78, 79. Ovate, rugoso-lamellated; superior valve flat or subdepressed; inferior valve concave, boat-shaped; umbo truncated, adhering; hinge depressed, oblique.

OSTRÆA SCAPHA, Roemer, die Versteinerungen des Norddeutschen Oolithen-Gebirges, p. 59, t. 3, fig. 1.

*The Ostræa scapha* is an Oolitic species with which the Syrian fossil closely corresponds, if it is not identical.

Local.: Bhamdûn, Mukhtârah.

### EXOGYRA.—*Say.*

*Exogyra Boussingaultii*, d'Orbigny, Pl. 1, fig. 9, and Pl. 2, fig. 10, 11. Oblong, arched, oblique; superior valve concave or nearly flat, irregular on the surface, concentrically laminated; cardinal tooth acute; inferior valve obliquely truncated or flattened on the sides, and carinated or angulated near the middle or anterior to the middle; posterior side furnished with large prominent irregular laminated ribs; beaks profoundly curved.

Local.: Mukhtârah, Bhamdûn, Mount Lebanon.

OSTRÆA BOUSSINGAULTII, d'Orbigny, Paléon. Franç., p. 702, pl. 468.

EXOGYRA BOUSSINGAULTII, ibid.; Fossils of Columbia, p. 57, pl. 3, fig. 10.

This species is well preserved and generally found with connected valves. It is abundant and frequently attached to various casts. It occurs thus on ***Echinus Syriacus***, ***Ammonites Syriacus***, ***Trigonia Syriaca***, and ***Turritella magnicostata***. As when attached, it is always to casts, it must have existed at a later period than the Jurassic species and may probably be the Cretaceous species to which I have referred it because I am unable to find a specific difference. D'Orbigny described his species from specimens found in Colombia. It also occurs in France. The ribs vary much in different specimens, some being much more profound or numerous, while in others slight undulations only mark the surface. In one small specimen the upper valve is strongly ribbed as in ***Ostræa Matheroniana***, d'Orbigny.

The Syrian shell is generally of a subfalcate outline, and the superior valve frequently thickened on the posterior submargin which is truncated and ribbed, the ribs crossed by closely arranged undulated laminæ.

Pl. 1, fig. 9, represents a variety more profoundly costate than usual, and has the superior valve deeply concave and ribbed, a character not occurring in any other instance among the numerous specimens in the collection.

### PECTEN.—*Gualt.*, *Lam.*

*Pecten* ———. A fragment of a valve shewing the interior surface. Form suborbicular; ribs nearly equal in size, except towards the anterior and posterior margins; one rib only is much smaller than the others. 1¾ inches long.

### NUCULA.—*Lam.*

1. ***Nucula submucronata***, Pl. 2, fig. 14. Elliptical, ventricose, anterior side short and pointed; cast of muscular impressions prominent; ligament margin slightly declining, nearly straight or slightly rounded; posterior end emarginate above, rounded inferiorly; basal margin nearly straight in the middle; summits angular.

Local.: Bhamdûn, Mount Lebanon.

No portion of shell remains on the cast, but the form of the cardinal teeth is very distinct.

2. *Nucula parallela*, Pl. 2, fig. 15. Subquadrate; convex; anterior side subrostrated; superior margin rectilinear and very oblique, extremity obliquely truncated; posterior side elevated, the end margin obtusely rounded; hinge and basal margins parallel; summits not prominent; beaks approximate; anterior basal margin rectilinear, oblique.

Local.: Bhamdûn, Mount Lebanon.

A cast somewhat distorted and compressed, but preserving nearly its original outline, which is peculiar.

3. *Nucula Syriaca*, Pl. 3, fig. 16. Triangular, ventricose, inequilateral; anterior side subcuneiform; basal margin tumid opposite the beaks; posterior end subtruncated.

Local.: Bhamdûn, Mount Lebanon.

This cast exhibits traces of the cardinal teeth.

4. *Nucula myiformis*, Pl. 3, fig. 17. Suboval, convex, inequilateral, anterior end truncated, nearly direct, slightly emarginate, angular where it joins the basal margin; beaks approximate; posterior end regularly rounded; basal margin rounded.

Local.: Bhamdûn, Mount Lebanon.

There is but one specimen of this species. It has an irregular carinated line anteriorly, which is partly and perhaps altogether owing to pressure which has distorted the cast. The form of the cardinal teeth is distinctly visible.

5. *Nucula perobliqua*, Pl. 3, fig. 18. Oblique; beaks nearly in a line with the anterior extremity; dorsal margin slightly curved; posterior extremity rounded.

Local.: Bhamdûn.

### TRIGONIA.—*Brug.*

1. *Trigonia Syriaca*, Pl. 3, fig. 19, 20, 21, 23. Triangular, very inequilateral, slightly ventricose; anterior margin truncated, direct; posterior margin very oblique, sinuous; inner margin entire.

Local.: Mount Lebanon, near Bhamdûn.

This species is abundant and remarkable for the wide and profound space made by the hinge between the umbo and the anterior muscular impressions. The cardinal teeth have been very large, and the muscular impressions rugose, like those in the thick-shelled species of *Unio*. The summits are elevated, distant and acute.

In the Appendix there is a figure and description of the external character of the shell.

2. *Trigonia alta*, Pl. 4, fig. 24. Elevated, subtriangular, equilateral, ventricose; anterior and posterior margins truncated, direct and nearly parallel; summits elevated, acute, very remote; basal margin obliquely truncated, entire within.

Local.: Aklîm el-Jurd, Mount Lebanon.

This species has a remarkable erect and elevated form.

3. *Trigonia cuneiformis*, Pl. 3, fig. 22. Subtriangular; anterior side short, obtusely rounded; posterior side cuneiform, somewhat contracted towards the submargin, or behind the umbonal slope; umbo ventricose, broad; posterior margin subtruncated? basal margin oblique and slightly rounded; inner margin entire.

Local.: Aklîm el-Jurd, Bhamdûn.

A single fragment of this species is all I have seen; the comparative thickness through the umbones is much greater than in either of the preceding species, and the form of the posterior side very different.

### Isocardia.—*Lam.*

*Isocardia crenulata*, Pl. 4, fig. 26. Obtusely subovate, inflated; anterior side very short, margin rounded; posterior end truncated; basal margin crenulated, contracted near the middle.

Local.: Bhamdûn, Aklîm el-Jurd.

There are a few casts of this species in the collection, all more or less distorted. The figure represents the original form as nearly as I could restore it.

### Astarte.—*Sow.*

1. *Astarte Syriaca*, Pl. 4, fig. 25. Suborbicular, compressed; summits approximate, acute; lunule acutely ovate; end margins obtusely rounded; basal margin rounded; beaks situated about one-third the shell's length from the anterior extremity.

Local.: Bhamdûn.

2. *Astarte orientalis*, Pl. 4, fig. 27. Subtriangular, convex; extremities acutely rounded; posterior margin rounded; basal margin regularly rounded.

Local.: Bhamdûn.

Resembles the preceding species, but is more convex, has less acute summits, more profoundly rounded base, etc.

3. *Astarte pervetus*, Pl. 4, fig. 28. Ovate, subtriangular, subequilateral; summits elevated, acute; anterior extremity acutely rounded; anterior and posterior hinge margins equally oblique; basal margin profoundly rounded.

Local.: Bhamdûn, Shâneih.

4. *Astarte engonata*, Pl. 4, fig. 29. Triangular; disk somewhat flattened; summits acute, direct; posterior side cuneiform, extremity angular; posterior basal margin rectilinear.

Local.: Bhamdûn.

5. *Astarte arctata*, Pl. 20, fig. 119. Triangular, compressed; valves flattened; end margins subtruncated.

Local.: Shore of the Dead Sea.

This is a water-worn cast, quite distinct from the preceding species.

### Arca.—*Lin.*

1. *Arca Syriaca*, Pl. 5, fig. 30. Oblique, subtriangular; anterior side short; summits elevated, rounded; valves flattened towards the base; beaks distant; inner margin crenate.

Local.: Bhamdûn.

An imperfect cast. The internal plate has formed an angular furrow, and traces of crenæ or large teeth are visible at the base.

2. *Arca brevifrons*, Pl. 5, fig. 31. Oblique; sides flattened below the umbones, which are slightly contracted anteriorly; beaks remote; summits very prominent, oblique, nearly terminal; posterior side elongated, end margin obliquely truncated or slightly emarginate, nearly straight in the middle.

Local.: Bhamdûn.

3. *Arca indurata*, Pl. 5, fig. 33. Trapezoidal; anterior side short, acutely rounded; posterior margin obliquely truncated or slightly contracted, extremity rounded; umbonal slope angular; beaks distant, situated about one-third the shell's length from the anterior extremity; summits elevated, rounded; umbo slightly flattened; posterior slope obliquely flattened; diaphragm impression profound; basal margin rounded.

Local.: Bhamdûn.

4. *Arca orientalis*, Pl. 5, fig. 36. Oblique, triangular, ventricose; anterior side short; posterior margin oblique, sinuous, extremity angular; basal margin rounded in the middle, obliquely truncated anteriorly.

Local.: Bhamdûn.

An imperfect cast with traces of radiating lines; it exhibits no trace of marginal crenulations.

5. *Arca declivis*, Pl. 5, fig. 32. Ovate-oblong; sides somewhat flattened; beaks situated about one-third of the shell's length from the anterior margin; posterior hinge margin declining, subrectilinear; posterior end obliquely truncated; basal margin straight; within entire; beaks approximate; lunule lanceolate.

Local.: Aklîm el-Jurd.

Of this species there is only one somewhat distorted cast.

6. *Arca subrotunda*, Pl. 5, fig. 34. Cordate-triangular, profoundly ventricose; umbo very prominent, obliquely rounded; umbonal slope angular; beaks separated; posterior extremity acutely rounded?

Local.: Bhamdûn.

A portion near the base of this cast retains imperfectly the original external character of the species. It appears to have had broad flat ribs, separated by an impressed line.

7. *Arca acclivis*, Pl. 5, fig. 35. Oblique, subovate, ventricose; anterior side very short; beaks distant; summits angular; posterior margin obliquely subtruncated, extremity angulated; basal margin rounded.

Local.: Bhamdûn.

### Corbula.—*Brug.*

*Corbula congesta*, Pl. 5, fig. 37, and Pl. 22, fig. 130. Subtriangular, ventricose, inequilateral; umbo broad; anterior side acutely pointed, recurved: (larger valve.)

Local.: Bhamdûn.

This species is abundant, exhibited in relief upon a piece of limestone. The shell in some instances is preserved, but weathered, and the lines, if it had any, obliterated.

### Cardium.—*Lin.*, *Lam.*

1. *Cardium biseriatum*, Pl. 6, fig. 38, 39, 40. Rotundate-cordate; ventricose, subequilateral; posterior side rather longer than the anterior; the margin subtruncated and nearly direct; summits prominent, acutely rounded; basal margin profoundly rounded anteriorly, obliquely truncated posteriorly; surface of the valves marked with concentric lines as far as the umbonal slope; posterior submargin with about 15 slender minutely echinated radii; posterior margin crenulated within.

Local.: Bhamdûn, Mount Lebanon.

This abundant species resembles *Cardium perigrinorsum* and *Cardium Hillanum*, but is proportionally more elongated and the sulci are much larger. The largest specimen measures 2½ inches in length.

2. *Cardium crebriechinatum*, Pl. 6, fig. 41, 42, 43, and Pl. 15, fig. 77; Appendix, Pl. 2, fig. 16. Cordate, elevated, inflated, slightly oblique, subequilateral; summit elevated, acute; hinge margin declining; posterior end obliquely truncated or slightly contracted, extremity acutely rounded; beaks not approximate; surface of the cast marked with slender, closely arranged echinated radii.

Local.: Bhamdûn and vicinity.

The echinated tubercles appear to have been prominent by the markings on the cast. The small portion of shell remaining has the character almost obliterated. Fig. 41 is taken from a specimen which appears to retain nearly its original outline, though one beak has been pressed below the level of the other. One small cast shows a single row of minute tubercles in each intercostal space.

Since the above was written, I have seen a more perfect cast in the Collection of Professor Silliman, which is represented on Pl. 2, fig. 16, of the Appendix.

3. *Cardium Syriacum*, Pl. 7, fig. 45. Obliquely ovate-acute, elevated, ventricose; summits prominent, acute; posterior margin and extremity rounded; lunule large, cordate.

Local.: Bhamdûn.

The impressions of the anterior lateral teeth in this cast show that they were very thick and prominent, and the lunule seems to have been deeply impressed.

4. *Cardium Hermonense*, Pl. 22, fig. 129. An impression of a species with squamose ribs, the interstices crossed by laminated lines.

Local.: Summit of Mount Hermon.

5. *Cardium ?* Pl. 15, fig. 76. From two imperfect casts I have endeavored to restore the outline of this fossil. A third specimen, much distorted, exhibits the mineralised shell, a portion of which is marked by fine concentric raised lines.

### PHOLADOMYA.—*Sow.*

*Pholadomya decisa*, Pl. 7, fig. 44. Ovate-ventricose; ribs about 18 in number, distant posteriorly, one or two obsolete ribs posterior to the umbonal slope which is undefined; anterior side short, abrupt or direct on the margin, which is somewhat contracted, and biangulated; dorsal line concave or curved inwards; basal margin rounded; beaks contiguous.

Local.: Bhamdûn.

There is only one specimen of this species in the collection.

### PANOPÆA.—*Ménard.*

*Panopæa pectorosa*, Pl. 7, fig. 46. Oblong-ovate, inflated; anterior side very short, margin obliquely truncated, obtusely subrostrated; extremity subangulated; beaks contiguous, summits acutely rounded, prominent, furnished with obscure concentric sulci, which are most conspicuous on the posterior side of the umbo; anterior basal margin obliquely truncated.

Local.: Bhamdûn.

This species resembles *Myacites elongatus*, Schloth, as figured in Goldfuss' Petrefacten, but is more ventricose and less elongated. There are two specimens, casts, and the one figured appears to have been altered little, if any, from its original form.

### Inoceramus.—*Sow.*

*Inoceramus Lynchii*, Pl. 8, fig. 47. Subovate, equivalve? slightly ventricose, compressed posteriorly; summits elevated; beaks approximate; posterior margin oblique, slightly rounded; basal margin rounded; surface of cast marked with numerous regular concentric sulci; muscular impressions undefined.

Local.: Mount Lebanon, Bhamdûn.

The character of the hinge of this fossil is unknown to me, and I have referred it to *Inoceramus* only on account of its form, and the sulci which resemble some species of that genus.

This species bears the name of the indefatigable explorer, Captain Lynch of the Palestine Expedition.

### Mactra.—*Lin.*, *Lam.*

1. *Mactra petrosa*, Pl. 8, fig. 48. Subtriangular, ventricose; beaks approximate, situated posterior to the middle of the valves; summits rounded, prominent; anterior side subcuneiform, extremity rounded; posterior margin direct, truncated.

Local.: Between Mukhtârah and Jezzîn.

2. *Mactra pervetus*, Pl. 8, fig. 49. Triangular, ventricose, inequilateral; summits prominent, rounded; umbo somewhat oblique; anterior end acutely rounded; basal and posterior margins rounded.

Local.: Aklîm el-Jurd.

This species is more ventricose than the preceding, the umbo oblique, which in the other is direct, and the anterior side is shorter. No trace of the shell remains on the casts of either species.

3. *Mactra arciformis*, Pl. 8, fig. 50. Subrhomboidal, inflated, inequilateral; disk with concentric lines; summits rounded; posterior margin obliquely rounded; umbonal slope undefined; basal margin regularly rounded.

Local.: Bhamdûn, Khân Hussein, near Bhamdûn.

In this cast no trace of hinge teeth is visible, and the general form is the only indication, and an uncertain one, of the generic character. It is, therefore, only provisionally that this and some other casts described in this work, are referred to particular genera.

4. *Mactra Syriaca*, Pl. 8, fig. 51. Subtriangular, slightly ventricose, equilateral; summits prominent, angulated, not approximate; anterior margin rounded; posterior margin very oblique, nearly rectilinear or slightly contracted below the umbo; posterior extremity truncated; basal margin rounded.

Local.: Bhamdûn.

### Venus.—*Lin.*, *Lam.*

1. *Venus Syriaca*, Pl. 9, fig. 52. Cordate, ventricose; margins rounded; umbo broad; summits rounded.

Local.: El-Jurd, el-Jurd el-Toqâny.

This is a somewhat distorted cast, resembling in outline *Cytherea Poulsoni*, of the Alabama Eocene. The inner margin appears to have been entire.

2. *Venus indurata*, Pl. 9, fig. 53. Subtriangular, ventricose; anterior margin rounded; posterior side cuneiform, extremity rounded; posterior margin oblique and nearly straight; basal margin rounded.

Local.: 'Aklîm el-Jurd, Jurd el-Toqâny.

The inner margin appears to have been crenulated, but the traces are obscure.

### CYTHEREA.—*Lam.*

*Cytherea Syriaca*, Pl. 9, fig. 54, 55, 56. Elliptical, slightly ventricose; extremities subtruncated; summits not prominent, rounded, situated about one-third the shell's length from the anterior extremity; basal margin rounded.

Local.: Bhamdûn, Mejdel Bâna.

This species is not uncommon, and the casts are frequently distorted.

### LUCINA.—*Lam.*

1. *Lucina Syriaca*, Pl. 10, fig. 57. Suborbicular, inequilateral, ventricose, suddenly contracted on the anterior and posterior submargins; umbonal slope angular; posterior margin subtruncated, direct; basal margin profoundly rounded.

Local.: Bhamdûn.

2. *Lucina? subtruncata*, Pl. 15, fig. 76. The figure represents a restored outline of this species as nearly as the fragments in the collection indicate it.

Local.: Bhamdûn.

### TELLINA.—*Lin.*, *Lam.*

1. *Tellina Syriaca*, Pl. 10, fig. 59, 60, 61. Subtriangular, convex; beaks distant from the anterior extremity; summits acute; anterior side slightly reflected; posterior margin rounded.

Local.: Bhamdûn, Khân el-Mezrâ'ah.

This fossil occuring only in casts, seems to be the most abundant of the bivalves in the collection, excepting *Exogyra Boussingaultii*, d'Orbigny.

2. *Tellina obruta*, Pl. 10, fig. 58. Triangular, rather elongated, posteriorly cuneiform; extremity subtruncated; hinge margin long and oblique; anterior extremity obtusely rounded; posterior side slightly reflected.

Local.: El-Ghŭrb el-Toqâny.

There is but one imperfect cast of this species; it presents traces of impressed concentric unequal lines.

### ORBICULA?—*Lam.*

*Orbicula subobliqua*, Pl. 10, fig. 61½. Oval, slightly oblique and somewhat ventricose, smooth, with indistinct lines of growth.

Local.: Bhamdûn.

A single valve of this species adheres to a piece of ferruginous limestone, containing specimens of *Ostræa scapha*.

## UNIVALVES.

### CHENOPUS.—*Phill.*

1. *Chenopus turriculoides*, Pl. 10, fig. 62. Turrited; volutions six; whorls of the spire slightly convex; beak short and straight.

Local.: Bhamdûn, head of Wâdy es-Shahrûr.

Traces of the expanded labrum are visible in a few specimens of this species. They are generally distorted casts, some of which have small perfect specimens of *Exogyra Boussingaultii* adhering to them. Other casts are studded with the same shell which seems to have existed at a later period than the associated fossils, as it is evident that their shells must have disappeared and the casts become indurated before the *Exogyræ* existed. Distinct periods or long intervals of time are seldom traced in a single group of fossils, and these specimens therefore have more than ordinary interest for the geologist.

2. *Chenopus induratus*, Pl. 11, fig. 69. Fusiform; volutions 5 or 6, those of the spire somewhat flattened laterally; spire conical; body-whorl ventricose, very large in proportion to the spire, regularly rounded inferiorly.

Local.: Bhamdûn.

3. *Chenopus Syriacus*, Pl. 12, fig. 71. Turrited; volutions 6 or 7. A cast, somewhat distorted, with the spire and body-whorl nearly equal in length.

Local.: Bhamdûn.

This species resembles the cast of *Natica prolonga*, Desh., figured in d'Orbigny's Paléontologie Française.

### NATICA.—*Lam.*

1. *Natica indurata*, Pl. 11, fig. 65 and 68. Subglobose, wider than high; volutions 4 or 5, ventricose; base widely umbilicated; aperture obliquely semicircular, rather more than half as long as the shell.

Local.: Mukhtârah, Mount Lebanon, Bhamdûn.

2. *Natica Syriaca*, Pl. 12, fig. 70. Ovate, ventricose; volutions 4 or 5, rapidly diminishing towards the apex; spire very short; base umbilicated? aperture acutely subovate.

Local.: Mukhtârah, Jezzîn, el-Judeideh, esh-Shûf, Mount Lebanon.

A number of this large species occurs, often so pressed out of shape as hardly to be recognised.

### PHORUS.—*Montf.*

*Phorus Syriacus*, Pl. 11, fig. 66. Volutions 5, those of the spire convex; body-whorl large and flattened.

Local.: Bhamdûn.

An imperfect cast representing a large species. The impressions of adhering bodies are few and large. The base is entirely concealed by the matrix.

### TURRITELLA.—*Lam.*

1. *Turritella Syriaca*, Pl. 15, fig. 75. Subalate; volutions 6 or 7, convex; suture deeply impressed; aperture subquadrangular; base umbilicated.

Local. Bhamdûn.

A specimen of this species exhibits traces of revolving lines which are very distinct on the body-whorl, and about 5 in number between the suture and upper margin of the aperture.

2. *Turritella magnicostata*, Pl. 10, fig. 63, 64. Turrited; volutions rounded, longitudinally ribbed; ribs large, distant, rounded; revolving lines prominent, some large and distant, with generally 3 finer, unequal intermediate lines.

Local.: Bhamdûn, Jezzîn.

The aperture is not preserved in any of the specimens, and I have therefore only provisionally referred it to *Turritella;* a specimen has a valve of *Exogyra Boussingaultii* attached to it.

3. *Turritella peralveata*, Pl. 20, fig. 120. Turrited; volutions 9 or 10, convex, with 3 equal and equidistant prominent revolving carinæ on each; space above and below the carinæ equal in width and concave.

Local.: Bhamdûn.

### Nerinea.—*Defr.*

1. *Nerinea Syriaca*, Pl. 12, fig. 72; Pl. 11, fig. 67, young. Turrited; volutions numerous; sulcus wide, excavated; volutions angulated nearly in the middle, the sides straight and oblique.

Local.: Near the Greek Church of Bhamdûn.

A cast of this species is represented in fig. 72, and it bears a striking resemblance to *Nerinea Gosæ*, *Roemer*, (Ool. p. 143, t. xi, fig. 27.)

2. *Nerinea Bhamdunensis*, Pl. 22, fig. 132. A comparatively small subulate species, the angle of the volutions being situated much below the middle.

Local.: Near the Greek Church of Bhamdûn.

The specimens are so imperfect that any other difference than the position of the angle between this species and *Nerinea Syriaca* is not distinctly visible.

### Strombus.—*Lin.*, *Lam.*

*Strombus pervetus*, Pl. 13, fig. 73. A large distorted cast, having a short spire with four or five volutions.

Local.: Aklîm es-Shûf, Lebanon.

### Ammonites.

*Ammonites Syriacus*, Pl. 14, fig. 74. Discoid, bicarinated, costate; ribs alternated in size, 6 or 7 of which become very prominent or tubercle-shaped on the inner submargin; some of the intermediate ribs short, acutely pointed interiorly, little prominent, sometimes obsolete; periphery bicarinated, each carina ornamented with compressed rounded tubercles, about 20 in number; back somewhat concave, nearly flat in the middle.

Local.: Bhamdûn.

Dr. Anderson informs me that this species occurs in some European collections under the name above given. It is in all probability somewhere described; but I have not the means of ascertaining in what work it is published. It is an abundant fossil and quite variable in the comparative size of the ribs and in its thickness, which in part may be owing to pressure. The figures represent two of the differences in form and ribs, and fig. *a* exhibits one to which a young *Exogyra Boussingaultii* is attached.

# ORGANIC REMAINS OF THE CHALK.

### Astarte.—*Sow.*

1. ***Astarte undulosa***, Pl. 16, fig. 81 and 86; Pl. 17, fig. 89, 90, and 99. Triangular, inequilateral, compressed, with concentric angular ridges; posterior extremity subtruncated; basal margin regularly rounded.

Local.: Near Deir Mâr Sâba, Desert of Judah.

2. ***Astarte mucronata***, Pl. 17, fig. 88. Triangular, elevated, compressed; beaks prominent, acute; posterior margin very oblique, straight; disk with concentric lines; posterior extremity truncated, direct; inner margin crenulated.

Local.: Wâdy Kidrôn.

### Corbula.—*Lam.*

1. ***Corbula sublineolata***, Pl. 16, fig. 83. A cast of the left valve. Suboval, equilateral, ventricose, marked with very minute, closely arranged concentric lines.

Local.: Wâdy Kidrôn.

2. ***Corbula Syriaca***, Pl. 21, fig. 125. Triangular, ventricose; surface with prominent angular concentric ribs; posterior end rounded.

Local.: Near Safed.

A cast of the larger valve, resembling *C. oniscus*, an Eocene species of Alabama.

### Opis.—*Defr.*

***Opis undatus***, Pl. 17, fig. 87. Triangular, compressed, with concentric irregular or unequal angular ridges; umbonal slope carinated, terminal; posterior slope or area excavated, angular; beaks curved forward, and the apex nearly on a line with the anterior extremity, which is regularly rounded; posterior extremity angular.

Local.: Mount of Olives.

This fossil has considerable resemblance externally to *Venilia Conradi* of Morton. The hinge is unknown, and it is referred to *Opis*, from its outline. It belongs no doubt to that genus or to *Venilia.*

### Nucula.—*Lam.*

1. ***Nucula perovata***, Pl. 17, fig. 91. Ovato-subtriangular, compressed? very inequilateral; posterior end subtruncated, direct; disk with concentric lines anteriorly; inner margin crenulated.

Local.: Wâdy Kidrôn.

This species is represented by one specimen which has been flattened by pressure. The original outline of the shell, however, has probably not been much altered.

2. *Nucula crebrilineata*, Pl. 17, fig. 92, 93. Subtriangular, ventricose; disk covered with fine very closely arranged regular concentric lines.

Local.: Deir Mâr Sâba.

Of this species the few specimens found have probably lost their original form. I have therefore figured two specimens, of which the upper figure is probably the least distorted. The shell is generally preserved.

3. *Nucula* ———, Appendix Pl. 1, fig. 5. An impression in chalk of a compressed, inequilateral species from Safed.

4. *Nucula perdita*, Pl. 17, fig. 96. Ovato-oblong, inequilateral; anteriorly acute; posterior end rounded; anterior side slightly contracted; disk with regular, closely arranged concentric lines.

Local.: Desert of Juda, Mâr Sâba.

The shell is well preserved in some specimens of this species, which is not a rare fossil.

5. *Nucula* ———, Pl. 19, fig. 111. A distorted and rather obscure cast from Safed.

### Cucullæa.—*Lam.*

1. *Cucullæa subrotunda*, Pl. 17, fig. 94. Suborbicular, inequilateral; disk flattened in the middle; umbonal slope angular; posterior hinge margin elevated; disk minutely striated concentrically, having fine obscure radiating lines; radii distinct and distant behind the umbonal slope.

Local.: Wâdy Kidrôn, 1½ miles below Jerusalem.

A portion of the shell remaining on the specimen figured exhibits traces of fine reticulated lines.

2. *Cucullæa lintea*, Pl. 17, fig. 95. Rhomboidal, very inequilateral, compressed, having fine radiating lines and transverse wrinkles; umbonal slope acutely carinated; posterior margin truncated, not very oblique; hinge extremity posteriorly forming a right angle with the posterior margin.

Local.: Between Mâr Sâba and the Dead Sea.

3. *Cucullæa parallela*, Pl. 17, fig. 98. Rhomboidal, compressed; posterior end truncated; umbonal slope carinated; posterior slope wide, flattened; disk having a few distant striæ radiating from the beaks; hinge line parallel with the basal margin.

Local.: Summit of Mount of Olives.

The specimen of this species is broken anteriorly, and it is doubtful to what genus it should be referred.

### Arca.—*Lin.*

*Arca fabiformis*, Pl. 17, fig. 97. Oblong-subovate; disk contracted from beak to base; marked with minute closely arranged radiating lines; umbonal slope slightly prominent, subangulated; posterior slope marked with more distinct lines than the disk; basal margin contracted.

Local.: Wâdy Kidrôn, near Jerusalem.

### Crassatella.—*Lam.*

*Crassatella Syriaca*, Pl. 17, fig. 100. Subovate, convex, marked with concentric lines, most prominent on the umbo; posterior hinge line straight, declining; posterior extremity subtruncated, direct; umbonal slope subangulated; anterior side short, margin rounded; basal margin rounded.

Local.: Deir Mâr Sâba.

This shell is perfectly preserved in the only specimen collected.

### Lithodomus.—*Cuv.*

*Lithodomus cretaceus*, Pl. 17, fig. 101. Subcylindrical, narrowed anteriorly, subrostrated.

Local.: South of Nabulûs, Mount Gerizîm.

A distorted and imperfect cast is the only representative of this species in the collection.

### Gryphæa.—*Lam.*

1. *Gryphæa capuloides*, Pl. 18, fig. 103, 104. Oblong-ovate; inferior valve profoundly ventricose; umbo narrowed, somewhat curved laterally, often truncated by adhesion.

Local.: El-Sîleh, Hills of Samaria.

This species occurs in chalk and is well preserved, but the hinge and the interior of the larger valve are concealed in the matrix. A variety can scarcely be distinguished from *Gryphæa vesicularis* by its outline and general character; but the species is much smaller.

2. *Gryphæa vesicularis*, Brown, Pl. 18, fig. 105. Semiglobose, retuse at base, smooth; inferior valve ventricose; subauriculated on one side; superior valve plano-convex, operculiform.

Ostræa vesicularis, Lam., Desh., ed. vol. 7, p. 246. Goldfuss' Petrefacten, 2, p. 23, No. 61, pl. 181, fig. 2, a, o.

Pycnodonta radiata, Fisher, Bull. de Moscow, 8, pl. 1.

Local.: Near Neby Mûsa, Mâr Sâba.

There is but one inferior valve of this shell in the collection, and it perfectly agrees with the common form of *Gryphæa vesicularis*, abundant in the chalk formation of Europe and the United States.

### Exogyra.—*Say.*

*Exogyra densata*, Pl. 18, fig. 102. Ovate-oblong; inferior valve ventricose, angulated about the region of the umbo where it is very thick; surface with concentric laminated lines; umbo narrowed, somewhat flattened laterally; superior valve flat or slightly convex, with closely arranged rugose concentric prominent lines.

Local.: Mountains of Moab, half way between the Dead Sea and Kerak.

A handsome species, well preserved, and remarkable for its proportional extension from beak to base.

*Exogyra densata, var.*, Pl. 18, fig. 106. A fragment of the larger valve. Thick, ventricose, regularly rounded; umbo very large and thick; beak much curved; second volution prominent and rounded; hinge area large and thick.

Local.: Wâdy Zerqa Ma'în; East of Dead Sea; found also near Kerak.

The description and figure are from a fragment of an inferior valve, remarkable for its great thickness about the hinge and umbo.

### Avicula.—*Lam.*

*Avicula Samariensis*, Pl. 19, fig. 107. Obtusely ovate, convex; margins rounded; ears short and elevated.

Local.: Wâdy Burkîn, Hills of Samaria.

The impression in chalk represents a squamose shell with five or six distant rays, slightly impressed and darker colored than the other portion of the valve.

### Pecten.—*Lin. Lam.*

1. *Pecten delumbis*, Pl. 19, fig. 110, and Appendix, Pl. 1, fig. 4. Suboval or suborbicular, compressed, rugose? ears small and equal.

Local.: Desert of Judah, Wâdy en-Nâr, Mâr Sâba, Safed.

An impression in chalky limestone. The valves were probably rugose on the exterior about the umbo, as all the impressions have fine wrinkles on that portion of the shell.

2. *Pecten obrutus*, Pl. 19, fig. 114. Ovate, convex-depressed; ribs about 22 in number, angulated, narrower than the interstices, smooth and destitute of distinct lines; ears unequal.

Local.: Bituminous limestone of Neby Mûsa.

### Cardium.—*Lin. Lam.*

1. *Cardium bellum*, Appendix, Pl. 1, fig. 3. Subovate, ventricose, with numerous regular concentric ribs, closely arranged and terminating on the posterior side of the umbonal slope; posterior slope marked with fine radiating lines.

Local.: Deir Mâr Sâba.

This beautiful species is allied to *C. Hillanum* and *C. perigrinorsum*, but is more ovate, with a more pointed apex and narrower umbo, and the posterior radiated space is much narrower.

2. *Cardium ovulum*, Pl. 19, fig. 108. Oblique, suborbicular, inequilateral, ventricose; anterior margin regularly rounded; surface concentrically striated.

Local.: Wâdy Zerqa Ma'în.

### Astarte.—*Sow.*

1. *Astarte lintea*, Pl. 19, fig. 109. Subtriangular, elevated, compressed, inequilateral; posterior margin very oblique, subrectilinear; margins rounded; surface with fine closely arranged concentric lines.

Local.: Hills of Samaria, el-Sileh.

2. *Astarte sublineolata*, Pl. 19, fig. 112. Triangular, compressed, inequilateral; surface with numerous minute regular closely arranged concentric lines.

Local.: Near Safed.

### Venus.—*Lin. Lam.*

*Venus perovalis*, Appendix, Pl. 1, fig. 2. Oval, inequilateral, ventricose, finely striate concentrically; summits and margins rounded.

Local.: On the road to Kerak from the Dead Sea.

The piece of limestone in which this shell is imbedded contains a very small smooth *Buccinum*, a small species of *Inoceramus*, very like a species found in Alabama, a small *Opis* and a *Corbula*.

I should infer from the few distinct forms in this small piece of limestone that the rock is of the era of the Upper Chalk.

INOCERAMUS.—*Sow.*

*Inoceramus aratus*, Pl. 19, fig. 113. A fragment; a dilated ventricose species with distant acute concentric ridges and concave interstices.

Local.: Near Neby Mûsa.

A small portion of the shell remaining exhibits minute concentric impressed lines, not very closely arranged; the cast anteriorly has a subtuberculated aspect on the ridges.

LUCINA.—*Lam.*

*Lucina Safedensis*, Pl. 19, fig. 115. Lenticular, compressed, subequilateral; surface with about fifteen prominent concentric striæ and intermediate minute concentric lines.

Local.: Safed.

TEREBRATULA.—*Lam.*

*Terebratula Hermonensis*, Pl. 20, fig. 123. Triangular, ventricose; ribs about 28 in number, narrow, the interstices transversely striated; lesser valve more ventricose than the other, with a broad flattened space in the middle, slightly raised, and having ten ribs upon it; umbones obtusely rounded.

Local.: Summit of Mount Hermon.

UNIVALVES.

FUSUS.—*Lam.*

*Fusus Ellerii*, Pl. 16, fig. 82. Fusiform; spire elongated; volutions convex, longitudinally ribbed; ribs large, rounded, on the body-whorl less prominent; surface of the shell, finely striated with reticulated lines; beak long and narrow.

Local.: Wâdy Burkîn, Hills of Samaria.

This fine species was discovered by C. Ellery Anderson, (Dr. A's son,) and is dedicated to him to commemorate his zeal in the pursuit of objects of Natural History, during a fatiguing and hazardous journey through parts of Syria not visited by the Expedition.

CHENOPUS.—*Phillipi.*

A species of *Chenopus* occurs with longitudinal ribs about 1½ inches long.

Local.: Between Kefr Hûneh and el-Judeideh, 'Ain el-Jîsh.

HIPPURITES.—*Lam.*

*Hippurites Syriacus*, Pl. 16, fig. 84. Dentiform, elongated, curved; side opposite the longitudinal furrow angulated; surface with distant annular impressed lines and longitudinal wrinkles; upper surface with oblique slightly curved numerous angular lines. (A cast.)

Local.: A little north of Bethel.

The cast of this species bears some resemblance in shape to the tooth of a *Mosasaurus.* The diameter of the thickness is of an acutely ovate outline.

NERINEA.—*Defr.*

*Nerinea cretacea*, Pl. 16, fig. 85. Turrited; volutions rounded, with a revolving series of tubercles near the suture.

Local.: Between Neby Samwîl and el-Jîb.

The figure represents the mould impressed by a species of *Nerinea*, but the cast was not found and the specific character is therefore obscure.

ANCYLOCERAS.—*D'Orbigny.*

*Ancyloceras Safedensis*, Pl. 20, fig. 117, 118. A fragment of a cast and an impression exhibit a species with prominent angular ribs, numerous and subequal or gradually lessening towards the apex.

Local.: Safed.

BACULITES.—*Lam.*

*Baculites Syriacus*, Pl. 20, fig. 121. A fragment of an ovate species with the shell well preserved and mineralised occurs. The shell is pearly, not very thin, and the lines of growth, fine and regular, are profoundly curved on the narrower portion of the shell.

Local.: The Cliff above 'Ain Terâbeh.

*Baculites* ——, Pl. 20, fig. 122. This represents the interior of a species, probably the same as the preceding, in which the septa are mineralised, and are remarkably thick and well preserved.

Local.: The Cliff above 'Ain Terâbeh.

AMMONITES.—*Brug.*

*Ammonites Safedensis*, Pl. 21, fig. 124. Flattened, ribs little prominent, generally about as wide as the interstices, subnodulous and terminating on the periphery in flattened tubercles with a rounded margin; inner submargin of the volutions tuberculated.

Local.: Safed.

A large species in chalk which seems to approximate *A. Rhotomagensis*, Defrance; but that species has a double row of tubercles towards the periphery, while the Syrian species apparently has but one.

NUMMULITES.

*Nummulites Arbiensis*, Pl. 22, fig. 127. Suborbicular, the annular lines appearing rugose and imbricated on the weathered surface; thickness unknown in consequence of all the specimens being greatly distorted; the transverse lines are minute and shew the septa to have been very numerous.

Local.: 'Arby.

This species occurs in great numbers in hard white limestone, standing in relief upon the weathered surface, various sizes crowded together, from one-eighth or less to three-fourths of an inch in diameter. Not a single one can be observed in its normal shape, all having been contorted by pressure.

### Dentalium.—*Lin.*

*Dentalium cretaceum*, Appendix, Pl. 1, fig. 1. Much curved, very tapering towards the apex, finely striated longitudinally and transversely wrinkled.

Local.: Safed.

## ECHINODERMATA.

### Echinus.—*Lin.*

*Echinus Kerakensis*, Pl. 19, fig. 116. Oval, convex; tubercles very small, closely arranged and equal; base concave.

Local.: Kerak.

This species is obscure, being worn at the base, and nearly all the upper surface is imbedded in limestone.

---

# RECENT SHELLS.

### Helix.—*Lin.*

1. *Helix lithophaga*, Pl. 22, fig. 128. Depressed-convex, moderately thin; volutions five, those of the spire flattened; suture margined by a carinated line; base convex; umbilicus rather large, but more than half covered by the lip which is widely reflected; color whitish varied with pale-brown irregular angular spots in series of revolving lines, four on the large whorl; base without colored markings.

Local.: Wâdy en-Nâr, below Deir Mâr Sâba.

This species is remarkable for its habit of penetrating limestone rocks. It has been supposed to be a variety of *Helix planospira*, *Muller;* but it appears to me quite distinct from that species. The carinated line, angular spots and widely reflected lip, which more than half covers the umbilicus, are sufficient to distinguish it from *planospira* independent of the habit of the animal which perforates indurated limestone and resides in the deep cavities it makes.

2. *Helix ligata*, *Muller*, Pl. 15, fig. 80. Globose, imperforate, striated; spire elevated, subturbinate, whorls four, somewhat convex, the large one inflated,s lightly descending; columella oblique, somewhat contracted; aperture lunato-rotundate; peristome slightly expanded; margin of columella dilated, widely callous.

Helix ligata, Muller, Verm. II, p. 58, No. 252. Chem. P. 2, p. 110, fig. 128. Férussac, Hist. t. 20, fig. 1, 2, 4. Lam., Desh. ed., 134, p. 90.

Local.: Between Mukhtârah and Jezzîn.

This species is nearly allied to *H. pomatia* and *H. cincta*, and inhabits Italy, Russia near Odessa, the Caucasus, Morea, etc. A slight trace of the colored bands is visible on the dead and bleached specimen from which the figure has been drawn.

### CARACOLLA.—*Lam.*

***Caracolla tuberculosa***, Pl. 22, fig. 129. Trochiform, minutely umbilicated; spire elevated, volutions each with a tuberculated carina above the suture and a revolving series of smaller tubercles in the middle; sides of volutions flattened and oblique, transversely rugose; periphery of body-whorl profoundly carinated, the carina reflected and furnished with numerous unequal tubercles; base convex, profoundly rugose; peristome reflected.

Local.: Shore of the Dead Sea.

A single specimen, with the two volutions nearest the apex broken, was obtained. The shell is bleached and remarkably similar in form to a species of *Trochus*.

### PALUDINA.—*Lam.*

***Paludina Phialensis***, Pl. 22, fig. 130. Turrited, volutions five, regularly rounded; suture profoundly impressed; base umbilicated; aperture ovate; labium reflected; labrum slightly reflected.

Local.: Lake Phiala.

This is a small species without any prominent character. It is thin and fragile and has traces of a pale-brown epidermis.

# APPENDIX.

Some interesting fossils have been sent to Dr. Anderson for comparison with those of the Expedition. Of these, a number were kindly furnished by Professor Silliman, and the others by a Society in Cincinnati, (Friends of Missions.) I have described some new species from both collections and add them in an Appendix. They are all Jurassic forms, with the exception of a species of *Janira*, which however is probably Jurassic, although lower in the scale of formations than the genus has hitherto been observed. Two species of *Polyparia* occur which have been omitted. On the first plate of the Appendix, fig. 1 to 5 represent Cretaceous shells of the Expedition.

## BIVALVES.

### Janira.—*Shum.*

*Janira Syriaca*, Pl. 1, fig. 6. Subtriangular, elevated; superior valve slightly concave, with rather narrow, unequal ribs and concentrically wrinkled, about twenty-six in number; inferior valve ventricose, with six large ribs, rounded and finely wrinkled; intervals with generally four rounded unequal ribs.

The genus *Janira*, according to d'Orbigny, commenced with the Cretaceous period, which is characterised by numerous species, and the *Janira Syriaca* may possibly belong to that era; but as it accompanied a group of exclusively Jurassic fossils, and its matrix is apparently of the same mineral character with that of the latter, I have supposed it to be Jurassic and arranged it accordingly.

Local.: 'Abeih.

### Ostræa.—*Lin.*, *Lam.*

*Ostræa corticosa*, Pl. 1, fig. 7. Subovate; superior valve flat, with very irregular radiating folds and numerous small scales; inferior valve not deeply convex, and with narrow, not prominent, irregular ribs and prominent large scales. This species is very perfect, generally showing a mark of attachment at the umbo of the inferior valve, and in general appearance is not unlike some forms of *Plicatula.*

*Ostræa virgata* ? Pl. 1, fig. 8. This I suppose to be the same species figured on Plate 1 of the Expedition, fig. 6 to 8. The figure on the Appendix plate represents the hinge and upper valve of a specimen in excellent preservation.

### Opis.—*Defr.*

*Opis equalis*, Pl. 2, fig. 9. Triangular, ventricose, beaks central; anterior end acutely rounded; posterior truncated; basal margin regularly, not profoundly curved.

*Opis orientalis*, Pl. 2, fig. 10. Triangular, inequilateral; anterior margin of umbo acutely rounded; posterior side cuneiform, slightly sinuous; posterior end obliquely truncated.

*Opis obrutus*, Pl. 2, fig. 12. Triangular, inequilateral, elevated; margins of umbo angular; basal margin nearly straight; posterior slope concave. On one of the casts of this species are traces of concentric lines.

Local.: 'Aleih.

### Astarte.—*Sow.*

*Astarte lucinoides*, Pl. 2, fig. 11. Orbicular or lentiform; inequilateral; beaks not prominent.

*Astarte subcordata*, Pl. 2, fig. 13. Subcordate, inequilateral; summits prominent; margins rounded.

### Inoceramus.—*Sow.*

*Inoceramus Syriacus*, Pl. 2, fig. 14. Subrhomboidal? ventricose, concentrically sulcated; ligament margin recurved; anterior and posterior margins abrupt; basal margin rounded.

The cast is considerably distorted, and the figure represents the original form as nearly as the specimen indicates it.

Local.: 'Aleih.

*Inoceramus elevatus*, Pl. 2, fig. 15. Suboval, equilateral? elevated, profoundly ventricose; umbo large and prominent with rather large concentric undulations, not profound; base and extremities rounded; beaks contiguous.

The cast of this species is broken anteriorly and somewhat distorted.

### Pholadomya.—*Sow.*

*Pholadomya Syriaca*, Pl. 2, fig. 17. Suborbicular, inequilateral, ventricose; valves with radiating tuberculated ribs, wanting on the posterior side where there are concentric lines or furrows of rather large size.

There is but one specimen of this cast, much distorted.

### Cardium.—*Lin.*

*Cardium crebriechinatum*, Pl. 2, fig. 16. This species is refigured here to represent a cast more perfect in its outline than those on Pl. 6.

### Arca.—*Lin.*

*Arca longa*, Pl. 3, fig. 18. Trapezoidal, inequilateral; sides flattened or slightly contracted; anterior extremity rounded; posterior slightly curved; basal margin slightly contracted. The figure of this shell is too angular and abrupt posteriorly, for the ligament margin forms a regular curve with the posterior margin.

*Arca Bhamdunensis*, Pl. 3, fig. 19. Elliptical, inequilateral, ventricose; posterior side cuneiform; basal margin curved.

Local.: Bhamdûn.

*Arca cuneus*, Pl. 3, fig. 22. Rhomboidal, inflated in the umbonal region; sides flattened; anterior side very short, extremity rounded; posterior side cuneiform, extremity angular; basal margin slightly curved.

### Cucullæa.—*Lam.*

*Cucullæa opiformis*, Pl. 3, fig. 21. Triangular, elevated, inequilateral; summits profoundly elevated; sides flattened.

An imperfect cast, remarkable for the elevation of the summits and the widely remote beaks.

### Nucula.—*Lam.*

*Nucula abrupta*, Pl. 3, fig. 20. Ovate, convex, inequilateral; anterior dorsal and ligament margins straight and oblique; posterior extremity much above the line of the base; basal margin rounded.

Local.: 'Aleih.

*Nucula ? obtenta*, Pl. 3, fig. 23. Ovato-triangular, ventricose, inequilateral; posterior side subcuneiform; extremities subtruncated; basal margin regularly rounded.

### Tellina.—*Lin.*

*Tellina Syriaca ?* Pl. 3, fig. 25. This appears to be a variety of *T. Syriaca*, a species represented on Pl. 10, fig. 59, 60, 61.

Local.: 'Aleih.

### Orbicula.—*Cuv.*

*Orbicula ? Syriaca*, Pl. 3, fig. 24. Obtusely ovate, convex, with concentric lines.

An obscure small species attached to a cast of *Inoceramus Lynchii.*

### Trigonia.—*Brug.*

*Trigonia Syriaca*, Pl. 4, fig. 26. This figure represents the external character of a species previously described and figured from casts. See Pl. 3, fig. 20, 21, 23. Here the shell though broken at the base is otherwise well preserved and mineralised.

Local.: 'Aleih.

*Trigonia distans*, Pl. 4, fig. 27. Ventricose, concentrically ribbed; ribs distant, narrow, prominent, somewhat undulated, terminating on the umbonal slope which is profoundly carinated; valves contracted anteriorly to the umbonial carina; posterior area contracted or concave.

Local.: Bhamdûn.

### Panopæa.—*Mén.*

*Panopæa orientalis*, Pl. 4, fig. 28. Oblong-ovate, inflated, very inequilateral; summits prominent; anterior basal margin obliquely truncated.

Local.: Bhamdûn.

An imperfect cast. In the figure the summits are not sufficiently elevated and the ligament margin is too much so.

## UNIVALVES.

### Nerinea.—*Defrance.*

1. *Nerinea? cochleæformis*, Pl. 4, fig. 29. Turrited; whorls obscurely crenulated or tuberculated; space between the ridges profoundly concave.

Local.: 'Ain 'Anûb.

2. *Nerinea* ——, Pl. 4, fig. 30, 31. A comparatively short species, too imperfect to describe.

Local.: Hadith, Lebanon.

3. *Nerinea? Orientalis*, Pl. 5, fig. 32. Sides of volutions straight, longitudinally ribbed; ribs rounded, slightly curved and but little prominent; volutions of the spire, with about six revolving lines on each.

Local.: 'Ain 'Anûb.

The description of this species refers to three or four fragments, two of which have the inferior volution scalariform.

4. *Nerinea Syriaca*, Pl. 5, fig. 33, 34, 35, 37, 38. Varieties of *N. Syriaca* previously described, and a cast figured on Pl. 12, fig. 72.

Local.: 'Ain 'Anûb, Lebanon.

5. *Nerinea abbreviata*, Pl. 5, fig. 36. Cylindrical; spire short, conical, scalariform; suture margined by a minute raised line; columella four-plaited.

Local.: 'Ain 'Anûb, Lebanon.

6. *Nerinea* ——. A fragment, representing part of a very large species occurs in the collection sent from Cincinnati. This fragment of the body-whorl measures 3½ inches in width; the base is strongly striated with revolving lines.

Local.: 'Ain 'Anûb.

### Actæonella.—*D'Orb.*

*Actæonella Syriaca*, Pl. 5, fig. 40. Ovato-oblong, smooth, acuminated above, dilated inferiorly; columella three-plaited.

Local.: Sabbatic River, Lebanon.

### Cerithium.—*Adans., Lam.*

*Cerithium bilineatum*, Pl. 5, fig. 39. Subulate; volutions 12, with straight sides, those of the spire having two distant, revolving lines on each; suture compressed; body-whorl rounded inferiorly.

Local.: 'Ain 'Anûb.

### Natica.—*Lam.*

*Natica Orientalis*, Pl. 5, fig. 41. Globose; volutions three, flattened above; spire not prominent.

Local.: 'Aleih.

### TURRITELLA.—*Lam.*

*Turritella Syriaca*, Pl. 5, fig. 42. A specimen of the species figured on Pl. 15, fig. 75.
Local.: 'Ain 'Anûb.

### CANCELLARIA.—*Lam.*

*Cancellaria petrosa*, Pl. 5, fig. 43. Subfusiform; turrited, spire scalariform; ribs large, distant, oblique.

## BIVALVES.

### LITHODOMUS.—*Cuv.*

*Lithodomus stamineus*, Pl. 5, fig. 44. Oblong; elegantly and profoundly striated concentrically; disk contracted in the middle; umbonal slope rounded, inflated; posterior margin oblique; slightly curved.

### CARDIUM.—*Lin.*

*Cardium biseriatum*, Pl. 5, fig. 45. Previously described and figured. See Pl. 6, fig. 38, 39, 40. Fig. 45 represents a specimen in which the markings or lines are very distinct.
Local.: 'Aleih.

## UNIVALVES.

### AMMONITES.

*Ammonites Libanensis*, Pl. 6, fig. 46. Compressed; obscurely ribbed transversely; whorls flattened, four or five in number; periphery of the umbilicus strongly ribbed; ribs of the volutions in the umbilicus with a prominent tubercle on each; septa unequal, three-lobate on the sides. Diameter eight inches, thickness near aperture 2½ inches.
Local.: Mount Lebanon, five miles East of Beirût.

### HIPPURITES.—*Lam.*

*Hippurites liratus*, Pl. 7, fig. 47, 48. Elongated, curved, imbricated, profoundly ribbed; ribs narrow, irregular, unequal, diameter ovate.

The cast, fig. 48, is longitudinally finely striated, and exhibits but faint traces of the longitudinal ribs on the shell.
Local.: Bhamdûn.

*Hippurites plicatus*, Pl. 7, fig. 49. Pyramidal, obscurely plicated longitudinally.
Local.: 'Aithâth.

### NATICA.—*Lam.*

*Natica ? scalaris*, Pl. 7, fig. 50. Short-fusiform; spire prominent, scalariform, consisting of 5 volutions with concave sides; body whorl with two distant revolving obtuse carinæ, the inferior one tuberculated.

### Chenopus.

*Chenopus* ——, Pl. 8, fig. 51, 52. These two figures represent two species too imperfect for description.

Local.: 'Abeih, Lebanon.

## BIVALVES.

### Corbula.—*Lam.*

*Corbula Aleihensis*, Pl. 8, fig. 53. Suboval, equilateral; both valves profoundly ventricose; posterior end obliquely truncated; beaks remote; anterior basal margin subtruncated.

Local.: 'Aleih, Lebanon.

### Orbicula.—*Lam.*

*Orbicula ?* ——, Pl. 8, fig. 55. A very small species with angular lines.

Local.: Mount Lebanon.

## ECHINODERMATA.

### Echinus.—*Lin.*

*Echinus Libanensis*, Pl. 8, fig. 54. Depressed; base deeply concave; primary tubercles small, the largest consisting of a single series, and rather closely arranged, whole surface minutely granulated; on the periphery and base, the primary tubercles consist of 4 or 5 series nearly equal in size.

Local.: Mount Lebanon.

*Echinus bullatus*, Pl. 8, fig. 56. Depressed-hemispherical; primary tubercles in two distant series, one tubercle in each series larger than the others and very prominent, only two of the primary tubercles large and situated about the periphery, secondary tubercles in two approximate series, rather large, closely arranged, and gradually increasing in size from apex to base.

Local.: Mount Lebanon.

The base of this specimen is concealed by a portion of the rock in which it was imbedded.

THE END.

# ERRATA.

| | | | | |
|---|---|---|---|---|
| Page 86, | line 9 from bottom, | *for* nearly ...... | *read* | nearly to. |
| " 87, | " 3 " | " Aklîm ...... | " | Aqlîm. |
| " 88, | " 9 ............ | " 'Aïthâth .... | " | 'Aithâth. |
| " 90, | " 10 from bottom, | " Area ........ | " | Arca. |
| " 91, | last line, .......... | " el-Dâmûr ... | " | ed-Dâmûr. |
| " 99, | line 18, ........... | " form ........ | " | forms. |
| " 105, | " 22, ........... | " 'Aîthath .... | " | 'Aithâth. |
| " 107, | " 2, ........... | " 'Ard ........ | " | Ard. |
| " 112, | " 7, ........... | " Hâsbeîya ... | " | Hâsbeiya. |
| " 126, | " 21, ........... | " souweîd .... | " | suweid. |
| " 127, | " 1 & 2, ....... | " Semu'y ..... | " | Semû'y. |
| " 160, | " 29, ........... | " Kharayan ... | " | Kharâyin. |
| " 169, | " 10, ........... | " to .......... | " | of. |
| " 169, | " 23, ........... | " Haneideh ... | " | Huneideh. |
| " 170, | " 9 from bottom, | " which ...... | " | while. |
| " 171, | " 1, ........... | " Mezeirat .... | " | Muzeirat. |
| " 174, | " 28, ........... | " crebrilineatae | " | crebrilineata. |
| " 184, | " 23, ........... | " Uheimĭr .... | " | Uheimir. |
| " 184, | " 7 from bottom, | " el-Dera'ah .. | " | ed-Dera'ah. |

Palestine Expedition. Pl. 1. Palæontology.

T. Sinclair's lith. Phila.

Palestine Expedition. Pl. 6. Palæontology.

38. 39. 40. 41. 42. 43.

T. Sinclair's lith. Phila.

Palestine Expedition. Pl. 2. Palæontology.

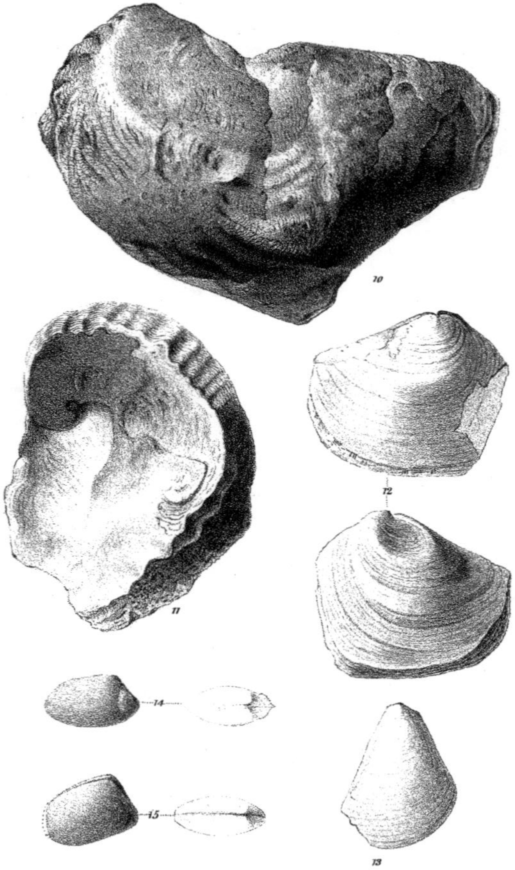

10
11
12
13
14
15

T. Sinclair's lith. Phila.

Palestine Expedition. Pl. 5. Palæontology.

30
31
32
33
34
35
36
37

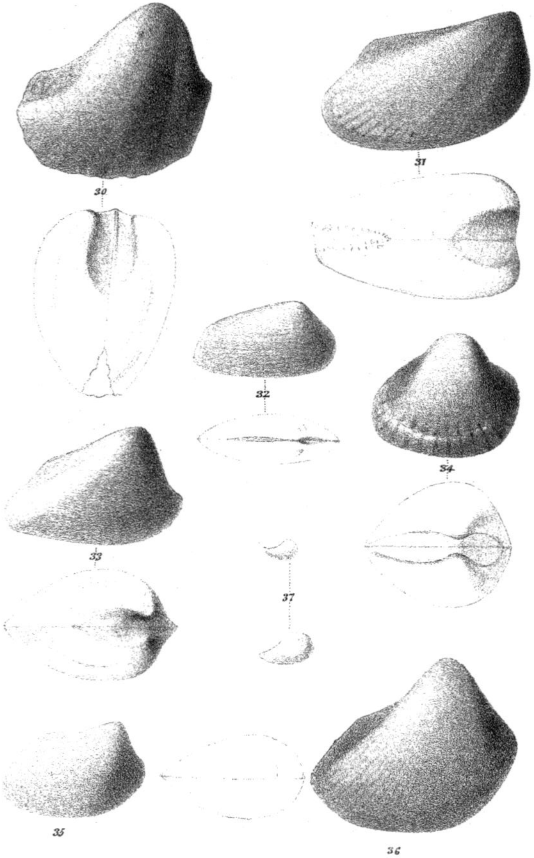

T. Sinclair's lith. Phil.

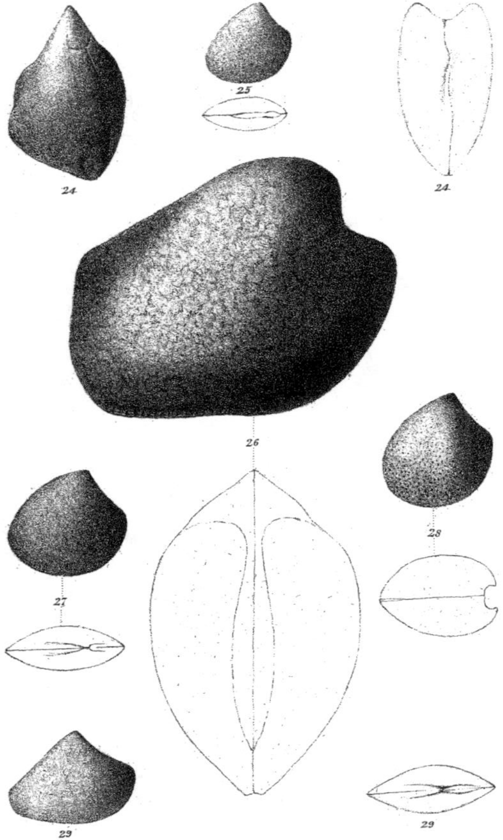

24 25 24

26

27 28

29 29

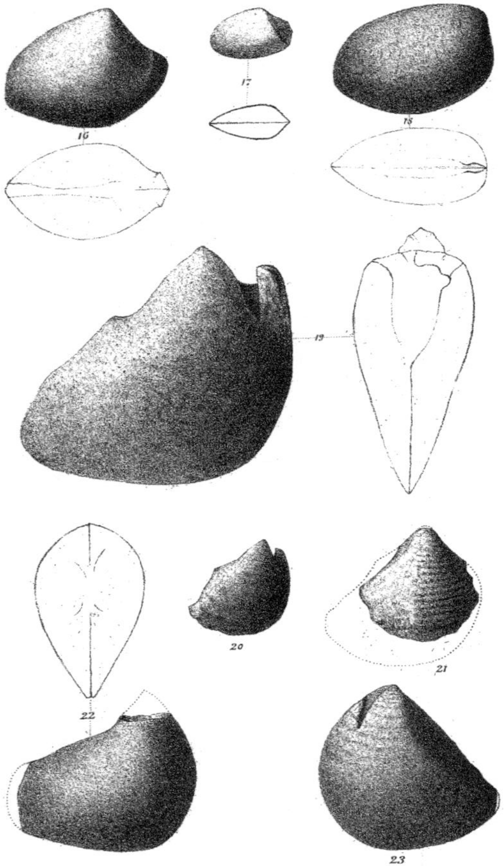

T. Sinclair's lith. Philada.



16 17 18

19

22 20 21

23

T. Sinclair's lith. Philada.

47

48

49

50

51

T. Sinclair's lith. Philada.



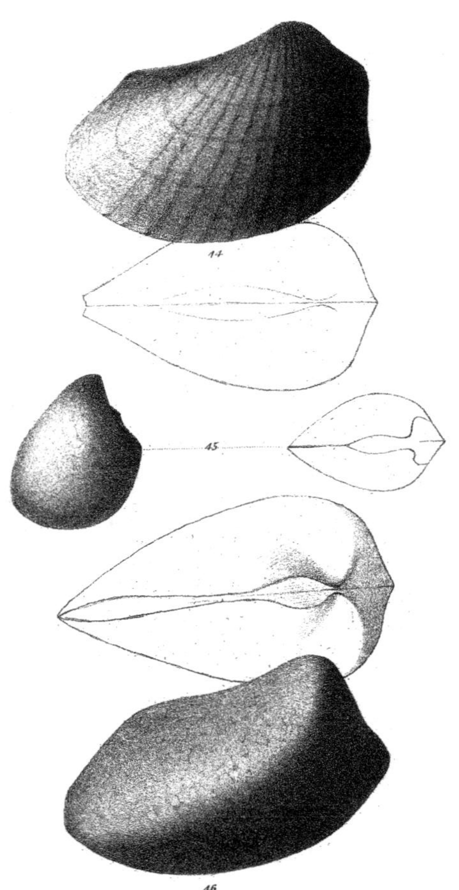


T. Sinclair's lith. Philada.

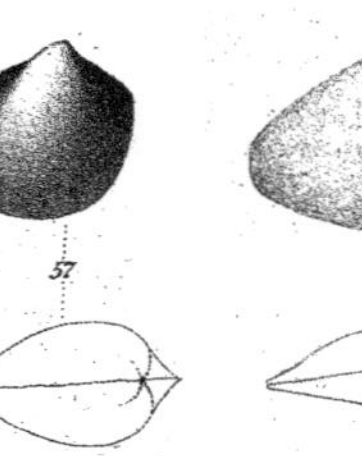
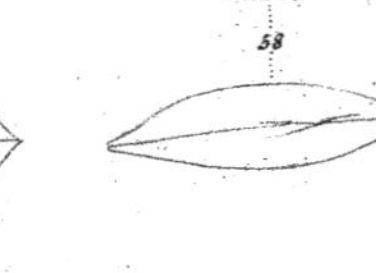
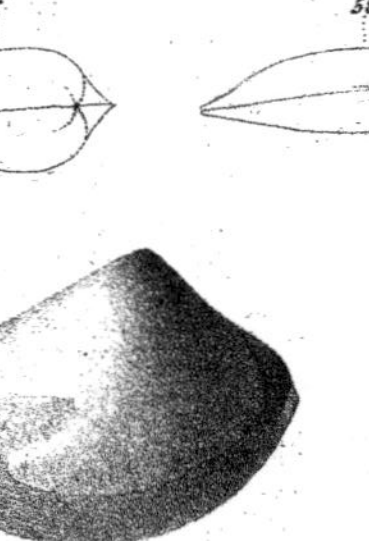
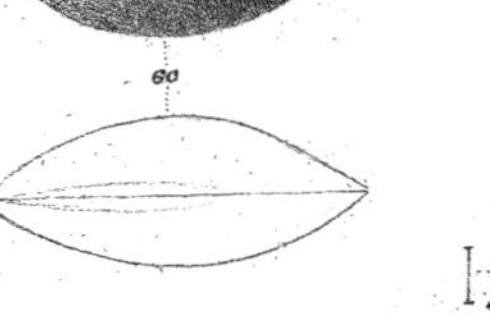

T. Sinclair's lith. Phila.



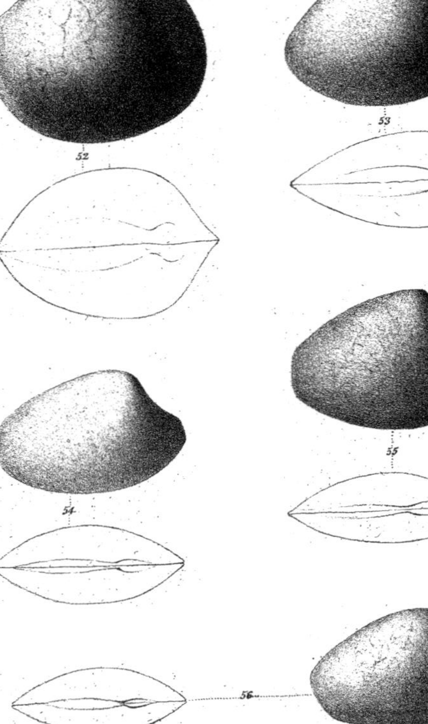

T. Sinclair's lith. Phil.

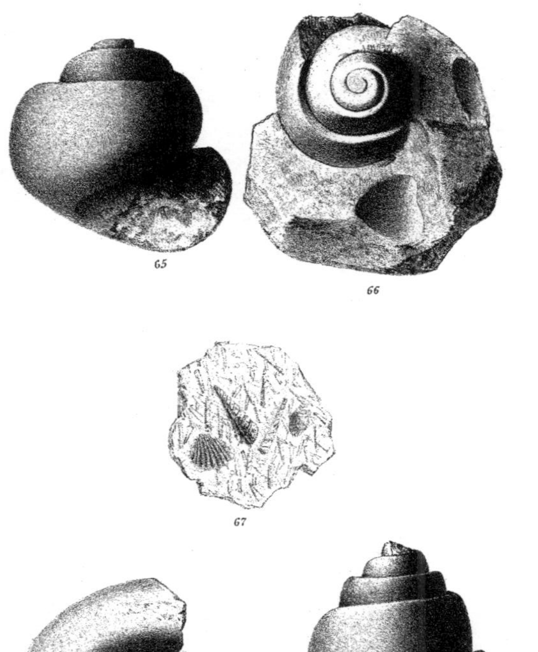

65

66

67

68

69

T. Sinclairs lith Phila.

70

71

72.

T. Sinclairs lith Phila.

73

T. Sinclair's lith. Phila.

Palestine Expedition. Pl. 14. Palæontology.

74

a

b

T. Sinclair's lith. Phila.

Palestine Expedition. Pl. 15. Palæontology.

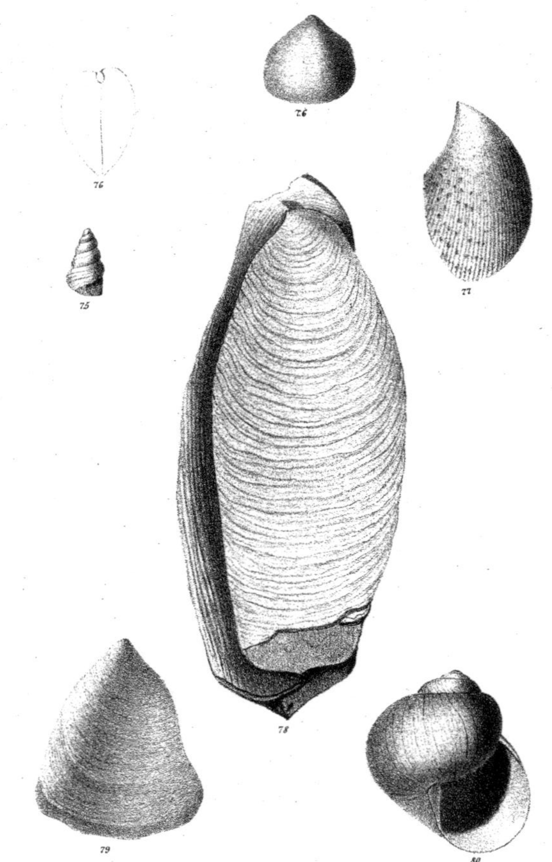


T. Sinclair's lith. Phila.

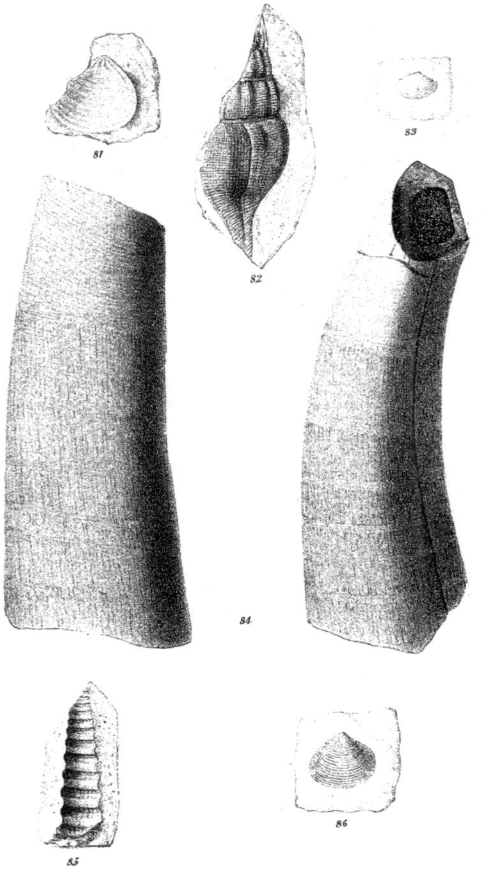

81 82 83

84

85 86

T. Sinclair's lith. Phila.

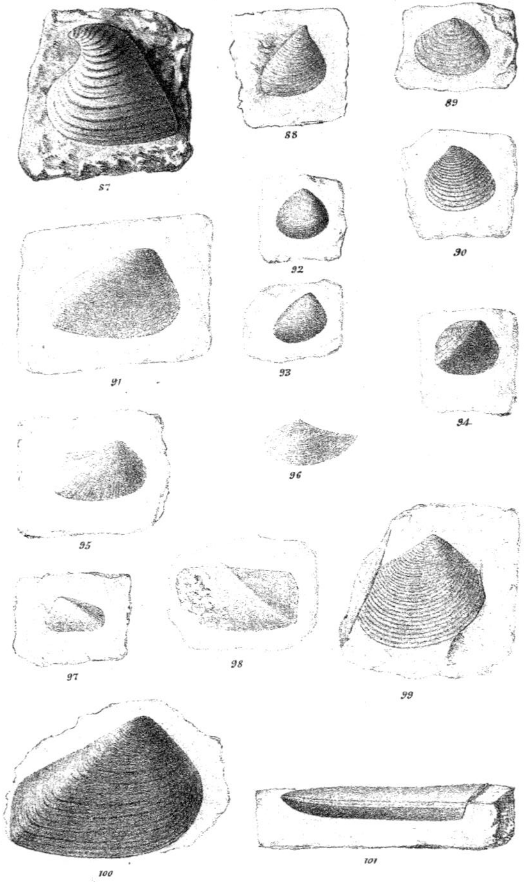

87 88 89

92 90

91 93 94

95 96

97 98 99

100 101

T. Sinclair's lith. Phila.

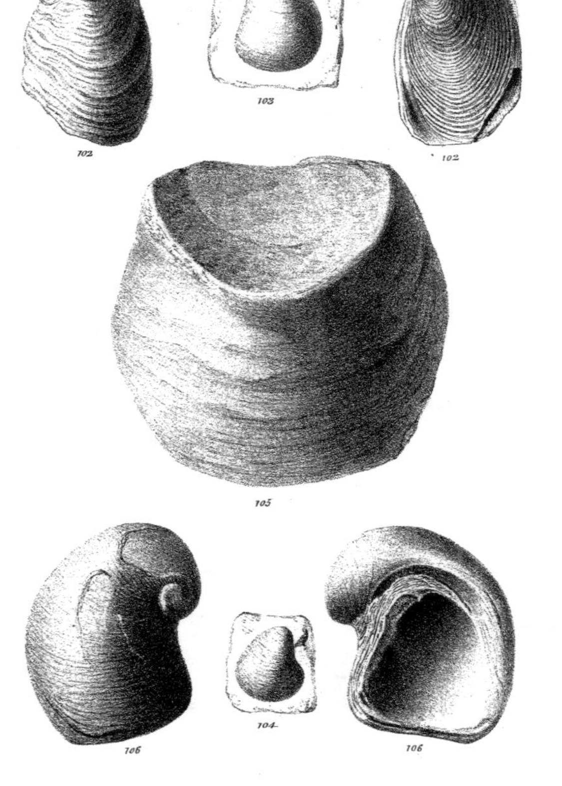


T. Sinclair's lith. Philad.

T. Sinclair's lith. Philad.

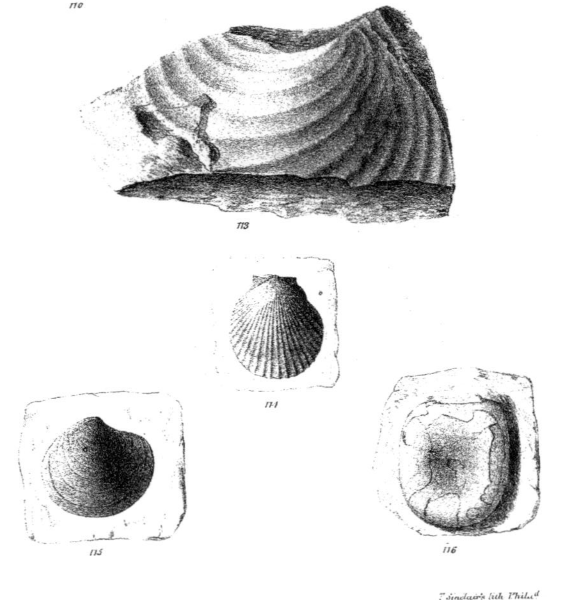


T. Sinclair's lith. Philad



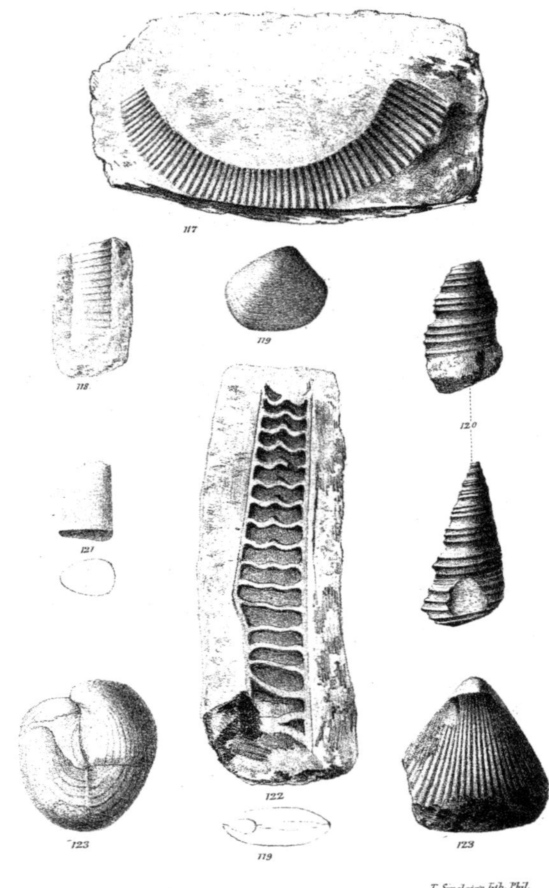


T. Sinclair's lith. Phil.

126 127 128 129 130

RECENT SHELLS.

131 132

133

Sinclair's Lith. Phil^a

Palestine — Appendix — Plate 1

1 2 3 4 5 6 7 8

Palestine — Appendix. — Plate 2.

9 10 11 12 13 14 15 16 17

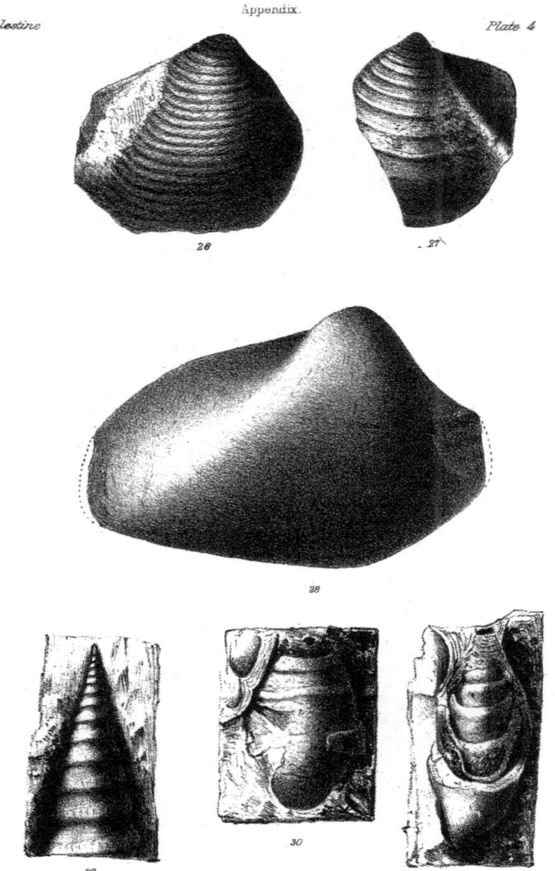




18 19

20

21

22

23 24 25

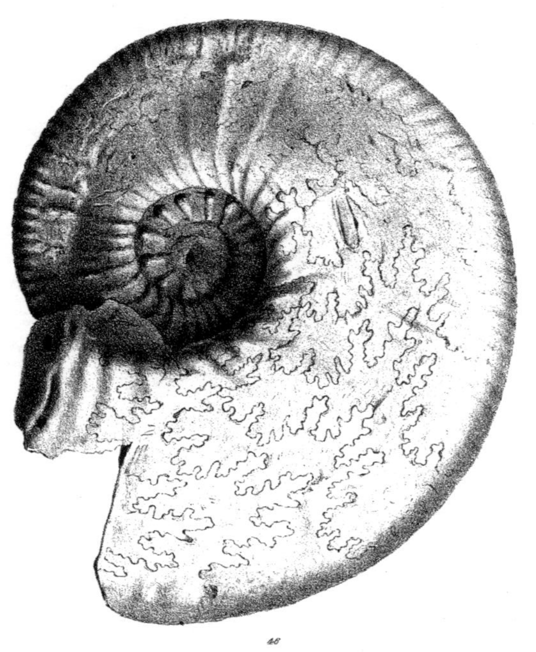
46

32
33
34
35
36
37
38
39
40
41
42
43
44
45
44

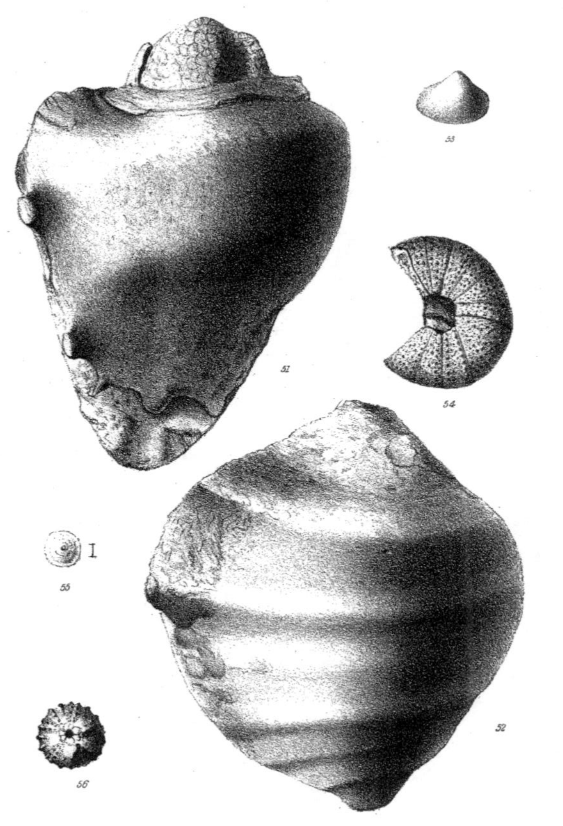
51
52
53
54
55
56



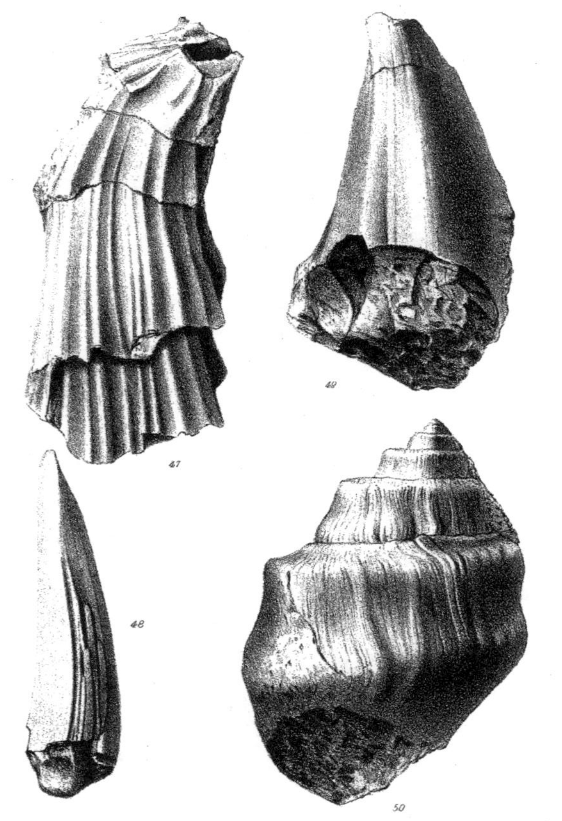
47
48
49
50

www.ingramcontent.com/pod-product-compliance
Lightning Source LLC
LaVergne TN
LVHW010242110826
845151LV00004B/1366